PENGUIN BOOKS

TO THE ENDS OF THE EARTH

'Fascinating and far-reaching, thoughtful and incisive . . . one of the deepest thinkers on Scottish identity and history'
Scottish Field

'Devine is not afraid to name and shame . . . he has a rare gift for detecting contradictions' *Herald*

'Devine is an admirable historian, acerbic in judgement, and a pleasure to read' *Spectator*

'*To the Ends of the Earth* is littered with compelling facts . . . Devine is at his best in capturing the sheer size, range and complexity of historical phenomena with prescient points'
The Times Higher Educational Supplement

'A large historical canvas requires bold and imaginative brush strokes, an art few historians can master. Devine is one of them'
Scotland on Sunday

'The key chapters – on slavery, technics and investment, and migration – are magisterial' *Independent*

D0184183

ABOUT THE AUTHOR

T. M. Devine is the Personal Senior Research Professor of History at the University of Edinburgh and Director of the Scottish Centre for Diaspora Studies. He is an honorary member of the Royal Irish Academy, a Fellow of the Royal Society of Edinburgh and a Fellow of the British Academy, the only historian elected to all three major national academies in the British Isles. In 2001, Professor Devine was awarded the Royal Gold Medal, Scotland's supreme academic accolade. Among Professor Devine's numerous publications is the bestselling *The Scottish Nation: A Modern History* and *Scotland's Empire: The Origins of the Global Diaspora*, both published by Penguin.

T. M. DEVINE

To the Ends of the Earth

Scotland's Global Diaspora
1750–2010

PENGUIN BOOKS

PENGUIN BOOKS

Published by the Penguin Group
Penguin Books Ltd, 80 Strand, London WC2R ORL, England
Penguin Group (USA), Inc., 375 Hudson Street, New York, New York 10014, USA
Penguin Group (Canada), 90 Eglinton Avenue East, Suite 700, Toronto, Ontario, Canada M4P 2Y3
(a division of Pearson Penguin Canada Inc.)
Penguin Ireland, 25 St Stephen's Green, Dublin 2, Ireland (a division of Penguin Books Ltd)
Penguin Group (Australia), 250 Camberwell Road, Camberwell, Victoria 3124, Australia
(a division of Pearson Australia Group Pty Ltd)
Penguin Books India Pvt Ltd, 11 Community Centre, Panchsheel Park, New Delhi – 110 017, India
Penguin Group (NZ), 67 Apollo Drive, Rosedale, Auckland 0632, New Zealand
(a division of Pearson New Zealand Ltd)
Penguin Books (South Africa) (Pty) Ltd, Block D, Rosebank Office Park, 181 Jan Smuts Avenue,
Parktown North, Guateng, South Africa 2193

Penguin Books Ltd, Registered Offices: 80 Strand, London WC2R ORL, England

www.penguin.com

First published by Allen Lane 2011
Published in Penguin Books 2012
004

Copyright © T. M. Devine, 2011

The moral right of the author has been asserted

Typeset by Jouve (UK), Milton Keynes
Printed in Great Britain by Clays Ltd, St Ives plc

A CIP catalogue record for this book is available from the British Library

978-0-141-01564-4

www.greenpenguin.co.uk

MIX
Paper from
responsible sources
FSC
www.fsc.org
FSC™ C018179

Penguin Books is committed to a sustainable
future for our business, our readers and our planet.
This book is made from Forest Stewardship
Council™ certified paper.

For
Cara, Erin, Rebecca and Thomas

Contents

List of Illustrations

List of Tables

Preface

In 1999 I published *The Scottish Nation 1700–2000*, an attempt to survey and understand the domestic history of Scotland over the last three centuries and more. Then *Scotland's Empire 1600–1815* appeared in 2003 and it described, explained and considered the effect, both on Scotland and abroad, of the nation's central role in the development of the British Empire to the early nineteenth century. This volume continues that narrative down to the present day. Its focus, however, over the last 250 years is global as well as imperial, incorporating the post-1783 USA and other non-British territories in the overall account. My contention here is that Scots were never limited to the formal empire as migrants and adventurers. They were a global people whose diasporic roots were established in medieval and early modern Europe and then spread across the world. On the face of it, therefore, this may now appear as the third volume of a trilogy, as my attempt to understand in its totality, through analysis of both home and overseas experience, the modern history of one country. If so, it was never planned thus, but evolved almost by accident.

The present study impinges significantly on areas and periods which I have considered before: the domestic history of Scotland from the eighteenth to the twentieth centuries and the nation's role in the imperial project in its earlier phase, *c.*1750 to 1815. Many studies of the Scots abroad examine the reasons for emigration from the homeland or the impact of them on the new lands. I have tried to combine both approaches in order to project a sense of interaction and the dynamic relationship between homeland and host-land. Scottish ideas and institutions have traditionally been regarded as important in the fashioning of new countries overseas, especially in the Empire. Much less attention has been given to how expanding settlements overseas were crucial to Scotland's own national history.

Purists may cavil at the word 'diaspora' in the subtitle. For some social scientists and historians the term must always relate to the experience of the Jewish people, a process involving the coercion, uprooting and forced removal of an ethnic group outside the boundaries of its established homeland. In that narrow definition there is danger in its use by an historian of Scottish emigration. To some, it may legitimize the popular myth that Scotland's great modern exodus was in large part due to the dispossession associated with the Highland Clearances. This is by no means my intention. It seems to me, however, that one rendering of 'diaspora' in the literature does suit the purposes of the narrative of this volume well. I seek here a return to the original etymological origins of the word, from the Greek 'to sow' or 'to scatter', a process of human dispersal which can be voluntary and opportunistic rather than necessarily governed by implacable expulsive forces. The primary objective, of course, is to examine the diaspora of people. But a secondary purpose is to consider the global 'scattering' and impact of Scottish religious and secular ideas, borne to several overseas countries by the emigrants and leaving a deep mark there, as well as commodities and funding exported from Scotland itself. Scottish overseas investment and capital goods production were often basic to the economic transformation of the new lands in the Victorian era and without which mass migration and settlement there would have been much diminished. These factors are therefore seen as an integral part of the history of diaspora as a whole. Viewed from this perspective, the Scots, in the same way as the Jews, the Irish, Chinese, Palestinians and others, can be rightly considered a diasporic people.

A striking feature is the remarkable longevity of the Scottish emigrations. From the thirteenth century to the present, Scots have been leaving their homeland in significant numbers. Throughout the last seven centuries movement to England has been a constant feature (and, though not considered here, I intend to return to the subject of Scottish migration to England in a future book), and until the few decades before 1700, Scandinavia, the Low Countries and Central Europe attracted large numbers. Even before the Union of 1707, however, the axis was shifting further afield, across the Atlantic and to

India, Asia, South Africa, Australia and New Zealand. By Victoria's reign Scots traders, missionaries, doctors, educators and engineers could also be found in China, Japan, Argentina and other Latin American states: truly a global people.

There is also the linked issue of scale and volume. When European emigration can be measured comparatively from the nineteenth century, Scotland had a higher rate of outward movement on a per capita basis of its population than virtually any other country of the time. Because of this, the history of the Scottish diaspora might not simply be of interest to Scots at home and abroad, but to all those seeking to understand international mobility, one of the great issues of this new century. Key aspects of human experience run through this book: transition, assimilation, identity, the relationship between host country and home country, nostalgia, emigrant cultures, adjustments to the new lands, the impact of Europeans on the lives of native peoples, the invention of traditions and mythologies and much else. The book can therefore be read from one perspective as a detailed case-study of how a single ethnicity, deeply involved in the historic process of the spread of European peoples across the globe, experienced one of the fundamental transformations in modern history.

Nonetheless, I am more than conscious of the weaknesses and gaps in the current text. The subject of Scottish diaspora studies is still in its intellectual infancy despite the immense contributions which some researchers have made over the last few years. There are so many questions to which the answers, rigorously based on representative evidence, are still impossible and will remain so until more systematic archival and comparative research is completed. As a result, this study is an interim statement, a tentative road map into often mysterious territory, much of which remains obscure, but at the same time potentially fascinating to researchers of the future.

Against this background I have tried to incorporate some principles in my approach. Many studies of emigration examine the origins of movement or the experience of settlers in the new lands. As mentioned already, this book seeks to integrate both approaches: the focus on homeland and host-land. I also believe that it is vital, whenever possible, to situate the Scottish experience in a comparative and international context in order to at least reduce some of the dangers of parochialism, introspection and exceptionalism. In addition, there seems to me to be a pressing need for Scottish historians to relate their specific discussions to the wider historiographical issues which currently attract the interest of international scholarship – to avoid so doing is to threaten the ghettoization of a subject which deserves to be part of such a wider discourse. Equally, the emigration saga of the Scots contains much which can enlighten historians of empire, settlement, identity, globalization, European expansion, relations with native peoples and many other topics. In my view another clear principle, obvious because it should be at the heart of all history writing, is to react as honestly as one can to the complexities and ambiguities of the evidence of the past when coming to interpretation and judgement. It will soon become apparent to readers of this book that the subject matter in it is sometimes contested and controversial territory. Scots emigrants often had a marked influence on the development of the countries where they settled. Conventionally this has been seen as being overwhelmingly for the good. But that was not always the case. The harsh realities of any migrant nation's past, particularly in relation to other peoples, need to be aired and debated. A mature democracy should require nothing else.

The book has another purpose. Much recent work on empire and globalization after c.1850 has rightly stressed the importance of the 'Anglophone World' and the 'British World' in explanations of nineteenth-century trade, migration and investment. Undeniably, there is much analytical and empirical merit in such an approach, as that period was indeed the great epoch of Britishness and of its worldwide global reach and impact. Yet the danger is that the different ethnicities within the United Kingdom may be subsumed, concealed and even forgotten within a British melange with only occasional illustrative references to their role as partial compensation. By focusing on the Scots, this volume, while maintaining the broader context, has the wider aspiration of trying to demonstrate that the individual nations of Britain still do merit specific consideration in their own right as part of the broader British dynamic. This is true in terms of the nature of their emigration, migrant identities and global impact because of the distinctive nature of their own economic, social and intellectual structures.

In writing this book I have had essential support from a number of sources. Catherine, our children and their own families – indeed all the rapidly expanding Devine kindred – were, as usual, the bedrock. Margaret Begbie has once again converted my hieroglyphics into impeccable typescript with her customary efficiency. My two assistants, Alex Hendrickson and David Ritchie, could not have been more helpful. Professor Angela McCarthy gave expert advice on New Zealand bibliography. Octavia Lamb skilfully researched the illustrations for the book, with ideas also coming from Douglas Hamilton and Eric Graham. Charlotte Ridings was a scrupulous copyeditor. Nicky Stonehill provided essential marketing and publicity support.

My agent, Andrew Lownie, was a sure guide. Simon Winder, editor par excellence, saved me from several gaffes and false trails. The wonderfully stimulating environment of the newly established Scottish Centre for Diaspora Studies, handsomely and generously endowed by the McFarlane family, in the University of Edinburgh, has provided me with ideas, questions and intellectual doubts in equal measure. I am grateful to all its members and numerous affiliated researchers in other institutions without whom writing this book would have been impossible.

Tom Devine
University of Edinburgh, October 2010

I

Imperial Scots 1750–1815

In 1815 Britain ruled over a global population in America, the Caribbean, Asia and the Antipodes of around 41.4 million people.[1] Contemporaries, such as Sir George Macartney in 1773, revelled in the scale of this vast empire 'on which the sun never sets and whose bounds nature has not yet ascertained'.[2] Patrick Colquhoun's *Treatise on the Wealth, Power and Resources of the British Empire* of 1814 had the revealing subtitle 'in every Quarter of the Globe'. But even these figures underestimated the real extent of British imperial influence. In addition to territories under formal rule there were other areas of 'informal' empire where Britain could, and did, impose its will. At the same time as British dominion was being carved out of the Mughal empire in India, commercial influence was spreading along the Malay coast and as far east as the Chinese port of Canton. Great Indian states such as Awadh (Oudh) and Hyderabad, which were still nominally independent, were nevertheless effectively brought within the sphere of hegemony through Britain's military and naval muscle. Again, in the Caribbean, Dutch or Danish sugar islands became dominated by British planters and capital. It was a similar story in parts of South America, where Britain also had substantial political impact.

Above all, perhaps, this unprecedented expansion of empire was most significant because it unambiguously confirmed the final victory of Britain over France, the great national rival in the epic struggle for global dominance. Seven times between 1689 and 1815 the two nations had fought each other in wars which extended well beyond Europe to North America, the West Indies and Asia. The final outcome always remained uncertain. France's population was substantially larger than Britain's and its martial power formidable. Britain was victorious in the Seven Years War (1756–63) and then annexed much French imperial territory in the Americas and the Caribbean. But the successful revolt of the American colonies after 1776, in alliance with France, came as a humiliating defeat for the British. Only success in the endlessly protracted and uncertain Napoleonic Wars and the signal triumphs at Trafalgar and Waterloo finally settled a global contest which had raged for over a century. By 1815 Britain had become Europe's most powerful imperial state. That provided the vital foundation for yet further territorial expansion in India, south-east Asia and Africa in the nineteenth century. By 1914 the remarkable edifice which was the British Empire approached the zenith of its territorial power. On the eve of the Great War, its extent had expanded to some 11 million square miles, containing 400 million subjects.[3]

Scottish legal and formal involvement in this extraordinary enterprise ultimately rested on the Treaty of Union of 1707. It ensured inclusion within the English system of tariff protection, free trade to the colonies and the support of the Royal Navy for the Scottish marine. Moreover, in an imperial context, in the final analysis, it was mainly English military and naval power that triumphed against the French by the early nineteenth century and set the scene for the massive territorial acquisition which in time was of great material benefit to the Scots.

There can be little doubt in retrospect that in 1707 Scotland had entered a parliamentary union with one of the most aggressive and expansionist nation states in Europe. By the later seventeenth century, England had already built the financial, political and military foundations for unprecedented territorial expansion overseas. This 'fiscal-military state' had revolutionary implications.[4] Like most European governments of the time, the English state spent most of its resources either in waging war or in preparation for future conflict. It has been reckoned that over most of the eighteenth century, between 75 per cent and 80 per cent of annual government expenditure went on current military needs or to service debt accruing from previous wars. For Britain, far and away the biggest outlay was on the navy, the 'senior service', vital for the home defence of an island people and for the prosecution of a 'blue water' policy around the globe, safeguarding trade routes and establishing secure overseas bases for the protection of colonies. Sir Walter Raleigh's dictum still rang true: 'Whosoever commands the sea, commands the trade; whosoever commands the trade of the world commands the riches of the world, and consequently the world itself.'[5] The problem was, however, that navies were fearsomely expensive. Wooden ships rotted fast, maintenance costs were enormous and the huge dockyards and shipyards required for repair and construction inevitably were a major drain on the public purse. Abundant finance rather than military force per se was therefore reckoned to be the crucial sinew of war.

The English state had been pursuing a policy of aggressively extending its economic and military resources since $c.1650$ and the process was virtually complete by the time of the Anglo-Scottish Union in 1707. It amounted to a financial revolution which made available to both the army and navy vast sums for the prosecution of war. The key components included a huge extension of the National Debt, sharp increases in taxation, a government bank (the Bank of England) and the flotation of long-term loans on the London capital market which also attracted funds from the Continent. No other state in Europe (apart perhaps from the Netherlands, which did not link its mercantile prowess so effectively to war strategy as England) was quite as successful in this financial transformation.[6] The costs of the revolution were borne mainly by taxes, especially customs and excise on imported and home-produced goods. Undeniably, as a result, Scotland was faced with an increased tax burden after 1707.

Scottish taxes did rise on consumer items, most notoriously with the salt and linen taxes of 1711 and the malt tax of 1725. Yet, one estimate suggests that, in the half-century after the Union, rather than being transferred to London up to 80 per cent of the revenue take was absorbed in Scotland itself to cover the routine costs of its own civil administration.[7] Moreover, before the 1740s, the Westminster government tended to tread carefully in Scotland, conscious of the extent of Jacobite disaffection there and of the popular fury the malt tax increases had provoked in 1725. Revenue burdens on a per capita basis were therefore much lighter than in the richer counties of southern England. In addition, the Scots customs service was much less effective in collecting revenue in the first few decades after union than its counterpart in the south. Underpayment and smuggling were endemic. A black economy ran through Scottish society from top to bottom at the time. To the anger of their rivals in the English outports, the Clyde tobacco merchants were reckoned to have paid duty on only half their imports in the first two decades after 1707. The Records of the Scottish Board of Customs also teem with cases of widespread intimidation, violent assault on officers and gang attacks on the warehouses of the Revenue.[8]

Tax evasion on this massive scale could not disguise the fact that union with England presented the Scottish elites with a golden opportunity. The benefit of naval protection for merchants engaged in the American trade was obvious. Even more fundamental, however, were the possibilities now opening up for the landed classes, the real masters of Scotland in this period. An historic anxiety for the aristocracy and the lairds was the challenge of achieving gainful employment for younger sons which would not only provide income but an acceptably genteel position in society. Landed estates in Scotland, whether great or small, descended by primogeniture on the eldest male child. His siblings had to make their own way in the world, either by the family acquiring some landed property for their remaining progeny or by younger sons achieving army and naval commissions, entering the law, the ministry or being apprenticed to a merchant house. This was the basic social dynamic which for centuries impelled the offspring of the Scottish gentry to seek careers and fortunes in Europe. But the European connection was fading fast in the later seventeenth century and there is some evidence that the decline of career opportunities there was beginning to stoke up anxieties among the laird classes. Something of this was revealed in the plans for the Scottish colony in East New Jersey in the 1680s. The project was dominated by landowners from the eastern counties of Scotland, especially the north-east region, formerly a major supplier of Scots army officers and merchants to Scandinavia. The proprietors envisaged a colony of landed estates, and among those who eventually emigrated to the New World were a very high proportion of younger sons of the north-east gentry. Thus, three members of the Gordons of Straloch purchased proprietary shares, but only the two younger bothers actually travelled to the colony. Several other emigrants can be identified as sons of minor, cadet branches of landed families. Robert Gordon of Cluny probably spoke for many of his fellow proprietors when he stated that his own reason for being attracted to the project of colonization was to provide land for his younger son, 'since I had not estate whereby to make him a Scotch laird'.[9]

But perhaps even more acute pressures were building up by the early eighteenth century. Scottish landed families were simply having more surviving adult children as infant mortality levels started to fall rapidly. No exact figures exist to prove the point conclusively from a specifically Scottish perspective. However, research on the demography of British ducal families for the period can provide a useful surrogate source of information on changing patterns of population growth among the nation's governing classes. Family size among this elite was relatively stable until the later seventeenth century. But a few decades later, rapid growth started among the aristocracy at a rate considerably higher than in the general population increase in the country as a whole. The percentage of children of the nobility dying under the age of sixteen was 31.1 between 1480 and 1679; from 1680 to 1779, the figure fell to 25.9 and declined further to 21.1 between 1780 and 1829. There were now many more sons surviving into adulthood. If this pattern was replicated across the Scottish landed classes, the concerns for placing younger sons in employment which was both gainful and socially acceptable must have become even more acute.

But this was not all. Changes in the composition of the Scottish landed structure added to the challenge. In 1700 there were around 9,500 landowners in Scotland, only about half of whom had the right to inherit or sell the land they possessed. The structure was dominated by the great aristocratic landlords and their associated kinship groups. This elite was expanding its territorial control at the expense of the lesser lairds between the later seventeenth century and the 1770s. Thus, the number of proprietors in Aberdeenshire fell by nearly two-thirds between c.1670 and c.1770 (621 to 250), and the steepest decline occurred among the smallest group of landowners. The trend was repeated all over Scotland. The total of 9,500 landowners at the beginning of the eighteenth century dropped to 8,500 by the 1750s and fell further to around 8,000 at the start of the nineteenth century. Manifestly, the minor lairds were under considerable economic pressure before the 1750s. Rental income was relatively stagnant and increases in farm productivity did not really encompass most of Scottish agriculture until the 1760s. At the same time, as the number of estates possessed by this class was squeezed, one traditional option exercised to solve the problem of younger sons – namely purchasing additional properties in their name – became much more difficult. In a sense, then, imperial employment after 1707 in the armed forces, colonial administration, trade and the professions came both as a crucial lifeline and a major opportunity. In the decades after the Union, streams of eager Caledonians from genteel but impoverished backgrounds poured into the British Empire at every point, from the Arctic wastes of Canada to the teeming cities of Bengal. The bureaucratic growth of the fiscal-military state ensured that career openings were now much more abundant than before and the Scots were very keen to exploit them. It was a form of resource transfer from the metropolis to Scotland, a kind of eighteenth-century variant on the twentieth-century Barnett formula, with the prime beneficiaries being the landed classes of the nation.

What one writer has described as the 'luscious opportunities' of empire became even more enticing in the second half of the eighteenth century.[10] Particularly after the Seven Years War, there were enormous British territorial gains as a result of conquest, annexation and victory over the French. By *c*.1770 the population of the North American colonies had grown to around 2.3 million. East and West Florida, Quebec and Nova Scotia had all been won from France and Spain. The American Revolution in 1776 and the emergence of an independent United States, born out of the thirteen British colonies, did provide a temporary setback. The colonies' departure left only a rump of under-populated territories in the north of the American mainland. Known as British North America they would in due course become the Dominion of Canada. Elsewhere, however, the momentum of territorial expansion seemed unstoppable. In the West Indies the Ceded Islands (Grenada, Tobago, St Vincent and Dominica) and Trinidad were acquired in 1763, while the most spectacular gains were achieved in India where the whole of the eastern subcontinent and a large part of the Ganges valley were under the administration of the English East India Company by 1815. At that date, it was reckoned that 40 million Indians were now living under British rule, which was also fast extending into Ceylon (Sri Lanka) and Mauritius. At the same time, the East India Company was raising some £18 million in taxation within its territories, a sum amounting to around one-third of peacetime revenue in Britain itself. Exploration had also been pursued in the vastness of the Pacific Ocean by the voyages of such famous navigators as Captain James Cook. A permanent British colony was established in Australia when the First Fleet arrived in New South Wales in 1788.

All this greatly increased demand for soldiers, arms and stores contractors, and the booming colonial bureaucracies with their serried ranks of officials: governors of huge territories at the top to humble clerks at the bottom of the administrative hierarchies. The numbers of men under arms rose from around 113,000 during the War of the Austrian Succession of 1740 to 1748 to 190,000 in the American War, while the cost of war, standing at £8.75 million per annum in the 1740s, spiralled to over £20 million in the 1770s. The fiscal-military state had never held out more alluring prospects for ambitious officers and colonial administrators.[11]

Moreover, in India, the victories at Plassey (1757) and Buxar (1764) became the military foundations for a veritable bonanza of pillage. The years from 1757 to 1770 were those when the subcontinent became notorious as the place where easy riches could be made quickly. Mortality rates among servants of the East India Company were horrendous, but there were compensations. As one historian has noted, 'these years were the only time during the eighteenth century when survival in Bengal virtually guaranteed that a man would return home with a fortune'.[12] It was not Company salaries which fuelled the rapacity but rather returns from private trade, prize money and tax revenues extracted from the newly conquered Indian territories. Edmund Burke summed it up as 'the annual plunder of Bengal'.[13]

In the final analysis, exploitation of these opportunities rested on the provisions of the Treaty of Union of 1707. Yet to Scots in the early eighteenth century there was nothing inevitable about the survival of the Union. Mere geographical proximity between two different states does not, of course, guarantee the durability of any political association. Indeed, far from being typical, it may well be that the Anglo-Scottish Union was unusual in this respect when seen in the context of European history. Christopher Smout, for instance, argues that 'unions between distinct and established medieval kingdoms of some reputation, like England and Scotland, to last for four hundred years (that is including the Regal Union of 1603) is a rare thing'.[14] He then cites the example of two well-known failed unions in Western Europe, the ephemeral connections between Spain and Portugal and Norway and Sweden which both came to an end in acrimonious divorce.

Indeed, the more closely one examines 1707 and its aftermath, the more unlikely seems the remarkable longevity of the Anglo-Scottish political association. The omens at that time were far from auspicious. Scotland's emergence as a nation made out of miscellaneous tribal groupings in the medieval period was in large part the result of a centuries-old struggle to defend the kingdom from English aggression. Moreover, a mere fifty-odd years before the Treaty of Union, Scotland had been conquered and subjected to a military dictatorship by the Cromwellian regime of the 1650s which left bitter memories. The prelude to 1707 itself was the legislation of 1703 of the Scottish Parliament, which in the key areas of foreign and dynastic policy suggested separation from England rather than union. The successful union negotiations were carried out by a tiny patrician elite, resulting in a marriage of convenience passed through the parliament in the teeth of both internal opposition and considerable external, popular hostility.

After 1707 the threat of 'the elephant' loomed closer in the form of the English constitutional principle of the absolute sovereignty of 'the Crown-in-Parliament'. Potentially this dictum was the most lethal threat to the new association. The old royal tradition of the Divine Right of kings to rule without constitutional limit was transferred in the Glorious Revolution of 1688–9 to the English Parliament and later the British Parliament after 1707. Given the dramatically different levels of parliamentary representation, whether based on population levels or property values of the two nations, this constitutional assumption could imply the imposition of unacceptable policies by Westminster on Scotland. That this was not simply a theoretical possibility became brutally clear very quickly. In London, the High Church Tories (who replaced the Whigs in government in 1710) passed the Patronage Act of 1712, re-establishing the legal right of local patrons (usually landowners) to appoint ministers to vacant church offices. This decision did not simply outrage pious Presbyterians. It also opened up a running sore which poisoned Church and state relations until the final crisis of the Disruption of 1843, when the established Church split and the Free Church of Scotland emerged as a powerful rival body. In addition, the Act confirmed unambiguously that the Treaty of 1707 was not, as many Scots believed, an inviolate, fundamental and supreme law; rather it was one which could be altered by the whim of any electoral majority in Westminster. This interpretation was confirmed much later by the most influential constitutional expert of the Victorian era, Albert Venn Dicey (1835–1922). Manifestly, this was a scenario for potential turbulence which became even more likely as taxation on such basic necessities as salt, linen, beer, soap and malt rose inexorably from the 1710s and the anticipated post-Union economic miracle failed to appear. The deep frustration was symbolized by the motion in the House of Lords of June 1713 to repeal the Treaty of Union, an attempt at dissolution only narrowly defeated by a mere four proxy votes. Even more crucially, dissent and anger helped to fuel the Jacobite movement and was one reason why Scotland became the great hope of the exiled Stuarts in the early eighteenth century.

But the febrile nature of anti-unionism should not obscure the fact that even in that volatile period the Union was gathering vital support. It came from two sources. First, just as enthusiastic Jacobites regarded 1707 as an effective recruiting sergeant, Presbyterian Scots (which meant the vast majority in the Lowlands) saw the Union increasingly as the best defence against the potential menace of a Catholic Stuart restoration. The more threatening Jacobitism became, the more these fears were reinforced. It helped that anti-Jacobite feeling was often strongest in some of the most economically advanced areas of the country. Glasgow's joyful relief when the news came of the happy deliverance at Culloden Moor was uninhibited. The town's newspaper, the *Glasgow Journal*, brought out a special large-print edition in celebration of Cumberland's victory to record 'the greatest rejoicings that have been at any time in the past'.[15]

A second factor was the effect which, in spite of public frustrations, the rewards of union was already having before 1740 on the country's business and landed elites. The 'golden age' of the tobacco business, the huge prize of the Union settlement, is often seen as an exclusively post-1740 phenomenon. In fact, recent evidence on the scale of smuggling and under-recording (an estimated average of 42 per cent of legal imports of tobacco leaf, 1715–31) in the trade suggests that the good times could be pushed much further back.[16] Even more crucially, the non-inheriting sons of the Scottish landed gentry, forced into other careers by primogeniture as described above, were already moving in significant numbers into imperial and London jobs before the mid-century.[17] The early emigration of these elites was noted everywhere from British North America to Asia. Later that link between elite careers, empire and union was to be strengthened even further. But it was already a remarkably potent force in the first three to four decades after 1707, and indeed had become significant even before formal union became a reality.

Yet, the final defeat of Jacobitism at Culloden in April 1746 and its brutal aftermath did not entirely end the tensions within the Union. True, the gravest threat to the relationship had been finally eliminated but, on the other hand, English suspicions of crypto-Jacobitism as a peculiarly Scottish disease lived on for some time. Scottish pride was offended by the Militia Act of 1757, which created a volunteer force for defence of the realm against foreign attack in England and Wales but not in Scotland. The conclusion drawn north of the Border was that the treacherous Scots could not yet be trusted with the bearing of arms.[18] Scotophobia then reared its ugly head in the early 1760s, during the government of John, Earl of Bute, the first Scottish-born Prime Minister after the Union. His tenure in this exalted position was brief – less than a year – but his influence endured through interest, networks and clientage. So too did the relentless attacks on him personally (his family name, Stuart, did not help) and on Scots in general. During the 1760s the number of Scots holding state office rose dramatically and it was easy to suspect that Lord Bute was favouring his own kind. In the vast array of cartoons turned out by the London press, the caricatures of the Scots were savagely racist in tone, portraying them as greedy mendicants growing wealthy on England's rich pastures.[19] Bute himself was satirized in one ribald print after another as the well-endowed seducer of the mother of George III, explicit sexual symbolism for the intolerable penetration of England and the Empire by ragged swarms of Scots crossing the Border in search of places and pensions:

> Friend and favourite of France-a,
> Ev'ry day may you advance-a,
> And when dead by tomb be writon,
> 'Here lies one whom all must sh-t-on,
> Oh, the Great, the Great North Briton'.[20]

The transformation in these strained relations began during the American War of Independence, and was completed, finally and emphatically, during the French Revolutionary and Napoleonic Wars. The vital contrast here was with Ireland, the more awkward neighbour. Between 1776 and 1783 the Scots were enthusiastically loyal to the British Crown. Even in the American colonies more loyalists were apparently born in Scotland than in any other country. They became the hated enemies there of the Patriot Party, denounced as natural supporters of tyranny because of Scottish support for the exiled Stuarts in 1745, a dynasty which was viewed as the very incarnation of absolute monarchy and Catholic autocracy by respectable Protestant colonists. At the same time, Irish politicians were seen to be behaving badly and attempting to extract advantage from England's travails.

That contrast between the two nations became starker during the Napoleonic Wars. With Napoleon's all-conquering armies encamped a few miles across the Channel the Irish committed the ultimate act of treachery, as the rebellion of 1798 gave the French the real chance of an effective flank attack. The contrast with the Scots could not have been clearer. Already over-represented among the officer class in the field armies, 52,000 Scots also joined the ranks of the volunteers. With around 15 per cent of the British population, this amounted to 36 per cent of all the volunteer soldiery in 1797, 22 per cent in 1801 and 17 per cent in 1804.[21] Scottish loyalty and the Scottish contribution in blood to the final victory had cemented the Union by 1815. If contemporary caricatures and cartoons are any guide, the 'venomous contempt' of the mid-eighteenth century now became the 'innocent humour' of the Victorian era.[22]

2

National histories can be prone to insularity, introspection and even chauvinistic triumphalism.[23] Perhaps the risks of committing these academic sins are greater when the country in question, like Scotland, is relatively small and in a full political union with a much larger and more powerful neighbour. There is a strong temptation towards boosterism and ethnic conceit about past achievements as a spurious compensation for the risks of inferiority and provincialism. Recently there has been a pronounced tendency in this direction in some works of popular history which focus on the Scottish impact on the world. Well-known examples of this genre include Duncan Bruce, *The Mark of the Scots. Their Astonishing Contributions to History, Science, Democracy, Literature and the Arts* (1996) and Arthur Herman, *The Scottish Enlightenment* (2002), modestly subtitled in the US edition *How western Europe's poorest country invented our world and everything in it*. Herman's book became a best-seller on both sides of the Atlantic. In Scotland at least, its publication seemed to coincide with a new national mood of self-confidence in the immediate aftermath of devolution and the establishment of the first Scottish Parliament since 1707. How to counter the vice of exceptionalism and avoid the pitfalls of what might be termed 'The Burns Supper School of Scottish History' is a major challenge for the scholar, especially when the Scottish impact on the British Empire is under consideration.

Three approaches might help to provide some balance: the provision of generalizations based on hard, statistical and representative evidence; construction of numerical ratios of the Scottish factor in imperial territories and occupations (such as merchants, soldiers, officials, plantation owners and professionals) in relation to the population of Scots in the UK population as a whole; and an attempt at impartial location of the Scottish contribution in comparative context with that of the other ethnicities in the British Isles.

Simply by dint of their demographic predominance within the UK, the English, of course, were likely to take the lion's share of the spoils of empire. But what of the Scots, Welsh and Irish? One imperial historian has recently claimed, 'Of all the peoples of the United Kingdom, it is the Scots' contribution to the empire that stands out as disproportionate. They were the first peoples of the British Isles to take on an imperial mentality and possibly the longest to sustain one.'[24] The same author considers that the Welsh, though by no means irrelevant to the imperial project, 'were more reticent'.[25] It was the Irish, however, who were potentially the main rivals of the Scots – ironically, because Ireland was a country which was itself subject to English colonization. Nevertheless, despite generations of collective amnesia over the British Empire, modern scholarship has identified a powerful Irish contribution to imperial expansion.[26] The Irish were far and away the largest group of emigrants in the eighteenth century to the Atlantic empire, significantly outnumbering the Scottish exodus of the time.[27] Moreover, despite the glamour and fame of the Highland regiments during the Seven Years War, the American War of Independence and, especially, the Napoleonic Wars, it was Ireland which provided most boots on the ground in the struggle for empire. Forty-two per cent of British soldiers were Irish in 1830, when Ireland accounted for one-third of the total UK population, while nearly half of the Bengal Army of the East India Company in 1825 was Irish-born.[28] There is no doubt either that, as has been argued, the Empire 'served as a vehicle for the upward mobility of the Irish middle classes, both Catholic and Protestant', and this was especially the case in India by the middle decades of the nineteenth century.[29]

But for reasons which will be examined below, the Irish never achieved the same preponderance in higher civil and military posts across the Empire as the Scots in the eighteenth century. Their commercial profile in British North America, the American colonies and the Caribbean in the late eighteenth century was lower than that of the Scots, and the Irish never forged anything like the same intellectual, educational and cultural impact on the Atlantic empire by before c.1800.[30]

The point comes through with even greater clarity when we turn to ethnic British Isles ratios in the imperial economy and service in the post-1750 period. At the census of 1801, England and Wales had a population of 8.9 million, Ireland 5.2 million and Scotland 1.6 million: a UK population of 15.7 million at that date. The Scottish proportion was around one in ten of the UK population. If the Scots managed to achieve substantially higher ratios than this in the various areas and sectors of empire, it would strongly suggest 'over-representation' or a 'disproportionate' ethnic presence. In order to identify whether this was or was not the case, the survey which follows will move from British North America, then south to the Caribbean islands (the USA having ceased to be part of the Empire in 1783) and finally to India.

British North America

By the end of the eighteenth century the Hudson's Bay Company (HBC) had established a commanding presence in the Canadian fur trade. It became more like 'an independent beaver republic' than a business firm, trading across 3 million square miles of territory and with an eventual domain that encompassed over a twelfth of the earth's land surface (or, as was once pointed out, ten times the circumference of the Holy Roman Empire at its height). When the HBC's overseas governor, the Scot Sir George Simpson, visited Norway in 1838 he was toasted as the head of the most extensive dominion in the world, 'the Emperor of Russia, the Queen of England and the President of the United States excepted'.[31]

Amid the bitter internecine rivalries and competition in the fur trade, the HBC's success crucially depended on the quality of its human capital, the directors and the servants who represented the company in the remote wastes of Canada. Perhaps not surprisingly however, it was plagued by an acute problem of manning its isolated trading posts in a subarctic region half-way across the world, although for such an international enterprise the staffing needs of the HBC were surprisingly small. As late as 1811 it had only 320 employees in its 76 Canadian posts. More important than numbers were the qualities of reliability, steadiness and loyalty under extreme circumstances. Many of the first recruits had come from the slums of London and the company's managers were soon vociferous in their complaints of their outrageous levels of promiscuity with Indian women and inordinate indulgence in alcohol. They therefore anxiously sought men 'not debauched with the voluptuousness of the city'.[32] The search brought them north to Scotland. Scots were being appointed as factors from the first decade of the existence of the HBC, several years before the Union, and were also active in the fur trade outside the company's ambit from an equally early date. Soon, however, Orkney became the great recruiting ground for most of the eighteenth century. The company's vessels sailing northwards from the Thames put in annually at the tiny town of Stromness to take on fresh water and supplies before embarking on the great circle route to Canada. From the later seventeenth century numerous Orkney lads from the neighbourhood were recruited as company servants, so that by 1800 the HBC had become almost an Orcadian dominion. In 1799, 78 per cent of the men on the overseas payroll were from Orkney.[33] It was a marriage of convenience. For the Orcadians even the wilderness of North America promised a better return than scratching a living from subsistence farming and fishing in the Northern Isles. Temporary migration was nothing new to them. Their ancestors had gone south to the Scottish mainland and east to Europe in search of work for centuries. Many also had worked in the icy waters of the Greenland fisheries long before the days of the HBC. For the company, Orkney was a fruitful source of more loyal and dependable servants than it was accustomed to, who also, in the Scottish tradition, possessed basic standards of literacy and the island experience of labouring on both the sea and land.

The North West Company (NWC), the great rival of the HBC, was formed in 1783 in Montreal but it always remained a loose confederation of small individual firms, each consisting of a few promoters, merchants and fur-trader explorers. The principals were essentially adventurers and gamblers who were devoted to free-market capitalism in its most ruthless and purest form. Its expansion in 1787 to include other syndicates came about because of the murder of a Scottish merchant, John Ross, caught up in the bitter rivalries of the fur trade in the northwest. Fearing that Ross's death would lead to bloody reprisals, and all-out war, the principals of several firms decided to unite rather than fight.

From the start the NWC was dominated by Highland Scots, their sons and grandsons. The prime mover was Simon McTavish, who with his nephew William McGillivray controlled the concern from the beginning. The other great names in the company's history, such as the two famous explorers Alexander Mackenzie and Simon Fraser, were from the same background. They looked to Scotland from which to recruit clerks and servants. As one writer has put it, 'the names of the North West Company partners sound like a roll-call of the clans at Culloden'.[34] Of the 225 men active in the firm, 62 per cent were Scots from Inverness, Banff and Aberdeenshire, normally from military, farming or small landed backgrounds. The ethnic invasion changed the character of Montreal: 'the country is over run with Scotchmen,' complained one Englishman.[35] Even contemporary critics, such as Washington Irving, who condemned the swelling and braggart style of those 'Hyperborean Nabobs', accusing them of behaving like latter-day Highland chieftains attended by scores of retainers in the wilderness, could still acknowledge them as 'the lords of the lakes and the forests'.

Indeed, long before Canada became synonymous with large-scale Scottish emigration it was seen as a land of opportunity for trade and profit. Mercantile interests, rather than statesmen and armies, were in the vanguard of imperial expansion. And, from the Scottish commercial perspective, British North America had several attractions. The country was open to direct trade, whereas India had a statutory monopoly that ensured all goods were channelled through London via the East India Company. In contrast, British North America was a level playing-field. Its partial annexation in 1763 had also come at a convenient time. Scotland was experiencing the early stages of economic expansion which in time would become a fully fledged Industrial Revolution. The search was on for ever more market outlets for the massive increase in volume output of linen, iron goods, woollens and a host of other consumer commodities. As a letter to the *Glasgow Journal* noted in 1760, three years before the war was finally won against the French:

> . . . of all our acquisitions the conquest of Quebec, and consequently of
> the country of Canada, is the most important and most beneficial to
> this Kingdom . . . and also such a source of trade and commerce opened

to us here, as will be fully significant, had we no other, to employ all our trading and commercial people; and find a vent or constant consumption for all our goods, products and manufactures.[36]

The editor of the same paper was positively euphoric at the prospects. To him Canada was a marvel:

An exclusive fishery! A boundless territory! The fur trade engrossed and innumerable tribes of savages contributing to the consumption of our staple!

These are sources of exhaustless wealth. Ignorant and despairing men have called this a quarrel for a few dirty lands or acres of snow, but the British public will soon have feeling proofs that Great Britain must sink or swim by her colonies.[37]

British North America became even more attractive a decade later. As relations between the old colonies and the mother country deteriorated into armed conflict in 1775, merchants in a number of Scottish ports began a feverish search for alternative trades and markets. Thus, during the last twenty years of the eighteenth century, a veritable frenzy of Scottish mercantile activity concentrated in the Canadian centres of Montreal, St John and Halifax. The Scots took advantage of the shorter sailing time to Canada from the Clyde than from the Thames and the relative indifference of the larger London firms to a trade that was still in its infancy.[38] Greenock and Glasgow merchants were already well established in this commerce in the late 1760s after the conquest of the French territories. The HBC and the NWC had already made fortunes in the fur trade and, as already seen, both were run by Scots. This undoubtedly spread knowledge of Canada across the nation's business classes. Others also saw the profit potential of the increasing emigrant trade to British North America after 1783. In the same period Scottish exiles from the former American colonies, such as James McGill and John Dunlop, helped to make Montreal something of a Scottish business enclave as they exerted control over the key export trades in grain, potash and timber to Europe.[39]

Nineteenth-century propagandists liked to give the impression of a monolithic Scottish-Canadian community held together by a shared sense of Scottish values. Mutuality in business, in the promotion of schooling and in the tight personal and kin networks of the Gaelic settlements was much in evidence and seemed to confirm the common contemporary criticism of Scottish clannishness and nepotism. In Upper Canada, for instance, in the early nineteenth century, the ruling political grouping was labelled 'the clan' or 'the Scotch faction'. But in other respects there was precious little sign of ethnic solidarity. Religious divisions and territorial allegiances in the Old World were often carried over to the New. Catholic Highlanders, who mainly supported Toryism, confronted Protestant Lowlanders, many of whom were committed to a more reforming agenda. The NWC, which for a time not only seriously threatened the hegemony of the HBC in the fur trade but nearly drove it to the brink of ruin, was itself almost torn apart by savage vendettas between members of its governing Highland families. The war between the HBC and the Nor'Westers was a ferocious struggle between different groups of Scots – the Orcadian servants of the Bay on the one hand and the Gaels who led the North West Company on the other. Ethnic loyalties on the wild frontier of British North America were easily fractured by the naked greed which fuelled the battle for trading supremacy.

To a much greater extent than in later times, transatlantic emigration from Scotland before 1815 was dominated by Highlanders who, especially from the 1770s, established strong enclaves of Gaelic culture in Upper Canada, Prince Edward Island, Nova Scotia and Cape Breton. But, although in a minority, the Lowland Scots of some means and education were already making their mark. The merchants and fur traders (by no means all from Lowland backgrounds) were prominent and successful members of Canadian society. But of almost equal significance were those involved in medicine, law, the ministry and journalism. These professions gave them an advantage in achieving access to positions of political authority. The Scots were significantly over-represented among elected politicians and holders of official appointments in Upper Canada between 1791 and 1841. The pattern became even more apparent in the higher rungs of the ladder of preferment.[40]

The most notable leaders of the early reform movements in almost every colony were Scots: William Carson in Newfoundland, James Glenie in New Brunswick, Thomas McCulloch in Nova Scotia, Robert Gourlay in Upper Canada and Angus Macaulay in Prince Edward

Island.[41] All five men were highly educated and had attended Scottish universities. Glenie, indeed, had won mathematics prizes while at St Andrews. This was a cut above the educational background of most other ethnic groups in Canada at the time and more than made up for their lack of earlier political experience in Scotland.

The early over-representation of Scots in the ranks of the politically powerful partly also reflected their loyalty during the American War of Independence. Attachment to the Crown had often been achieved at great personal sacrifice between 1775 and 1783 in the embattled thirteen colonies. Many thousands of Scots paid for their loyalty by losing both land and position in an independent USA and were forced to flee as refugees across the border to Canada. Their steadfastness earned them the gratitude of the imperial government and ensured that many educated Scots of social standing quickly rose to prominence in both local government and public office. Through these positions of influence they were also able to introduce Scottish institutions into the fabric of early colonial society. Most often this meant foundations in both the religious and educational spheres. Nearly half the institutions of higher learning across the greatly expanded British North America before the Great War had Scots intimately involved in their foundation.[42]

The Caribbean and Asia

After the independence of the American colonies in 1783 and the decline of direct importations of tobacco to the Clyde ports (now traded direct to Europe) the Caribbean emerged as a surrogate source of Atlantic trade in sugar, cotton and rum. The Scottish connection with the islands was long-standing and went back before the Union of 1707. But after the Seven Years War and the annexation of the Leeward Islands of Dominica, St Vincent, Grenada and Tobago from France in 1763, Scottish interest multiplied in terms of migration, plantation ownership and trade. Historians estimate that there were between 15,000 and 20,000 Scots in the West Indian empire in c.1800.[43] By the same date, Caribbean commerce had become by far the dominant sector of overseas trade, while throughout the British islands Scots were significantly over-represented in the ranks of colonial officials, including those of governors, plantation managers, overseers, military officers and physicians (see Chapter 2).

In Asia, the second half of the eighteenth century saw the power and function of the East India Company (EIC) transformed. The success of the Company's forces against the Nawab of Bengal at Plassey in 1757 coincided with victory over the French in the same area and in Madras during the Seven Years War. After these triumphs the EIC was no longer simply a great trading organization. Instead, it had become an expansionist territorial body which in these years laid down the military and political foundations for the British Empire in India. By 1815, around 40 million Indians were living under the authority of the EIC.[44]

This massive increase in territorial and commercial power inevitably demanded more personnel in the EIC service, whether in the Company's civil administration, armed forces, shipping fleets or the professional cadres, such as physicians and surveyors. By 1800, for instance, the Company's army had grown into one of the largest military formations in the world, with numbers multiplying from 8,000 men in 1783 to over 154,000 by 1805. Most of the rank-and-file soldiers were native Indians (sepoys) but the officers were European, and the Company also employed 10,000 white soldiers in the 1770s. In addition, Crown forces also expanded in the same period, as the age-old struggle with France took on an Indian dimension during the American War of Independence and during the worldwide struggle for naval and military supremacy of the Napoleonic Wars.[45]

As the Empire expanded, it steadily became less English and more British. Even the East India Company, which had jealously guarded its English status against all interlopers from elsewhere in Britain in the later seventeenth century, had been transformed a mere few decades later. By the mid-eighteenth century, the English empire had been transformed slowly, almost imperceptibly, into a multinational business and military enterprise.[46] Nowhere was this more true than in the bureaucracies of the EIC. There the Scots were to the fore in exploiting the huge expansion in career opportunities. Sir Walter Scott once famously remarked that 'India is the corn chest for Scotland where we poor gentry must send our younger sons as we send our black cattle to the south'.[47] Such was the scale of the Caledonian invasion of the Indian empire that jealous reaction to it in London helped to fuel the Scotophobia of those years and the fiery campaigns of John Wilkes against the supposed political incursion of the despised North Britons.[48] Indeed, an additional factor in the opposition to *arriviste* wealthy nabobs, returning from the subcontinent with plundered fortunes, was that many of the most prominent were Scots. One correspondent to the *Public Advertiser* argued passionately that the EIC had to be reformed because the 'Scotch' were 'so deeply interested in our commerce and great trading concerns'.[49]

The fears of English contemporaries about a growing Scottish presence in the Company and the Crown forces in India have been fully supported by modern research. In Bengal, the richest of the EIC's provinces, 47 per cent of Writers (the highest administrative grade) appointed between 1774 and 1785 were Scots. Earlier, in 1750, the Caledonian influx was already marked, with three out of every eight Writers in the province young men from Scotland. It was a similar pattern in the commercial sphere. By 1813, 37 per cent of the private merchant houses in Calcutta were Scottish concerns. Nowhere, however, was the Scot more prominent than in the officer class of both the Crown and Company armies. Fourteen royal regiments helped to garrison the Indian provinces of the EIC between 1754 and 1784. Of these, seven had been raised in Scotland and were led by Scottish officers. Scottish physicians were not only to be found throughout the Indian empire but were also prominent in the great shipping fleets of the Company. As early as 1731, John Drummond of Quarrell, a major patron of Scots in the EIC, asked one of his kinsmen not to recommend any more surgeons to him: 'all the East India Company ships have either Scots Surgeons or Surgeon's mates, and till some of them die I can, nor will look out for no more, for I am made the jest of mankind, plaguing all the Societys of England with Scots Surgeons'.[50] From 1720 to 1757 also, all the Principal Medical Officers in Madras were Scots, while by 1800 they made up nearly 40 per cent of the province's total medical establishment. A strong Scottish presence was also noted in the 1740s and 1750s in the elite ranks of the captains of the East Indiamen which plied the lucrative trade between Britain and

Asia. Scottish over-representation in the EIC persisted: in 1806, 22 per cent of Writers' appointments were Scots, 16 per cent of Cadets' and 27 per cent of Assistant Surgeons'.[51]

Several conclusions emerge from this evidence. First, Scots achieved a much higher recruitment to Indian posts than might have been expected from the Scottish share of the population of the British Isles, which, as indicated earlier, stood at around 10 per cent of the total in the middle decades of the eighteenth century. Nevertheless, it must be remembered that the ratio of Scots fluctuated over time and between the different sectors of Indian employment. It was a pattern of complexity rather than one of remorseless progress to ethnic hegemony. Secondly, the Scottish penetration of the Indian empire was all pervasive, encompassing the civil service, merchant classes, the armies, the professions and the shipping services, and it is also apparent that these recruits came from all areas of Scotland. Thirdly, while some accounts suggest that the Scottish role became decisive only after c.1760, there are clear indications of a visible Scottish presence in the EIC from the 1720s, several decades before the era of significant territorial expansion in India. Fourthly, Scottish success in the higher echelons of the Company was not mirrored by any comparable achievements by the Welsh or the Irish. The presence of the former on the subcontinent was hardly noticed, while the Irish, although very significant in the rank and file of the army – by 1815 over 50 per cent of the Crown forces in India were Irishmen – were notable by their virtual absence in the EIC civil service and the commercial sphere, in large part because of constraints on the recruitment of Catholics.[52] Until the mid-nineteenth century members of the Indian Civil Service were recruited from Haileybury College in a patronage system controlled by the EIC. Between 1809 and 1850, after which Irish numbers did increase, the Irish-born made up only 5 per cent of new recruits.[53] It was partly because of this extensive Scottish presence in the governance of the subcontinent that Scottish philosophical ideas, framed and developed within the eighteenth-century Enlightenment, left such a deep impression on Indian administrative history, as Scottish officials such as Sir John Malcolm, Sir Thomas Munro and Mountstuart Elphinstone applied a whole range of ideas from the Scottish Enlightenment to issues of land tenure, administration and judicial systems.[54]

3

In accounting for Scottish over-representation in the management of the eighteenth-century British Empire, the focus has traditionally been on the Anglo-Scottish Union of 1707, the legal foundation for engagement with the Empire. Comparison with the Irish commercial relationship with the Empire does confirm the Scottish advantages gained in 1707. In the later seventeenth century, English protectionist policies in trade were aimed both at the Irish and the Scots. Through a series of legal prohibitions from the 1660s, Westminster tried to prevent the direct participation of the two nations in England's jealously guarded colonial commerce. This did not, however, prevent a burgeoning clandestine Scottish trade with the Americas.[55] In 1707, however, the Scots formally became part of a new British empire which allowed unrestricted and protected access to Atlantic trade, but this was not the case for the Irish. By an Act of 1696 no goods from the American plantations could be landed in Ireland and this prohibition endured until 1731.[56] Even then, only commodities of lesser value from the colonies were allowed to be imported to Ireland. This ruling remained in place until 1780 and meant that the Irish were legally prevented until that date from direct involvement in the lucrative tobacco and sugar trades, which were so crucial to the Scots in the eighteenth century.[57]

The Irish did take part in Atlantic commerce through the export of provisions (butter, pork and salted beef) and coarse linens, but not in the carrying to Irish ports of those of 'high value'. The constraints therefore conflicted with Sir William Petty's forecast of 1672 that Ireland would have a golden future in the Atlantic because, as he argued, the country 'lieth Commodiously for the Trade of the new American world which we see every day to Grow and Flourish'.[58] For the Scots, therefore, these controls on the Irish plantation trade largely removed a potentially powerful rival in the struggle for transatlantic commercial dominion. After all, in the later seventeenth century, Ireland was reckoned to have better economic prospects for the future in American trade and already had many more settlers in the islands of the Caribbean than the sister kingdom.[59] However, as one Irish scholar has concluded:

> ... while Scottish merchants revelled in the opportunities afforded by the expanding re-export trade in tobacco and, to a lesser extent, in sugar, Irish merchants were firmly excluded ... a substantial trade centred on Glasgow promoted the growth of sophisticated financial services and institutions; lacking any re-export trade Ireland signally failed to develop a similar infrastructure in the eighteenth century ... While individual Irish merchants, and small houses, were to be found throughout the chief trading ports of the empire, the Irish colonial trade was dominated by English merchant houses, English intermediaries and English capital.[60]

The advantageous terms of the Treaty of Union were, therefore, undeniably crucial to Scottish commercial success. Scotland had entered into a partnership with England, albeit an unequal one; Ireland was still regarded by London as a colony which should be policed and kept in check. Nonetheless, union, though a necessary condition, was not a sufficient explanation for Scottish over-representation in empire. Even the tobacco trade was not an inevitable or guaranteed success story. The eventual pre-eminence of the Clyde ports by the 1770s depended in the final analysis on innovative commercial practices and institutional advantages.[61] Union alone cannot account for the high visibility of the Scots in almost every aspect of imperial expansion.

Also worthy of consideration, therefore, is the age-old Scottish connection with Europe. Even before the Union, these ancient links were crumbling as the axis of commerce started to shift from the east to the Atlantic west in the 1670s. Perceptive commentators of the time, such as the Glasgow merchant John Spreull, were aware of the new possibilities. He queried in 1705: 'Although [the English] gain more lands and islands, where have they the people to inhabit them and defend them without Scotland to assist them?'[62] It was an implicit acknowledgement of the vast and time-honoured experience of the Scots as migrants since the thirteenth century in England, Europe and Ireland. Any future role in empire was likely to be as much an extension of this earlier history as an exploitation of new opportunities in the Americas and Asia.

For the four centuries before 1707, the main destination of Scottish migrants had been Europe.[63] Their experience there was very relevant to their later high-profile role in the British Empire. Two particular emigrant 'streams' to the Continent were key: first, the movement of soldiers attached to European armies and, secondly, the persistent emigration of Scots pedlars, tradesmen and merchants into the commercial networks of Scandinavia, the north German states and the interior areas of Poland-Lithuania.

Scots had sold their martial expertise to Irish chiefs, English kings and French monarchs since the fourteenth century. The professional soldier was not only an accepted figure but also a respected part of the Scottish nation. Before 1600, and in some parts for even longer, warrior societies thrived in most of the Highlands. The *Buannachan*, or mercenary corps, were the Hebridean clans' acknowledged spearhead of ferocity.[64] The landscape of the Scottish Borders was studded by a remarkable proliferation of tower-houses and other fortifications. The military architecture confirmed the region's notoriety before 1600 as a centre of murder, cattle thieving, assault and vicious family vendettas that were on a par with the Sicilian Mafia in the twentieth century. Proficient swordsmen were also a common breed in seventeenth-century Lowland Scotland. Thus when Europe entered its greatest-ever military recruitment boom during the Thirty Years War, Scots soldiers were at a premium. One modern estimate suggests that between 1618 and 1648, over 112,000 men from the British Isles were raised for service by the various European powers in this conflict. Of these, around 60,000 (or 54 per cent of the total) may have been Scots.[65] Thus, long before they became British imperialists, the Scottish elites and their family regiments had become a force to be reckoned with in Europe. This was especially the case in Scandinavia where close relationships were forged with the Protestant powers of Norway-Denmark and Sweden. The Oldenburg and Vasa dynasties in particular relied heavily on Scottish military support. In return, Scottish officers became integral to the Scandinavian state systems as senior military and naval commanders and as regional governors. Entire military dynasties were built up around this tradition. One of the most renowned, the Munro lineage from Easter Ross, was reputed to have had three generals, eight colonels, five lieutenant colonels and thirty captains serving in the Swedish armies of Gustavus Adolphus.[66]

Militarism on this scale suggests that soldier employment abroad was built into the social structures of Scotland. Thus, when the end of the Thirty Years War came in 1648 and the military labour market in Europe temporarily collapsed, Scots officers and rank and file began to search for other opportunities. After 1688 they were once again drawn into large-scale European conflict. But this time, most soldiers joined the armies of William III, in his crusade against the French King Louis XIV on the battlefields of Flanders during the War of the Spanish Succession. In this war William created a new British army almost from scratch. To do so, he used Scottish soldiers, which were his by right as king of both England and Scotland, as a single royal force. They fought with the long-standing Scots Brigade in Dutch service against the French. By the time of the Union of 1707, therefore, Scots officers and men had had substantial experience in the European service of a British army. They included established formations with distinguished lineages stretching back to the Wars of the Covenanters in the 1640s and before that to the European theatre in Scandinavia. Both old and new regiments, like the Cameronians, Scots Guards, Royal Scots Greys, Royal Scots (1st Regiment of Foot), King's Own Scottish Borderers (Earl of Leven's) and the Royal Scots Fusiliers (Earl of Mar's), were to achieve even greater celebrity in the eighteenth and nineteenth centuries as the military cutting-edge of the British Empire.[67]

Scottish traders were just as visible in Europe as Scottish soldiers. Commercial links were especially strong with Scandinavia, the Baltic and the Low Countries. Significant Scottish mercantile communities had developed in the port towns of these areas. They were especially well represented in Rotterdam, Veere, Copenhagen, Gothenburg, Hamburg, Bremen, Danzig and Königsberg. From the last of these, Scots pedlars and small traders penetrated deep into the heartlands of Poland-Lithuania in what became, for roughly the period 1600 to 1660, probably the single largest Scottish civilian diaspora, though modern research has shown that they were not quite as numerous as some contemporaries and some later scholars have claimed.

The Polish commercial structure was stagnant with few towns

established across the countryside. At the same time, the Polish aristocracy were marketing the surplus wheat and rye of their great estates at a time of population increase and urban growth in Western Europe. The potential for gain was immense. Scots merchants moved in first from Danzig along with the Dutch and other nationalities. Credit was advanced to grain producers, in a manner not unlike the relationship between Glasgow tobacco lords and Virginian planters in the following century. One suggestion is that at the peak of the grain trade's prosperity in the early seventeenth century there was reckoned to be over four hundred small Scottish settlements in Poland and along the Prussian coast. The success of these ethnic communities was demonstrated by the rise of the twelve 'Scottish Brotherhoods', each organized by an elected committee of 'Elders' drawn from all the Scottish 'colonies'. It was also confirmed by the ascent of a few Scots to positions of real power in Poland. Perhaps the most famous was Alexander Chalmer (Czamer), born in Dyce near Aberdeen, who made his pile in textiles and then served four terms as Mayor of Warsaw. Some, like Robert Gordon, a wealthy Danzig merchant who endowed Robert Gordon's College at Aberdeen, invested some of their riches back home. Yet others entered the ranks of the Polish nobility. But these were not the typical Scots. The majority were packmen, plying their trade on horseback, selling cheap household wares into the remotest parts of the country.[68]

This commercial experience in Europe provides one explanation for Scottish economic success in the eighteenth-century empire. The Scots had cut their teeth for many generations in long-distance overseas trade in alien environments. Thus, they were no strangers to the challenges posed by transatlantic commerce in frontier lands. Indeed, several of the techniques refined and perfected in Europe were simply transferred *en bloc* to the Americas. These included the use of family, local and regional networks; tramp-trading (conveying goods to and from several ports rather than directly across the Atlantic); circumventing competition by expanding into peripheral areas where rivals were weaker; the systematic extension of credit in order not only to gain custom, but to maximize loyalty when it had been achieved; and concentrating on low-cost goods in volume rather than the quality end of the trade.[69]

But the European centres were not simply sources of commercial expertise. They were also platforms from which the Scottish trading empire in the West could be expanded. Here, Scottish expatriates in Holland were to the fore. In 1700 the Scottish Kirk in Rotterdam had around 1,000 communicants. The merchants and seafarers who belonged to it were well placed to benefit from Rotterdam's emergence as a vibrant Atlantic and Asian trade centre with global connections to Brazil, the Caribbean, North America and India.[70] The city's main employers were the navy, the Dutch East India Company and innumerable private merchant houses, all of whom had need of skilled and experienced sailors. Indeed, communions in the Scots Kirk tended to be held in spring and autumn because so many members of the church were sailors serving in the Dutch merchant service and were away in Arctic waters in summer and in the Mediterranean and elsewhere all winter.[71] According to some reports, the Dutch marine employed as many as 1,500 Scots in 1672. Recent research has also uncovered Scottish involvement in the Dutch East India Company and some instances where individual Scots rose to high naval and administrative positions.[72]

This was one advantage of a close connection with the Dutch Empire. Another was the experience gained by being at the heart of one of the world's most sophisticated economies. Rotterdam had a stock exchange in 1598, a chamber of insurance in 1604 and a bank by 1635. Sons of Scottish merchants were often sent to commercial academies in the Low Countries to learn accounts and cyphering.[73] The experience of one family, the Livingstons, shows the advantages that could accrue to those Scots schooled in such a context. John Livingston was a Covenanting cleric who took refuge in Holland in 1663. One of his sons, Robert, became a leading merchant in Rotterdam before moving back to Scotland and then to Boston. By 1674 he had settled in New York where his fluent Dutch, Scots and English were a decided asset amid the ethnic diversity of that city. He married Alida Schulyer in 1678, a bond which connected him with three of the most powerful Dutch New York families. Ultimately, Livingston became a successful transatlantic trader, maintaining close ties with both Scotland and Holland, and founding a family which attained eminence in American politics during the revolutionary era.[74]

However, the over-representation of Scots in influential posts in the expanding empire cannot simply be explained as the consequence of centuries of military and commercial apprenticeship in Europe, although well-born and educated Englishmen were more likely to have the pick of the jobs at home through established networks of personal connection and patronage. It tended to be the 'outsiders' within the British Isles who were most willing to abandon their home country for overseas adventures which, especially in India and the Caribbean, could often end in early death. From England, at least in the eighteenth century, the less affluent and the less able were attracted to the frontiers of empire. Equally, Scots excelled because even the most talented among them had fewer prospects in the metropolis and elsewhere in the homeland and were more easily seduced by opportunities in the colonies.[75]

Of course, the majority of Scottish emigrants were from the lower ranks of society – small farmers, artisans, labourers and the like. Yet, there was also a substantial minority who came from more genteel backgrounds. They conformed on the whole to a classic Scottish pattern, already long-established in movement to the European continent. Many were from families of some social standing but modest means. A large number were well educated, including significant groups who had had the benefit of some university instruction. They were migrants from a society which produced too many trained professionals for too few jobs at home. This, for instance, was at a time when, in one estimate, Scotland was able to retain no more than a third of the physicians it educated.[76] Increasingly, the fairest prospect in all of Scotland was not, as Dr Johnson famously alleged, the road to London, but rather the way to the Clyde ports and the chance there of taking ship for the Americas and Asia.

Over the century between 1680 and 1780 a careful estimate suggested some 818 college- or university-educated men came to the American colonies from Britain and Europe. About a quarter of this total (211) had been educated at just three Scottish universities: Glasgow, Edinburgh and Aberdeen, and most of these (about 75 per cent) went to the Chesapeake colonies of Virginia and Maryland, with only a minority going to New England. New England was well supplied with educational institutions of quality including Harvard and Yale, Dartmouth and the College of Rhode Island (now Brown). The Chesapeake, however, was attractive to Scots not only because of the tobacco connection between Glasgow and Virginia but because, despite the best efforts of the College of William and Mary, demand for higher education significantly exceeded supply. At one point in the seventeenth century, for example, the Virginia legislature was forced to offer ships' captains a bounty of £25 on the delivery of a live minister of religion to the colony. The geographical skew of 'learned' Scottish migration meant that the Scottish intellectual influence was mainly confined to the middle colonies and had less effect on New England. Between 1680 and 1780 some 443 college- or university-educated men settled in the Chesapeake, recruited from institutions in Scotland, England, Ireland and Europe. Nearly 40 per cent were Scottish-trained, by far the largest group. Oxford and Cambridge together sent 153.[77]

Recent scholarship has provided new insights into the educational training and character formation of these elites.[78] Many would have experienced the remarkably rigorous curricula of the Scottish burgh grammar schools, in which they would spend five to six years after leaving the parish system at the age of eight or nine. By the end of that period pupils were expected to be able to converse and write fluently in Latin. The hours of work and study were truly draconian, more than twice the average of equivalent French provincial schools of the time. Such was the discipline of thought and mind embedded in the products of this education system that they were able to cope with enormous volumes of dedicated work in later life and be adept at the 'brain-intensive' activities of administration, accounting, commercial management and the like. It was an educational process admirably suited to producing future functionaries of empire and was further strengthened by the inherited values of Scottish Calvinism:

> [Calvinism's] discipline instilled in believers the need for a life centred on devotion and duty; all had a moral duty to follow God's instruction to work to the best of their ability ... and to practise providence and frugal living. Time must be used fruitfully, to work at one's lawful calling, whether as the servant to the plough, the teacher or the magistrate ... or live off your own, not taking from neighbours or family: 'in the sweat of thy brow shalt thou live'.[79]

The competitive edge in imperial labour markets was also refined for some in the middle ranks of Scottish society by university training. The four universities were transformed in the eighteenth century. No longer were they mainly seminaries for the education of divines and clerics. 'Useful learning' became the watchword as medicine, law, natural philosophy and chemistry flourished, so attracting the professional and mercantile classes who were keen for some form of practical training. Student numbers were on the increase. Edinburgh had 400 students in the 1690s but over 1,300 a century later. Glasgow's student population stood at 250 in 1696 but 1,240 in 1824. Instruction was revolutionized as dictation from set texts in Latin was abandoned and the specialist professorial system allowed for more discursive and specialist teaching, sometimes delivered by such giants of the Scottish Enlightenment as Adam Smith, William Robertson, Francis Hutcheson and Joseph Black. By the early nineteenth century, Scotland had a higher ratio of university places to population size than any other nation in Europe.[80] The impact of the intellectual migration which such educated numbers encouraged was soon apparent. More than 150 Scots doctors left for the American mainland in the eighteenth century, and before 1775 almost all the colonial medical profession were Scots or had been trained in Scottish universities. Scottish educators and ministers were commonplace throughout, and in particular at some of the great institutions of higher learning in America – the College of New Jersey (later Princeton), William and Mary and the College of Philadelphia (later the University of Pennsylvania).[81] Thus it was that Scottish civil institutions began to make a deep mark on the expansion of empire only a few generations after the union with England.

2

Did Slavery Help to Make Scotland Great?

In his *magnum opus*, *The Wealth of Nations*, Adam Smith famously declared that: 'Under the present system of management, therefore, Great Britain derives nothing but loss from the dominion which she assumes over her colonies.' Yet, even Smith's authority could not lay to rest the question of whether empire in the later eighteenth century was a drain on the metropolis or a priceless resource of great material advantage to the mother country as it moved towards economic transformation.

Much later in time, in 1944, the West Indian historian Eric Williams published his seminal *Capitalism and Slavery*.[1] In it, he not only made a stimulating contribution to the intellectual debate which Smith's assessment had encouraged but raised the issues to a much more polemical and controversial level. His focus centred on the role of African people in the development of the world's first Industrial Revolution in Britain. Williams himself described his book as 'an economic study of the role of Negro slavery and the slave trade in providing the capital which financed the Industrial Revolution in England'.[2] Ironically enough, however, despite its later fame, if not notoriety, this thesis formed a relatively small section of a much broader study which also included an analysis of how mature industrial capitalism was itself ultimately responsible for the destruction of the slave system. At first, the book provoked little published reaction in scholarly circles and it was only in the 1960s that a robust response began, which proved to be unambiguously negative. A series of thoroughly researched and carefully argued articles stretching from the 1960s to the 1990s sought to demonstrate that 'the Williams thesis' did not stand up to serious scrutiny.[3] Thus, one contribution published in volume 2 of *The Oxford History of the British Empire* series concluded that the slave trade, though immense in scale, might have added only a mere 1 per cent to total domestic investment in Britain by the later eighteenth century.[4] Scholarship seemed to have delivered a conclusive verdict on the Williams thesis.

However, that judgement proved to be premature. During the 1980s, new perspectives began to emerge as some scholars argued that the approach of the sceptics was much too narrow. Not only should the slave trade itself be considered but also (as Williams himself had implied) the total impact of the slave-based plantation economies of America and the Caribbean on Britain. These could not have existed and, even more importantly, could not have grown so enormously in scale over time but for the labour input of untold numbers of black slaves. If the American colonies and the islands of the British Caribbean contributed markets, profits, capital and raw materials to industrialization in the mother country, then those gains ultimately depended on the enslaved workers of those territories.[5] It was an important shift of conceptual direction which gave a new and invigorating lease of life to the entire debate.

A stream of books and articles soon helped to place the Williams thesis firmly back on the historical agenda. Even long-term sceptics were forced to partially recant, at least to the extent of a cautious realignment of argument:[6] 'African slavery thus had a vital role in the evolution of the modern West, but while slavery had important long-run economic implications, it did not by itself cause the British Industrial Revolution. It certainly "helped" that Revolution along, but its role was no greater than that of many other economic activities.'[7] Others were less restrained. In 2002, Joseph E. Inikori published a lifetime's work on the subject under the title, *Africans and the Industrial Revolution in England*.[8] Inikori's conclusion, after presentation of a vast array of statistical and empirical evidence, was unequivocal: 'the contribution of Africans was central to the origin of the Industrial Revolution in England'.[9] The critical response to his work nonetheless demonstrated that debate on these contentious issues was far from over.[10]

The Scottish dimension never really featured in these discussions. Perhaps this is not surprising given the persistent Anglo-centric nature of a good deal of modern English history, the cordon sanitaire between much of the historiography of England and Scotland, and the continued commitment of many Scottish historians to stick to their own patch and refuse to engage in major British and international debates. This is a pity, because, as will be argued in this chapter, the Scottish experience has much to contribute to the discussion of the broader issues of slavery and capitalism which currently interest a very wide audience of scholars. Several of the participants in the debate refer to 'British' or 'Britain' in their analysis. Yet, in their contributions there is precious little sign of any material being deployed for and against opposing views from north of the Border.

This may not be entirely the fault of colleagues in English and American universities. There has been a long tradition in Scotland that Glasgow and other ports, unlike Bristol, Liverpool and London, took little or no part in the mass transportation of Africans to the plantations of America and the West Indies. Even modern historiography, as recently as the early years of the new millennium, suffered from this nineteenth-century amnesia. Much more attention was paid both to the role of the thinkers of the Scottish Enlightenment in their intellectual destruction of the moral and economic foundations of slavery and to the leadership of the Scottish churches in the abolitionist movement and the cause of black emancipation.[11] As a result, darker aspects of the Scottish connection with the slave economies tended to be either played down or ignored altogether. In 2001, a major compendium of modern scholarship, *The Oxford Companion to Scottish History*, provided striking confirmation of this neglect. The index to the volume contained only one reference to the Caribbean sugar plantations. That related to the sale of Scottish linens in the West Indies. No index entry to 'slavery' appeared and the single reference to the 'slave trade' was exclusively concerned with the abolition campaigns of the early nineteenth century, in which the Scots did indeed play an important and influential part.[12]

In the last few years, however, the research agenda has changed dramatically. Studies have now started to be published on the Scottish connection with the West Indian sugar colonies, and the extent of Scottish involvement in slave trading, either itself or, by proxy, in Bristol, Liverpool and London. A new interest has also developed in the impact of the slave-based economies on Scotland which connects with older work on the relationship between the imperial trades and Scottish development.[13] In consequence, there is now enough material to consider, if only in a preliminary fashion, the ways in which slavery may have been a factor in the eighteenth-century Scottish economic revolution.

I

It is unlikely, even if some new facts come to light, that Scottish involvement in *direct* slave trading from Africa to the Americas was of any great significance. Current research confirms the Victorian belief that Scottish ports played only a very minor role in that commerce. Around 3.5 million Africans are estimated to have been shipped across the Atlantic in British vessels before the slave trade was finally abolished in 1807. The table below indicates the minute level of direct Scottish participation in that traffic.

This low rate of participation was not caused by any ethnic or moral opposition to the trade, however, as there was little hint until the 1760s of significant opposition to the idea of black men and women being used as slaves.[14] Rather the explanation seems to be that London and

Table 1: Known slave voyages direct from Scottish ports, 1706–66

Port	Number of voyages	Period
Port Glasgow	7	c.1717–30
Greenock	14	mainly 1760s
Montrose	4	1760s
Leith	2	1706; 1764

Total slaves embarked: c.4,500

Sources: M. Duffill, 'The Africa Trade from the Ports of Scotland 1706–66', *Slavery and Abolition*, 24 (December, 2004), pp. 102–22; D. Eltis *et al.*, *The Transatlantic Slave Trade*. A database on CD-ROM (Cambridge, 1999).

the English outports were already so well established in the Africa trade by the end of the seventeenth century that during the subsequent decades Scots had to find their primary Atlantic commercial niches in tobacco and sugar importation. A form of port specialization developed along the west coast of Britain in the eighteenth century, with Bristol and Liverpool emerging as the premier slaving centres, and Glasgow more and more active in the tobacco trade, at least until the outbreak of the American War of Independence in 1775.[15]

Nevertheless, Scots expatriates did have a notable role in the slaving activities of English ports. In Liverpool at least five Scots managed slaving firms. Of the 128 slaving captains sailing from the port during the later eighteenth century who mentioned their origins, 25 were from Scotland, as were no fewer than 136 ships' surgeons. Many were in the employ of the two dominant Scots trading houses in Liverpool – Samuel McDougal of Wigton (later a pre-eminent opponent of abolition) and the Tod brothers from Moffat.[16] Scots were equally prominent in Bristol. One of the most powerful merchant dynasties in the north of Scotland, the Baillies of Dochfour, near Inverness, was partially founded on slave trafficking from Bristol.[17] Robert Gordon from Moray was among the owners who managed ten or more slave-trading vessels in the city and between 1745 and 1769 profited from eighteen different voyages to East Africa.[18]

It was in London, however, that the Scots really made their mark. Around one in ten of the African traders in the capital were Scots in the early 1750s, a number which increased in later decades.[19] They were similarly heavily involved in the governance of the Company of Merchants trading to Africa as elected members of the Company's committee of management. Scots were factors and surgeons in the Company's ports where slaves were collected, and also private traders searching the coasts of Sierra Leone and the Gold Coast for human cargoes. One of the most notable enterprises was founded in 1748 when a consortium of five Scots, led by Richard Oswald, Augustus Boyd and Alexander Grant, took possession of a slave 'castle' on the Sierra Leone River at Bance Island which was linked to a dozen 'out-factories' or slave-gathering points in the interior. The enterprise was staffed mainly by kinsmen and associates of the principals. Between 1748 and 1784 the firm and its satellite companies shipped nearly

13,000 Africans across the Atlantic, many of them to Scots plantation owners in the Caribbean.[20]

Hence Victorian assumptions about Scotland's peripheral role in slave trafficking were largely unfounded. There was full and enthusiastic Scottish engagement at every level of the trade, even if direct trading from Scottish ports was minuscule. Yet, while the business may have made some Scots merchants rich, its scale was unlikely to have had a profound impact on the overall economy of Scotland itself. To evaluate the connection between slavery and Scottish development, it is therefore necessary to look more closely at the plantation systems in the West Indies and the American Chesapeake colonies whose very existence depended on slave labour. The sugar, tobacco and cotton produced by these slave-based economies were absolutely central components in Scottish overseas commerce for most of the eighteenth century, and the dominant factors in the country's international trade to a much greater extent than even the equivalent sectors south of the Border.

2

The trade in tobacco became the most remarkable example of Scottish commercial enterprise in the imperial economy during the course of the eighteenth century. In one year, 1758, Scottish tobacco imports from the colonies of Virginia and Maryland exceeded those of London and the English outports of Bristol, Liverpool and Whitehaven combined. Three years later, the highest-ever volume of tobacco leaf was landed in Scotland, a staggering 47 million lb, which amounted to a third of all the nation's imports and, when then sold on to European and Irish markets, no less than two-thirds of its exports. On the eve of the American Revolution, the Scots were reckoned to control over half the trade in the key areas of colonial tobacco production in the interior districts. Little wonder that one planter, William Lee, could proclaim: 'I think it self-evident that Glasgow has almost monopolised Virginia and its inhabitants'.[21]

Lee's reference to Glasgow was telling. Although in earlier years other Scottish towns, such as Ayr, Dumfries, Bo'ness, Leith, Dundee and Aberdeen, were actively importing tobacco, the Glasgow merchants, through their two outports of Greenock and Port Glasgow, increasingly established a virtual stranglehold on the trade. As early as the 1710s the Clyde's share of Scottish imports was already around 90 per cent, and by the 1760s that figure had climbed to 98 per cent. Glasgow was Scotland as far as the tobacco trade was concerned. It was not simply that the city's merchants were adept at crushing competition across the country; they were also formidable rivals within the broader imperial system. Over the middle decades of the century they carved out an ever-larger share of the British trade. As late as 1738 the Scots controlled only 10 per cent of official UK tobacco imports but this figure then rose to 20 per cent in 1744, stood at 30 per cent by 1758 and topped 40 per cent in 1765. Voices were raised in alarm in London, Bristol and elsewhere that if this trend continued for much longer, the Glaswegians would surely possess one of the nation's most lucrative Atlantic trades in its entirety.[22]

In an important sense, however, this dynamic business was much more than the simple acquisition of tobacco leaf from colonial planters, based on slave-labour cultivation, followed by sale to the burgeoning consumer markets of France, Scandinavia, Holland and the German states. The tobacco trade was Scotland's first global enterprise. Because of it, Glasgow became a player on the world commercial stage by the 1770s. To establish and refine their competitive position in the international marketplace, the city's merchants had to ensure they were able to service the needs of the colonial planter class for domestic articles, plantation equipment, household plenishings, clothing, luxuries and a host of other items. American consumers became increasingly sophisticated purchasers as their material standards rose in the wake of expanding markets in Europe for colonial sugar, tobacco, timber, cotton, rice and indigo. Some sense of the new consumerism comes from the New York press. In the 1720s merchants there described only fifteen different manufactured goods in newspaper articles. By the 1770s they were selling over 9,000 different imported items, many of which had highly specific descriptions. Expanding custom in the tobacco colonies, therefore, increasingly meant that Scottish factors and storekeepers had to offer the widest possible range of goods to satisfy the new demands. That in turn

meant that their Glasgow principals had to create secure lines of supply not just for tobacco but for the vast array of consumer goods
needed across the Atlantic. A global business emerged. Wine came
from Madeira and the Canary Islands; sugar and rum from the Caribbean; linen from Ireland; luxuries from Holland, and so on. The
sources of supply ran from the Mediterranean to Russia and across
the Atlantic to the West Indies and Canada: 'the shipping routes
stretched out from Glasgow like the ribs of a fan'.[23] And, at home,
tobacco merchants set up many of their own centres of production by
investing heavily in tanneries, bottleworks, linen manufactories,
sugar-refineries, breweries, ironworks and other enterprises in Glasgow itself and in the counties around.[24]

The impact of all this was deeply felt on the other side of the Atlantic. If the needs of the colonial planter class for consumer goods and
agricultural equipment were great, their requirements for credit were
even more pressing. Especially in the newer areas of tobacco cultivation, such as the backcountry of Virginia, where the poorer planters
concentrated, credit was the lifeblood of the local economy. With capital provided by British merchants, planters could purchase slave
labour and the tools necessary to expand cultivation and clear virgin
land. In addition, the credit advanced meant that the colonists could
work through the months between harvests without denying themselves clothing, food and other items. Credit made it possible to
cope with the inevitable differences in timing inherent in the tobacco
economy – before the return for one year's crop had been harvested,
the planter had to live and plant the next crop. In a sense, then, by
extending liberal amounts of credit the Scottish tobacco houses provided the development capital for many parts of the Chesapeake.
The resulting level of debt owed to the Scots rose steeply, from an
estimated £500,000 in the early 1760s to £1.3 million when the Revolution broke out in 1775.[25]

Credit on this scale provides evidence of another close Scottish
link with the slave economies. It was not simply the merchant houses
who gained but those on whom they relied upon as sources of capital
for transatlantic investment. As a late eighteenth-century historian
of Glasgow observed, 'the strength of the monied interest of the west
of Scotland was embanked in it'.[26] The account books of the big

companies reveal their remarkable capacity to attract interest-bearing loans on personal bond from a very wide social circle far beyond the active managers and partners of the firms. The funds which helped to lubricate the Chesapeake trade were drawn from landowners, trustees, tradesmen, physicians, military officers, spinsters, widows and university professors among others. That also meant the returns from the tobacco business were widely distributed, through these financial networks, beyond the ranks of the merchant community.[27]

In the West Indies, as well as trading with the Caribbean sugar colonies, Scots were heavily involved in plantation ownership there (which was less common in the American colonies), and were also widely engaged in the management of the islands as government officials, military men, merchants, attorneys, surgeons, physicians, shopkeepers and overseers. It was striking that, although the commercial relationship went back to the later seventeenth century, the connection strengthened considerably from the 1760s. This was especially so after the end of the Seven Years War in 1763, precisely at the time when the transformation of the Scottish domestic economy gathered pace. In total there were an estimated 4,500 Scots in the British Caribbean at the time of the Union. These numbers remained relatively stable until the 1760s and then rose steeply about 17,000 new emigrants between 1750 and 1800.[28] Especially after the collapse of the American tobacco trade in 1775 (and its only muted recovery after 1783), the Scottish commercial relationship with the Caribbean achieved a new significance. The export share of British goods from Scottish ports to the islands accelerated dramatically. It rose from 21 per cent of official value in 1781, to 42 per cent by 1801 and then to 65 per cent in 1813. The tonnage of Scottish shipping bound for the Caribbean by that date was no less than 50 per cent greater than that to the European continent combined during the key period of radical economic transformation in Scotland itself.[29]

In the eighteenth century, Britain's West Indian colonies were universally regarded as crucial to the Empire. Even Adam Smith, one of the most eminent contemporary critics of the colonial system, as already seen, waxed eloquent about their immense value: the profits of a sugar plantation in the Caribbean, he admitted, 'were generally much greater than those of any other cultivation that is known either in Europe or America'.[30] Edmund and William Burke also asserted in 1757 that nowhere in the world could great fortunes be made so quickly as in the West Indies. Their importance to the British state and economy was widely and fulsomely acknowledged. In 1700 the British islands accounted for about 40 per cent of all transatlantic sugar consignments; by 1815 the figure had reached 60 per cent. At the end of the eighteenth century the Caribbean colonies employed, directly or indirectly, half Britain's long-distance shipping, their fixed and moveable wealth was reckoned at more than £30 million, duties on West Indian produce accounted for an eighth of Exchequer revenues and the credit structures linked to the plantation economy were crucial elements in UK financial markets.[31]

The expansion of the British West Indian colonies was forged in the violent crucible of the conflicts with France over transatlantic hegemony. By the 1760s, the Leeward Islands (Antigua, St Kitts, Nevis and Montserrat) and Jamaica had all been conquered or annexed. Further large-scale territorial gains took place after the Seven Years War and the Napoleonic Wars. As a result of the first, Britain added Grenada, Dominica, St Vincent and Tobago (the Ceded Islands) in 1763. Thanks to the second, the Empire absorbed Trinidad, St Lucia and the South American mainland colony of Demerara. The British Laws of Trade and Navigation gave the islands a virtual monopoly of the protected home market for the products of tropical agriculture, where by the 1750s commodities such as sugar were selling at prices some 50 per cent higher than in continental Europe. The West Indies at that time also exported rum and molasses and, especially after c.1760, fed the factories of the early Industrial Revolution with cargoes of raw cotton. But sugar was king. Between 1771 and 1775 colonial imports topped 1.8 million cwt. Annual consumption per head in Britain rose spectacularly from about four pounds in 1700, to ten pounds by 1748 and then to twenty pounds in 1800.[32]

The Caribbean response to the burgeoning sugar markets in Europe was built on two key foundations: the evolution of the plantation system and the intensive use of black slave labour. Some islands soon became little more than vast sugar plantations. It was said, for instance of Antigua in 1751, that the land was 'improved to the utmost, there being hardly one Acre of Ground, even to the Top of the Mountains, fit for Sugar Canes and other necessary Produce, but what is taken and cultivated'.[33] These were 'slave societies', in the sense of being human communities that depended above all else on unfree, forced labour for their very existence. Without the slave, the sugar econo-mies of the Caribbean would have been impossible. By 1750 black Africans comprised about 85 per cent of the population of the British West Indies. It was scarcely surprising, then, that the contemporary commentator Malachy Postlethwayt, writing in 1745 in *The African Trade, the Great Pillar and Support of the British Plantation Trade in America*, could report that the nation's transatlantic commercial empire ultimately rested on an African foundation. Slaves outnum-bered whites by six to one in 1748 and by twelve to one in 1815. Most whites were transients, hoping to make a quick fortune and return home as soon as possible with their profits (although, despite the fabled riches of the Caribbean, not many actually managed to achieve their dreams). One consequence, however, was that British West Indian whites failed to develop 'integrated, locally rooted socie-ties, comparable with the North American colonies'.[34] Even Scottish migrants failed to leave much of the classic ethnic stamp of schools and churches on the Caribbean islands where they settled.

This was not the only point of distinction between the two colonial systems. Another was the dramatic difference in the treatment of blacks. Not for nothing was the Caribbean known as the graveyard of the slaves. Even by the standards of unfree labour in the North Ameri-can plantation colonies, human suffering in the West Indies was especially horrendous. In *c.*1830, crude death rates in the USA and Jamaica were 20 and 26 per thousand respectively, and the differences in birth rates were even more dramatic – 50 and 23 per thousand respectively. It was reckoned in the 1750s that a quarter of all slaves died within three years of arrival. But averages often conceal: on the Codrington plantations in Barbados between 1741 and 1746, 43 per cent of all African Negroes died within three years of arrival. Partly this was caused by an inhumane calculation. Planters generally believed until the later eighteenth century that buying 'salt-water' blacks straight off the slave ships was 'cheaper' than encouraging family life and reproduction of the existing stock. Thus, it was com-mon practice for plantations to buy in slaves at crop time and set them to work with little or no time spent on 'seasoning' (acclimatization). By definition, also, slavery was an oppressive regime where work was always managed by the threat of severe punishment. Coercion reached especially rigorous and exacting levels in the Caribbean because the grossly skewed ratios of whites and blacks generated rancorous fear and paranoia among British planters about the potential menace of slave rebellions.

Essentially, however, the high levels of slave mortality were caused by the unrelenting nature of the plantation regime. The slave gangs on the sugar estates toiled from dawn to dusk in land preparation, harvesting the canes and sugar boiling. In the Caribbean about 90 per cent of the slaves worked in these tasks. One scholar estimates that it was 'probably one of the highest labour participation rates anywhere in the world'.[35] The arduous toil helps to explain why about half British West Indies slave women never bore a child in the mid-eighteenth century. On the American mainland there was not the same intensity of work on a single crop. Tobacco cultivation, tending farms, cutting timber and domestic service were just some of the varied range of tasks undertaken. Recent work by nutritionists and anthropologists on slave skeletal remains in Barbados' burial grounds has added a new dimension to an understanding of slave mortality in the Caribbean. These results point unambiguously to malnutrition as a vital factor in reducing the immunity of the black population to the epidemic diseases which infested the low-lying plantations and their malignant environments.[36]

The Caribbean was notorious for planter absenteeism. In 1832, 540 (84 per cent) of a total of 646 sugar estates were owned by absentees or minors. Proprietors were normally keen to escape back home (because of the low life expectancy in the tropics) as soon as they had managed to make enough for independent, leisured living in Britain. By 1800 it was their attorneys, managers and overseers who actually ran most plantations in the West Indies and in these positions Scots were often pre-eminent. This class was committed to maximizing production, not simply to satisfy the expectations of their masters, but because they were also determined to get rich as quickly as possible and so return home to spend their last years in more congenial surroundings. Thus a pervasive culture of avarice engendered a regime of unrelenting and pitiless rigour on the slave plantations. Untold numbers of blacks were quite literally worked to death. It is hardly surprising, therefore, that modern scholarship has identified the islands of the British West Indies as the location of the most deadly and destructive systems of chattel slavery in the New World. Only in the later decades of the eighteenth century, when the policy on most estates altered in favour of breeding new generations of black labour, rather than simply purchasing 'salt-water' slaves off the ships from West Africa, did a distinct trend develop towards amelioration. After 1807, when the slave trade to British territories was outlawed, that process became unstoppable.[37]

By the 1770s Jamaica had become the dominant island in the British Caribbean economy, its wealth estimated at over £28 million, compared to £50 million for the whole of the rest of the West Indian empire combined. Jamaica alone accounted for 40 per cent of the slave population of the British West Indies in the same decade. It was described in the mid-eighteenth century as a 'Constant Mine, whence Britain draws prodigious riches'.[38] The island, by the later eighteenth century, had replaced Barbados as the economic powerhouse of the British Caribbean. White Jamaicans became the richest citizens in the Americas 'with individual wealth and income exceeding by a significant margin those of whites in mainland British America'.[39] And it was, of course, slavery which made all this possible.[40]

In this 'famous fount of profit', the Scots were very active. Edward Long, the planter-historian of the colony, famously claimed 'Jamaica, indeed is greatly indebted to North Britain, as very nearly one strand of the inhabitants are either natives of that country or descendants from those who were. Many have come from the same quarter every year, less in quest of fame than of fortunes.'[41] The evidence of wills and testaments confirms Long's assertion. Between 1771 and 1775 Scots accounted for nearly 45 per cent of all inventories at death valued at more than £1,000 sterling. Further, roughly two-fifths of personal property inventories belonged to Scots in the same period.[42] The Scottish connection went back as far as the ill-fated attempts to create a colony at Darien in the 1690s and before. Some of the survivors of the disaster settled in Jamaica and one of the most prominent was Colonel John Campbell from Inverary, who had been captain of troops at Darien. By his death in 1740 he had become a member of both the Jamaica Assembly and Council and the influential patron of large numbers of young kinsmen and associates on the island from Argyll and Jura. Edward Long noted in 1774: 'I have heard a computation made of no fewer than one hundred of the name Campbel [*sic*] actually resident in it [Jamaica] all claiming alliance with the Argyle family.'[43] The Scots were also over-represented among the ranks of the professional classes – physicians, surgeons and attorneys – who actually managed the sugar estates on behalf of absentee owners. In 1750 over 60 per cent of doctors in Antigua were Scots or Scottish-trained, and there is no reason to believe the pattern in other British islands was very much different. Some of these physicians also diversified into merchanting, slave-trading and plantation ownership.[44] The common view was that attorneys and overseers in Jamaica were usually men from Scotland. Lady Nugent, soon after her arrival on the island in 1801, took the view that 'almost all the agents, attornies, merchants and shopkeepers, are of that country [Scotland] and really do deserve to thrive in this, they are so industrious'.[45]

A strong Scottish presence was noted in other islands. When St Kitts was ceded to Britain in 1713, half the land divisions of 100 acres and above went to Scots.[46] In the later eighteenth century most of the white population of Tobago were Scotsmen, while in Grenada, by 1772, fifty-four Scots (over half of British landowners) possessed 40 per cent of all land planted in sugar and coffee.[47] As more and more territory was won from the French from the 1760s, so it too offered fresh opportunity for Scottish investment in Antigua, Dominica, St Vincent, Trinidad, Demerara and Guyana. As Sir William Forbes, the distinguished Edinburgh banker, recorded in his *Memoirs*: 'extensive speculations were entered by some Scotsmen for the purchase and cultivation of lands in the newly acquired West India Islands'.[48] A distinctive profile began to emerge. Unlike the pattern in the Chesapeake, Scots in the Caribbean became major owners of both plantations and the armies of slave labourers who worked them. In these islands the Scottish connection with slavery was direct, unambiguous and immediate.

In another sense, however, the Scottish links with the West Indies had important parallels with those to the American colonies.[49] If the American trade had its rich 'tobacco lords', West Indian commerce could boast its 'sugar princes'. Both produced merchants and firms of immense wealth. Glasgow's sugar merchants were a small elite numbering around eighty individuals in the partnerships which dominated the trade. Among them was an inner group of only a couple of dozen families who ran much of the business. The biggest firm was Alexander Houston and Company with assets in trade, land and industry in both Scotland and the West Indies, valued at £630,000 in 1809. When it showed signs of collapse in the 1790s the government itself was forced to step in, so disastrous would its failure have been deemed for the Scottish economy as a whole. Immediately below the Houston organization were firms such as John Campbell Sen. and Co. (with assets of £179,000 in 1814); Robert Dunmore and Co.; Dennistoun, Buchanan and Co.; Leitch and Smith; Robert Mackay and Co.; and Stirling, Gordon and Co.

Several of the merchant dynasties who made up these partnerships also owned Caribbean plantations, but the primary function of the firms was essentially to act as the selling agents in the UK and Europe for sugar, rum and coffee, provide credit and advances for slave purchases and organize the Scottish export trade to the West Indies. From their ranks were also drawn Glasgow's political elite after c.1780 – the provosts, councillors and officers of the Merchants' House and the Chamber of Commerce who governed the city down to the early nineteenth century. They established the Glasgow West India Association in 1807, which by the 1820s had become a vocal and robust opponent of the movement for slave emancipation.[50] While anti-slavery petitions were being generated from all over Scotland, the Association and its loyal press ally, the *Glasgow Courier*, vigorously defended the interests of the slave-owners against 'the spread of evil, so much to be dreaded' which, in their view, if emancipation came, would be catastrophic for the fortunes of the city.[51]

3

The evidence surveyed thus far suggests that Scotland had a deep and growing association with the two principal slave-based economic systems in the eighteenth-century Atlantic empire: Virginia, Maryland

and North Carolina on the American mainland, and the sugar islands of the Caribbean to the south. But what impact did this relationship have on Scotland's domestic transformation in this period? In England, the debate on slavery and industrial capitalism remains unresolved. Indeed, one very recent contribution to the discussion has insisted that 'sugar cultivation and the slave trade did not form an especially large part of the British economy'.[52] Such a conclusion is hardly surprising because the revisionists who search for a link between slavery and capitalism in England face considerable evidential and conceptual difficulties in their attempts to produce a convincing thesis. On the eve of the Industrial Revolution, England already had a rich, highly developed and sophisticated economy with substantial urban growth and a highly commercialized agriculture system, making the country one of the most materially advanced societies in Europe.[53] Hence English industrialism probably had little need of finance from external sectors like the colonial trades to move forward by that period. The system was quite capable of replenishing itself from the re-ploughing of profits to provide for further growth and from the existing surplus wealth of the contemporary domestic economy. In addition, econometric studies suggest that the idea of a radical change in economic direction during this period in England, at least implied by the term 'revolution', is overdrawn. The route to economic modernity was long and evolutionary rather than one of short-term dramatic transformation. In this perspective, once again, the resulting modest increments in capital supply could easily be achieved from within the existing domestic system: 'there were enough rich people in the country [England] to finance an economic effort far in excess of the modest activities of the leaders of the Industrial Revolution'.[54]

However, it may be that Scotland can provide more fertile ground for revisionist analysis. It was a country which was in much greater need of external markets and supplies of capital during the industrialization process than its much richer and more advanced neighbour to the south. North of the Border, and up until the early nineteenth century when convergence between the two countries accelerated rapidly, the structures of the Scottish economy were distinctive and different. First, as indicated by contrasting wage rates and the persistence of subsistence relationships in much of agriculture, Scotland *c.*1750 was a much poorer society.[55] Indeed, a few decades earlier in the 1690s, a series of harvest failures and trade crises had unambiguously demonstrated the fragility of the nation's economy. It took at least a generation for Scotland to experience sustained recovery from these disasters.[56] Secondly, from around the 1750s and the 1760s a clear and decisive break with the past was taking place. The comparative evidence suggests that not until forced Soviet industrialization in the 1920s and 1930s few societies, if any, in Europe could equal the speed and scale of the Scottish transformation in the eighteenth century.[57] In other words, the term 'Industrial Revolution' can still be considered to have profound and legitimate resonance in a Scottish context.

Thirdly, the fundamental extent of these rapid changes needs to be stressed. Growth was not simply confined to a 'leading sector' of textile-based industrialization in cotton and linen, where it may indeed have been at its most dynamic. The whole of Scottish society was being recast between the mid-eighteenth and early nineteenth centuries. A key indicator of the dash towards modernity was the pace of urbanization. In 1750 only one in eight Scots lived in towns (defined as urban communities of 4,000 or more inhabitants): a very much lower proportion than that of England. By the 1820s it was more like one in three.[58] Further, the transformation was not confined to manufacturing industry and the urban areas. In the two decades after *c.*1760 the Scottish countryside took on a recognizably modern form with enclosed fields, trim farms and separate individual holdings – a set of changes which had taken many generations to achieve south of the Border. North of the Highland line, Gaeldom moved from tribalism to capitalism over less than two generations.[59]

Fourthly, again unlike England, the Scottish domestic market was relatively small and grew only slowly in the eighteenth century. In the 1750s the population was around 1.25 million and had only risen to 1.6 million in 1801. The annual growth rate of 0.6 per cent was just over half that of England, primarily because of high net levels of emigration, and significantly behind the Irish increase of 2.1 per cent over the longer period of 1791 to 1821. Not surprisingly, therefore, there was far more emphasis on external markets, partly in England but more commonly across the Atlantic, as the strategic sources of demand for the increasing flow of goods now turned out by the nation's textile mills, weaving shops and iron works.[60] Throughout the nineteenth century, this overseas orientation became even more evident. Against this background, it can be argued that the slave-based economies of the Atlantic had a powerful impact on Scottish economic growth as a source of raw materials for the new industrialism and of market expansion and capital transfers to manufacturing, mining and agriculture.

Before the 1830s, the Scottish Industrial Revolution was mainly limited to the textiles of cotton and linen. Metal manufacture only came into its own from the 1830s and 1840s onwards. The establishment of the famous Carron Company in 1759 and a flurry of iron works opened before 1801 proved to be a false dawn. No new companies were floated between that date and 1824. While output did rise for a time, the rate of expansion was markedly slower than that in England.[61] On the other hand, textiles were dominant, accounting for the employment of 257,900 workers, 89 per cent of all recorded manufacturing jobs. Much the fastest rise was in mechanized cotton spinning, which in turn depended on the expansion of raw material supplies from the plantation economies of the West Indies and the American South.[62]

In fact, the connection can be considered catalytic. During the American War, several Glasgow tobacco houses switched their interests to the sugar islands of the Caribbean. Merchant correspondence reveals that while the most lucrative opportunities lay in the importation of sugar, planters drove hard bargains and forced firms to take the less desirable and marketable raw cotton as well. In consequence, cotton coming into the Clyde virtually halved in price between 1776 and 1780, a factor which encouraged many former linen and silk merchants and manufacturers to concentrate activities on cotton spinning and weaving.[63] Until well into the 1790s, 'sea island' cotton from the Caribbean provided the leading sector of the Scottish Industrial Revolution with the vital raw material for its mills and workshops, until being replaced as a source of supply after that period by the southern states of the USA, another slave-based economic system.[64]

These economies were also key markets for Scottish textile producers and other manufacturers. While the domestic market for English producers was dominant it was a different story for Scotland, especially when the populations of the American tobacco colonies are added to those of the West Indian islands.[65] Between 1651 and 1851, the population of England rose from 5.2 million to 16.7 million.[66] Scotland's population was 1.2 million in 1755 and by 1801 had only grown to 1.6 million. In 1851 the total stood at 2.8 million.[67] For such a less-populous country, the Atlantic markets came as a much bigger and decisive bonus than for England. In 1770, the population of the British American colonies was 2.7 million and that of the British Caribbean 760,000 in 1801, most of them slaves who represented a potentially enormous market for provisions and cheap clothing. By 1810, the number of Africans in the sugar islands and the plantation areas of North America had risen to just over 2 million.[68]

Scottish exports to the American mainland colonies at official values averaged £97,962 from 1740 to 1744, then tripled to £298,922 from 1770 to 1814.[69] This was significant, but even more crucial to the domestic economy was the market for 'slave cloth' in the Caribbean. Demand there helps to explain why, as already seen, the West Indies took such an increasing share of exports from Scotland of home-produced goods in the later eighteenth century, rising from 21 per cent (at official values) in 1781 to 65 per cent in 1813. Here, the strategic factor was linen manufacture. Linen was by a long way Scotland's largest manufacturing industry and biggest industrial employer in the eighteenth century. Between 1746 and the 1790s, the output of cloth more than doubled in volume and trebled in value. Even after the 1780s, when the dramatic expansion of cotton captured attention, linen production continued apace. Official output again rose threefold to reach nearly 27 million yards annually in 1813–17. Work in linen spinning, weaving and finishing was critical to the way of life of countless Scottish families. Contemporary estimates suggest that about 40,000 weavers worked for the market in the 1780s and just under 170,000 women found their 'chief employment' in the spinning of linen yarn. When some of the finishing trades are included, full and part-time linen employment in that decade may have occupied more than 230,000 men, women and children.[70] Little wonder that John Naismith could remark in 1790: 'The linen manufacture has been the most universal source of wealth and happiness introduced into Scotland. To how many thousands has it afforded bread for these forty years past?'[71]

In broader terms, the industry was divided into two types of specialization. Most Scottish production concentrated on the cheaper and coarser linens which in turn were heavily geared to satisfying the needs of the export market. Fife, Angus and Perthshire were the dominant centres for these trades. Fine manufacture for lawns and cambrics tended to focus more on Glasgow and the western counties of Renfrewshire and Lanarkshire. The finer production was more oriented to the home market than in the regions of east-central Scotland. In that area, the imperial factor was crucial in three ways. First, the industry enjoyed the protection of a high tariff wall against European competition. Secondly, the system of subsidies through bounty payments set up by the state in 1743 to boost cloth exports to the colonies, was vital. From 1745 bounties were also extended to low-priced cloth, which generated a dramatic increase in linen exports to the plantations across the Atlantic in the years that followed. Throughout the eighteenth century, 80 to 90 per cent of these exports were supported by the bounty and when it was temporarily withdrawn in 1754 the output of some of the coarser linens halved, only to recover vigorously when the subsidy was restored two years later.[72] Thirdly, the colonial markets were critical to growth. European consumption was marginal and Ireland's of minor significance. Nine-tenths of all Scottish linen exported from Scotland went to North America and the West Indies. After the American War, the Caribbean became even more important. In the last quarter of the eighteenth century, the standards of living of countless working-class families in the eastern Lowlands of Scotland came to depend on the huge markets for cheap linen clothing among the slave populations of Jamaica and the Leeward Islands.[73] Moreover, out of this specialization came the global industry of jute, centred on Dundee. Jute in the Victorian era was to that city what shipbuilding was to Glasgow and Clydeside. In due course, Dundee came to rejoice in the name 'Juteopolis'.

The final issue to be considered is that of capital transfers from merchanting and plantation ownership in the slave-based economies to Scotland. There is evidence of very significant investment by tobacco and West Indian traders in Scottish industry, commercial infrastructure and land in the key decades of economic transformation between c.1750 and c.1800.[74] Manufacturing industry in Glasgow and the west of Scotland gained much from colonial merchant capitalization after c.1730. Around eighty industrial units in iron-working, sugar houses, glassworks and soapworks gained substantial investment, but the decisive capital transfers were in textiles where no fewer than forty-six enterprises were involved. Above all, West India merchant capital was often vital for the big cotton-spinning firms which dominated the industry before 1815.

Two merchant houses, Leitch and Smith and Stirling, Gordon and Co., were key shareholders in James Finlay and Co. which by the early nineteenth century owned three major mill complexes and was probably the single largest producer of cottons in Scotland.[75] Similarly, two of the partners in John Campbell Sen. and Co. and one of the members of Dennistoun, Buchanan and Co. contributed £70,000 of the total capital of £150,000 in the New Lanark Company between 1810 and 1812.[76] The two last-mentioned West India firms were also connected through Alexander Campbell and Robert Dennistoun with Robert Humphrey and Co., cotton-spinners of Hutchesontown, Glasgow, in which West India interests held £20,000 of the £32,000 capital in 1816.[77] The Dennistoun family were involved in a variety of other firms, such as John Monteith and Co. and Reynolds, Monteith and Co., cotton-spinners of Renfrewshire (c.1795) and, more importantly, in the formation of the company which developed the major Stanley Cotton Mills in Perthshire.[78] Monteith, Bogle and Co., the owners of the cotton complex at Blantyre in Lanarkshire, also drew on the resources of two West India houses – Alexander Garden of the Caribbean firm of Francis Garden and Co. became a member of Monteith, Bogle and Co. through his marriage with the daughter of its leading partner, Henry Monteith;[79] and Adam Bogle, the other major partner, was not only a scion of a long-established merchant family in Glasgow, but was also a member of Robert Bogle Jun. and Co., a leading West India house in the city.[80] Furthermore, it was reckoned that Alexander Houston and Co. had about £20,000 invested in the cotton industry at the time of the firm's bankruptcy; and Robert Dunmore was the leading figure behind the establishment of the Ballindalloch Cotton Co. in Stirlingshire.[81]

Other spin-offs from the tobacco and sugar trades were the foundation of Glasgow's first three banks and investment in both the Forth–Clyde and Monkland canals. There was also a great outflow of funds from colonial commerce into the purchase of landed estates, with well over half of the Glasgow colonial merchant elite involved and a grand total of at least 140 properties acquired in the burgh itself and the surrounding counties.[82] Even this impressive figure, however, does not do full justice to the capital repatriated from the Caribbean because it is confined to merchant portfolios and does not include possible investments by plantation owners in Scottish land. Initial investigations not only suggest that this was very significant but, unlike that of the merchant princes considered here, spread across Scotland and was not limited in any way to the west-central region.[83] Here was a telling difference with Ireland's connections to the Atlantic slave economies. In one sense it too gained from demand from the West Indies for butter, salt meat and fish as well as linen cloth. The port of Cork grew in the eighteenth century to become the greatest provisioning centre for transatlantic commerce. The agrarian hinterland of the city was developed and, like Glasgow, several wealthy merchant tycoons began to emerge as dominant figures in the economic life of Cork. But the impact was much weaker than in the west of Scotland. The depth of Irish investment penetration into manufacturing, banks and other financial institutions was muted by comparison with Scotland, and failed to generate structural change in the regional economy of south-west Ireland. Moreover, Irish merchants, though very active in the Caribbean were much less visible than the Scots in the slave-based tobacco colonies of the American mainland. Scotland, therefore, had the decisive strategic advantage of market stimulus and capital flows from both Atlantic economies.[84]

The strategic connections between the Atlantic slave-based economies and Scotland's Great Leap Forward in the second half of the eighteenth century were undoubtedly potent ones, especially in relation to raw material supply for cotton manufacture, expanding and new markets, and capital transfers to industry and agriculture. These external influences were especially vital to Scottish development given the country's traditional poverty and relatively small population size. They were not the only factors, however. The commitment of the landed elites to economic transformation, indigenous levels of skills and education, the dissemination of Enlightenment thought and a favourable natural endowment, *inter alia*, were all part of the mix. Also, the slave-based economies were of fundamental importance in the first textile-dominated phase of Scottish industrialization but had little relevance to the second, after *c.*1830, based on iron, steel and engineering, not least because by then the capital resources of the nation were much enhanced. Recent research has also shown that the Indian empire was a further source of external funds; by no means did the Atlantic have a monopoly. Yet, it would seem, on current knowledge at least, that Asian resources, repatriated by Scots in the East India Company's service and by private merchants, tended on the whole to be invested in landownership rather than directly in industry.[85] So the story is a remarkably complex one but even when all the necessary qualifications are made, the central argument remains that the Atlantic slave-based economies were indeed important to Scotland's eighteenth-century transformation.[86]

There is a final irony here. Scotland's growing prosperity increasingly rested after *c.*1760 on the profits and markets of these trades. Yet, precisely at that time, some of the towering figures of the Scottish Enlightenment were building a formidable moral, economic and philosophical case against black slavery.[87] Scottish empirical philosophy, notably in the writings of Francis Hutcheson, emphasized sympathy and fellow-feeling between human beings as the keystone of proper ethical behaviour. That idea of benevolence was in direct conflict with the slave system. Adam Smith also attacked it from the standpoint of economic pragmatism: 'the work done by slaves, though it appears to cost only their maintenance, is in the end dearest of all'.[88] Equally, one of Smith's star pupils, John Millar, in his influential *Observations concerning the Distinction of Ranks* (1771), argued that slavery was a cancer in the very heart of any civilized society, likely to cause continuous rebellion from those subject to coercion and inducing luxury among those who owned them. In time, these contributions fed into the great arsenal of ideas which destroyed slavery in the British Empire and ensured that Scots became significant in the struggle for emancipation, which finally ended in victory in 1833.[89]

But in the short term the intellectual assault on slavery seems to have remained insulated from the daily existence of those Scots employed in the plantation economies and the Africa trade. For a time, indeed, the enormous vested interests involved won over abstract theory. The correspondence of Scots merchants and managers to their relatives at home reveals little concern with the morality of slavery in the later eighteenth century, even among those who had been exposed to the condemnations of the intellectuals. One of the most forthright opponents of black slavery was James Beattie, who held the Chair of Moral Philosophy in Marischal College, Aberdeen. In his *Elements of Moral Science* (1790) he fulminated against this outrageous moral evil, which he described as 'utterly repugnant to every principle of reason, religion, humanity and conscience'.[90] But Beattie also admitted that some of his students found employment in the slave-based societies of the empire despite his 'pleading the case of the poor Africans' in his teaching. He recognized that 'many of my pupils have gone to the West Indies' and he could only maintain the pious hope that, while there, the principles he had enunciated would guide 'their conduct to their unfortunate brethren'.[91]

3

Industrial and Financial Sinews of Scottish Global Power 1815–1914

The eighteenth century can, in retrospect, be seen as the classic period of British imperial expansion. The following one hundred years maintained the territorial momentum but at the same time saw unprecedented British influence expand across the globe, even over nations where the United Kingdom claimed no sovereign authority. This has been aptly described in recent historical writing as the rise of 'the British World-System'.[1]

In the later decades of the eighteenth century, and arguably until c.1830, Britain was an Atlantic power with a great empire, expanding also into parts of the Indian subcontinent. The West Indies and the American colonies were by the 1770s the key elements in her external trading connections. At that point, the Caribbean plantations alone supplied a quarter of Britain's imports and, with the American colonies, around a fifth of her exports.[2] From 1783 the American possessions became independent and by 1815 the future of the remaining colonies of settlement was uncertain. Populations in British North America, South Africa and New South Wales were small and their economies still fragile. There was little indication yet of the extraordinary transformation in economic and territorial influence which was to come. Indeed, the great source of eighteenth-century imperial riches, the West Indies, descended into rapid decline after 1815. They still contributed £15.4 million, or 17.6 per cent of Britain's trade in that year, but soon lost their previous importance. A century later, the Caribbean colonies generated trade with Britain to the value of a mere £6.6 million, less than 1 per cent of the national total.[3]

Yet, in 1869, in his *Greater Britain*, Charles Dilke could proclaim the British 'a world people' because of the enormous scale of their commercial activities in East Asia, the Pacific, south-east Asia, East Africa, the Middle East, Latin America, the USA and the old colonies of settlement.[4] Sovereign control of territory not only continued but expanded. Yet, the hegemony to which Dilke referred was both economic and territorial. The rapid growth of British foreign trade from the 1780s was based to a great extent on developments outside the formal empire. The principal markets by the 1830s were the USA, Western Europe and Latin America.[5] Three decades later, four 'great zones' had become important: the Middle East, tropical Africa, China and South America.[6] All were beyond the imperial frontier. The old colonial system was shattered by this new globalization of British commerce. By 1914, Argentina and parts of China had become more important for British trade and investment than Canada and the West Indies.[7] This was not to say that the Empire had ceased to be relevant or significant. Its share of British total trade in the 1850s was 23 per cent for imports, 30 per cent for exports and 14 per cent for re-exports. These proportions changed little in the years before the Great War. Then the Empire's share of Britain's imports was around 25 per cent, for exports 35 per cent and 12 per cent for re-exports.[8] Manifestly, however, unlike the eighteenth century, the Victorian epoch of commercial success did not alone depend on imperial access, tariff control and territorial rule. Little wonder that the nation's merchants could claim 'this country is more than ever the entrepôt of the world'.[9] That pinnacle had been reached on the back of a truly colossal growth in world trade values, which rose tenfold between 1850 and 1913. Britain was to be the main beneficiary of that increase.[10]

Of paramount importance in explaining this outcome was early British industrialization. Even in the last quarter of the nineteenth century Britain was still ahead of rival nations in the depth, range and complexity of its manufacturing production. By 1881, 44 per cent of the labour force was employed in industry or industry-related occupations, compared with 26 per cent in the USA and 36 per cent in Germany. At the same time only 13 per cent of British workers were in the agricultural sector. The comparative figures for the USA and

Germany were 52 per cent and 43 per cent respectively.[11] In 1840 Britain accounted for as much as 45 per cent of world industrial production and still nearly 30 per cent of a far larger total in 1880. From this huge capacity of industrialism came the upward swing in exports, rising in nominal value from around £38 million in 1840 to £112 million by 1857. Other measures tell a similar story. The tonnage of shipping leaving British ports increased fourfold between 1834 and 1860.[12] Even peasant production in Asia and Latin America could not compete with the price of British products. Especially in textiles, UK producers, with the benefits of technology, could undercut local workers while at the same time break into new markets.

The great river of wealth flowing from industrialism and commerce then fed the projection of military and naval power across the oceans, propelled the transport revolution in steamships and railways and, by the 1870s, enabled UK banks, finance houses and investment companies to export capital to developing countries on an unprecedented scale.

Several other factors added to these key economic advantages. Of central importance was the revolution in global trade. A new and dynamic set of commercial relationships was forged between Europe and the Americas, Asia, the Pacific and Australasia, based on volume exchange of foods and raw materials for manufactured goods and investment capital. Grain, meat, raw cotton, timber, wool and numerous other commodities went to Europe. In return, the primary producers acquired ships, locomotives, bridges and railroads which then went to build the infrastructure in the New World for yet further expansion in global trade. The entire system was lubricated by the revolution in transportation and the flow of information: improvements in the design and speed of sailing ships; the arrival of the ocean-going steamships; the crucial invention of the telegraph, at a stroke providing instant commercial intelligence; and the construction of transcontinental railways, such as the Canadian–Pacific. These unlocked the production potential of vast territories, from the prairies of North America to the plains of India, while the opening of the Suez Canal transformed the connections with Asia and the East. In the centre of all this, like the proverbial spider in the web, was Britain, as the main entrepôt for world trade and finance.[13]

At the same time, the system of tariffs, regulations and controls which had been at the heart of the old imperial system in the eighteenth century were all swept away by the 1850s. The Navigation Acts were abandoned, chartered companies lost their privileges, and the East India Company conceded its monopoly in Indian trade in 1813. Colonial preferences and import duties on many commodities were consigned to history.[14]

However, to conclude that government was but a marginal and passive player in the new economic order would be mistaken. True, the geopolitics of the first half of the nineteenth century worked in favour of the British state. Trafalgar and the final defeat of Napoleon ensured that Britannia did rule the waves for the foreseeable future. By 1815, too, most Latin American countries were liberated from their European masters and became tempting markets for British merchant houses. France, the old imperial enemy, was profoundly weakened for over a generation. Yet, to make free trade and the Pax Britannica work, force, or the threat of it, sometimes still had to be employed. Treaties of commerce with foreign powers were indeed preferred to outright territorial annexation, but even they had sometimes to be backed with armed intervention and gunboat diplomacy. The most striking example of the deployment of British military power to protect the interests of trade was in China. An expeditionary force extracted major concessions from the Chinese Empire in 1842 via the Treaty of Nanking. By this action, half a dozen 'treaty ports' were created where British merchants were shielded from Chinese jurisdiction, maximum tariffs on goods imported to China were established and the harbour at Hong Kong transferred to the British. After a second conflict in the 1850s, the number of these treaty ports increased and internal travel in China conceded.[15]

The final context for British hegemony was demographic. The estimated population of the world rose from 906 million in 1800 to around one and a half billion a century later.[16] Demand for foodstuffs, housing and clothing at this global level therefore rose exponentially. Then there was the great movement of European peoples across the Atlantic and, to a lesser extent, to the southern hemisphere, where they helped to populate some of 'the empty lands' of the American West, the Canadian prairies and Australasia. The number of European migrants to the USA alone between 1820 and 1930 totalled 32.1 million. This was part of the biggest and most rapid demographic transformation in human history. Britain contributed disproportionately to the exodus. By the mid-1870s, over 8 million people (75 per cent of them from the home countries) left UK ports for non-European destinations. This great surge in emigration hugely expanded the productive capacity of the receiving countries while at the same time offering fresh opportunities for British and, in the case of this particular study, Scottish merchants and manufacturers.[17]

2

In 1888, amid great celebrations, the Glasgow City Chambers were formally opened by Queen Victoria. The lavish internal decoration, imposing façade and marble staircases symbolized Glasgow's extraordinary progress in the previous decades and its eventual claim to the status of 'the second City of the Empire'. Earlier, in 1883, at the foundation ceremony, overwhelming civic confidence was also visible. About 100,000 spectators in George Square watched a ceremonial march by the skilled workers from the heavy industries which by the later nineteenth century had made Glasgow one of the wonder cities of the world. In 1901 the second International Exhibition, staged in Kelvingrove Park, conveyed similar images. It was the largest of its kind ever held in Britain and attracted 11.5 million visitors, including the Tsar of Russia. The focus was on the city's economic and industrial achievements. The Machinery Hall and the Industrial Hall were particularly dedicated to Scottish prowess in the arts of engineering and science.[18]

These events were striking confirmation not only of Glasgow's economic success but of the remarkable material progress of Scotland as a whole since 1830. Then the jewel in the nation's economic crown had been the textile industries, with cotton manufacture in particular in a pre-eminent role. The later nineteenth century, however, was the era of triumphant advance in the heavy industries in which Scotland developed a position of global dominance in several key sectors. By 1914, Glasgow and its satellite towns in the surrounding region of industrialization produced one-half of British marine-engine horse-power, one-third of the railway locomotives and rolling stock, one-third of the shipping tonnage and about a fifth of the steel. On the eve of the First World War the Clyde shipbuilders not only built a third of British output but almost a fifth of the world's shipping, a record that was greater at the time by a considerable margin than all the German shipyards combined. At the heart of the heavy industrial complex with its worldwide markets was the huge range of engineering specialisms in engines, pumps, hydraulic equipment, railway rolling stock and a host of other products. Three of the four greatest firms building locomotives were in Glasgow; in 1903 they came together to form the North British Locomotive Company, 'the Titan of its trade' with a capacity to produce no fewer than 800 locomotives every year. This made the city the biggest locomotive-manufacturing centre in Europe with engines being produced in large numbers for the Empire, South America and continental countries. In civil engineering, too, the west of Scotland was a famous centre of excellence symbolized by the career of Sir William Arrol (1839–1913), the builder of the Forth Bridge, the Tay Bridge, Tower Bridge in London and numerous other major projects in many parts of the world.[19]

Cotton-spinning, 'the leading sector' of the first Industrial Revolution, was in some difficulty from the 1850s when the embroidered muslin trade dramatically collapsed. Although 131 cotton mills still operated in Scotland in 1868, the industry came under intense pressure from foreign competition, assisted by tariffs and the impact of Lancashire producers at the finer end of the trade. By 1910, cotton-spinning had declined in Scotland to the point where only nine firms survived, its demise accelerated by a failure to maintain earlier patterns of innovation, low levels of investment and a labour force which, the owners asserted, was unwilling to accept the measures necessary to achieve higher productivity.[20]

The collapse of cotton-spinning, however, was more than compensated for by virtuoso performances in other textile sectors. When Coats of Paisley amalgamated with Patons in 1896, the world's biggest thread-making producer was created. Archibald Coats (1840–1912) came to be known as the Napoleon of the thread trade and his business was so profitable that eleven members of the family became millionaires. When faced with American tariffs, Coats audaciously set up factories in that country and soon dominated the market in thread across the Atlantic. The firm eventually controlled no less than 80 per cent of global thread-making capacity.[21]

Just as remarkable was the development of jute manufacture in the coarse linen areas of Dundee and the surrounding districts. Jute was a fibre used in bagging and carpeting and was imported from Bengal. The Cox Brothers' Camperdown Works in Lochee in the 1880s employed 14,000 (mainly women) workers, making it the biggest single jute complex in the world. Again, the product was sold throughout the globe, with booming markets in the United States and the British colonies.[22] Other Scottish towns and cities had their own textile specializations: Kirkcaldy in floor coverings and linoleum; Galashiels, Hawick and Selkirk in the Borders with tartans, tweeds and high-quality knitted goods; Kilmarnock and Glasgow in carpets (in Glasgow, Templetons was the largest carpet manufacturer in Britain by 1914); and in Darval and Galston in Ayrshire, fine lace-curtain manufacture employed around 8,000 people just before the Great War. This range of activity ensured that textiles remained an integral part of the Scottish economy despite the malaise in cotton-spinning. Indeed the numbers employed in thread and lace-making in the 1910s in the west of Scotland fell little short of the labour force in both cotton-spinning and weaving in the 1870s.[23]

Diversity was not confined to the textile sector. James 'Paraffin' Young (1811–83) pioneered the exploitation of the shale oil deposits of West Lothian through a series of inventions which led to the growth of a substantial industry producing 2 million tons of shale by the 1900s. Whisky distillation was, of course, a Scottish specialization, with over 20 million gallons charged for duty in 1884. At Clydebank, the American Singer Company developed the world's largest complex for the manufacture of sewing machines with a labour force that numbered over 10,000. Further evidence that heavy industry did not have a complete monopoly was the Barr and Stroud optical factory, the Acme wringer factory and the experiments in new ventures such as automobile and aircraft manufacture on the vast 45-acre site of the engineering giant, William Beardmore and Co. During the Great War Beardmore alone supplied no fewer than 650 planes.[24]

The decades before 1830 had seen radical changes in the Scottish economy and society. However, major industrial development was mainly – though not exclusively – confined to cotton and linen, with only sluggish growth in coal and metals. What happened after 1830, and more especially in the second half of the nineteenth century, was a truly massive increase in the scale of development. Coal, iron, steel, shipbuilding and engineering took off and transformed Scotland into a manufacturer for the world. All these sectors (and others) were emphatically committed to the export market. A small country of fewer than 5 million people in the 1900s emerged as a key player in the global economy, linking the primary producing regions of America, Africa, Australasia and Asia to the industrializing regions of Europe. Such a development was bound to have deeply significant effects on the nature and structure of Scottish society.

First, the employment generated by the new industrial economy permitted a substantial increase in Scotland's population. Between the 1750s and 1831 this had risen by 88 per cent to 2.374 million. In the next 80 years, 1831–1911, the population doubled to 4.761 million. Some of this was accounted for by an upsurge in immigration from Ireland after the Great Famine and in subsequent decades, attracted by the employment opportunities in Scottish industry. Secondly, the national redistribution of population that was already under way before 1830 became even more marked in the second half of the nineteenth century. The concentration of people in the central Lowlands accelerated. The eastern region, centred on Edinburgh, grew from 785,814 to 1,400,675, but the increase in the heartland of heavy industry in and around Glasgow was much more spectacular. The western zone expanded from 628,528 to nearly 2 million people by 1901. At that date the western counties had boosted their share of national population to an astonishing 44 per cent. At the same time the overall share of the eastern Lowlands remained virtually static. Elsewhere the pattern was one of general haemorrhage. The population of the Highlands peaked in 1841 and then went into absolute decline. The far north reached its maximum population level in 1861, the Borders in 1881 and the north-east in 1911. The clear gainers were the counties where manufacturing and mining dominated. For instance, the population size of Fife, Angus, Renfrew and Stirling more than doubled; West Lothian trebled and Dumbarton increased fourfold. Remarkably, numbers in Lanarkshire rose by 356 per cent. Rural depopulation is often associated with the Highlands, but it is clear that hardly any area of Scotland escaped the full impact of demographic transformation in this period. Special study of one decade, the 1860s, has revealed that the overwhelming majority of parishes in all parts of the country were losing people, especially in the south-west and in the east from Moray to Berwick. It was only the textile towns of the Borders and parts of the central Lowlands which experienced significant levels of inward migration.[25]

Thirdly, and almost an inevitable corollary of the point already made, agriculture as an employer was in rapid retreat as mining, building and manufacturing established a hegemony in the labour market. As late as the census of 1851, more men and women were engaged in farming than in mining and textile work combined. Thereafter the pattern altered radically. The proportion of the population working in agriculture fell from 25 per cent in 1851 to 11 per cent in the early twentieth century. Fourthly, the drain of people from the land was the essential precondition for a continued expansion in urbanization. Scotland had already experienced a rapid rate of urban growth in the early nineteenth century. By 1851 it was second only to England and Wales and significantly ahead of the Netherlands in a league table of 'urbanized societies' in Europe. Yet, as late as the 1830s, just over one-third of the Scottish population lived in towns of over 5,000 inhabitants. By 1911 this proportion had risen to nearly 60 per cent. This explosion of urban development was generated primarily by the expansion of the 'big four' cities – Glasgow, Edinburgh, Dundee and Aberdeen – where more than one in three Scots lived by the beginning of the twentieth century. Once again, Glasgow stood out in the colossal and continuous nature of its exuberant growth. An army of men and women flooded into the city from the farms and small towns of the Lowlands, the Highlands and Ireland to satisfy the enormous appetite of the great staple industries for both skilled and unskilled labour. In the 1830s there were already over a quarter of a million Glaswegians. By 1871, the total had reached half a million, and just before 1914, partly as a result of boundary extensions, the magical figure of 1 million inhabitants was attained. Elsewhere, agricultural and market centres such as Lanark, Dumfries and Haddington continued to thrive, but the urban dynamic was, in the final analysis, primarily generated by the power of industry. Outside the 'big four', the most significant rates of growth were experienced in the Border textile towns, the iron, steel and mining centres of Lanarkshire (such as Coatbridge, Motherwell and Airdrie) and the Fife burghs.[26]

The new industrial and urban society depended on a number of important foundations. Most crucially of all, it relied overwhelmingly upon access to overseas markets. Some 38 per cent of all Scottish coal production went abroad or to the coast in the 1910s, apart from that consumed by the export-orientated iron, steel and other industries. The giant North British Locomotive Company sent nearly half its engines to the British Empire in the years before the First World War, with India as the primary destination. The rise of Dundee jute was generated from the 1840s by the demand for bagging for international commodities as varied as East India coffee and Latin-American guano, as well as the enormous market for sandbags during the Crimean War, the American Civil War and the Franco-Prussian War. At the end of its first major phase of precocious growth in the 1840s, two-thirds of Scottish pig-iron were exported, a significantly higher proportion than the pattern elsewhere in Britain. Even in the later 1860s, around a half of total production was still being sent overseas. The yards that poured out ships on Clydeside also relied for orders on the condition of international trade, even if increasingly from the 1890s the needs of the Admiralty for naval vessels were becoming ever more significant. It was the same story elsewhere, from quality Border knitwear to malt and blended whiskies.

But that market was increasingly global and not simply colonial, as had overwhelmingly been the case in the eighteenth century. The destinations of shipping tonnage clearing from the Clyde between 1886 and 1911 can shed some light on this important point. The decline of the West Indies colonies, described earlier in this chapter, is plainly visible from these data. In this period, the volume of shipping for the Caribbean islands from the Clyde was significantly behind most other destinations, including Canada, Australasia and even Africa – a stark contrast to the early nineteenth century when the West Indies were the single largest external markets for Scottish manufacturing. The tables below, while confirming the significance of the imperial factor, also demonstrate that by these measures at least, the west of Scotland was much more than 'the workshop of the British Empire'. In terms of cargo tonnage, Europe and the USA were of crucial importance, more so than imperial destinations.

Table 2: Tonnage of shipping with cargo clearing from the Clyde to foreign destinations, 1886–1911

Non-imperial

	1886	1891	1896	1901	1911
Europe	407,805	506,293	651,374	n.d.	948,587
USA	305,356	308,466	358,635	n.d.	865,258
South America	60,760	88,495	161,892	n.d.	482,723
China, Japan and the Pacific	38,480	53,542	124,692	n.d.	175,182
Total out	812,401 (58%)	956,796 (58%)	1,296,593 (66%)		2,471,750 (59%)

Imperial

	1886	1891	1896	1901	1911
India and East Indies	320,628	350,712	303,489	n.d.	616,684
Canada	117,369	176,669	160,489	n.d.	427,504
Australasia	99,084	79,660	70,438	n.d.	192,182
West Indies	25,042	45,907	48,140	n.d.	91,998
Africa	20,261	46,718	80,843	n.d.	382,217
Total out	582,384 (42%)	699,666 (42%)	663,399 (34%)		1,710,585 (41%)

Source: Mitchell Library Glasgow, Clyde Navigation Trust Shipping Returns

Table 3: Tonnage of shipping clearing from the Clyde to foreign destinations, cumulative percentages, 1886, 1891, 1896, 1911

Destination	Percentage cumulative tonnage
Europe	27
USA	19
India & East Indies	17
Canada	9
South America	8
China, Japan, Pacific	7
Africa	6
Australasia	5
West Indies	2

Source: Mitchell Library Glasgow, Clyde Navigation Trust Shipping Returns

Table 4: Tonnage of shipping entering Glasgow from foreign destinations, 1911

Destinations	Tonnage	Percentage of total
Europe	1,279,346	44
USA	549,176	19
Canada	394,645	13.5
India & East Indies	391,379	13.5
South America	121,301	4
Australasia	73,818	2.5
Africa	48,733	1.5
China, Japan, Pacific	42,666	1
West Indies	1,002	0.03

Source: Mitchell Library Glasgow, Clyde Navigation Trust Shipping Returns

Industrialism had dramatic consequences for Scottish manufacturers. On the one hand, the earnings which accrued to the world's primary producers enabled them to purchase more capital goods. On the other, the investments in the global transport system opened up a voracious demand for ships, locomotives, railways, bridges and jute bagging. Scottish investors added to this momentum by themselves putting money into American, Australian and Asian railway stock, land and cattle companies, mining ventures, tea plantations and state bonds (see Chapter 11). This outflow, from what for the majority of the population was still a relatively poor country, had a circular impact on the development of the Scottish economy, as these investments then helped to fuel demand for Scotland's industrial staples. As one scholar has put it: 'The wheat of the Canadian or American prairies, for example, had to be taken by rail to eastern ports, and in Canada the locomotive could well be made in Glasgow while both in Canada and in America the sacks holding the grain were quite likely to have been manufactured in Dundee. The ships which crossed the North Atlantic with the grain were often enough built and engineered on the Clyde.'[27] The New World economic context was the essential precondition for economic success; what of the domestic factors which made this possible?

3

A prime foundation was the rich heritage from the decades before 1830.[28] Scotland's early industrialization had given the country a head start over virtually all European rivals – with the exception of its nearest neighbour, England. A number of key advantages were already in place which helped to provide a platform for the industrial achievement of Victorian times. These included a large and experienced business class; a political and social elite committed to national economic growth; a labour force which had already developed skills in engineering, mining and textiles and, crucially, had become accustomed to the more rigorous time and work disciplines of industrial capitalism; a sophisticated infrastructure of ports, roads and canals; and an international network of trading connections, not only to Europe and

North America but increasingly to the countries of the Empire and beyond. The meteoric rise of Dundee was in large part based on these relationships. Samples of jute were first sent from Bengal by the East India Company to leading textile centres in Britain in the hope that the cheapness of the coarse fibre might prove attractive to manufacturers. Dundee was the first to solve the technical problem of the dryness and brittleness of the new fibre, not only because the city and the surrounding region specialized in coarser linens but because raw jute was softened by the process of 'batching' or applying a mix of whale oil and water. Since the later eighteenth century Dundee had become a leading whaling centre in Scotland.

An even closer link can be established in shipbuilding, which in the second half of the nineteenth century became the strategic heart of the west of Scotland's heavy industrial economy. In the early decades there was little competitive advantage in ship construction. In fact, the Clyde had limited traditional expertise in building modern ships and as late as 1835 it launched less than 5 per cent of total British tonnage. The crucial advantage was the Clyde's pre-eminence in the development of steam engines for ships, which in turn depended on the range of engineering skills that had accumulated in the region during the first epoch of industrialization. Steam engines were used in the pits to pump water and raise coal and in the cotton factories they were becoming increasingly common. The foundries and workshops of the region not only built but repaired and improved engines. As James Cleland remarked in the early 1840s, 'Glasgow ... has already large establishments for the manufacture of Steam-Engines and Machinery, and for making the machinery employed in the process of Cotton-Spinning, Flax-Spinning and Wool-Spinning. In these works everything belonging to, or connected with, the Millwright or Engineer department of the manufacture is fabricated.'[29] It was perhaps almost inevitable that from these skills in precision engineering would come an interest in the application of steam propulsion to ships. Henry Bell's historic launch of the steamboat *Comet* in 1812, followed by the successful voyage across the Clyde, demonstrated that it could be done. By 1820, 60 per cent of all British steam tonnage was launched on the Clyde, even if all these vessels were small, had low boiler pressures and consumed huge amounts of coal. The foundation of later greatness depended upon an effective solution to these basic problems of high cost and low performance. It is acknowledged that an important catalyst was the Napier family, headed by David and, later, by his cousin Robert, who pioneered key technical improvements at their Camlachie foundry and Lancefield yard. The Napier firm became a kind of advanced school of marine engineering and construction and David Napier became the first to combine engineering and shipbuilding in one firm. Many other foundries became active in the supply of boilers and engines for ships as well as for their traditional markets in the mines and mills. What is striking, however, is that virtually all these engineering firms were clustered in the cotton districts of Glasgow, such as Tradeston and Camlachie. The close connection between the textile industries of the first Industrial Revolution and later fame in shipbuilding in the west of Scotland was confirmed.

These were the foundations, but a number of basic influences then helped to accelerate the transformation of Scotland into a world economic power in the next few decades. A primary factor was a remarkable rate of strategic invention and innovation in metalworking and ship construction. In iron, the seminal advance was made by James Beaumont Neilson (1792–1865), the manager of Glasgow Gasworks who had developed considerable expertise as a chemist and engineer. He revolutionized the iron industry through his hot-blast process. It resulted in great savings in material, costs and fuel and also in increased production per furnace. Neilson's invention was the basis of the exceptional growth of pig-iron manufacture in Scotland. It allowed the Scots ironmasters to undercut their English and Welsh rivals significantly. Between 1825 and 1840, Scottish output expanded twentyfold to 504,000 tons. Growth was concentrated in Ayrshire and, to a much greater extent, in Lanarkshire, where the Bairds of Gartsherrie built the core of their great iron-producing empire in the Monklands area. In just forty years from the 1830s this family developed a reputation as the world's leading pig-iron producer with, in 1870, 42 furnaces with a capacity of 300,000 tons per annum and a profit in that year alone of £3 million. Thomas Tancred, the commissioner appointed to report on conditions in the mining districts, described the Monklands in graphic terms in 1841:

... the groups of blast furnaces on all sides might be imagined to be blazing volcanoes at most of which smelting is continued Sundays and weekdays, by day and night without intermission. By day a perpetual steam arises from the whole length of the canal where it receives waste water from the blast engines on both sides of it and railroads traversed by long trains of waggons drawn by locomotive engines intersect the country in all directions.[30]

Here indeed was the scarred industrial landscape of Victorian Scotland in its classic form.

The rate of innovation in shipbuilding was unrelenting from the 1830s. The Clyde achieved worldwide renown because of its capacity to produce radical and ingenious modes of propulsion and at the same time pioneer new materials of construction. There was a remarkable list of Clydeside firsts which kept the Scottish yards at the leading edge of the burgeoning global market for ships. These included the development of the screw propeller in place of the paddle, which increased speed, the compound marine engine which dramatically expanded power, and the use of new materials such as iron and then steel in ship construction. In the second half of the nineteenth century the fortunes of shipbuilding, iron and steel became very closely linked, primarily because the Clyde yards were so keen to pioneer new materials. In the 1840s almost all iron tonnage was launched on the Clyde and between 1851 and 1870 accounted for over two-thirds of all British production. Steel-making was established in Scotland in the 1870s. Expansion was constrained because Scottish iron ores were phosphoric and the main steel-making techniques – the Bessemer converter and the Siemens-Martin open-hearth process – relied on low-phosphoric ores. This problem was remedied by the Gilchrist-Thomas process of the 1880s. In the event, however, the Scottish industry developed by using the open-hearth process and imported ores. By 1885 there were already ten firms producing almost half of all British-made Siemens steel. The link between the open-hearth process and shipbuilding is very significant. Essentially, steel was the child of shipbuilding and the result of the determination by the major yards to use metal plates of even greater strength, lightness and durability in order to maintain their leading position in world markets.

The economic achievements of Victorian Scotland were also built on local supplies of fuel, raw materials and the low costs of labour. Coal reserves were abundant throughout the central belt and had helped to power the steam-driven textile mills of the early nineteenth century. However, with the vast expansion of iron-making, coal came into its own. In 1800 there were probably around 7,000–8,000 miners in the country. By 1870 this labour force had risen to nearly 47,000 men, working in over 400 pits. The Baird ironmasters accounted for their extraordinary success in large part on the fortuitous presence of rich seams of the invaluable splint coal in close proximity with reserves of blackband ironstone in Lanarkshire. From the later eighteenth century, access to coal and iron ore supplies had been radically improved with the development of a network of roads and canals. From the 1820s, however, the railway added a new dimension to the transport of heavy raw materials and finished products. It is significant that the earliest ventures, such as the Monkland and Kirkintilloch Railway (1824) and the Garnkirk and Glasgow (1826), were promoted in order to maximize the exploitation of mineral deposits. Capital raised by Scottish railway companies was a mere £150,000 in 1830. By 1850 it stood at over £20 million and at nearly £47 million in 1870. Trunk lines were promoted linking Glasgow, Edinburgh, Paisley, Greenock and Ayr as early as the 1830s, followed thereafter by the creation of coastal routes to England. The railways had far-reaching effects on almost all aspects of Scottish life but their impact on the heavy industrial economy was particularly profound. They were more reliable than canals, which were likely to freeze in winter. Like them, they could shift bulk goods at low cost but did so much more rapidly and with greater regularity. It was also technically much easier for industrial and mining plants to connect to an intricate network of railways by sidings and spur lines than to a system of canals. The mineral riches of particular localities were unlocked and industries with complementary specializations could concentrate together on an unprecedented scale. It was the railway more than any other factor that helps to explain the sheer density of industrial activity in parts of Glasgow, Ayrshire, West Lothian and Lanarkshire.

In spite of the marvels of the new technology, most industries still depended on human labour. Shipbuilding was to a significant extent a huge assembly activity in which skilled workers were much more crucial than machine tools. Coal-mining, despite significant advances in cutting machinery from the later nineteenth century, remained a 'pick and shovel' industry. In 1890 one estimate suggests that labour costs constituted around half the overall cost of finished steel and anything between one-third and two-thirds in shipbuilding. The engineering, tool-making, metalworking, furniture, woodworking and printing industries could function only on the basis of skilled labour. In 1911, seven out of every ten men and women in Glasgow found employment in a range of manufacturing activities. Those sectors where skilled male workers were dominant or significant accounted for almost a quarter of the entire Glasgow workforce compared to only 10 per cent in 1841.

Furthermore, Scottish labour worked for lower wages than the average in England, the country which was Scotland's main competitor for much of the Victorian period. Scholars are agreed that this gave Scottish industrialists a strategic cost advantage, even if the Anglo-Scottish gap narrowed somewhat in the later nineteenth century. Scottish wages were low in comparison to the average for the United Kingdom in iron and steel, shipbuilding, cotton and brewing, according to data for the 1880s. In the crucial sectors of iron and steel and shipbuilding, the Scottish average was £70 per annum compared to £76 for the UK. In textiles there was an even more entrenched system of low pay, based on the widespread employment of female labour. By the 1880s two-thirds of the 100,000 workforce in textiles were women. The cotton-masters in the west had embarked on a strategy of hiring low-paid women operating self-acting spinning mules rather than men, while in Dundee the employment of poorly paid female labour was the city's first line of defence against the continuing threat of Indian competition.

Any bottleneck in recruitment to the collieries was eliminated in two stages. The first was the ending of collier serfdom by legislation in 1775 and 1799. These measures were not enacted in a spirit of philanthropic benevolence but rather to recruit more labour, destroy the collier trade unions or 'brotherhoods' and keep wage claims in check. The second was through the increase in Irish immigration, which helped to solve any problem of labour shortage in the long term as coal production grew rapidly after *c.*1820. There is little doubt that the swelling coal- and iron-mining communities of Lanarkshire and Ayrshire depended heavily on the Irish as production levels escalated. In 1861 in Coatbridge, fewer than half of the colliers and miners were Scots-born. The rest were Irish migrants.

It was not simply the cost and availability of labour that was of critical importance to these great staple industries. Also of relevance was the response of the workforce. By the early twentieth century, trade unionism was expanding and labour relations became more tense. This was symbolized by the foundation of the Scottish Trades Union Congress in 1897. But the later militant image of 'Red Clydeside' did not at all fit the west of Scotland in earlier decades. The Glasgow Cotton Spinners' Union had successfully resisted the introduction of self-acting spinning mules, but in the strike of 1837 and the aftermath it was effectively destroyed and never again represented a threat to innovation. There were stoppages among Clydeside engineering and shipyard workers in the 1860s and again in the 1880s, and Dundee female jute workers did strike at regular intervals. But during the 1860s 'trade unionism was all but wiped out in the shipbuilding and mining industries'.[31] Union membership was low by the standards of England and Wales and the usual pattern was one of small, local unions with few members and little muscle. Demarcation disputes were common, especially in metals, shipbuilding and building, while occupational sectionalism was aggravated by sectarian tensions between Irish Catholics and Protestant Scots workers. For these reasons Scottish labour seemed to employers to be both cheap and docile. It was because of this reputation that the American Singer Sewing Machine Company was attracted to Clydebank in 1900, where its factory soon achieved the capability of turning out 13,000 sewing machines a week.

In general, indeed, during the golden years of the Scottish economic miracle the employers held the whip hand. Some, like Bairds and the Neilsons, were resolutely opposed to trade unions as an unmitigated evil, but virtually all of them took a hard line in industrial disputes, sometimes pooling their strength in such alliances as the Shipbuilders' Employers Federation, the National Association of Master Builders and the East of Scotland Association of Engineers. Employers were therefore in a virtually impregnable position. Edward Young reported to the United States Congress in 1872 that the Clydeside worker 'must work for a mere pittance, to enable his employer to sell his goods abroad at low rates, or there will be no work for him to do, and he will be left to starve'. He added that the worldwide success of Clyde-built ships was to be explained in the final analysis by 'the abundance of skilled workmen and the low wages paid to them'.[32]

4

The scale of Scottish activity in nineteenth-century shipping and merchanting, both within and beyond the formal empire, has tended to be neglected by British historians. This is not surprising since London and the Home Counties, the heartlands of Victorian imperialism, were mainly bypassed by Scottish syndicates both in trade and overseas investment, at least before 1900. The well-known work of P. J. Cain and A. G. Hopkins has added to this relative oversight, not only of the Scottish factor but also of the significance of the English regions.[33] They see the drive to British overseas expansion as firmly rooted in the 'gentlemanly capitalism' of the city of London and its affiliates in finance and services rather than in the manufacturing dynamic of the provinces. Scottish enterprise does not fit into this London-centric model. Indeed, the evidential base on which it is founded cannot capture the global range of Scottish activity which emanated not simply from the homeland but from expatriate Scottish firms that were firmly lodged within the business communities of Liverpool and Manchester, as well as in the numerous port cities of Canada, south and south-east Asia and Latin America.[34] The Cain-Hopkins thesis has not been accepted uncritically since publication and it is possible that one of its most significant weaknesses is the marginalization of the Scottish contribution to British expansion.[35]

Ship-owning is one of the sectors where this was most prominent. Until 1914, Glasgow ranked third in the UK after London and Liverpool when measured by shipping tonnage registered in British ports. In addition, Glasgow was the only other UK city, apart from London and Liverpool, to have a Lloyd's Committee. At the industry's peak, in

1910, there were no fewer than 182 management firms in Glasgow and Greenock. The heart of the industry was a core group of forty-three companies, each of which managed five or more vessels over 1,000 tons.[36]

Some of the giant firms had a global reach. The most impressive in this respect was the huge conglomerate headed by Sir William Mackinnon who, in one opinion, could 'lay claim to being the greatest Scottish tycoon of all time'.[37] By 1890, this entrepreneurial and puritanical Gael from the Kintyre peninsula owned five great shipping companies, with a total fleet value of over £3 million.[38] The Mackinnon group straddled a web of interrelated shipping lines that connected London, Lisbon, Sydney, Fiji, Basra in the Persian Gulf, Singapore, Hong Kong, Rangoon and many other locations. The main area of concentration was the immense expanse of the Indian Ocean from East Africa to India and then onwards to Burma, the Indonesian archipelago and as far as eastern Australia.[39] From the Mackinnon companies emerged the Inchcape Group which survives to the present day.

The Peninsular and Orient shipping company was formed in 1840 by Arthur Anderson from Shetland out of his original firm, the Peninsular Steam Company, which had specialized in trade with the Iberian Peninsula. In due course, another Scot, Thomas Sutherland from Aberdeen, helped develop P&O operations to the Far East and Australasia. Its Scottish roots soon disappeared into the past but as late as 1900 half of the firm's fleet was registered at Greenock.[40] Another famous name, Cunard, had extensive Glaswegian connections during its first forty years of commerce from 1840. Samuel Cunard himself was from Nova Scotia but the founding partnership also involved George and James Burns and David and Charles MacIver from Glasgow. The company retained a strong Scottish complexion during its climb to ascendancy in the transatlantic shipping routes before c.1880, after which Cunard based itself in Liverpool.[41] It was a rival of the Glasgow-based Allan Line in the Atlantic emigrant trade to Canada. By 1880 the company was operating thirty-nine vessels, making it the seventh largest shipping firm in the world, and its offices were to be found in the Americas, in Montreal, Boston, Philadelphia and Buenos Aires.[42] Other notable Scottish syndicates in global shipping included the Anchor Line to the Orient; the Donaldson Line, plying between the Clyde and the River Plate; the Glen Line with a specialization in the importation of Chinese tea; the Albion Line, which played a pioneering role in the shipping service to New Zealand from where it brought the first cargo of refrigerated mutton in 1882; and the famous Irrawaddy Flotilla Company, its paddle steamers immortalized by Rudyard Kipling as they traversed the route from Rangoon to Mandalay.[43]

Doubtless the rise of these major shipping lines in part reflected Scotland's long tradition as a seafaring nation with centuries-old connections to Europe and, in more recent times, to the Americas and beyond. But there was more to the story than that. At its heart was the historic expansion in the exchange of manufactured goods with the primary producers of the world in return for their foods and raw materials. Scotland, as a notable centre of industrialism, needed sea transportation to convey its exported goods across the oceans. In addition, because of the Clyde's pre-eminence at the cutting edge of shipbuilding and ship propulsion, Scottish ship-owners were able to fully exploit the maritime revolution in steamship design at an early stage. The technological lead in marine engineering, hull design and dockside cargo-handling machinery meant the Scottish and other British companies were extremely well placed to exploit the new opportunities in Asia and Australasia when the opening of the Suez Canal in 1869 cut 4,000 miles off the old route around the Cape of Good Hope. The shipping firms were among the best customers of the Clyde yards. The Mackinnon group, for example, was the first to transfer Scottish technology in iron-hulled steamers to the East. Indeed, no shipping magnate ordered more tonnage from Clyde yards after c.1850 than William Mackinnon's five companies.[44] It was also common for the shipbuilders and ship-owners to make common cause. Dennys, for instance, had connections with nearly twenty shipping lines and sold over 770 vessels to many of them, valued at more than £20 million between 1880 and 1913.[45]

The steep increase in emigration to the Americas and the Antipodes after 1850 also came as a godsend. Some firms, such as the Allan and Donaldson lines to Canada or the Albion Line to New Zealand, became specialists in the emigration business, with the space on the return voyage to British ports filled with primary produce from these overseas territories. Many of the shipping lines, like their counterparts in overseas investment, relied heavily on contacts among expatriate Scots in positions of influence in the Indian and Asian ports where they provided advice, introductions and commercial intelligence. These ethnic relationships were founded ultimately on the earlier growth of Scottish influence in the eighteenth-century East India Company and in the private trading houses of Asia.[46] The networks were much less pervasive or traditional in Latin America and that fact may help to explain the greater Scottish focus on Asia and Australasia as commercial activity expanded beyond the frontiers of empire in the course of the nineteenth century.[47]

Leading the economic charge were the agency houses which, though primarily trading concerns, also often developed functions as bankers, ship-owners, bill-brokers, insurance agents and purveyors. Some were simply the agents of British industrial firms, especially in cotton manufacture, which depended on them to sell their products in distant and alien markets because they possessed the specialist knowledge and local connections in these territories.[48] They spread from India into Burma and other parts of south-east Asia in the first half of the nineteenth century. Even before the East India Company monopoly on trade with China ended in 1833, agency houses were already actively engaged with Chinese merchants and customers.[49]

Scots companies became pre-eminent in the Eastern trade. A striking example is the colony of Singapore, founded in 1819. Twelve of the first seventeen trading partnerships set up there were predominantly Scottish.[50] One of the greatest was Guthrie and Co., established in 1821 by the young Alexander Guthrie from Brechin and managed by members of his family for over a century thereafter. After dealing in sugar, spices, vegetable oil and coffee, Guthries moved into investment in Malayan rubber plantations in 1896. By 1913, the company owned 25 per cent of the land in that colony possessed by British agency houses, by far the greatest share.[51] Especially impressive was the move of the great Scottish textile firm of James Finlay and Co. from specialization in cotton to investment in Indian tea and jute.[52] Other famous names were also established in this period. Thomas Sutherland, chairman of P&O, founded the Hong Kong and Shanghai Bank in 1864, with the help of several fellow Scots. Predictably it was run on 'Scottish principles' with a heavy reliance on joint-stock company traditions, acting as a bank of issue through a broad network of branches and with the aspiration to attract both British and Chinese capital.[53] At the time of writing, HSBC, long shorn of its Scottish roots, is both the world's largest banking group and the world's sixth largest business corporation.[54] Another eminent name, the Burmah Oil Company, the parent of British Petroleum, developed out of the Rangoon Oil Company. The latter was itself a marriage of two leading Scottish ship-owning firms, Hendersons and the Irrawaddy Flotilla Company. Progress was at first halting, until, when taken over by David Cargill of Glasgow, the Burmah Oil Company was incorporated in 1886. Two decades later it produced the largest output of oil in the British Empire.[55]

First in fame (and notoriety) of the Scottish houses at the time, however, was Jardine, Matheson and Co. It has survived the vicissitudes of war, revolution and economic crisis over nearly two centuries and still flourishes to this day, but with the direct Scottish connections long ended, though not forgotten. (The Chinese junk the company owns today in Hong Kong is named *Highland Thistle*.) The company was formally established in Canton under the saltire flag in July 1852, though the earliest of the partnerships from which it grew date back as far as 1832. Known as 'The Firm', Jardine Matheson has had a longer continuous existence than any other British or European business in the China trade and is the only survivor from the Treaty of Nanking in 1842 which opened China to foreign commerce. Originally based in Canton, it soon moved after the treaty to the new colony of Hong Kong and remained the most important commercial enterprise there for most of the nineteenth and twentieth centuries.[56]

The two leading partners came from opposite ends of Scotland.[57] William Jardine was born near Lochmaben in Dumfriesshire in 1784. Trained in medicine at Edinburgh University, he became a ship's surgeon with the East India Company at the age of eighteen. Employees on the Company's ships were granted the privilege of carrying some cargo on their own account and it was through this mechanism that Jardine first entered the China trade. He did so well that he left the Company in 1817 to start up as a private merchant. Jardine was by reputation stern, unbending and formidable. The Chinese were said to call him 'Iron-Headed Old Rat' because of an incident at the gates of Canton when a heavy bar fell on him from a scaffold. The story goes that Jardine walked on undaunted. He combined a devout Christian commitment with the capacity for ruthless rapacity which drove The Firm to early dominance over all other rivals.

James Matheson was born in Lairg in Sutherland in 1796, the bastard son of a Highland gentleman. Like Jardine, he too was an alumnus of the University of Edinburgh, though he studied arts rather than medicine. Family connections facilitated a post in India from where Matheson also branched into the lucrative China trade after 1819. Despite their profound differences in personality (Matheson was reckoned to be personable, suave, and with real intellectual interests), both he and Jardine were unrelentingly committed to making money by either fair means or foul. One writer has described them as 'utter rascals' who 'distinguished themselves by a ruthlessness bordering on infamy'.[58] When both eventually retired to Britain with great fortunes, the principal source of the massive profits earned by The Firm was the opium trade to China.

For the Scots merchants in the East, the opium business was the equivalent of tobacco for their predecessors in the eighteenth-century Atlantic trades: namely a quick route to unimaginable riches. James Phipps, the contemporary compiler of commercial handbooks, took the view that the trade in opium 'can scarcely be matched in any one article of consumption in any part of the world'.[59] For William Jardine it was 'the safest and most gentlemanlike speculation I am aware of'.[60] Success arose from a traditional problem in the China trade. The East India Company wanted China tea and plenty of it. But China required little in return other than Indian raw cotton. The Company was therefore forced to pay in bullion to make up the deficit. The discovery of the insatiable appetite of the Chinese for Indian-produced opium changed all that. Between 1800 and 1810, China had gained something like $26 million in her world balance of payments. From 1828 to 1836 this surplus was turned into a deficit of $38 million, such was the impact of the massive increase in opium imports.

The sale of opium had been prohibited by the Chinese from 1799 and partly for that reason the East India Company preferred to deal in the trade through private merchants rather than via its own employees.

As a contraband commerce, precise and definitive figures on opium imports are elusive but what is not in doubt is the astronomical increase in sales. From 1800 to 1821 the opium traffic was estimated at around 4,500 cases (140 lbs or 63.5 kg per case), while by 1840 the trade had swollen to 40,000 cases. A decade earlier it alone was contributing one-seventh of the total revenues of the East India Company, and therefore indirect surpluses for the British Exchequer. The Chinese monied upper class was the target market and so it was alleged that, by mid-century, 20 per cent of the officials of the central government were smokers as well as 80 per cent of the clerks at lower levels of administration. The damage done to the elite of the nation by the drug trade was incalculable, even to the extent of threatening imperial rule and national administration itself.

Jardine, Matheson and Co. were the kings of this trade with only one other British firm, Dent and Co., coming close to their hegemonic status. In the financial year 1832–3 the company's net profits stood at £309,000. Their interests soon diversified into shipping when they developed a large and impressive fleet of opium clippers.[61] After one of the Emperor's sons died of an overdose of opium, however, China finally moved to try to suppress the trade in 1840. Jardine Matheson and other British houses immediately sought to portray themselves as victims of Chinese aggressors who were attacking the sacred British principles of free trade and universal access to markets worldwide, especially after merchants were shut up in their Canton factories for twelve weeks by the Chinese government when they refused to hand over their opium stocks. This became a pretext for the extremely one-sided First Opium War which ended with the signing of the Treaty of Nanking, ceding sovereignty to the British over Hong Kong and admitting foreign commerce on a legal basis. It was a signal victory for The Firm and their supporters. Lord Palmerston thanked William Jardine for 'the assistance and information so handsomely afforded us' in these 'satisfactory results'. He went on: 'There is no doubt that this event [Nanking], which will form an epoch in the progress of the civilisation of the human races, must be attended with the most important advantages to the commercial interests of England.'[62]

Jardine returned to London, set up a banking business specializing in oriental trade and became a favoured member of the ruling Whig party. In 1844, Matheson came back as well and purchased the island of Lewis in the Outer Hebrides for half a million pounds. During the Highland Famine of the 1840s his riches from the opium trade were employed to support the people of the estate. For these endeavours he was knighted and entered Parliament for Ross and Cromarty in the Whig interest between 1847 and 1862.[63] Yet, the failure of attempts at 'improvement' on his Lewis estate resulted in a reversal of his policy of benign support for the crofters. From the early 1850s, eviction and 'compulsory emigration' caused an outflow of nearly 2,400 inhabitants of Lewis across the Atlantic to Canada (see Chapter 5). Matheson was immortalized in the pages of Disraeli's novel *Sybil* as 'a dreadful man. A Scotchman richer than Croesus, one Macdrugy, fresh from Canton with a million of opium in each pocket, denouncing corruption and bellowing free trade.' Meanwhile, control of The Firm passed to Matheson's three nephews, led by Alexander, the eldest. When he retired in 1852, a clutch of William Jardine's nephews ran the business until the 1880s.

These ship-owners and merchant adventurers of the East in the nineteenth century were following in an age-old tradition which stretched back to the Scottish traders of medieval and early modern Europe. Their counterparts of the Victorian era shared the view that the best prospects lay outside the homeland. James Lyle Mackay, the formative influence on the creation of the Inchcape Group (and himself created the first Lord Inchcape in 1911), recalled his reasons for leaving Scotland in a speech at his old school later in life. He had worked as a scrivener in Arbroath and then for a firm of rope and canvas makers, toiling for a relative pittance from nine in the morning until eight at night. His employer described 'Jeemie' as 'no a bad laddie, but a damed sicht ower-ambitious'. His ambition took him overseas. As he put it to the pupils of the new generation: 'Let me recommend you not to be afraid to go out into the world. There is no scope in Scotland for the energy, the brains, the initiative and the ambition of all the youth in the country . . . if there is no prospect for you here, the sooner you get away the better.'[64]

There were other links to the older times of Scottish merchanting. Private family partnerships remained dominant, dependent on a network of recruitment from kindred at home. It was that way in seventeenth-century Scandinavia and Poland and remained so in Asia into recent times. The writer Neal Ascherson recalls meeting 'Lofty' Grant, the senior partner in Guthries of Malaya, during his national service there in the 1950s:

> I had been given a taste of the Scottish colonial network which I never forgot. Guthries ... was a private partnership which remained patriarchal: firmly in family hands. Its recruitment, still mainly from the north-east of Scotland which Alexander Guthrie [the firm's founder] had left more than a hundred years before, was operated through a network of friends and relations back in Scotland who recommended likely lads on the basis of intelligence and moral character.[65]

Such systematic nepotism had its uses in volatile and alien environments where trust between trading partners was so crucial. But family links in themselves were not enough. Recruits also had to have ability and reliability. William Jardine warned one correspondent from Dumfries that he had 'a strong objection to extravagance and idleness' which, he trusted, would be impressed on the minds of his relatives at home: 'I can never consent to assist idle and dissipated characters however nearly connected with me, but am prepared to go to any reasonable extent in supplying such of my relations as conduct themselves prudently and industriously.'[66]

Thus it was that family control in many of these firms proved enduring. The tradition was established that the principals, if they survived, usually had relatively short careers in the tropics before retiring to Scotland. Their companies were therefore continuously replenished with new blood as opportunities became available for younger men of ambition, ability and loyalty. Again, parallels can be drawn with the Scottish sojourners in eighteenth-century Bengal and the Caribbean islands who also endeavoured to come home as soon as a fortune had been made. But there was a single but important difference between the two groups. As argued in the previous chapters, overseas profits often funded the industrial and agricultural transformation in eighteenth-century Scotland. Research on Victorian returnees remains very limited, but the available evidence suggests that their investment behaviour diverged from that of the merchant princes of the century before. Profits often seem to have been ploughed back to promote further growth in the family companies in Asia and, when repatriated, were mainly used to purchase landed estates, enhance a leisured style of life and also to leave significant sums to kinsfolk. This was the pattern associated with such figures as Matheson, Jardine, Mackinnon, William Burrell (the ship-owner who spent his fortune on an art collection before gifting it to the city of Glasgow), and several others.[67] It may well be that the Scottish industrial economy by the 1850s had generated such resources from its own extraordinary development that it had much less need for external capital sources. Indeed, the trajectory was soon towards large-scale Scottish investment overseas, rather than building and expanding the economy at home (see Chapter 11).

4

The Great Migration

The Scots had been a migratory people since medieval times, but by the later seventeenth century the axis was beginning to shift from Europe towards the west. Emigration to Ulster became dominant, especially so in the 1690s, while in the following century the Americas, the Caribbean and, for some sojourners, India exerted the greatest attraction. However, against the background of this long record of migration, the nineteenth century and several decades of the twentieth still stand out in terms of both the scale of movement and territorial spread across the globe. Between 1825 and 1938, over 2.3 million people left Scotland for overseas destinations.[1] When the estimated 600,000 who moved across the border to England between 1841 and 1911 are included in the total it is little wonder that Scotland can be regarded as the European country of emigration over this period.[2] The numbers are very striking and the change in scale from the eighteenth century very marked. Eighty to ninety thousand departures for overseas have been estimated between 1700 and 1815 from the fragile and incomplete data which are available.[3] The exodus after c.1840 was massive by comparison. At its peak, in the 1920s, over 363,000 Scots left for the USA and Canada in a single decade, although some soon returned as employment conditions across the Atlantic deteriorated during the Great Depression.[4] These figures have to be set against a national Scottish population size of only 4,472,103 at the census of 1901. Even before the huge losses of the interwar period, emigration was still immense. In the eight decades before the Great War, for instance, somewhat more than half of the natural increase in population was likely to leave Scotland.[5]

This huge expansion in numbers was accompanied by the territorial expansion of the migrations across the globe. Indeed, it has been claimed that Scots went to a greater range of overseas destinations than probably any other European group over these years.[6] Throughout the period the USA and, to a lesser extent, Canada remained dominant. But Australia and New Zealand started to attract significant numbers from the 1830s and '40s. During the gold rushes of the 1850s Australia alone was the preferred destination for around 90,000 Scots, while by the end of the century New Zealand settlers from the British Isles were more than twice as likely to be Scottish as the homeland UK population itself.[7] In contrast, Scots proportions of emigrants to South Africa were always much lower than for the other colonies of settlement. In the census of the South African Union in 1904, the percentage of whites born outside the country was 20.4, of which the English made up nearly 50 per cent and the Scots 14.3 per cent, nearly three times the Irish figure.[8]

These countries experienced the main concentrations, but Scottish emigrants were also to be found by 1900 in places as varied as the cattle estancias of Argentina and Uruguay, the merchant communities of the River Plate, as coffee and tea planters in India and Ceylon and as merchants, ships' officers and engineers in the China and south Asian trades. Though the numbers in the countries outside the Empire and the United States were never large, the qualitative impact of some Scots émigrés was sometimes disproportionate in the places where they settled. Thus, Admiral Thomas Cochrane, Earl of Dundonald, a daring naval officer during the Napoleonic Wars of such high reputation that he eventually became the inspiration for such fictional heroes as C. S. Forester's Horatio Hornblower and Patrick O'Brian's Jack Aubrey, played a central part in the victories of the Chilean and Brazilian navies against Spain and Portugal which paved the way for the eventual independence of the two nations. Cochrane was even alleged to have made plans to free Napoleon from exile on St Helena, but before these could be implemented the former Emperor died on the island in 1821. At the other end of the world, in Japan, another high-profile Scot, Thomas Blake Glover from Fraserburgh, became a legend in that country's history in the second half of the nineteenth century. Glover was a key influence in early Japanese industrialization, transferring the latest cutting-edge technology from the Clyde and elsewhere in the West, having originally begun his connection with Japan as a buyer of green tea for the great Scottish merchant house of Jardine, Matheson and Co. His shipbuilding enterprises eventually developed into the Mitsubishi Company of Japan, a key motor of Japanese economic transformation. Glover's house and gardens in Nagasaki are said today to attract 2 million visitors annually.[9]

Only by analysing the Scottish emigration experience in a British and European context do the distinctive features of the exodus really become apparent. Of sixteen Western and Central European countries considered, three – Ireland, Norway and Scotland – consistently topped the league tables as the source of proportionately most emigrants. Ireland headed the list in most years. Norway and Scotland fluctuated in their relative positions. However, in three decades, 1851–60, 1871–80 and 1901–10, Scotland was second only to Ireland in this unenviable championship. In 1913, the year before the start of the Great War, Scotland had an even greater outflow than either Ireland or Norway.[10] The upward trajectory was temporarily interrupted by four years of conflict and then by the short-lived postwar boom until 1921. Thereafter, the dynamic of mass emigration reasserted itself. Between 1920 and 1929, those leaving averaged 46,876 per year, a figure which specifically excluded cross-border migration to England. Scotland accounted for about one in ten of the UK population in that decade but contributed 28 per cent of all British and Irish emigrants to the USA, 26 per cent of those to Canada and 20 per cent of migrants to Australasia.[11] The nation now headed the international league table of emigration to overseas destinations ahead of both Ireland and Norway. For the first time since the eighteenth century, the Scottish population actually fell in the 1920s, by over 40,000. The writer Edwin Muir was only one of several commentators to voice deep alarm: 'my main impression ... is that Scotland is gradually being emptied of its population, its spirit, its wealth, industry, art, intellect and innate character. If a country exports its most enterprising spirits and best minds year after year, for fifty or a hundred or two hundred years, some result will inevitably follow.'[12]

More emigrants came from mainland Britain after c.1850 than from most other European countries. But Scottish emigration, at least from the 1860s, was significantly higher per head of population than that of England and Wales. From 1881 to 1931, Wales lost an average of 17 inhabitants per thousand, England 14; but the Scottish figure was 35 per thousand.[13] Over the longer period, from the 1850s, the pattern was similar. Annual emigration from England and Wales in the second half of the nineteenth century was 1 per thousand. For Scotland the figure was 1.4, and nearly 2 in some decades. Overall, England and Wales lost 9 per cent of natural population increase (i.e. births over deaths). In Scotland the fall was around a quarter.[14]

The high rate of emigration was probably the single most distinctive Scottish feature but there were also others of significance. Much of European migration, especially from Scandinavia, Spain and Italy, was distinguished by visible differences inside countries, with regions of high activity existing alongside others where levels of out migration were demonstrably lower.[15] The evidence contained in the Poor Law Commission Report of 1844 suggests a different pattern in Scotland. There, emigration was noted as being common throughout the country, with over two-thirds of parishes reporting losses over the previous few years.[16] Studies of movement to New Zealand confirm that emigrants' last places of residence in Scotland were spread relatively evenly across the country and represented the broad demographic structure of the nation.[17] It is true that the central Lowlands, and especially the towns and cities of the industrial areas, were producing disproportionate numbers of emigrants after c.1860 and that was particularly the case with the movement to the USA. But this concentration was primarily a result of changing population settlement within Scotland, as urbanization and industrialization intensified and the exodus from rural counties diminished in relative terms.[18]

There is also evidence from some European countries that higher per capita incomes as a consequence of industrial growth could restrict the urge to emigrate. This response is often used to explain the relatively low migration rates of Belgium, France and the Netherlands in the nineteenth century.[19] Similarly, north-western Italy was a key source of emigration, but as that area experienced the spread of industrial development so the axis shifted to the poorer central and southern regions of the country. The same process has been detected in Catalonia.[20] Economic growth, so it is argued, provides alternatives to emigration and absorbs those who might have left before the onset of better times. These perspectives, however, conflict with the history of emigration from Scotland. Certainly, in the later eighteenth century and possibly through to the 1850s, the Highlands, the poorest region of all, produced more emigrants per head of population than any other.[21] But as the Scottish exodus reached unprecedented proportions, depopulation in the north and west inevitably meant a relative decline in the Highland factor. Generally, after c.1860, Lowland emigration exceeded that from the Highlands by a factor of seventeen to one.[22] Industrialization radically reshaped Scotland. By 1910, only one in ten Scots were engaged in agriculture or related employment. At the census of 1911, 60 per cent of the Scottish people lived in towns and cities (defined as settlements of 5,000 inhabitants or above). But the economic revolution had not stemmed the tide of emigration. On the contrary, by the later nineteenth century the outward movement reached levels never seen before. This is a conundrum which will be addressed later in this chapter.

There is one final peculiarity of the Scottish case. By the Victorian era, Scots emigrants were less likely to be common labourers and more to be skilled or semi-skilled artisans from both town and country. This was the pattern even in relation to emigrants from England and Wales, countries which had a broadly similar social and economic structure to Scotland. Information on occupations is not reliable before 1912. However, in 1912 to 1914, nearly half of all Scottish male emigrants were skilled artisans, and one-fifth claimed white-collar status. In both these categories, the Scottish proportions were greater than the English and Welsh. Around 30 per cent were classified as 'labourers' but since the majority were from an agricultural background many were probably farm servants who often had significant skills in horse management. Of the women, 10 per cent had professional occupations, 19 per cent did garment work and the remainder were domestic servants.[23] Unlike several European countries, notably Ireland, Russia, Italy and Spain, the marginalized and the poor do not surface to the same extent in the Scottish statistics, at least not after the Great Highland Famine of the middle decades of the nineteenth century (see Chapter 5).[24]

Despite these distinctive features, however, Scottish emigration was also an integral part of the much greater movements from Europe to the New World. One estimate suggests that between 1821 and 1914 about 44 million people emigrated from the continent, a demographic phenomenon unprecedented in human history over such a relatively short period.[25] Scotland had its own experience of emigration, but, before exploring that fully, it is necessary to address the broader influences which affected all European peoples and provided the essential infrastructure for international migration in the nineteenth century and thereafter.

I

An important precondition for mass emigration was the removal of the constraints of the later eighteenth and early nineteenth centuries. Those decades between 1775 and 1815 had been times of intense global hostilities, only interrupted between 1783 and 1793 and then again, briefly, in 1801–3. During wartime British emigrant traffic was suspended. In contrast, no global conflict broke out in the rest of the nineteenth century. Wars were regional and local and the transoceanic sea lanes were kept secure by the Royal Navy and the Pax Britannica. Emigration became safer. Emigration also had an image problem in earlier centuries. Lord Sheffield famously remarked in the 1780s: 'Emigration is the natural recourse of the culprit, and those who have made themselves the objects of contempt and neglect.'[26] New South Wales was still a penal colony and British North America, to which thousands of Scots émigré loyalists had fled after the American Revolution, continued to be portrayed in British popular magazines as a cold, intimidating and daunting wilderness. Long after many Scots had settled there, a Canadian government minister could admit in 1897 that, 'Owing to the persistent representation in Britain of Canada as a land of ice and snow, emigration has been chiefly going to Australasia and South Africa, and it is now the endeavour of the department to counteract the effect of such literature.'[27] Even in 1902, a Canadian official complained that despite the government's best marketing efforts in the UK, much ignorance prevailed. People believed 'a man would have to hew his way through timber, cut down trees, clear his land and end his life before he emerged from the wilderness'.[28]

Another huge psychological obstacle was the duration and hardships of the sea voyage to the New World. It may be that most journeys were uneventful and boring but plenty of horror stories still surfaced in print, bringing into stark focus the perils of ocean travel. Notices of ships 'lost at sea' and of passengers killed in storms abounded in the British and colonial press. Infectious disease, smallpox, typhus, influenza and assorted 'fevers' were always a potential threat. Once an epidemic broke out, virtually nothing could be done to contain it: 'death stalked these voyages'.[29] As late as 1847 to 1853, fifty-nine wrecks of emigrant vessels were reported in the press. During the same period, the horrendous stories of the 'coffin ships', sailing from Ireland in the wake of the Great Famine, gripped the public imagination. Even emigrants who successfully made it across the Atlantic had sometimes experienced great trauma during the long weeks of the voyage.[30] There were also ideological constraints. In the Scottish case this comes through most clearly in the attitude of landowners and government to the mounting evidence of a Highland exodus before 1815. The eighteenth-century mind considered population as an invaluable military and economic resource. For north-west mainland and Hebridean landlords in particular, people were needed for kelping and fishing and to man the family regiments during the Napoleonic Wars. There were a few exceptions, but, for the most part, landlords regarded emigration as anathema. Some were even prepared to consider rent abatements and the breaking up of land to accommodate smaller tenants who were tempted to move away, though such policies of appeasement did not always work. The concerns of the elite were intensified because it was the middle rank of the peasantry, those with some resources above subsistence level, who were more likely to go first.[31]

The British state was equally opposed to emigration. Before 1775 there was increasing concern that an empire of colonization would cost Britain dearly because it would lead inevitably to huge increases in expenditure on army and naval resources. The American Revolutionary War and the emergence of an independent United States of America confirmed the criticisms of the sceptics that colonial expansion could only end in disaster. Thus government continued to enforce – somewhat ineffectually – an anti-emigration strategy from 1775 (when emigration to America was banned during hostilities) until the 1810s. This was the political background to the Passenger Vessels Act of 1803 and the attempt by Henry Dundas, Scotland's most powerful political figure, to introduce yet another prohibition on emigration in 1786. Highland emigration fell to a low level in the 1780s in large part because the loss of the old empire broke the transatlantic connection built up over earlier decades. During the Napoleonic Wars, however, especially when Highland emigration once again reached significant levels in 1801–3, the state became even more alarmed about the potential loss of a militarily valuable population. Parliament was even prepared to vote vast amounts of money (over £½ million for roads and bridges alone) to promote communications development in the Highlands, including the construction of the Caledonian Canal, which through the release of enlisted men would help check 'the present Rage for Emigration and prevent its future Progress'.[32]

The age of mass emigration from Europe was, then, ushered in by a series of interconnected transformations. As national populations rose and social tensions increased because of economic change, so governments became more interested in emigration, seeing it not as a source of loss, as previously, but rather as a potential safety-valve for emerging demographic problems. In Britain, the ideology of 'systematic colonization' became a fashionable set of ideas and theories associated with Edward Gibbon Wakefield and others. Building on the theories of Thomas Malthus, it was argued by advocates such as Wakefield that emigration could be a blessing rather than a curse, creating markets abroad for British industry while, at the same time, easing population pressures at home. These views became widely influential and in 1837 the New Zealand Association was formed in London along the lines suggested by Wakefield to support emigration to the Antipodes. The new ideas also inspired government intervention in the emigrant trade, particularly to Australia, thought too distant and unappealing to attract unsubsidized immigration. Between 1828 and 1842, 180,000 emigrants sailed for Australia.[33] Many were assisted through a scheme of bounties whereby colonial governments paid ships' masters and merchants a fee to recruit potential settlers from Britain and Ireland.

However, changes in elite attitudes to colonization were less significant than advances in communications.[34] The steamship is rightly regarded as a key development but it is important that the earlier and parallel improvements to sailing-ship design are recognized too; bigger vessels, wooden hulls with iron all helped to prolong the age of sail, particularly for long-distance voyages, until the 1880s.[35] Related developments in commerce were also deeply significant. During and after the Napoleonic Wars, British North America became the nation's main source of timber, accounting for 75 per cent of all such imports in 1819–23. This was a boon to the Atlantic emigrant traffic because empty timber ships took a human cargo on their return voyages.[36] Similarly, emigrants filled the clippers en route to Australasia while on the return journey the steerage berths were removed and the 'tween decks stored with bales of wool.[37] Indeed, it was, above all, the profitability of the wool trade that made the long-distance emigration to New Zealand a lucrative enterprise over several decades.

Of course, the arrival of the ocean-going steamship was catalytic. Although the cost of steamship travel was actually about a third dearer than crossing by sailing ships, the new vessels soon radically increased speed, comfort and safety. In the 1850s it took six weeks to cross the Atlantic from UK ports. By 1914 the average voyage time had fallen to around a week. By drastically cutting voyage times the steamship also removed one of the major costs of emigration: the time between embarkation and settlement during which there was no possibility of earning.[38] This was especially crucial for the skilled and semi-skilled urban tradesmen who comprised an increasing proportion of Scottish emigrants in the later nineteenth century. They were now able to move on a temporary basis in order to exploit high wages or labour scarcities at particular times in North America. This factor also explains the increasing scale of return emigration. By 1900 it is estimated that around one-third of those Scots who left came back sooner or later.[39] The evidence from New Zealand suggests that returns became more common over time. Returnees rose from only 36 per cent of outward sailings between 1853 and 1880, to 82 per cent of the 1 million outward sailings between 1881 and 1920. The increases corresponded exactly to the impact of transport innovation on the New Zealand route.[40]

The steamship was the most dramatic and decisive advance but it was paralleled by the railway and canal, which made it possible for emigrants to be quickly and easily transported from all areas to the port of embarkation. Agreements were commonly made between shipping and railway companies allowing emigrants to be transported free to their port of departure. The expansion of the railroad in North America brought similar benefits. By the 1850s, the completion of the Canadian canal network and the associated railway development facilitated access to the western USA by allowing emigrants to book their passage to Quebec and Hamilton and then to go on by rail to Chicago. The links between steamships and railways led to the provision of the highly popular through-booking system by which emigrants could obtain a complete package, with a ticket purchased in Europe allowing travel to the final destination in America. *Chambers' Journal* in 1857 described it as a 'prodigious convenience' which would 'rob emigration of its terrors and must set hundreds of families wandering'.[41]

Scots emigrants had a particular advantage because the railway system existed alongside a number of major shipping lines operating from the Clyde which by the 1850s had developed a worldwide network of services. The significant passenger companies were the Allan, Anchor and Donaldson lines, sailing mainly on a number of routes across the Atlantic; the City Line to India; the Allan Line to South Africa and, from the 1860s, the Albion Line to New Zealand. In addition, some of the major railway companies in Canada played a vigorous proactive role in the emigrant business. They recognized that the railway was not simply an easy and rapid mode of transport for new arrivals from Europe but was also the most effective way of opening up the wilderness and prairie territory to permanent settlement. The mighty Canadian Pacific Railway Company (CPR) became very active in the promotion of emigration because of this. In 1880 it had been allocated 25 million acres of land between Winnipeg and the Rocky Mountains by the Dominion government. In order to generate profit, the company had to increase traffic through expanding areas of settlement and to achieve this goal it embarked on an aggressive marketing campaign in Britain designed to stimulate emigration to the prairies. Scotland was specifically targeted, and agents of the CPR toured country areas giving lectures and providing information. The CPR even sought to reduce the hardships of pioneering by providing ready-made farms in southern Alberta, with housing, barns and fences included as part of the sale.[42]

These initiatives by a large organization in attracting settlement to the prairie provinces were but one manifestation of a wider revolution in communicating the attractions of emigration to the peoples of Europe. The letters of emigrants to their families at home had always been the most influential medium for spreading information about overseas conditions. With the steamship, railway and telegraph, this traditional form of communication became even more effective as postal services became more frequent, increasingly reliable and speedier. Emigrant letters, coming as they did from trusted family members, retained great significance as the more credible source of information on overseas employment, prices and wages. Letters were sometimes supplemented by remittances sent home to relatives.

Returning migrants were also a key source of information. It is wrong, for instance, to assume that those who came back did so because they necessarily experienced failure and disillusion in the New World, although some were indeed in this category. The Scottish press printed articles from time to time about emigrants who had returned with 'blighted hopes and empty purses'. The steamship revolution was bound to mean that the number of emigrants returning could increase markedly when conditions in the receiving countries temporarily deteriorated. However, many 'returnees' had originally left Scotland with no intention of settling permanently in America. This was especially the case with tradesmen and semi-skilled workers. In the north-east, for instance, several hundred granite workers migrated annually to American yards each spring, returning to Aberdeen for the winter. Coal miners from Lanarkshire also developed a tradition of temporary movement for work in the USA. Masons and other skilled building workers were in great demand on a seasonal basis. By the 1880s there seems to have been a willingness to go overseas at relatively short notice. In the latter part of that decade, for example, scores of Scottish building tradesmen, who had responded to press adverts, descended on Austin, Texas when work on the state capitol was halted by a strike by American workers. Evidence from Scandinavia, Italy, Greece and England suggests that the 'failed' returning migrants were usually in a minority. There seems no reason to suppose that the Scottish pattern was any different. 'Successful' returnees must indeed have been a potent source for spreading knowledge of overseas conditions in local communities, and a positive influence in encouraging further emigration.[43]

To these personal and family networks was added in the later nineteenth century a veritable explosion in the quality and quantity of information available to potential emigrants. The Emigrants' Information Office opened in 1886 as a source of impartial advice and information on land grants, wages, living costs and passage rates. Circulars, handbooks and pamphlets were made available in greater volume and were valued because of their avowed objectivity. Even more important were local newspapers. Advertisements for ships' sailings, information on assisted passages, numerous letters from emigrants and articles on North American life were very regular features as the country population was relentlessly bombarded with all the facts of the emigration experience. Overseas governments and land companies also became more aggressive, professional and sophisticated in promoting emigration. In 1892, for instance, the Canadian government appointed two full-time agents in Scotland who undertook a tour of markets, hiring fairs, agricultural shows and village halls. The illustrated lecture, using the magic lantern, was a favourite device. W. G. Stuart, the agent for the north, was even able to deliver his presentation in Gaelic if the audience required it.

From the 1870s to the Great War, the Canadian government's aim was to settle the Prairie West with immigrants who would establish an agricultural foundation for the Dominion. The key influence on the strategy was Clifford Sifton, the Minister of the Interior from 1896 to 1905. He pioneered the first emigration communications plan by flooding selected countries with appealing literature and advertisements in the press, arranging tours for journalists who then filed flattering copy on their return home, paying agents' fees on a commission basis for every immigrant who settled in Canada and giving bonuses to steamship agents for promoting the country in the United

Kingdom. The rural districts of Scotland were especially targeted because of their historic links with Canada and the country's reputation for experienced farmers and skilled agricultural workers.[44]

Yet, even the revolution of communications and information would have been insufficient if it had not been for the gargantuan increase in demand from the industrializing countries of Europe for the raw materials and food produce of the new lands. It was the explosion in the export of timber, wool, mutton, cotton and other staples to feed the industries and rising populations of Europe which powered the new economies and so made them increasingly attractive places in which to settle and work. The transformation was fuelled by the massive export of capital from Britain after c.1850, a process in which Scotland had a leading part (see Chapter 11). Between 1865 and 1914, the UK invested over $5 billion in the USA alone, facilitating the construction of railways, the reclaiming of land and the building of towns without which large-scale settlement from the Old World would have been impossible. In turn, the great migrations were not uniform or persistent, but were, rather, triggered intermittently by a series of booms which sucked in labour at different times, in different countries and in diverse regions of each country. Some of these could last for several years, others were more short-lived. When they collapsed, return migration, especially in the later nineteenth century, tended to occur.[45] In essence, the combination of better communications, superior flows of information and the huge rise in staple exports from the primary producers had created a new international labour market in which workers were no longer constrained by national frontiers. This pattern goes a long way to explaining the changing attraction of different destinations, as the syncopation of boom and bust was often different in the various settler societies. The model helps us to understand why Scottish emigration shifted rapidly from the USA to Canada in the years before the Great War but back again to the USA in the 1920s.

This then was the new context for mass international migration which deeply influenced the Scottish exodus as well as that of other nations. What it cannot explain, however, is why Scotland, by any standards a successful industrial economy in the vanguard of Victorian modernity, lost so many more of its people than the European or mainland British average before 1930. The puzzle is compounded by two additional aspects. Unusually, Scotland was also a country of immigration as well as emigration. By 1901, around 205,000 Irish had made their homes in Scotland. Indeed, Irish immigration was proportionately greater in Scotland than England. Only 2.9 per cent of the population of England and Wales were Irish in 1851. The Scottish figure was 7.2 per cent. To the Irish should be added about 40,000 Jews, Lithuanians and Italians, who mainly arrived between 1860 and 1914, together with an unknown number of English moving from south of the Border.[46] That is one part of the conundrum. The other is that, after c.1860 at least, the existence of a poor and deprived Highland region within the country cannot be used to fully explain the emigration paradox. Certainly the Highland factor did loom large in the eighteenth-century movements and in the decades up to the 1850s. The famine period between 1846 and 1856 saw particularly high levels of population loss from the region, as detailed in the next chapter. Thereafter, however, the Highland share of overall Scottish emigration became minimal. It might be suggested that Highlanders who moved to the Lowland cities and then emigrated were concealed within the numbers of those who left directly from urban areas. But the proportion of first-generation Gaels in Lowland towns and cities in the 1851 census was rarely more than 10 per cent and in Glasgow, for instance, significantly less even than that.[47] Scots who gave a town or city as their last place of residence before departure, though born in country districts, were much more likely to have originally moved from a Lowland farm or village than a Highland croft. The Highland Clearances, therefore, cannot explain, either directly or indirectly, mass Scottish emigration after c.1860. If we are to reach any substantive conclusions on the origins of these movements, the clues from the Lowland countryside and the urban/industrial areas are the ones which need to be considered.

To a significant extent the very nature of Scottish economic transformation in the period after c.1760 became the vital context for extensive emigration. Far from restraining outward movement by providing new employment and material improvement, as in some parts of Europe, Scottish industrialization may have actually stimulated a continuing exodus of people. Basic to the Industrial Revolution

in Scotland was profound change in rural social and economic structures. In the Lowlands, farms were consolidated, sub-tenancies
removed and the terms of access to land became more rigid and regulated.[48] Over time fewer and fewer had legal rights to farms as
consolidation accelerated and subdivision of holdings was outlawed.
As numbers rose through natural increase, mobility of people became
inevitable. Peasant proprietorship in Scotland (commonplace throughout central and southern Europe) was unknown, and by 1840 most
Lowland rural Scots were non-inheriting children of farmers, farm
servants, country tradesmen, textile weavers or day labourers. The
Scottish Poor Law before 1843 was also notoriously hostile to the
provision of relief for the able-bodied unemployed though, in practice, modest doles were often given. In this context, the majority of the
population of the Lowland countryside relied mainly on selling their
labour power in the market to survive. The ebb and flow of demand
for labour inevitably enforced movement upon them. Even before
1800 such domestic mobility was already present and probably gave
Scotland a higher incidence of internal migration than such countries
as France or the German states.[49]

In the nineteenth century this certainly intensified. There were at
least five reasons for this.[50] First, population was rising while both
agricultural and industrial opportunities in rural areas were stagnant
or, especially after c.1840, contracting rapidly. In consequence, the
proportion of natural population employed in agriculture declined
markedly, from 24 per cent in 1841 to 10 per cent in 1911. Secondly,
most permanent agricultural workers on Scottish farms were 'servants'
hired on an annual or half-yearly contract who received accommoda-
tion as part of their labour contract. The unemployed farm worker,
who inevitably had lost his home, had no choice but to move to seek
a job. Thirdly, Scottish urbanization was notable for its speed and
scale. The proportion of Scots living in settlements of over 5,000 rose
from 31 per cent in 1831 to almost 60 per cent in 1911. The vast
majority of the new urban populations were from the farms, villages
and small towns of the Lowland countryside. Fourthly, the first phase
of industrialization down to c.1830 had extended manufacturing
employment, especially in textiles, in rural areas. During the coal,
iron and steel industrialization phase, production concentrated more

intensively in the central Lowlands, the Border woollen towns, Dundee, Fife and Midlothian. Indeed, one of the most striking features of Scottish industrial capitalism was its extraordinary concentration. This process ensured a rapid shedding of population from areas of crumbling employment to the regions of rapid growth in the Forth–Clyde valley. Lastly, in the last quarter of the nineteenth century, clear evidence emerged of a growing rejection by the younger generation of the drudgery, social constraints and isolation of country life. The towns had always had an attraction but now they seduced the youth of rural society as never before.

The interaction of these influences produced an unprecedented level of mobility. The 1851 census shows that no less than a third of the Scottish population had crossed at least one county boundary. Demographic research has demonstrated that in the 1860s, the vast majority of parishes in all areas were experiencing net outward movement of population. Heavy losses in the Lowlands were especially pronounced in the south-west region and in many parts of the east from Berwick to Moray. The only areas attracting people were in the central zone and the textile towns of the Borders.[51] This demographic pattern is crucial to an understanding of the roots of Scottish emigration. Scots were mobile abroad in part because they were increasingly very mobile at home.[52] No comparative index exists of national rates of European internal migration. If it did, it might well put the Scots near the top. Emigration, then, could be seen as an extension of migration within Scotland, and one that was much less challenging after 1860 with the revolution in transatlantic travel associated with the steamship and railways. Such a suggestion is entirely consistent with the point made earlier that most emigrants in the later nineteenth century were urban in origin, because almost certainly concealed within this category were many born into an agricultural or industrial artisan background in the countryside and who had moved to the towns before emigrating.

Equally, some evidence suggests that from the later nineteenth century the volume of emigration varied inversely with internal migration. People in country farms and villages searching for opportunities elsewhere seem to have been able to weigh the attractions of the Scottish towns against those of overseas destinations, and come to a decision on the basis of these comparisons. In the decades 1881–90 and 1901–10, for instance, there was heavy emigration, with 43 and 47 per cent respectively of the natural population increase leaving the country. In the same periods, movement to Glasgow and the surrounding suburbs fell to low levels, while there was actual net movement out of the western Lowlands. On the other hand, during the 1870s and 1890s emigration declined, but larger numbers moved to the cities and towns of the west.[53] This pattern suggests an informed and mobile population which had access to sources of information such as newspapers, letters from relatives and intelligence from returned migrants that enabled judgements about emigration to be considered.

Lowland rural emigration was not induced so much by destitution or deprivation – as in the Highlands for long periods – as by the lure of opportunity. Throughout the nineteenth and early twentieth centuries, Canada and Australasia were the great magnets for those who wished to work the land, while rural tradesmen and industrial workers tended to opt more for the USA. From emigrant letters and newspaper articles one can piece together the attractions of emigration for both small tenants and farm servants. A primary incentive was the possibility of owning land that was cheap to acquire and was increasingly made available for purchase in developed form by land companies and by the Dominion and provincial governments. In Canada and Australia land was plentiful, whereas in Scotland even wealthy farmers were dependent on their landlords, with tenure regulated by a detailed lease enforceable at law and other sanctions. The Scottish tenants' agitation of the 1870s shows the tensions that these relationships could sometimes generate. In the colonies, on the other hand, owner-occupation, the much desired 'independence' and the right to bequeath the hard-worked land to the family were all on offer and at reasonable rates. The strains imposed by the agricultural depression of the 1880s added to discontent in some areas and further increased the attractions of emigration. The Board of Agriculture in 1906 reviewed the reasons for the decline in the rural population and concluded with respect to Scotland that:

Many correspondents refer to the absence of an incentive to remain on the land and of any reasonable prospect of advancement in life, and it is mentioned in some districts, particularly in Scotland, many of the best men have been attracted to the colonies, where their energies may find wider scope and where the road to independence and a competency is broader and more easy to access.[54]

This can be seen most vividly in the pages of the weekly *People's Journal*, Scotland's most popular periodical, selling at one penny per issue. Its impact was extraordinary. By 1890 its total circulation over a six-month period reached 5½ million at home and abroad, with an average of 212,000 copies printed each week. The *Journal* proudly boasted that it 'enters more Scottish Households than any other Newspaper' and was 'sold by 10,000 Newsagents'. It was 'specially designed to promote the interests of the working classes' and, crucially, virtually every issue had articles on emigration worldwide, providing comment, advice on changing employment conditions and the opportunities available overseas for people from both town and country.

Ironically, the dynamic heart of the Scottish economy, the regions of advanced industrialism, were the main sources of emigrants after *c*.1860. But, when the nature of urban and industrial society is probed more deeply, key fault lines are revealed which make the exodus more comprehensible. For a start, huge social inequalities were entrenched in those manufacturing districts of the nation where armies of semi-skilled, unskilled and casual labourers serviced the mining, shipbuilding, engineering and textile industries. Notoriously, west-central Scotland, and the Dundee area in particular, had proportionately few members of the professional, commercial and managerial classes.[55] Some of the lower-middle class might have had the chance to move up the social scale with energy, talent and connections. But it was much more difficult (and often impossible) for those below to 'get on' and achieve advancement. The barriers, even to minimal social mobility for the vast majority of the population of Victorian Scotland, were huge and enduring.

One telling indicator was the background of students in the Scottish universities. They did attract students from a much broader social range than Oxford and Cambridge but, even so, the hard evidence does not entirely support the myth of the 'democratic intellect'. The Argyll Commission's 1867 analysis of Scottish education concluded that a third of students in the nation's universities came from professional families and over a half from the middle classes as a whole. The sons of skilled artisans with traditional skills – carpenters, shoemakers and masons – were also represented. But the offspring of miners, farm servants and factory workers were notable by their virtual absence. It has been remarked that the son of a church minister was a hundred times more likely to go to a Scottish university than a miner's son. Most working-class students were drawn from the skilled and artisan families. The rural poor and the unskilled workers in the towns were hardly represented at all.[56] The celebrated 'lads o' pairts' (boys of talent) did exist but they were few and far between. Against this background, the aspirational attractions of the overseas territories, even if much exaggerated in the booster literature, must have struck a chord with many.

Another factor of considerable relevance was the reward to labour ratio. Relative to England and Wales, industrial Scotland was a low-wage economy. Despite variation between sectors, Scottish wages were often up to 20 per cent below the equivalent in English trades.[57] The evidence suggests a degree of convergence from the 1880s yet, when costs of living are taken into account, on the eve of the Great War most earnings in Scottish manufacturing still lagged 10 to 12 per cent behind those in English industrial areas.[58] Of course, there is no inevitable correlation between low wages and emigration. What is crucial is the relative differential between opportunities at home and overseas. In the second half of the nineteenth and early twentieth centuries, that differential between Western Europe and the New World became greater. Wages and opportunities were increasing at home but they were doing so with even greater speed overseas, because the American economies were very rich in resources but grossly underpopulated. Those with industrial skills and experience were especially in demand.[59] The scenario for mass emigration from societies such as Scotland was clearly emerging as the previous constraints on movement crumbled. Ignorance of conditions across the Atlantic and in Australasia diminished further as more and more information was disseminated through the press, government sources, emigration societies and advice from previous emigrants. This was widely absorbed in this highly literate society. Emigration therefore became available to many more as income levels rose in the later nineteenth century – the sheer cost had been a significant obstacle to many in previous times. Detailed analysis of migration in Scottish rural society after 1870 has suggested a marked increase in social expectations, a change partly related to higher wages but also to the expansion in educational opportunities after the Elementary Education Act of 1872.[60] It may have been the case that there were similar attitudinal changes among many urban and industrial workers which made the lure of greater opportunities overseas more attractive. This was where the transport revolution became of critical importance, since now the essential infrastructure had emerged to define and shape a truly transatlantic labour market.

Thus, the habitual and historic internal mobility of the Scots could now be translated fully into international movement. In the same way as they had long compared wages and employment within Scotland, it was now easier than ever before to evaluate opportunities in New York, Toronto and Chicago in relation to those in Glasgow, Dundee and Edinburgh. The income differentials were often so enormous and the skills shortage in the New World so acute that many thousands could not resist the temptation, especially since, in the event of failure, the return journey home was but the price of a steamship ticket. The chances were also there, of course, for the skilled of that other advanced economy, England. But it is hardly surprising that the Scots found it more irresistible. Scotland was still a poorer society than England and the difference between opportunities at home and abroad was greater for its people. Quite simply, they had more to gain by emigration. The proof of this was the migration from Scotland to England before 1900. For the period 1841 to 1911, according to one estimate, about 600,000 Scots-born persons moved to England and Wales.[61] This was around half of the total net emigration from Scotland in the nineteenth century and was not paralleled by any similar significant movement from the south to the north. It was eloquent testimony of the perceived differences in standards of life between the two societies, especially when it is remembered that, from the 1870s, many Scots who moved to England were skilled and increasingly settled in the mining and heavy industrial areas of England and Wales.

But Scottish emigration was not simply because the rewards of industry could not compete with those abroad or in England. It attained such high levels because of the peculiar economic structure of Scottish society. It had a higher proportion of its inhabitants employed in industrial work by 1871 than any other country in Western Europe apart from England. But, unlike in England, the majority of the employed male population in Scotland was heavily concentrated in the capital goods sector of shipbuilding, coal-mining, metals and engineering. In addition, to an unusual extent, many of these activities were heavily dependent on the export market. The Scottish economy lacked the cushion of a strong service sector and a range of industries catering for the domestic market.[62] After 1830 the British economy as a whole became subject to more extreme fluctuations in the trade cycle; in Scotland the amplitude and duration of cyclical changes were felt more severely because of the tight interrelationships within the heavy industrial structure, the bias towards foreign markets, which were inherently fickle, and the relative weakness of domestic demand. This economic insecurity was basic to emigration. Violent fluctuations in employment were integral to Scottish industrial 'prosperity' even in the heyday of Victorian and Edwardian expansion. Their scale and frequency can be seen in the building industry, which employed about 7 per cent of the occupied male labour force in the 1880s. Between 1881 and 1891 the numbers employed fell by 5.1 per cent; they rose by 43.3 per cent during 1891 to 1901 and contracted again by a striking 21.4 per cent over the years 1901–11.[63] Not surprisingly, emigration was at its height at the bottom of these cycles. Because fluctuations were probably more savage and longer lasting in Scotland it is reasonable to assume that the volume of outward movement would be greater than south of the Border. The dramatic peaks in Scottish emigration – the late 1840s and early 1850s, the mid-1880s, 1906–13 and the 1920s – all took place in periods of serious industrial depression at home.

In the final analysis then, it would seem that, after c.1860 at least, Scots left their native land in search of more opportunity, 'independence' and through an ambition to 'get on', aspirations which, for the reasons described above, could not easily be satisfied in Scotland itself. It is significant that the very poor and destitute of the towns and cities were not usually counted among the emigrants in large numbers. Most of those who left may have had few resources but they had some modest means. Pressure to go was not irrelevant – as witnessed by the correlation of economic downturn at home and increased emigration abroad – but what comes through strongly from the evidence is the central importance of individual human choice and decision, albeit powerfully fashioned by the prevailing structural forces of society, ideology and economy.

5

Human Selection and
Enforced Exile

Until the later 1850s, emigration from the Scottish Highlands was an important aspect of the Scottish exodus as a whole. In the last four decades of the nineteenth century, however, and thereafter, the contribution of the region to the general outflow of Scots diminished dramatically as the towns, cities and Lowland countryside became by far the dominant sources of Scottish emigration. Yet, for a period in the later 1840s and early 1850s, the Highland diaspora reached truly unprecedented levels. While much of Scotland's international mobility throughout the nineteenth century was led by the search for opportunity overseas, as already argued, in this case the great wave of Highland emigrants was driven on in addition by subsistence crisis, clearance and peasant expropriation.

The essential background was the lethal impact of the potato blight which had so devastated Ireland and some other parts of Europe in the years after 1845. The Highlands were affected from the autumn of 1846. Press reports described the stench of rotting potatoes, the key subsistence crop of the region, in numerous crofting townships, particularly in the Hebrides and the coastlands of the western mainland.[1] In this area, with its moderate winters and rainy summers, the climatic conditions were exactly right for the rapid and destructive spread of the fungal disease *phytophthora infestans*, to which there was no known contemporary antidote. Early estimates suggested the potato crop had failed entirely in over 75 per cent of crofting parishes. The newspaper of the Free Church, the *Witness*, reported in apocalyptic terms: 'The hand of the Lord indeed touched us', and proclaimed the calamity 'unprecedented in the memory of this generation and of many generations gone by, even in any modern periods of our country's history'.[2] Unambiguous signs of famine emerged. While burial registers for most Highland areas in the 1840s are few and far between, in those that have survived deaths among the old and the very young rose significantly in late 1846 and the first few months of 1847. *The Scotsman* in December 1846 described how deaths from dysentery were 'increasing with fearful rapidity among the cottar class'.[3] In the Ross of Mull, government relief officers advised that the mortality rate during the winter months was three times the normal. Elsewhere, in Harris, South Uist, Barra, Skye, Moidart and Kintail, influenza, typhus and dysentery were spreading unchecked among the poor. The awful possibility was that the Highlands might be engulfed in a human tragedy of Irish proportions.

That potential disaster was averted, despite the fact that the potato blight continued to ravage the Highlands for almost a decade after 1846–7. By the summer of 1847, death rates had returned to normal levels and the threat of starvation receded. The mortality crisis had been contained. The different experiences of Ireland (where over 1 million died) and the Highlands in this respect can be explained by a number of influences. An important factor was that of scale. In Ireland, the blight brought over 3 million people to the edge of starvation. In the Highlands, on the other hand, around 200,000 were seriously as risk, and this number diminished over time as the crisis increasingly centred on parts of the north-western coastlands, the northern isles of Orkney and Shetland and the Hebrides. By 1848, only around a quarter (or fewer than 70,000) of the total population of the Highland region were still in need of famine relief.

The map of distress was in fact a complex one. The southern, central and eastern Highlands did not escape entirely unscathed, but after 1847 relief operations were wound down there. This reflected the more resilient economies of these areas. There was less potato dependency and more reliance on grain and fish, a better ratio of land to population and stronger alternative occupations, such as commercial fishing and linen manufacture, in southern Argyll, Perthshire and eastern Inverness-shire. The concentrated and relatively small-scale nature of the Scottish famine meant that the emergency could be managed more easily by the relief agencies of the day than the great crisis across the Irish Sea. The Scottish authorities were dealing with many thousands of potential victims, the Irish several millions. The vastly different magnitude of the two famines is best illustrated by the role of government. In Ireland the state, both local and national, was the principal source of relief over several years, whereas in the Highlands direct government intervention began in late 1846 and ended in the summer of 1847. Two vessels were stationed as meal depots at Tobermory in Mull and Portree in Skye to sell grain at controlled prices. Landowners in the stricken region were able to make application for loans under the Drainage and Public Works Act to provide relief work for the distressed populations of their estates.

These initiatives apart, the main burden of the relief effort was borne by three great charities, the Free Church of Scotland and the Edinburgh and Glasgow Relief Committees, which came together in early 1847 to form the Central Board of Management for Highland Relief. The Central Board had the responsibility for relieving destitution until its operations came to an end in 1850. The programme of support went through several phases. First in the field was the Free Church, eager to come to the aid of its numerous loyal congregations in the north-west and the islands. The schooner *Breadalbane*, built to carry ministers around the Hebrides, was pressed into service to take emergency supplies to the most needy communities. The Free Church was the only active agency during the most critical months of late 1846 and early 1847. Through its intelligence network of local ministers it was able to direct aid to those areas where the risk of starvation was greatest. The Free Church's relief operation was also free of any sectarian bias. Grateful thanks for supplies of grain were received from such Catholic areas as Arisaig and Moidart. Not the least of the Free Church's contribution was the imaginative plan to transport over 3,000 able-bodied men from the Highlands for temporary work on the Lowland railways.

The Central Board assumed control of relief operations in February 1847 and by the end of that year had established a huge fund for the aid of distress of nearly £210,000 (over £16 million at today's values). This was probably the greatest sum ever raised in support of a single charitable cause in nineteenth-century Scotland. With this resource it proceeded to divide responsibility into two sections, with Edinburgh entrusted with Skye, Wester Ross, Orkney, Shetland and the eastern Highlands, while Glasgow took charge of Argyll, western Inverness, the Outer Hebrides and the Inner Hebrides apart from Skye. The distribution of meal was managed initially under the sections' Local Committees, appointed from each parish or district from lists supplied by local clergymen. The aim was to do enough to prevent starvation, with allowances limited to one pound of meal per adult male per day and half a pound per female. In order to ensure that the people were not to be corrupted into a state of indolent dependence, work was supposed to be given in return for food. In the spring and summer of 1847, gangs of men, women and children could be seen labouring all over the western Highlands, the northern isles and the Hebrides at 'public' works, laying roads, building walls, digging ditches and constructing piers. Several of these 'destitution roads' survive to this day as physical memorials to the greatest crisis in the modern history of the region.

The relief effort contained the threat of starvation and the spread of famine-related disease. In the spring of 1847, for instance, the Glasgow Section dispatched 15,680 bolls of wheatmeal, oatmeal, peasemeal and Indian corn to the distressed districts. But critics in the hierarchy of the Central Board were soon complaining that the Highlanders were being encouraged to rely on 'pauperizing' assistance, the 'labour test' was often ignored and the distribution of meal too lavish. A campaign to establish a more rigorous system of relief started to gain momentum, partly inspired by the belief that destitution was likely to endure for much longer than one season and so some effort had to be made to ensure that the Gaels could support themselves in the future. Latent racism also came to the surface. Vitriolic attacks against the 'lazy' Highlander who was supported by the 'industrious' Lowlander appeared in the pages of *The Scotsman*, the *Glasgow Herald* and other newspapers. Sir Charles Trevelyan, Assistant Secretary to the Treasury and the key figure in the famine relief strategies in Ireland, was a powerful influence on the men who ran the Central Board. Trevelyan's position was unequivocal. He regarded both Irish and Highland Celts as profoundly racially inferior to Anglo-Saxons. In his view, the potato famine represented the judgement of God on an indolent people who now had to be taught a moral lesson to change their values and attitudes so that they might support themselves in the future. Gratuitous relief was a curse; as Trevelyan put it, 'Next to allowing the people to die of hunger, the greatest evil that could happen would be their being habituated to depend upon public charity.'[4]

The outcome was the imposition of the hated 'destitution test' throughout the distressed region. By this system of extreme stringency a whole day's work was required in return for a pound of meal, the theory being that only those facing starvation would accept help on such terms. Trevelyan stressed that 'pauperism', or dependency on relief, could be avoided but insisted that 'the pound of meal and the task of at least eight hours' hard work is the best regime for this moral disease'.[5] An elaborate bureaucracy was set up to enforce the new approach, consisting of an Inspector-General, resident inspectors, relief officers and work overseers. Most were retired or semi-retired naval officers ('heroes of the quarter-deck' as one observer put it) who were accustomed to maintaining strict discipline among their inferiors. Meal allowances were issued only once a fortnight in order to impose habits of prudence by teaching the poor to spread their means over an extended period rather than relying on being fed on a daily basis. Labour books were kept by the overseers in which the hours of work of each recipient were faithfully recorded, the fortnight's allowance for each family calculated with care and tickets issued for presentation to the meal dealers. The destitution test was resolutely enforced by relief officers who saw it as their duty to teach the people a moral lesson. Not surprisingly, however, it provoked deep hostility. One critic commented acidly that the scheme was 'starving the poor Highlanders according to the most approved doctrines of political economy . . . the Highlanders upon grounds of Catholic affinity, were to be starved after the Irish fashion'.[6] Free Church ministers protested loudly at the programme of 'systematized starvation', which provoked angry opposition among the people of Skye and Wester Ross. Nevertheless, the test was enforced through 1848 and into 1849. In essence a great philanthropic endeavour had been transformed into an ideological crusade to reform a population represented as inadequate and in need of improvement. It was an extraordinary outcome.

However, the reasons why the Highlands did not starve were wider and deeper than the relief effort itself. Many landowners were active, at least for a period, in supporting the inhabitants of their estates in the early years of the crisis. For instance, only 14 per cent of all west Highland proprietors were censured by government officials for negligence, though in several other cases pressure had to be brought to bear to ensure that landowners met their obligations, while in later years, as will be described below, estate policy in general became much less benevolent and more coercive. Civil servants even contrasted the positive role of Scottish landowners with the indifference of many of their counterparts across the Irish Sea. A prime factor in the Scottish case was that many proprietors had the financial resources to provide support to their small tenants. Since the early nineteenth century there had been a great transfer of estates from the indebted hereditary landlord class to new owners who were often rich tycoons from outside the Highlands. Over three-quarters of all estates in the famine zone had been acquired by merchants, bankers, lawyers, financiers and industrialists by the 1840s. These men were attracted to the Highlands for sport, recreation, the romantic allure of the region and, not least, the basic desire for territorial acquisition. Typical of the breed was the new owner of Barra and South Uist, Colonel John Gordon, dubbed 'the richest commoner in Scotland', and Sir James Matheson, proprietor of Lewis and partner in Jardine, Matheson and Co. The economic muscle of this elite complemented the relief programmes of government and the charities, at least in the first years of the disaster.

The different stages of economic development of Ireland and Scotland were also a crucial factor. The Scottish famine took place in an industrialized society with urbanization occurring at a faster rate than in virtually all other European countries. By the 1840s Scotland had much greater per capita wealth than Ireland and an industrial economy that offered a range of jobs in general and casual labouring to temporary and permanent migrants from the Highlands. Agricultural work (especially at the harvest), the fisheries, domestic service, building, dock labouring and railway navvying were just some of the outlets available in the booming southern economy. By the 1840s, temporary migration had become a very well-developed feature of

Highland life. Not only did it provide a stream of income from the Lowlands, but the peak months for seasonal movement – May to September – were also the times of maximum pressure on food resources, when the old grain and potato harvests were running out and the new had still to be gathered. These migration networks were of key importance during the potato famine. The years 1846 and 1847 were, by happy coincidence, a phase of vigorous development in the Lowland economy, stimulated in large part by the greatest railway construction boom in Scotland of the nineteenth century. Inevitably, therefore, there was an unprecedented demand for navvies, but fishing and agriculture, both traditional outlets for Highland seasonal migrants, were also very buoyant. The combination of a very active labour market in the south and the unremitting pressure of destitution in the north prompted a huge exodus from the stricken region.[7] In a sense, however, this early two-year phase of the Great Highland Famine was, despite acute distress, the relative quiet before the storm. Intense increase in social dislocation soon threatened to overwhelm entire communities in Scottish Gaeldom.

2

The benevolence of urban philanthropists and several Highland landowners in providing support for the stricken population in 1846–7 cannot be denied. However, the voices of disquiet and criticism started to become louder from 1848. This was partly because Scotland as a whole was plunged into a deep industrial recession in that year which was accompanied by serious cholera epidemics in some of the larger Lowland towns. 'Donor fatigue' started to set in, not least because it was increasingly questioned why the Gaels should be offered such 'generous' support while many industrial communities also suffered extreme distress with only limited help.[8] The Scottish Poor Law reform of 1845 had set its face against relief for the able-bodied unemployed and, as a result, countless families now sank into miserable destitution in the manufacturing areas.

The Central Board had sought to divert its resources to economic improvement but, apparently, to little effect. *The Scotsman* thundered in editorials that the charity of industrious, hard-working Lowlanders had been wasted on the support of 'Celtic laziness'.[9] On some of the great estates of the Highlands, where large sums had been spent on both famine relief and public works, the impact on long-term improvement was slight. Sir James Matheson had invested over £107,000 in the island of Lewis between 1845 and 1850, or some £68,000 more than the revenue derived from the entire estate over that period.[10] Similarly, between 1846 and 1850 £7,900 was spent by the Duke of Argyll on famine support on his Tiree and Ross of Mull properties, together with road and agricultural improvements.[11] Expenditure on this scale helped to maintain the people but, to the critics, the continuance of the crisis into its third and fourth years, despite such levels of funding, seemed to confirm that deployment of resources alone, however great they were, could not solve a problem now deemed to be chronic and deeply entrenched in the very fabric of the society.

The decision of the Central Board to give notice of the termination of its activities in 1850 finally concentrated minds. For the old and infirm, the only alternative was the Poor Law which, of course, meant a direct rising cost to local rate payers. Ominously, numbers on the local poor rolls rose dramatically from the early months of 1850.[12] Now an even worse scenario presented itself to the landed classes of the region. It began to be rumoured that, with the demise of the Central Board, the government was contemplating the introduction of 'an able-bodied poor law' to combat the threat of starvation and the continued serious destitution in the Highlands. This would have given entire destitute communities the legal right to claim relief. One observer alleged that such measures 'were being talked of in high quarters as a remedy for the grievances' of the Highlands.[13] If implemented, a drastic increase in poor rates would have had a catastrophic impact on the already weakened financial position of many landowners. Such a possibility was too awful to contemplate. Strategies on several estates now started to swing away from containment of the crisis to dispersal of the people by mass eviction and emigration. Contemporaries argued that 'the terror of the poor rates' and 'the retribution of the poor' were the fundamental reasons for the harsh measures soon to be enforced.[14] From his vantage point in Whitehall, Sir Charles Trevelyan, who maintained a keen interest in Highland affairs, concurred that the possibility of a sharp rise in the poor rates 'would give a motive for eviction stronger than any which has yet operated'.[15]

It did not help that in these shifting political circumstances the price of black cattle, the main source of income for the crofters, fell on average by more than 50 per cent between 1846 and 1852. The spiralling increases in tenant arrears could not be halted or reversed in such conditions. Ironically, during the same period prices for both Cheviot and Blackface sheep, which had fluctuated earlier in the century, now recovered and went on an upward curve from the later 1840s until the early 1860s.[16] Market forces were dictating investment in sheepwalks and, with it, policies of clearance of small tenants and cottars as the most secure route back to financial stability for landowners.

Another factor was likely to have a key influence on the unfolding trauma of the population. Several large Highland estates were virtually insolvent and under trusts. They included the lands of Walter Frederick Campbell, who owned most of Islay; Norman MacLeod of MacLeod and Lord Macdonald in Skye (and North Uist); Sir James Riddell (Ardnamurchan); the Macdonnels of Glengarry (Knoydart); and the Maclaines of Lochbuie (Mull), among others.[17] Management under a trust was much more rigorous in law than where a solvent landowner had personal freedom of action. When a voluntary trust was established, the trustee, normally an Edinburgh accountant or lawyer, possessed all power of decision-making and the owners did not exercise any control. In law, the responsibility of the trustee was to raise funds to repay creditors, organize the property to enable its sale in whole or in part to pay debts, and to maintain revenue enough at least to cover public burdens, interest payments and the costs of management. In particular, when the estate was administered under a judicial trust, the trustee was exempted from any law requiring the use of estate revenues for the relief of the poor.[18] Not surprisingly, most trustees were inclined to remove crofters and cottars to convert their lands to profitable sheep farms as the surest and quickest method of maximizing income. As one contemporary newspaper put it:

> When the lands are heavily mortgaged, the obvious though harsh resource is dispossessing the small tenants, to make room for a better class able to pay rent. This task generally devolves on south country

managers or trustees, who look only to money returns, and who cannot sympathize with the peculiar situations and feelings of the Highland population.[19]

A similar comment came from Professor John Stuart Blackie, the advocate of the rights of the Gael, some years later: 'A trustee on a bankrupt's estate . . . cannot afford to be generous: women may weep and widows may starve; the trustee must attend to the interest of the creditors.'[20] Historians have noted that some of the most draconian evictions of these years, such as those in North Uist and Knoydart, took place on lands administered by trustees.

In the gathering storm, a deep conflict of values and ideologies emerged and became as relevant as economics and law to the final outcome for the people of Gaeldom. Articulate Lowland attitudes to the Highlands in the Victorian era were profoundly ambivalent, and varied in tone and emphasis over time. On the one hand, romantic Highlandism had made the region a fashionable tourist destination for the elites of British society, while the Highlands were also seen as the kindergarten of elite imperial regiments which had brought fame and distinction to Scotland and helped confirm Scottish identity within both the Union and the Empire. But there was also a much darker side to Lowland perceptions which became increasingly dominant and influential during the famine years. One of the first published works arguing for the innate inferiority of the Celtic race was John Pinkerton's *Dissertation on the Origin and Progress of the Scythians or Goths* of 1787. He described the Celtic peoples as the aborigines of Europe, fated to be relentlessly displaced by the superior Anglo-Saxon Teutonic race until forced to retreat to the fringes of European civilization in Ireland and northern Scotland. He considered that the expected final disappearance of the Celtic races was also confirmed by the nature of their poetry and song which were 'wholly melancholic' as might be expected of 'a weak and dispirited people', unlike that of Lowland Scotland 'replete with that warm alacrity of mind, cheerful courage and quick wisdom which attend superior talents'.[21] Pinkerton's analysis was founded on eighteenth-century Enlightenment beliefs on different societies developing at different stages. The new science of anthropology was also interested in the classification of races and the ways in which the Enlightenment idea of man as the product of his environment could best be understood.[22] Even if the views of Pinkerton and his ilk were shared by only a small intellectual minority in the eighteenth century, they still helped to lay one of the key foundations for the later flourishing of racist thought: the assumption that the Celt was inferior to the Anglo-Saxon. In Scotland, this distinction came to be seen by some as a racial divide between the Highlands and the Lowlands.

In the first half of the nineteenth century, race became an even more central part of medical and scientific research.[23] George Combe's *The Constitution of Man* (1828) was one of the best-sellers of the age and was followed by Robert Knox's 'mono-maniacally racialist and virulently anti-Celticist volume', *The Races of Men* (1850). Knox, one of Edinburgh's leading medical teachers and anatomists, had moved south to London in the wake of his notorious role in the Burke and Hare scandal of 1828. The Teutonic-Celtic distinction was further refined, the former associated with industriousness, a strong work ethic and enterprise, the latter with indolence, sloth and dependency. The remarkable advances of Lowland commerce, industry and agriculture were regarded as proof-positive of the impact of positive racial attributes. On the other hand, the economic failures of the Highlands came to be explained by some as a result of Celtic inadequacy rather than a consequence of environmental constraints.[24]

The famine crisis made these views even more influential. The two most important Scottish newspapers, *The Scotsman* and the *Glasgow Herald*, supported them, as did the *Inverness Courier*. In their columns, the new orthodoxy of the famine experience from 1847–8 was reiterated time and again, often in the most vitriolic terms. The Gael was now perceived as naturally indolent, his laziness encouraged by the liberal distribution of Lowland charity and revealed by the failure of the Highlands to recover despite the massive dispensation of aid. This was argued to be unambiguous confirmation of the racial inferiority of the population of the region. Coincidentally, too, the 1840s were, in the view of one historian, 'a watershed in the surging growth of Anglo-Saxonism', as ideas of Teutonic greatness developed by comparative philologists were combined with notions of Caucasian superiority in the work of those interested in the science of man.[25] In

Scotland, these perspectives were often analysed in territorial and ethnic terms. *The Times* of London dispatched a special 'commissioner' to the north to investigate why Britain, a country so pre-eminent and advanced, could possibly contain within its borders an area of such profound poverty and threatened starvation. His explanation was couched in terms of racial difference. The journalist stressed that not all of the north of Scotland was afflicted. In parts of the region 'the Danish or Norwegian race' of Aberdeen, Caithness, Shetland and Orkney was thriving because they were accustomed to hard work. In a racial and physical sense, they were also clearly identifiable by their fair hair and blue eyes. Despite the bleak and inhospitable environment in which they lived, there was no famine in these areas. By contrast, in the neighbouring county of Sutherland, the land of the Celt, poverty was endemic, the turf huts smoky and filthy and the failure of the potatoes catastrophic.[26] The inference was clear. The famine was not the result of biology or economics. Fundamentally, it came about because of racial differences of character, values and attitudes.

What had emerged then, by 1848–9, were irreconcilable differences between the traditional values of Gaeldom and the prevailing ideologies of contemporary capitalism, improvement and social morality. Those who subscribed to the latter seemed to have little comprehension of the Highland cycle of labour involving considerable effort in spring, summer and autumn but much less activity during the winter months. These seasonal rhythms were intrinsic to a pastoral economy, subsistence agriculture and the climatic challenges of daily life in the Western Highlands and Islands. But to many outsiders, they conflicted with the Victorian belief in the moral and material value of regular and disciplined toil. Also offensive to this mentality was the traditional expectation of the Celt that his social superiors had a responsibility to offer support in times of need.[27] It was a clash of two world views but one in which those who were committed to the virtues of self-help, independence and initiative had the power and authority to enforce action.

Apart from landowners, their factors and the Lowland accountants and lawyers who became trustees of insolvent estates, the two key players in the unfolding scenario were the public officials Sir Charles Trevelyan and Sir John McNeil. Both had had a major influence on the policies of the Central Board and even when its operations ceased in 1850 they maintained a strong interest in the Highlands. It was McNeil's *Report to the Board of Supervision in Scotland of 1851* which finally discredited charitable relief as a solution to the Highland problem and presented a powerful case for the large-scale emigration of the 'surplus' population as the only way forward. His *Report* led to the passing of the Emigration Advances Act which provided loans at low interest to those proprietors willing to 'encourage' emigration from their estates. The legislation can be seen as a catalytic factor prompting a new wave of clearances and 'compulsory' emigration. Moreover, both McNeil and Trevelyan then became deeply involved in the foundation and then the management of the Highland and Island Emigration Society, which supported an exodus of nearly 5,000 people to Australia between 1851 and 1856. Trevelyan was the chairman and the principal influence on the Society while McNeil was his trusted lieutenant.

By 1850, Trevelyan was convinced that mass emigration, including, if warranted, the use of coercive means, was the necessary corrective to the social ills of the Highlands. The failures of charity and relief had already inflicted moral damage: 'The only immediate remedy for the present state of things . . . is Emigration, and the people will never emigrate while they are supported at home at other people's expense. This mistaken humanity has converted the people . . . from the clergy downwards into a Mendicant Community.'[28] He proposed instead a grandiose programme to 'emigrate' 30,000 to 40,000 of the people of the Western Highlands and Islands. 'A national effort' would now be necessary in order to rid the land of 'the surviving Irish and Scotch Celts'. The exodus would then allow for the settlement of a racially superior people of Teutonic stock. He welcomed 'the prospects of flights of Germans settling here in increasing numbers – an orderly, moral, industrious and frugal people, less foreign to us than the Irish or Scotch Celt, a congenial element which will readily assimilate with our body politic'.[29] *The Scotsman* agreed with the diagnosis that expulsion was now vital: 'Collective emigration is, therefore, the removal of a diseased and damaged part of our population. It is a relief to the rest of the population to be rid of this part.'[30] In the later twentieth century this approach might be described as a strategy of ethnic cleansing.

3

Over the two decades from 1841 to 1861 many west Highland parishes experienced an unprecedented fall in population, principally through emigration. Uig in Lewis lost almost a half of its total population, the island of Jura almost a third, several parishes in Skye a quarter or more and Barra a third. In the whole of the region covering the west coast north of Ardnamurchan and the Inner and Outer Hebrides, the total population decline averaged a third.[31] It was the greatest concentration of out-migration, not only in the nineteenth-century Highlands, but in the modern history of Scottish Gaeldom. Over 10,000 emigrants were 'assisted' to leave, mainly from four great landed estates – those of the Dukes of Argyll and Sutherland, John Gordon of Cluny and Sir James Matheson. A further 5,000 emigrated to Australia under the auspices of the Highland and Island Emigration Society. Overwhelmingly, this was an exodus from the Hebrides, and especially from those islands which had suffered most acutely during the potato famine, namely Lewis, North Uist, South Uist, Barra, Tiree, Mull and Skye.

Some went willingly. In other cases, however, coercion was employed widely and systematically. The officials of the estates reckoned that it was the poorest who were most reluctant to move, even if they were in desperate circumstances.[32] The mechanism employed to ensure that they did so was what some called 'compulsory emigration'. Crofter and cottar families were offered the bleak choice between outright eviction or assistance to take ship across the Atlantic with their costs of passage covered. As the Chamberlain for the Matheson estate in Lewis, John Munro Mackenzie, put it in April 1851: 'none could be called to emigrate and they need not go unless they please but all who were two years and upwards in arrears would be deprived of their land at Whitsunday . . . the proprietor can do with his land as he pleases'.[33] Thirty years later, a Church of Scotland minister in Lewis recalled:

> Some people say it was voluntary. But there was a great deal of forcing
> and these people were sent very much against their will. That is very

well known and people present know that perfectly well. Of course, they were not taken in hand by the police and all that, but they were in arrears and had to go, and remonstrated against going.[34]

Mackenzie had identified around 2,500 men, women and children for emigration. However, of the first 1,512 selected, only 45 were willing to take up the estate's offer of supported emigration. But by 1855 Mackenzie had virtually reached his target of 2,500, through a combination of threats of eviction, confiscation of cattle stocks and suspension of famine relief.[35]

So it was that a huge increase in clearance throughout the region ran in parallel with the dramatic expansion in emigration. In early 1848, William Skene, Secretary of the Edinburgh Section of the Central Board, had predicted that the termination of relief operations proposed for 1850 would immediately cause 'a very great and very extensive "Highland Clearing"'.[36] He was soon to be proven correct. Of the summonses or writs of removal granted at Tobermory Sheriff Court on Mull, a mere handful were awarded to proprietors in 1846 and 1847. Over 81 per cent of those issued between 1846 and 1852 were granted between 1848 and 1852.[37] This was a typical pattern. The processes of coercion reached unprecedented levels as the intensity and scale of clearance became evident. Between 1848 and 1851, Sir James Matheson in Lewis obtained 1,367 summonses of removal against his tenants.[38] In some districts in Skye, it was reckoned that eviction had become so widespread that men feared to leave their families to go south to search for seasonal work. The highly experienced official and lugubriously named Sir Edward Pine Coffin, who had been involved in famine relief in Mexico and Ireland as well as Highland Scotland, was so alarmed that he expressed himself in unusually colourful prose. He condemned the landed classes for seeking to bring about 'the extermination of the population', and thought eviction was so rampant it would lead to 'the unsettling of the foundations of the social system' and 'the enforced depopulation of the Highlands'.[39]

Three key sources provide considerable insights into how the managers of Highland estates went about the business of removal and 'compulsory emigration'. The first is a report by Thomas Goldie

Dickson, a trustee of the Ardnamurchan Estate of Sir James Riddell, written in 1852; secondly, the diary of John Munro Mackenzie, Chamberlain of the Matheson estate on Lewis, for 1851; and thirdly, the correspondence of John Campbell of Ardmore, Chamberlain of the Duke of Argyll's properties in Tiree and the Ross of Mull.[40]

A striking feature in all three cases was the careful investigations carried out of the population before decisions were made about individual removals. The economic conditions of each tenant and ability to pay rent were of paramount concern but they were by no means the only evidence to be considered. Character, age and health were among the other matters given considerable weight. Each household was visited and detailed enumerations collected. On the basis of these facts, the future of families and whole communities was decided. The poorest were always the targets. The Duke of Argyll put the issue directly in a note to his Chamberlain in spring 1851: 'I wish to send out those whom we would be obliged to feed if they stayed at home – to get rid of that class is the object'.[41] He had earlier issued John Campbell with instructions to completely remove and 'emigrate' crofters paying below £10 rental and all cottar families.[42] On Lewis, a special feature of the clearance programme was the eviction of those townships formerly involved in the now-redundant kelp industry and, at the same time, the building up of other communities on the island which were committed to the more profitable fishing industry.

But decisions were not simply based on disinterested economic calculation. Ideologies, values and attitudes also entered the equation. Some Lowland trustees, in particular, came north with a set of social and moral values about the racial inferiority of the Gael which undoubtedly influenced their thinking. One of the leading accountants of the time, George Auldjo Jamieson, in an address to the Royal Society of Edinburgh, noted the contrast between the Saxon race of the Lowlands, lauded as the land of independence and progress, as opposed to the Gaelic Highlands, inhabited by a Celtic race degenerate by dependence and backwardness.[43] It was also significant that in 1851 Sir James Matheson advised the immigration authorities in Quebec in advance of the arrival of the first shiploads of people from his estate that they should be dispersed rather than be allowed to remain together in the same communities. He contended that would be 'the best means of eradicating those habits of indolence and inertness to which their impoverished condition must in some measure be attributed'.[44]

These attitudes coloured the decision-making processes to a considerable extent. Indeed, estate managers often come across in the sources as the rigorous guardians of Victorian morality rather than as impartial administrators. While the 'respectable poor' might be protected and saved from removal, others were less fortunate. In April 1850, for instance, John Campbell issued 'a goodly number' of 'removing summonses'. Some were for rent arrears but others were for such offences as 'selling whisky', 'unruly conduct' and 'extreme laziness and bad conduct'. 'Bad characters' were also likely to be removed.[45] Thomas Goldie Dickson also made life-changing decisions for the people of the Ardnamurchan estate on grounds which were far removed from economic rationalism.[46] Dugald McDonald, the blacksmith at Sunart, had few rent arrears but 'was of intemperate habits' and so 'must be removed and another Smith procured'. Another unfortunate was James McMaster, who not only had substantial rent arrears but 'was living with a Woman not his wife'. Even more extraordinarily, Duncan Henderson of Kilmory was described as 'a clever man, a little too much so'. The decision was therefore that he 'must be sequestrated for safety'. Hugh McPherson 'does nothing all winter ... An ill-dressed and evidently lazy fellow.' In this and other estates, managers had almost literally the power of life or death over crofters, who held land on an annual tenure, and cottars, who had no legal tenurial rights at all. Several used this authority to impose the virtues of self-help, the work ethic and 'respectability' on a population deemed to be inferior in all these respects. Also striking was the callousness of the decisions; the very old, the sick and even the dying were not exempt from removal.

For a people already brought low by years of failing crops this must have seemed akin to the imposition of a reign of terror and, not surprisingly, long after these events their infamy lived on among the emigrant communities overseas. The following satirical poem, suffused with anger, was penned by Eugene Ross (or Rose), a native of Ardtun in the Ross of Mull to mark the death of the aforesaid John Campbell of Ardmore, known widely as the Factor Mòr, the Big Factor, because of his height. The 'Big Angus' referred to in the text was Angus McVicar, Campbell's sub-factor. Both were natives of the island of Islay.

Lament for Factor Mòr

There is news in the land that we rejoice to hear –
that the Factor is laid out without a stitch on him but a shroud,
without the ability to speak and unable to read or write;
the champion of the Islay folk is laid low, and will never rise again.

When they go to the boat we will laugh with glee,
and when we gather together, we will drink toasts to one another
with a good Highland whisky, with strong wine and cider,
and we will not be worried any longer, since that beast has been
  vanquished.

The Factor will have the pre-eminence in Satan's pit,
and Big Angus will be right behind him, with a flame of fire up
  his buttocks,
because of all the oppression that you inflicted on women and children,
and the people of the country that you drove mercilessly overseas.

When they heard in Canada that that beast had expired,
bonfires were lit and banners were attached to branches;
people were cock-a-hoop with joy, as they met one another,
and they all got down on their knees and praised God that you had
  died.[47]

6

In the Land of the Free: Scots and Irish in the USA

The Irish and the Scots were among the world's most renowned diasporic peoples. Their wanderings had begun long before the age of mass emigration, with the Scots very active in medieval and early modern Europe as soldiers, merchants and scholars and the Irish having long traditions of movement to southern and central European countries. It was, in crude terms, a kind of continental division of movement after the Reformation: the Protestants tending to concentrate in the north in Scandinavia and Poland-Lithuania; the Irish more visible in the Catholic countries to the south, though the frontiers between each region remained porous. When the axis of emigration started to swing to the Atlantic the Irish became even more numerous at an early stage in the seventeenth-century Caribbean than the Scots, though that ethnic balance did change significantly in subsequent generations.[1] In the eighteenth and early nineteenth centuries the Protestant Irish became far and away the largest group of emigrants from the British Isles in the American colonies, vastly out-numbering Scots in the transatlantic movement before 1815.[2] When it becomes possible to chart comparative emigration from European countries after 1861, Scotland and Ireland were always among the leading nations in terms of net outward movement.[3] Irish and Scots also converged in terms of migrant destinations after the 1840s. For the Catholic Irish, the USA was always the most favoured country. It was also most popular among the Scots, except in the decade before the Great War. More than half of all emigrating Scots embarked for the USA between 1853 and 1914. A higher proportion made it their final destination, after having first crossed the Atlantic to Canadian ports before moving south across the border.

There were, therefore, profound similarities between the Irish and Scottish emigrant experiences over long periods of time. Despite this, as will be seen below, significant differences emerged in the countries of settlement, where divergence rather than convergence was often the norm. The United States is perhaps the most interesting example of these patterns.

I

The potato blight struck Ireland repeatedly in the late 1840s with devastating consequences on a society where deep poverty and low standards of living already prevailed. During the famine decade between 1846 and 1855, somewhere between 1.1 and 1.5 million died, out of a national population of 8.5 million. Another 2.1 million left Ireland during these terrible years, of whom 1.8 million made the transatlantic crossing to North America. It was by far the largest and most concentrated exodus of human beings to the New World in European history. In all at least 1.5 million sailed directly for the USA. In the 1840s, the Irish alone accounted for nearly 46 per cent of all immigrants to the USA.[4]

Apart from sheer scale, there were other key differences from the well-established migrations before the famine. In the past, northern Protestants had made up the majority of emigrants from Ireland, but during the historic crisis nine out of ten of those who left were Catholic. Large numbers of them were also Irish speakers: in one plausible estimate, as many as half a million.[5] Again, before the famine, emigration had tended to centre on the provinces of Ulster and Leinster. The famine migrations, however, were heaviest from the poorer provinces of Connacht and Munster, in the west and south-west, where the potato disease had had its most lethal impact. Indeed, Connacht lost around a half of the population aged twenty-five and below at this time. Thereafter, during the post-famine decades of recovery, the poorer counties of these provinces would continue to dominate the movement to the USA.[6] But it was not the most deprived, but people of some modest means who were able to scrape together limited funds for the transatlantic passage. As one Irish historian has put it: 'In the

1. Bute: John, 3rd Earl of Bute and the first Scottish Prime Minister after the Anglo-Scottish Acts of Union. He was accused by political opponents of furthering the interests of his fellow Scots in London and the Empire.

2. 'A Flight of Scotchmen' (1796). Swarms of Scottish adventurers make their way south hoping for rich pickings in London and the Empire.

3. Sugar mill, slaves and overseers in Antigua, a Caribbean island extensively settled by Scots planters from the 1760s.

4. Bance Island slaving fort off the mouth of the Sierra Leone river. Between 1749 and 1784 its Scottish owners sold over 12,000 blacks into slavery across the Atlantic.

5. New Lanark Mills. The most renowned textile complex of the Scottish Industrial Revolution, famous for Robert Owen's social experiments but partly funded from the profits of Caribbean trade.

6. Poltalloch House, Argyll. Built by the Malcolm family, who made a great fortune from West Indian plantation ownership and commerce.

7. Glasgow International Exhibition, 1901, main entrance.
The Second City of the Empire revels in its global status.

8. Weaving shed, Baxter Brothers, Dundee. The city became 'Juteopolis',
famed globally for its processing of Indian jute into sacking and largely
dependent on the employment of women workers.

9. Dignitaries at a launch on the Clyde, 1891, when the river built a fifth of the world's ships.

10. William Jardine (1784–1843). The co-founder (with James Matheson) of the immensely successful Asian firm of Jardine, Matheson and Co., which made vast profits in the opium trade to China.

11. Thomas Blake Glover (1838–1911) with Iwasaki Yanosuke, son of the founder of Mitsubishi, c. 1900. Glover became a key figure in the industrialization of Japan.

12. *State Visit of Queen Victoria to the Glasgow International Exhibition 1880*, by Sir John Lavery. The monarch is welcomed by the imperial elites of Scotland.

WE`VE GOT JOBS IN CANADA
WE DON`T WANT THE DOLE!

13. The depression of the 1920s hit Scotland hard.

14. Emigrants waiting for transport across the Atlantic at the Broomielaw, Clydeside. In the 1920s Scotland topped the league table of European emigration.

15. On boat to New Zealand. The development of New Zealand, like that of Canada, was profoundly influenced by mass immigration from Scotland.

16. The *Hercules* carried several hundred destitute emigrants from the Hebrides to Australia in 1852. The voyage was notorious for the large numbers of deaths on board caused by typhus and smallpox.

17. The ruins of Shiaba township, Isle of Mull. The people were mainly cleared in 1847 and 'emigrated' by the Duke of Argyll to Canada.

hierarchy of suffering the poorest of the poor emigrated to the next world; those who emigrated to the New World had the resources to escape.'[7]

The famine years were unprecedented, but after 1860 the tide of migration, albeit at a lower level, was maintained. Emigration became part of the expected cycle of life: 'growing up in Ireland meant preparing to leave it'.[8] By 1901 the population of Ireland had collapsed from its high point of over 8 million in 1841 to just under 4.5 million. Different destinations attracted people at different times and they included England, Scotland, Canada, South Africa and Australasia. But nowhere across the globe could match the irresistible lure of the USA. From 1851 to 1921, of the 4.5 million who left Ireland (including a million Ulster Protestants), about 3.7 million settled in the United States.[9] Typically, they consisted of cottars, smallholders and middling farmers rather than the landless at the very bottom of the social scale. These emigrants may have been a cut above the substratum of Irish society but by American standards they were still miserably poor and vied only with African Americans as the most impoverished in the country.[10] During the famine years, their low material status was aggravated by disease, trauma and the speed with which they had had to uproot themselves. Nearly all were described as labourers or servants on arrival at American ports, with only one in ten named as tradesmen or artisans.[11] This was a pattern which persisted even after some years of settlement in the United States. As late as 1870, four out of every ten Irish-born men and women employed in the USA worked as unskilled labourers or domestic servants.[12] In New York City they comprised three-quarters of the labourers and, while the first-generation Irish did somewhat better the further west they moved (for instance, in Denver, Detroit and San Francisco), more worked as unskilled labourers in the 1870s than any other white ethnic group of the time.[13]

Although the Great Famine was by no means the only factor propelling these great movements across the Atlantic, it was such a dreadful and cataclysmic experience that it, more than any other influence, shaped the identity and memory of Catholic Irish America for the rest of the nineteenth century and beyond. The Irish came to see themselves as exiles, banished from their native land by a crisis which, so they believed, could in large part have been averted or at least alleviated by the British state.[14] The Irish-American nationalist John Mitchell spoke for many when he wrote, 'The Almighty indeed sent the potato blight, but the English created the Famine.' A popular ballad among the Irish in the United States put the same point even more powerfully when it recalled the visitation of famine in the town of Skibbereen:

O Father dear . . . the day will come when vengeance loud will call
And we will rise with Erin's boys to rally one and all.
I'll be the man to lead the van beneath our flag of green,
And loud and high will raise the cry, 'Revenge for Skibbereen'.[15]

The sense of exile was compounded by the fact that Irish emigrants had one of the lowest return rates to the homeland of any other nationality in Europe. At most, 10 per cent came back, in contrast to the Italians and East Europeans of whom it is reckoned that more than half eventually returned home.[16] This explains the tradition of the 'American wake' which was especially common in the Irish-speaking communities of the west of Ireland in the later nineteenth century, 'modelled on the Irish wake for the dead, only in this case it was the living dead who received the send-off, in the knowledge that they would not be seen in Ireland again'.[17] The combination of a sense of exile and the belief that the Irish people had been betrayed by the British government during the famine had a potent effect. Both deep sentimental attachment to the 'ould countrie' and hostility to the British oppressor inspired generations of Irish immigrants to support the nationalist cause at home. Support for Irish Home Rule did not emerge fully-formed until the 1860s and thereafter, but it was in embryonic form in the hearts and minds of many emigrants before that.

Personal links with families in Ireland, however, were not entirely severed by distance, as is evidenced by the truly remarkable scale of postal correspondence with kinsfolk. The Irish post office distributed 7 million letters in 1857, a figure which increased to 20 million by 1914.[18] The messages did not simply renew and maintain contact between loved ones separated by an immense expanse of ocean. They also formed an integral part of the mechanism of continued migration from poor communities, as large amounts of money and pre-paid tickets were sent back to Ireland to enable family members who could not afford the costs of transport to embark on the transatlantic journey. These remittances became the lubricant of 'chain emigration' which smoothed the transfer of family networks from Ireland to North America. It is reckoned that between 1848 and 1900 as much as $260 million was posted to Ireland from across the Atlantic, of which 90 per cent came from the USA.[19]

In the United States, the rural Irish peasantry for the most part became an urban people. By 1920, 87 per cent of the first-generation migrants lived in American cities. The Northeast and Mid-Atlantic tended to be the favoured region of settlement so that even at the end of the twentieth century, New York, Philadelphia and Boston remained the destinations of choice. But as the frontier expanded so the Irish also pushed west, and Chicago and San Francisco soon attracted large numbers of immigrants.[20] Their urban preferences made them stand out from the American-born population as a whole. Indeed, in 1850, fewer than one American in every ten lived in towns and cities of populations of 25,000 or more. Yet, on one estimate, 75 per cent of the American-born Irish lived in urban-industrial areas in 1870.[21] Within the cities, Irish-dominated localities and neighbourhoods were common – essentially village communities reconstructed behind the apparent anonymity of urbanism. These offered the new immigrants friendship, contacts and housing. But the fundamental reason for urban concentration was probably grounded more on economic than on social factors. The explosive growth of American towns and cities – a ninefold expansion between 1830 and 1860 – promised unskilled and semi-skilled jobs aplenty in construction and transportation. The urban focus probably also reflected the poverty of the Irish. The start-up costs of farming in virgin territories were beyond their means while the type of peasant cultivation they had been accustomed to in the smallholdings of rural Ireland hardly prepared them for the different challenges of American capitalist agriculture.[22]

The sheer volume and urban concentration of their immigrations gave the Catholic Irish high visibility in nineteenth-century American cities. Their Catholicism and predominantly lower-class status combined to fortify the stereotype of the Irish as inferior, ignorant, violent and drunken, a serious menace to Anglo-Saxon Protestant standards of civilization. This, after all, was the age of Darwin and Huxley, of evolutionary, racial and ethnological studies. These new 'sciences' helped to provide seemingly authoritative support for notions of Irish inferiority. Popularized in cartoons and the popular press, such ideas were commonplace in nineteenth-century America.[23] The Draft Riot of 1863 in New York (which left 105 people dead), the Orange Day riots in 1870 and 1871 and the terrorizing by the notorious Molly Maguires (a violent secret society) in the 1860s of some of the Pennsylvania coal-mining districts consolidated the public image of the Irish as a lawless race.[24] Almost inevitably this fuelled nativist antagonism, in the first instance through the Know Nothing movement of the 1840s and 1850s, which was defined by a virulent anti-Catholicism and deep-seated hostility to immigration. By 1855 the organization had 10,000 lodges and over a million members, although it eventually collapsed, broken into opposing factions over the contentious issue of slavery.[25] Ulster Protestant immigrants, their descendants and the Orange Order then played a key leadership role in the American Protective Association. Founded in 1877, it claimed to have attracted 2.5 million members at its zenith two decades later. The Association's members pledged not to hire Catholics or vote for Catholic candidates in either local or national elections.[26]

Perhaps inevitably the lives of the majority of Irish who emigrated to the USA in this period are lost to history. But for those which are recorded, it was probably predictable that the evidence suggests a strong response of ethnic solidarity to the widespread hostility which was experienced by the first generation of immigrants. A coherent sense of collective identity was at the heart of the Irish experience in the USA, a form of social defence against an unfriendly world. One of the most telling indicators was the formation and popularity of Irish regiments in the Civil War. The immigrants joined both sides but Irish Catholics were more drawn to the Union Army. At least thirty-eight Union regiments had 'Irish' in their names and around a quarter of a million Irish-born Americans served in the same army along with countless others from the second generation of immigrants.[27] This war experience was at once an affirmation of Irish ethnic identity while at the same time helping to forge an important route from the margins to the mainstream of American society in the north of the country. Moreover, the sheer scale of immigration, especially focused as it was in urban America, provided the Irish, when they were organized, with considerable demographic muscle which could be employed to decisive effect in both city politics and trade union affairs. At the core of this emerging Irish-American identity was the Catholic faith.

One notable date in the history of Irish America is 25 May 1879. That day marked the public opening of St Patrick's Cathedral on Fifth Avenue, New York, destined to become the most famous Catholic church in the country and a celebration in stone of the dominance of the Irish in American Catholicism. By the 1850s there were more Catholics in the United States than any other denomination, as immigration from Europe had resulted in a great surge in numbers of the faithful, from 1.6 million in the middle years of the nineteenth century to 3.1 million by the 1860s. Germans and Poles were in a minority in this rapidly expanding church. For every German Catholic in New York there were as many as seven Irish, a pattern which was duplicated in Boston and Chicago. By 1900, two-thirds of American Catholic bishops were of Irish birth or descent.[28]

The 'devotional revolution' in Ireland had instilled a much greater public commitment to Catholicism among post-famine immigrants to the USA. The architect of that liturgical transformation was Paul Cullen, archbishop of Dublin from 1852 to 1878. Regular attendance at Mass, frequent recourse to the sacraments and public commitment to the faith became the key hallmarks of his strategy and took the place of the more informal approach to piety and belief of earlier times. By the end of the century, Ireland had become one of the most observant Christian countries in the world, with more than 90 per cent of the people estimated to be regularly attending Sunday Mass.[29] The scale of apostasy after emigration is unknown but the communal loyalties to Catholicism in post-1850s Ireland ensured that religion would play a central part in the emerging world of Irish America.

In essence, Catholicism had three main effects on the Irish in the United States. First, allegiance to the faith became 'a badge of identity', defining what it meant to be Irish in America. An enduring link was renewed between 'Irishness' and Catholicism which had earlier been forged in the politics of Irish nationalism and Daniel O'Connell's campaign for Catholic Emancipation in Ireland. The Church buttressed the ethnic sense of Irish tribalism, fortified also by the growing hostility from nativism as many imagined that Popery was on the march in America.[30] The link with Ireland was also preserved through the numerous Irish-born priests and nuns who came to minister to the spiritual needs of the immigrants. The number of Catholic priests in the USA rose from 480 in 1840 to 1,500 a decade later. At least a third of this increase were Irish-born.[31]

Secondly, by the 1880s the Irish city parish had become much more than a religious entity. Instead, it developed wide communal responsibilities and established a whole series of social functions, including care of the poor, charitable activities, cultural and entertainment provision and much else. By this expansion into other areas of life the parish soon took centre place in the world of Irish Catholics. One New York priest remarked that by the 1920s the network of parish organizations 'aimed to meet every need of the parishioner and to deal with every condition'.[32] At the same time, the building of innumerable Gothic-style churches throughout the Irish urban neighbourhoods, paid for primarily from Sunday collections by the working classes, fortified ethnic pride and a sense of immigrant achievement in adversity.

Thirdly, the Catholic Church became a powerful engine of educational expansion, which eventually helped to sustain the social mobility of the community in later times. By the 1860s, the Church was committed to a separate educational path. The parish school was to take the place of the non-Catholic public school, even if aspirations sometimes remained pious hopes, dashed by lack of resources and the other claims on the pennies of the poor. Yet, in 1900, 37 per cent of American Catholic parishes were supporting their own schools, though the Irish still had fewer than the Germans who were even more committed to separate education because of the incentive towards language preservation.[33]

The decades from c.1860 to c.1910 saw significant changes in the social and economic status of second- and third-generation Irish Catholics in the USA. The first generation had experienced little occupational mobility, burdened as they were by low skills, poor education and discrimination, although not all were at the bottom of the urban labour force. Skilled and semi-skilled Irish have been identified in San Francisco, New York and New Orleans. There was also a small sprinkling of middle-class Irish in white-collar positions, though these remained a small minority within the immigrant community.[34]

However, by the early twentieth century the American Irish had, in the words of one scholar, 'achieved rough occupational and educational equality' with the US population as a whole.[35] The new immigrants were still concentrated in menial jobs, but the second and third generations did better. It was not so much 'a rags to riches' story or a movement from the working class to the middle class. Rather, the experience was one of more modest mobility, from the unskilled through to semi-skilled and skilled status. The further west they went, the better the Irish did. The San Francisco Irish, for instance, prospered more quickly than those in the old migrant centres of New York and Boston.[36] But the new arrivals tended still to be immersed in the poverty of the Irish slums where unemployment, alcoholism and ill health remained endemic. It was the children and grandchildren of the immigrants who fared a little better. The differences came out with clarity in a major academic study of the Boston Irish focused on the year 1890. Two of every three of the first generation were unskilled labourers, compared to one out of three of those who had been born in the USA.[37]

There are many explanations for this trend towards upward mobility. In part it reflected the enormous and extended boom in the post-Civil War period which expanded opportunities at all levels of the labour market. Also, the Irish were no longer at the bottom of the immigrant heap. New arrivals were starting to pour into the United States in their millions from Eastern and Southern Europe. The Catholic Irish may still have been outsiders from the Anglo-Saxon mainstream but they were recognizably less alien than the Poles, Italians and Russians who now became the new, favoured targets for resurgent nativism. Indeed, the Irish would be numbered among those who were the most virulently hostile to the new arrivals.[38] But the move into more skilled occupations also came out of collective self-help. The investment in human capital through their system of parochial schools and colleges did pay significant dividends over time for the Irish. They became, in addition, the leading practitioners par excellence of 'machine politics'. They settled in the growing urban areas precisely at the same time as modern systems of city governance were beginning to take shape. The success of the Irish machines lay in their capacity to organize and provide a disciplined vote in elections in return for jobs, patronage and contracts for their loyal supporters. Often this was done with the Democratic Party, which for a time became almost an Irish fiefdom in the northern cities.[39] The most notorious and successful of the machines was Tammany Hall in New York, which controlled that city for eighty years, from the 1850s to the 1930s. But Chicago, Boston and San Francisco were equally part of a vast network of corruption and patronage. Tammany's system of votes in return for jobs in the police, public services and with contractors was said to command 40,000 posts to offer supporters in the 1880s.[40] It was a classic case of how ethnic and religious solidarity could blatantly and ruthlessly pursue advantage for sectional interests.

By 1914, Irish Catholic loyalty to the USA was unmistakable. But for many, at least until the emergence of the Irish Free State in the 1920s, adherence to America was perfectly compatible with a commitment to Irish nationalism. In part, and possibly for a majority, this was simply the cultural reaffirmation of an older ethnic identity. The annual St Patrick's Day parades were the most striking public and popular manifestations of this. But for others the struggle for Irish Home Rule and independence was a lifelong commitment. The Fenian Brotherhood, Clan na Gael and the Irish Republican Brotherhood (among others) all flourished in the later nineteenth century in Irish communities in America. It is also apparent that these organizations had a transatlantic dynamic. Many of the leading lights of Irish nationalism, such as Michael Davitt, Charles Stewart Parnell and John Devoy, were as deeply involved in the political life of America as they were that of Ireland. The bond between some emigrants and the home country was not simply sentimental but also resolutely political. Thus, when the Easter Rebellion broke out in Dublin in 1916, the proclamation declared how the rising was 'supported by her [Ireland's] exiled children in America'. Indeed, much of the impetus for 1916 came from America and a remarkable number of the leaders of the insurrection had either lived or travelled in the USA.[41] As will now be seen, this robustly political connection between the old and the new country was but one of the many ways in which the experience of Scots emigrants to America fundamentally differed from the Catholic Irish.

2

That the Protestant Scots, unlike the Catholic Irish, were well received in America is a stereotype of United States history, not least because a number of hagiographical works have uncritically celebrated the contribution of Scottish immigrants to American education, economy, culture and politics.[42] For President Woodrow Wilson, as for so many others, his country's history 'was a line colored with Scottish blood'.[43] But it was not always thus. Especially at the birth of the new nation in the later eighteenth century, Scots were bitterly reviled as the enemies of American freedom and patriotism. Ironically, at that time it was not uncommon to praise the Irish while denouncing the Scots. Thus, the *Virginia Gazette* reported in October 1774:

> *Irish influence* is of the downright, genuine and unadulterated sort. *The Scotch Influence* is of a different species. A *Scotchman*, when he is first admitted into a house, is so humble that he will sit upon the lowest step of the staircase. By degrees he gets into the kitchen, and from thence, by the most submissive behaviour is advanced to the parlour. If he gets into the dining room, as ten to one but he will, the master of the house must take care of himself, for in all probability he will turn him out of doors, and, by the assistance of his *countrymen*, keep possession forever.[44]

Two aspects of the anti-Scots image come through here strongly. First, was their perceived grasping and rapacious nature, which threatened a kind of Scottish economic hegemony in the colonies. Indeed, in terms of Scottish success in the tobacco trade in the south, there was more than a degree of truth in such accusations. In November 1777, for example, the president of Yale, Ezra Stiles, fulminated that 'the Scotch had got <u>Two Thirds of Virginia and Maryld</u> mortgaged or otherwise engaged to them or <u>was owned in Scotland</u>'. He went on to assert, 'I have had it often suggested to me by Scotch

Merchants and Factors that the Scotch would in a very few years have all the property in Virginia if not in Gen. of No. America.'[45] The second aspect, and a perennial part of the same negative contemporary stereotype, was the supposed clannish behaviour of the Scots, seen to be supporting one another against non-Scots and engaged in an ethnic conspiracy of exploitation against the greater good of colonial America.

Hence dislike of 'the Scots nation' became integral to the political landscape of the USA in its early years of existence. A statute of the Assembly of Georgia of August 1782, for instance, banned Scots from settling or trading in the colony unless they declared themselves as American patriots. The reason was simple – they were acknowledged as the enemies of the Revolution: 'the People of Scotland have in General Manifested a decided inimicality to the Civil Liberties of America and have contributed Principally to promote and Continue a Ruinous War, for the Purpose of Subjugating this and another Confederated State'.[46] The flight of innumerable Scottish loyalists from Upper New York and the Cape Fear territory in the Carolinas during the latter stages of the war for refuge in places as far apart as Canada and the Caribbean told a similar story. They feared retribution for themselves and their families in the aftermath of an American victory. After all, Thomas Jefferson's first draft of the Declaration of Independence contained the notorious reference to 'Scotch and other foreign mercenaries who were being sent by the British government to invade and destroy us'.[47] John Witherspoon, one of two Scottish-born signatories, secured the deletion of this insult to his fellow countrymen in the final version. Nevertheless, 'A free exportation to Scotchmen and Tories' became a favourite revolutionary toast.[48] Even the master works of the Scottish Enlightenment did not escape censure. The Library Society of Charleston proposed in 1778 that Adam Ferguson's book *Essay on Civil Society* (1766), written by one 'of the Kingdom of Scotland', should be condemned and publicly burnt.[49]

The loyalist sympathies of most colonial Scots partly help to explain these xenophobic reactions. The fact that Witherspoon from Paisley was one of the most eloquent speakers favouring American resistance to imperial authority, or that John Paul Jones from Kirkcudbright became America's first naval war hero, did not weigh much in the overall balance. A leading historian of colonial loyalism notes that more loyalists were born in Scotland than in any other country outside America.[50] In Virginia the Scots were the backbone of loyalism and were also significant in the Carolinas, Maryland and parts of New York. One analysis of loyalist claims on the British government after the war shows that Scottish claimants accounted for nearly 37 per cent of all those made by persons born outside America,[51] a much higher proportion than the Scottish-born share of the colonial population. In some areas the Scots were divided. In Georgia, for instance, some Highlanders supported the Revolution, while in the Carolinas most, but not all, were loyalists. But most Scots engaged in proactive loyalism and their role in the notoriously violent loyalist militias of the backcountries of North Carolina and New York is well documented. Others joined the North Carolina Highlanders or the Queen's Own Loyal Virginians and died in battle defending King and Country against the rebels.[52]

Scottish loyalism rested on a number of foundations. The American Revolution would have jeopardized the remarkable success of Scottish transatlantic trade and emigration, as British Atlantic commerce rested on the Navigation Acts which directed that American commodities should first be shipped to British ports. An independent America could deal directly with Europe with Scotland rendered irrelevant in this new commercial scenario. Imperial law also secured the whole superstructure of credit and debt on which trade depended and on which much of Scottish success was founded. On the face of it, therefore, freedom for the Americans threatened a catastrophe for the Scottish economy.

In addition, many Scottish factors and merchants had come to the colonies as sojourners with the objective of making money and building a career. Most never intended to settle permanently and as temporary residents had an obvious vested interest in British victory. In the 1770s, many Scottish merchant houses were owed large sums by colonial debtors, especially in Virginia and Maryland. It did not help that the great economic crisis of 1772–3 had forced them to try to foreclose on some of their debts. The Scots factors were therefore easily stereotyped as a collective alliance of unyielding and grasping creditors.[53] Scottish imperial officials could be placed in the same negative category as they filled an inordinate number of governorships in the colonies. Many appointed a considerable number of their fellow countrymen to fill more junior positions in local courts and in the colonial bureaucracies of trade and customs, especially in the southern colonies of Georgia, Virginia, South Carolina and North Carolina. It was therefore easy for the patriot tendency to label these functionaries as imperial lackeys. Men like Henry McCulloch, James Glen, Alexander Spotswood and James Abercromby were uncompromising administrators who were determined to uphold British authority.[54] Scottish settlers were more committed to life in the New World but they, too, were loyalists for the most part and fitted the patterns outlined in general studies of American loyalism. Immigrants were more likely to be loyalist than the native-born, and the more recent the immigrant, the greater the chances of loyalty. Mass Scottish emigration to America came relatively late. Those who came in larger numbers between the end of the Seven Years War in 1763 and the beginning of the American War in 1775 may have still felt closer emotional ties with the home country rather than their adopted land.

A case in point was the well-known response of the Highland emigrants in North Carolina and New York. Their loyalism is bewildering for some. After all, they were popularly associated with Jacobite opposition to the House of Hanover. Why, then, did they fight for their former enemy?[55] The question is partly based on a false premise. Highland society was divided during the '45. Some clans fought for Bonnie Prince Charlie, others for the Hanoverians, and most were neutral.[56] The Jacobite connection in the colonies attracted interest because the legendary Flora MacDonald, heroic companion of the 'Prince in the Heather', and her husband, Allan, were prominent loyalists. Allan became second-in-command of the militia raised by his cousin, Brigadier Donald MacDonald, which was made up of emigrant Gaels from the Cape Fear region of North Carolina. The Highlanders met a force of rebels at Moore's Creek in February 1776 and were defeated with heavy losses. But Highland loyalism is not so puzzling. The Gaels were very recent emigrants and led by clan gentry to whom they owed traditional loyalty. They had benefited from generous and substantial land grants from the imperial government and some had served at officer level in the British army between 1756 and

1763. The opportunities now flowing from emigration depended on political stability and strong government. Revolution not only threatened all this but was instinctively obnoxious to an old gentry class imbued with strong hereditary feelings of social hierarchy.[57]

Yet the public loyalism of so many Scots was not in itself sufficient to account for the rampant Scotophobia which swept America in the later eighteenth century. Anti-Scots feeling became a marked strain in colonial popular culture and could be seen in such popular stage successes as Robert Munford's *The Patriot*, with starring roles for such Scottish mercantile stereotypes as McSqueeze, McFlint and McGripe. Another example would be the mock dedication in John Leacock's *The Fall of British Tyranny* (1776) to 'Lord Kidnapper, and the rest of the Pirates and Buccaneers, and the innumerable and never-ending clan of Macs and Donalds upon Donalds in America'.[58] These popular manifestations of prejudice suggest that in some quarters Scots were seen as natural supporters of tyranny, a charge apparently confirmed by the support of some for the exiled Stuarts in 1745, a dynasty which was bent on re-imposing absolute monarchy and Popery on Britain and its colonies. The 'plot' was said to have continued under the guidance of the Earl of Bute, the first Scottish Prime Minister and (more importantly) a man with the family name of Stuart. Even when he left office, Bute and his Scottish accomplices were still seen as the real powers behind the throne. The injustices done to the American colonies since the Stamp Act of 1765 were laid at their door. Apart from Bute's guiding hand, the other suspects were the King's mother, widely believed to be Bute's mistress, and another Scot, Lord Mansfield, Lord Chief Justice of the King's Bench. These beliefs, however bizarre, were given added power by the venomous anti-Scottish rhetoric of the London politician John Wilkes, whose views were widely reported in the colonial press. The American Benjamin Rush, who had studied medicine at Edinburgh, met Wilkes in 1769: 'He spoke with as much virulence as ever against Scotland, for . . . all the Scotch members of Parliament in both Houses, are against America.'[59]

However, by the early years of the new century such rabid hostility was already fading into the past, though suspicions did not entirely disappear and were briefly reawakened by the outbreak of war between Britain and the United States in 1812, which Americans saw as 'a second war of independence'. British-born immigrants were now regarded as aliens and potential enemies. Males aged fourteen and over were required to register at US marshals' offices and, later, British immigrants had to sign special oaths of loyalty. But these antagonisms were ephemeral.[60] Soon a more positive stereotype of the Scot started to emerge and, in contrast to the prevailing indigenous attitudes of hostility towards the Catholic Irish, was more or less fully formed by the middle decades of the nineteenth century.

Eulogistic books and articles began to be published, sometimes often specifically outlining why the Scots were more desirable than the Irish as new Americans.[61] Thus, one Peter Ross praised the Scots as 'good, exemplary citizens' and, unlike some other immigrants, 'unswayed by any claims of nationality'. In an implicit reference to the Irish political machines, he stressed that, 'No politician so far as is known, ever figures on the "Scotch vote", nor did any Scotch aspirant for political office ever count on the solid support of his countrymen.' Ross concluded:

> In all matters pertaining to the country the citizen of Scottish birth completely sinks his own original nationality and takes his place simply and individually with the other citizens in whatever matter is at issue.
>
> Consequently, no new citizens are more cordially welcomed to the great republic than those who hail from the Land o' Cakes. All over the country the Scot is looked up to with respect.
>
> From time to time movements have sprung up in America directed against a particular race or nationality but no such attack has ever been made directly or indirectly upon those hailing from Scotland ... the claim is generally allowed even by the most rabid believers in "Know Nothingism".[62]

The United States Consul in Glasgow was equally fulsome in his own tribute, asserting that 'the great body of the American people not only entertain a feeling of friendship for the people of Scotland but also a sense of obligation, for much of what they are they owe to the teaching and example of Scotland'.[63] One American historian has even gone so far as to claim that 'by *c.*1920 the Scots had become America's favourite immigrant group'.[64] How is this transformation in attitude to be explained?

The literary scholar Andrew Hook has provided at least part of the answer to this question by demonstrating the changing influence that Scotland began to have on American social and political elites by the early nineteenth century.[65] The old negative images faded away, to be replaced by a view of Scotia first as 'the land of Rationalism' and then 'the land of Romance'. It was soon recognized that the Scottish Enlightenment had been an important foundation for American intellectual and political culture. The writings of the Scottish literati were not only widely read but also had practical effect, notably in the way they influenced the curricula of American universities. Indeed, Scottish institutions were recognized as the models for leading American centres of learning such as Princeton, Brown, Columbia, William and Mary and Pennsylvania. Scottish medicine too had an enormous impact on medical education, either through Scots emigrant doctors or American students being trained in the Scottish universities, notably at Edinburgh.[66]

Over time, however, this intellectual appeal was first paralleled and then subordinated to the new romantic image of Scotland. There had long been an American readership for Scottish literature, particularly the works of Allan Ramsay, James Macpherson, John Home, Jane Porter and Robert Burns. With Sir Walter Scott, however, this interest became a burning fascination. The Waverley Novels were immensely popular. One contemporary estimate in *Blackwood's Magazine* had it that 'half a million of the great Scotch novels, we dare say, have issued from the American press'.[67] Even if this figure was no more than informed guesswork, there can be little doubt that Scott made a huge popular impact well outside the ranks of the American intellectual and literary elite. His skilful recreation of a romantic and idealized past had powerful appeal in societies, both in Europe and America, experiencing revolutionary and sometimes threatening changes. Above all, 'Scott consummated a cultural tradition which converted Scotland into the most romantic country in Europe ... for many Americans Scott endorsed, confirmed and authenticated what they long suspected – that Scotland was beyond compare the land of romance'.[68]

The effect could be seen everywhere in American life. Mark Twain famously contended that Scott was responsible for the American Civil

War because his romantic nationalism inspired the South with a bogus sense of identity based on notions of nobility, loyalty and honour. The point may be wildly exaggerated but plantations, and even children, in the southern states did frequently owe their first names to characters and places in Scott's novels. Moreover, his success ensured that he became a model for American writers and a flood of romances cast in the mould of the Waverley Novels soon poured from the presses. The most significant and enduring figure in this new literary fashion was James Fenimore Cooper, known (to his personal irritation) as 'the American Scott'. Such was Scott's unparalleled fame and the admiration for his works that those American tourists who travelled to Europe began to visit Scotland in large numbers. Scott's home at Abbotsford on the Tweed became a place of pilgrimage, and was reckoned to be second only to Shakespeare's birthplace as the most popular site in the cultural grand tour of Britain. Another great magnet was 'the sacred ground' of the Highlands, which so enchanted readers of Scott's epic works.[69]

These favourable changes in the perception of Scots and Scotland may have eased the reception of many immigrants to the New World. But they were not by any means the only reasons why Scots had a much more positive image in the USA than the Irish or, indeed, other European immigrants. The Catholic Irish were unambiguously alien, 'the other', not only because of their faith but as poor and unskilled and, especially during the famine years and afterwards, arriving destitute in such massive numbers that they inevitably caused immense social problems in the American cities where they first settled. The Scots, on the whole, like the English and Welsh, shared the Protestant traditions of the American majority, were much fewer in number and tended not to concentrate in semi-ghettoized urban areas. Five million Irish entered the United States between 1820 and 1930. The Scots numbered one-seventh of that, or 726,000 immigrants over the same period. Indeed, the peak percentage of the US population of Scottish birth was reached as early as 1791. Thereafter, it was a mere 3.1 per cent in 1850, 2.4 per cent in 1900 and 1.9 per cent in 1920. They settled mainly in New York, New Jersey, Pennsylvania, Massachusetts and California. At the time of the 1930 Census, seven states had Scots-born populations of more than 10,000: the most numerous was New

York (with 37,654), followed by Massachusetts (28,448) and then Pennsylvania (18,448).[70] But the Scots were also more scattered than the Irish. Over a quarter of those who settled in the middle of the nineteenth century pushed on to Indiana, Ohio, Wisconsin and Illinois. In addition, despite their marked preference for employment in manufacturing and mining, unlike the Catholic Irish, Scots could also be found in the mainly agricultural states of Montana, eastern Oregon, Idaho, western Washington state and southern California. 'Although never a statistically large group, Scots pioneered in the West as explorers, fur traders, gardeners, farmers, clerics, miners, cattle-ranch managers and especially sheepmen.'[71] Numerous Scottish place-names spread across the country and some concentrated settlements of Scots clearly did exist on the frontier. But territorial integration rather than ethnic separation was the norm for the majority.

Perhaps, however, the differentiation in the immigration experiences of the two peoples derived in the final analysis from the deeply contrasting paths of development of the countries from which they had come after the 1850s.[72] At that time Scotland had become one of the most advanced industrial societies in the world, with over 43 per cent of the country's male workforce employed in either mining or manufacturing (compared to a 41 per cent average for the UK as a whole). In 1860, almost 40 per cent of Scots lived in towns and cities of populations of 5,000 or above. The skills base, both in industry and agriculture, was deep, wide-ranging and sophisticated. There were rich resources of 'social capital', as illustrated by the fact that even before compulsory education was established in 1872, Scottish levels of school attendance were only matched in Europe by Prussia, where compulsion was already in place.[73] Striking confirmation of the advanced structure of the Scottish economy came in the 1840s. Like Ireland, Scotland also suffered the potato blight, though there the crisis was more localized and was limited mainly to the Western Highlands and Islands. Despite experiencing a serious industrial recession in 1848–9, however, the nation was able to contain the disaster with minimal loss of life. There was a great exodus from the stricken districts, as shown in the previous chapter, but this was overwhelmingly channelled to British North America and Australia rather than the USA.[74]

By 1901 Scotland and Ireland had virtually the same population numbers, in large part due to the unprecedented and sustained volumes of emigration from Ireland. But Scotland had an industrial sector about four times the size of the other country, and an agriculture sector around twice as productive.[75] Indeed, from the 1820s the Irish manufacturing base had shrunk as textile production retreated to Belfast and east Ulster. For most of the period considered here, Ireland remained a rural economy, dominated by agriculture, with its population concentrated in the countryside rather than in the towns and with deep pools of endemic poverty. These marked contours of economic and social difference between the two nations were to have a decisive impact on the life-chances of their emigrants as they made their way from homeland to host-land.

The key material fact of American history after 1860 was the unprecedented expansion of manufacturing industry. Production quadrupled by 1900 and US output exceeded that of all competitors, including the original British Workshop of the World, by that date. Indeed, in the years before the Great War American industrial production had become larger than that of Britain, France and Germany combined.[76] It followed from this gigantic leap forward that the United States developed a voracious appetite for labour, particularly that of skilled and semi-skilled workers.

Several aspects are therefore clear. Between 1875 and 1914 around a half of male Scottish emigrants to the United States were deemed to be 'skilled', and a substantial number 'semi-skilled'.[77] In 1885–8, eight out of ten Scottish emigrants to America were from 'industrial' counties at home.[78] They were not fleeing subsistence crises, or even, for the most part, escaping grinding poverty into 'exile'. Instead, they were drawn by higher wages (often three- to fourfold increases), opportunity, advancement and the search for 'independence'. And again, unlike the Irish, middle-class emigrants from 'commerce, finance, insurance and professional' sectors can also be traced in the passenger lists. Indeed, between 1875 and 1914 Scotland provided the highest proportion of professional and business emigrants of all the four UK nations.[79] Not surprisingly, therefore, Scots in the USA were to be found in skilled jobs in shipbuilding, construction, granite-working, engineering and mining. Like the English and Welsh (but unlike most

Irish) they tended to end up in the better-paid working-class occupations.[80] Often, indeed, employers in the United States had recruited them directly from Scotland.[81] Their privileged position did not always go down well. One American journal complained bitterly in 1865:

> They are arrogant, boastful and continually prating about 'the Clyde' and what wonderful achievements are performed on that classic stream, or else eternally sounding the praises of Maudsley and Fields, Napier-rs, etc. – to the disgust of our own mechanics who think not unreasonably, that what 'Napier' may do or not do is of very slight importance.[82]

It would be surprising if all of these immigrants succeeded. But on average, Scots did have a clear head start on the Catholic Irish. Ironically, this is partly shown by the much higher rate of Scottish return migration from the USA. Skilled and semi-skilled masons, granite workers and miners were able to exploit the shorter Atlantic crossings by steamship to spend the busy seasons working in America and then return to a more leisurely life in Scotland during the quieter months much more easily than low-paid common labourers.[83]

The Scots were also much more in evidence in American agriculture than their Irish counterparts, another confirmation of their superior standing. Scottish shepherds and gardeners were highly regarded, as were Scottish ranch managers in New Mexico, Colorado, North Dakota, Wyoming and the Texas Panhandle, often indeed overseeing the great holdings in the west established by Scottish investment companies after c.1870[84] (see Chapter 11). These niche roles also reflected the international reputation for innovation and excellence in agronomy established by Scottish breeders and agriculturists during the Victorian era. But Scots also bought into land. They were very active in Illinois, Wisconsin, Iowa and western New York State. Some rose to positions of significant wealth and eminence. Several Scottish émigrés established huge sheep empires, and men like Robert Burnett, Alan Patterson and Robert Taylor ranked among the largest sheepmen in the west.[85] However, none could match the remarkable success of Andrew Little from Moffat. At one time Little owned 165,000 sheep in Idaho, his flocks producing a million pounds of wool in the 1920s. On his death, the press dubbed him the 'Sheep King of Idaho, and possibly of the United States'.[86]

Another striking feature of Scottish emigration to the USA in the decades before 1914 was the evidence of middle-class occupational penetration, which was very rare in the first generation among the Irish. They may have been a small minority of the whole, but Scots could be found in American banking, accountancy, insurance, the drapery business and much else. It was from their ranks that the office-bearers of the numerous Caledonian, St Andrew and Burns societies which began to proliferate in the USA were drawn. These were not organizations of political, religious and ethnic solidarity, like those of the Catholic Irish surveyed earlier, but rather focused on cultural and sentimental expression. Scots immigrants could also bathe in the reflected glory of their fellow countrymen who had made a mark on American society. These included the father of the conservation movement, John Muir from Dunbar, and the enigmatic figure of Andrew Carnegie. The son of a handloom weaver in Dunfermline, Carnegie became the world's richest man primarily on the basis of ruthless and innovative management at his huge steel complex at Pittsburgh. In 1892 his managerial style triggered one of the most notorious strikes in American history, which ended only after several deaths and many wounded among his workers. In retirement, Carnegie underwent a metamorphosis by becoming the world's greatest philanthropist, generously endowing numerous libraries, universities and other charities. Doubtless to many Americans he encapsulated the stereotype of the Scot: hard-working, able and, above all, successful. In 1940, for instance, 45 per cent of the notables listed in *Who's Who in America* had either fathers or mothers bearing Scottish surnames. In time, descendants of the immigrant Irish would also be counted among the elite of the United States, but that would take somewhat longer to achieve.

Finally, a note of caution should be added. The discussion in this chapter has been conducted at a general level of analysis in order to draw out the main differences between Irish and Scots immigrants. Inevitably, the distinctions within each ethnicity and over time are obscured as a result. While most Scots seem to have had an initial advantage over most Irish Catholics in the United States, that conclusion is not intended to imply that the majority of Scottish immigrants adjusted quickly, easily and successfully to American life. There are at least four reasons why such a judgement is not yet possible in the current state of knowledge. First, unlike the Irish, who have attracted an extensive and impressive scholarly literature, serious academic research on the Scots is still at an early stage. The fact that what has been published in recent years often tends towards boosterism, hagiography and uncritical reiterations of the achievements of 'Great Scots' hardly improves the possibilities for balanced and evidence-based conclusions. Secondly, not all Scots immigrants were aspirational, ambitious young men with the skills to succeed in the American labour market. A minority of males who arrived in the USA after c.1860 from Scotland were classified as general labourers, while most unattached women were former domestic servants or factory workers. Nor should we overlook those less fortunate emigrant Scots of the kind whom the great novelist Robert Louis Stevenson encountered on his American travels in 1879, and who were then graphically described by him in *The Amateur Emigrant* published in 1895:

> around me were for the most part quiet, orderly, obedient citizens, family men broken by adversity, elderly youths who had failed to place themselves in life, and people who had seen better days ... We were a company of the rejected; the drunken, the incompetent, the weak, the prodigal, all who had been unable to prevail against circumstances in one land, and were now fleeing pitifully to another; and though one or two might still succeed, all had already failed. We were a shipful of failures.

Thirdly, the important factor of change over time has to be considered. American scholars do suggest that skilled and semi-skilled Scots were in considerable demand in American industry in the 1840s through to the 1870s and were likely to have done well as a result. But in the later 1880s, and for the rest of the century, the onset of rapid and extensive mechanization in American manufacturing made for de-skilling and more difficult times. Indeed, this process may have helped to drive Scottish emigration more in the direction of Canada in the years between 1900 and 1914. Finally, there is the key issue of volatility in the American labour market between departure and resettlement. In the 1920s, serious industrial depression after the immediate post-war boom resulted in an unprecedented increase in emigration from Scotland. Indeed, during that difficult decade no country in Europe lost as many of its citizens as a proportion of its population. The nation at that time achieved the unambiguous but unenviable reputation of being the emigration capital of the developed world. In the peak year of 1924, 80 per cent of the emigrants to the USA were skilled men from the depressed shipbuilding and engineering industries of Clydeside. They may have fared better for a few years across the Atlantic but then were soon faced with the economic crash of 1929. Many returned to Scotland as unemployment rocketed in the United States.[87] All these complexities must be considered in any overall reckoning of the American experience of these two ethnicities, and that can only be achieved satisfactorily when the current narrow base of knowledge, especially for the Scots, is significantly expanded.

7

The Emigrant Experience in the New Lands

The renowned actor Sir Henry Irving memorably commented in 1896 on 'the capacity of the Scot for ... transporting Scotland all over the earth. I have an idea that when the North Pole is discovered, it will be found to bear a strong resemblance to Arthur's Seat.'[1] That global scattering of the Scottish people is easily confirmed by the available evidence, as this book has tried to demonstrate. Perhaps more contentious, however, are the popular features of the ethnic stereotype which began to develop in the nineteenth century. The Scots were said to have punched well above their numerical weight and hence to have had a quite disproportionate impact on the new lands. One of the early sheep lords of Australia, John Peter, had become very rich in New South Wales after arriving there in 1832. One contemporary explained: 'You must recollect that he is a Scotchman which is in itself a sort of passport to fortune.'[2] While touring the Empire in 1867, Sir Charles Dilke also concluded that 'wherever abroad you come across a Scotchman, you invariably find him prosperous and respected'. He was not certain, however, whether this ethnic pre-eminence was to be accounted for by the famous educational traditions of the Scots or by their work ethic. Nevertheless, he went on to assert that 'for every Englishman that you meet who has worked himself up from small beginnings, without external aid, you find ten Scotchmen'. Dilke wondered as a result that it was 'indeed strange that Scotland has not become the popular name for the United Kingdom'.[3] The stereotype, once established, proved enduring. One essay collection, published in 1976, could assert that 'the history of Canada is to a certain extent the history of the Scots in Canada'.[4] When the great Australian poet Les Murray, himself of Scottish descent, was asked by some Irish-Australians what the Scots had done in Australia, he was said to have replied: 'Well, we own it.'[5] He was perhaps recalling the opinion of James Collier, who stated 'with pardonable exaggeration' in his *The Pastoral Age in Australia* (1911) that 'the Scots own all the land in Australia, while the Irish own all the public houses!'[6]

Two other elements buttressed this Scottish image of exaggerated success in the New World. First, Lowland Scots were often regarded as the most desirable immigrants of all by the colonial authorities in their search for fresh stock. They were apparently considered industrious, respectable and able to accommodate themselves to the challenges of frontier life to a much greater extent than other ethnic groups. In the later nineteenth century, for instance, both Canada and New Zealand specifically targeted Scotland in their attempts to attract an increasing number of immigrants. Scots were explicitly seen to be much preferred to the Catholic Irish. Indeed, the myth of the successful Scot was partly built up in opposition to the racial stereotype of the supposedly inadequate Irish. Vilification of the Catholic Irish went hand in hand with praise for the worthier Protestant Scots. Anthony Trollope, touring Australia in the early 1870s, could assert that 'in the colonies those who make money are generally Scotchmen and those who do not are mostly Irishmen'.[7] The Scots for many officials in the Empire had an attractive brand image. Thus, in 1885, one Australian small-town mayor enthusiastically proclaimed to his English visitor, J. A. Froude: 'We want more Scots. Give us Scots. Give us the whole population of Glasgow.'[8]

Secondly, the assumed extent of Scottish achievement in the new lands was usually explained by the values, character and attitudes believed to be intrinsic to the Scottish people. At a time when theories of Social Darwinism and discussions of racial differentiation were popular, it was not surprising that national achievements were often understood and portrayed in this way. The cultural stereotypes beloved by the Victorians saw the Scot as canny, serious, hardworking and successful, and these have partially survived in modern historiography. Thus, the biographer of one Scottish-Australian notable described his subject as possessing the 'Scottish values of prudence, application, doggedness and endurance, self-discipline and the capacity for preferring work to the call of pleasure'.[9] Another scholar depicted Neil Black, from Argyll, who made a fortune in the pastoral lands of western Victoria and entered the ranks of the colonial plutocracy there, as 'the very type of a Scots pioneer – righteous, frugal, hard-working, no one's fool . . . every risk he took was a calculated one'.[10] This same image was repeated time and again in other parts of the Empire.[11]

But not all were impressed by Scottish élan. There was an alternative and much more negative stereotype which was more reminiscent of the Scotophobia which thrived in the American colonies during the later eighteenth century. This was the image of the Scot as greedy, rapacious, mean and unrelentingly avaricious. Thus, in the pages of the New Zealand *Otago Daily Times* at the end of the nineteenth century, an anonymous correspondent under the pseudonym 'Staunch Englishman' denounced the Caledonians as 'mean, close, bigoted . . . porridge-eating and minding the "sixpences"'.[12] An even more vehement diatribe against Scots of Pictou in Canada has them as a 'canting, covenanting, oat-eating, money-grabbing tribe of second-hand Scotch Presbyterians; a transplanted degenerate, barren patch of high cheek bones and red hair, with nothing cleaving to them of the original stock, except covetousness and that peculiar cutaneous eruption for which the mother country is celebrated'.[13] Some modern critics have also seen through the Scotch mist towards more jaundiced perspectives. The Scottish hero Mackay, in Wayland Drew's Canadian novel, *The Wabeno Feast* (1973), is made to utter a memorable judgement on the business record of his fellow Scots: 'We have skewered this country like a fat ham from Quebec to the Athabascas.' On the same theme, an enraged reviewer of Marjorie W. Campbell's celebratory biography of William McGillivray, a famous figure in the fur trade and leading partner in the North West Company, was scathing in his condemnation:

> What follows is another astonishing exercise in Canadian double-think, another failed attempt to manufacture a Canadian hero out of a greedy, selfish, small-minded, unimaginative, disagreeable Scots clerk . . . Tough, intrepid phooey.
>
> The fur traders who rose to become robber barons were distinguished primarily by their ability to rob the Indians, cheat their competitors and shaft their friends.

A more reprehensible lot would be hard to find in any nation's iconography. [McGillivray] owed his success to nepotism, the North West
Company owed its success primarily to rum.[14]

A final complication is the notion of the immigrant as victim, a
tradition in obvious and direct conflict with the image of the Scot as
grasping, successful and ambitious. Probably this particular permuta-
tion of the Scottish myth has had an even more potent and enduring
influence among many in recent years, both in the homeland and the
emigrant territories, than some of the self-aggrandizing narratives of
the Victorian era. It is rooted in two popular assumptions. First, the
notion persists that Scottish emigration was extensively Highland in
origin. In this tradition the story of Lowland business elites, artisans,
farmers and agricultural labourers is marginalized to the point of being
largely ignored. The Highland exodus itself is portrayed in terms of
tragedy, pathos and involuntary exile. In the final analysis, it is assumed
the Scots emigrated because of the notorious Highland Clearances.
They are stereotyped as the victims of landlord greed and of economic
forces outside their own control. In this narrative, any voluntary quest
for self-improvement is rarely mentioned. The emotions are those of
nostalgia, loss and yearning for the old country.

The second factor is the powerful impact of the invention of a
Highland tradition within Scotland, which was later exported,
extended and embroidered within the expatriate Highland communities. It was mainly in the first half of the nineteenth century that
'Highlandism' became an integral but manufactured part of Scottish
identity. Tartan, bagpipes, kilts and the bens and glens of the Highland landscape were the instantly recognizable symbols of Scottishness
in the Victorian era. In essence, Scotland, through an extraordinary
alchemy, was transformed into a 'Highland' country. Clan associations and Highland games, which soon proliferated in many parts of
the settlement colonies, helped to embed this link between Highlandism, Scottishness and heritage deep within the consciousness of the
descendants of the emigrants and the wider community.

The popular conception is to see these movements in terms of
'emigration as tragedy', an assumption deeply embedded not only in
some aspects of the historiography but even more significantly in

Scottish culture and its relationship with the national past. Highland emigration in particular was depicted essentially as a forced exodus. This is the governing assumption behind the immensely influential books of John Prebble, more especially *Culloden* (1961) and *The Highland Clearances* (1963), which continue to have potent effect on the Scottish diaspora to this day. It also resonates from the works of such artists as Thomas Faed in *The Last of the Clan* and *Oh, Why Left I my Hame?*[15] Popular song conveys the image of loss and exile especially effectively. 'The Canadian Boat Song', first published in *Blackwood's Edinburgh Magazine* in 1829 and ostensibly from the Gaelic, has become the single most popular commentary on the Highland immigrant experience in Canada, despite its entirely bogus origins as the invention by a non-Gael who was not even an emigrant:

> I've looked at the ocean
> Tried hard to imagine
> The way you felt the day you sailed
> From Wester Ross to Nova Scotia
> We should have held you
> We should have told you
> But you know our sense of timing
> We always wait too long

A sentimental version of Scottish emigration also flourishes within the current renaissance in folk music in the Canadian Maritimes while, in Scotland, the Proclaimers' 'Letter from America' (1987) links the forced Highland diaspora of the past with Lowland deindustrialization in the modern era. The chorus of the song, starting with 'Lochaber no more', is followed by the melancholy litany of industrial closures in the 1980s: 'Methil no more', 'Bathgate no more', 'Linwood no more' and 'Irvine no more'.[16]

So what was the impact of Scottish immigrants on Canada, South Africa, Australia and New Zealand in the nineteenth century? Did they, as at least part of the stereotype has it, leave a deep and distinctive mark on these societies? What light can modern research cast on the oft-quoted but rarely rigorously supported idea that the Scots 'punched well above their weight' in colonial business, the professions and politics?

I

One area where there is little scholarly controversy concerns the Scots dominance of the life of the mind in the settlement colonies. Scotland grossly over-produced university-trained men in comparison to the rest of Britain. Even as late as the 1920s Scotland, relative to population size, educated three times as many university students as England.[17] By some measures, the nation had six institutions of higher learning when England had two, if we count the two colleges at Aberdeen – King's and Marischal – separately and include the Anderson Institution in Glasgow, alma mater of David Livingstone and a notable centre for the training of doctors and engineers in the Victorian era.[18] In addition, the Scottish educational philosophy, based as it was on 'useful learning', talent and meritocracy rather than class, tradition and extreme specialization, was admirably suited to the needs of the new lands for professionals and experts of every conceivable type.[19] So many educated Scots were to be found in every corner of the Empire and beyond, as their predecessors had been in the eighteenth century, that the Scottish engineer, doctor, teacher, accountant and banker became icons of imperial literature in the works of Kipling, Conrad, Buchan and others.

The outpouring of trained minds was also powerfully influenced by the distinctive Scottish intellectual ethos. The impact of the eighteenth-century Enlightenment was still enormous, as seen by the central place of Scottish Common Sense philosophy in many colonial universities and some of the staple readings in the Arts curricula, which continued to include the writings of such giants as Smith, Robertson, Miller and Hume. But nineteenth-century Scotland was also a place of remarkable innovation in science, medicine, philosophy and social enquiry, much of which was exported abroad by the mass emigration of university alumni. For too long Victorian Scotland has been considered an intellectual wasteland, a twilight period after the triumphs and glories of the eighteenth century. Nothing could be further from the truth.[20] Its world-class reputation was sustained by some remarkable scholars and their acolytes. They included William Thomson (later Lord Kelvin) and William McQuorn Rankine, whose combined talents made Glasgow Britain's leading centre for applied science and engineering. James Clerk Maxwell, Scotland's greatest scientist and a figure now compared to Newton and Einstein, was the most distinguished mathematical physicist of the age whose theory of electromagnetism was basic to the later development of the radio and many other modern marvels. In medicine, Joseph Lister pioneered antiseptic surgery, and Sir James Simpson was the first to apply anaesthetics to childbirth. But technical virtuosity was not confined to the university laboratories or the great teaching hospitals and infirmaries. The Clyde shipbuilding yards had for a time undisputed world pre-eminence in marine engineering design, while Scottish civil engineers were in demand throughout the globe for the building of bridges, docks and other capital works. They achieved their apotheosis in the completion of the Forth Bridge in 1890, justly regarded as the single greatest civil engineering triumph of the Victorian age in Britain.

The profile of Scottish philosophy in the nineteenth century has suffered because of the inordinate attention devoted by scholars to the golden age of the eighteenth century. Entire academic journals are devoted to some of the thinkers of the Enlightenment period but little has been published thus far on their successors of the Victorian era. This is a pity, because figures like J. F. Ferrier, acclaimed by some in his own time as the most significant philosopher in Europe, and Alexander Bain, Regius Professor of Logic at Aberdeen, also with a distinguished international reputation, are very worthy of serious academic consideration. So too is Edward Caird, leader of the 'Scottish Idealists'. In social studies, Sir James Frazer was a pioneering anthropologist. Educated at both Glasgow and Cambridge, his background in classical studies was also influenced by Kelvin, who stimulated him to search for the absolute laws of nature. His seminal work was the monumental two-volume *The Golden Bough*, first published in 1890, which gave powerful new insights into the study of early societies. His contemporary, Patrick Geddes, also established a world-class reputation through his studies of the new cities that were transforming all the industrializing countries and his conviction that life for their citizens could be improved through effective planning and a serious effort to understand the environment. Today Geddes is recognized as a central influence on sociology and planning and as the father of urban environmentalism, whose American disciple, Lewis Mumford, shaped our understanding of the modern city. Thus it was that nineteenth-century Scotland became the progenitor of a range of exciting new disciplines. There was little evidence of academic inertia or moribund thinking.[21]

The impact abroad of this domestic intellectual energy was partly manifested in institutional form. Nearly half of the centres of higher education in Canada had Scots intimately involved in their foundation, including elite establishments such as Dalhousie, McGill and Queen's universities.[22] Such academic developments were no Presbyterian monopoly. The Catholic hierarchy in areas of Hebridean settlement in Ontario, Prince Edward Island and Nova Scotia was also active in the creation of colleges, academies and seminaries. From this emerged the first-ever Scottish Catholic foundation of higher education in Canada, St Francis Xavier University, formally established in 1853.[23] Throughout the developing Canadian system, curricula continued to be built around the Scottish tradition of moral philosophy. It was a similar pattern in other colonies, in part because the Scottish model of tertiary education was more easily exported across the Empire than the collegiate structures of Oxford and Cambridge. In South Africa, nearly half of the first intake of academic staff in 1873 at the University of the Cape of Good Hope had Scottish degrees.[24] One modern commentator on that country concluded that 'no student of our university system can fail to be struck by the high proportion of Scotsmen who have, over the years, aided its development'.[25] Scottish missionary effort in South Africa, surveyed in Chapter 9, also had a profound educational impact. At the institutional level, the Scottish connection may have been weaker in Australian universities. Both Sydney (founded in 1852) and Melbourne (1855) drew more on English universities as their model. But even there, a huge Scottish professorial presence existed, especially in Sydney.[26] In New Zealand the Scottish educational ethos left more of a clear and definite imprint: Otago, the country's first university, was founded by Scots; the Scottish conception of broad-based higher education prevailed in other institutions; and Scots immigrants were to the fore in promoting secondary education for girls and schooling in general as a public good to which all should have access.[27]

Part of this Scottish world-of-the-mind was its remarkable influence on environmental ideas and the proactive role in the precocious development in an imperial context of the sciences of agriculture, forestry, animal husbandry, hydrology and geology.[28] Richard Grove, the distinguished environmental historian, concluded that 'the emergence of a critique of the environmental impact of settlement in the British colonial empire was pre-eminently a Scottish phenomenon'.[29]

A mix of influences came together here. In the eighteenth century, the Scots had turned their hard and demanding land into a source of more plentiful returns in grain and stock. The Scottish Enlightenment thinkers had both legitimized this quest and encouraged it and so Man's relationship to his environment was radically altered. Nature was no longer to be regarded as fixed and preordained but instead could be changed for the better by rational, planned and systematic intervention.[30] The striking success of the agricultural revolution in Scotland was such that by the early nineteenth century admiring visitors came from far and wide to learn how a formerly poor country with much marginal, hilly and uncultivable land had managed to achieve such a miracle. As a spin-off, Scottish practitioners – from animal breeding through to gardening – gained worldwide fame. It was perhaps predictable that these skills would then be disseminated overseas. Both veterinary science and agriculture were also established by the later nineteenth century as formal disciplines in the Scottish universities. The influence of medical men was also paramount. Since the earliest of times, physicians had to be concerned with herbs and plants in the 'physic gardens', the source of their medications and treatments. John Mackenzie estimates that around 600 medical men, either Scots or trained in Scotland, arrived in South Africa alone between 1815 and 1914.[31]

The environmental history of Scotland also pointed to an interest in the natural world. The country was virtually treeless by the early eighteenth century. It is reckoned that at the time of the Act of Union in 1707 only 5 per cent of Scotland had forest cover.[32] A key interest of the Improving Movement was afforestation, not simply for the profit to be gained by investing in the production of construction materials and fuel supplies but for reasons of aesthetic appeal in the policies of the gentry and the great estates of the aristocracy. Once again, an interest in conservation and improvement was stimulated. Influential Scots in the colonies in this area, such as Robert Moffat and John Crombie Brown, linked environmentalism to their Christian commitment. For Moffat, environmental degradation was a manifestation of God's punishment on human husbandry and the consequence of original sin, a moral evil which had to be confronted and destroyed.[33]

This global network of Scottish thinkers and experts (coupled with the renown of such Scottish-originating publications as the *Encyclopaedia Britannica*, *Blackwood's Magazine* and the *Edinburgh Review*) burnished the reputation of Scotland among global intellectual elites as a land of academic, scientific and medical excellence. In turn, this favourable ethnic image gave Scottish professional emigrants a decided competitive advantage in achieving suitable employment overseas. Also, in the professions of accounting, banking, education, engineering and medicine, chains of patronage and connection between fellow Scots, often from the same extended families, localities and universities, built up strong Scottish niches of worldwide influence which again facilitated the migration process for their fellow countrymen. It was a practice that had evolved from the old Scottish networks of adventurers and traders in Europe and the Americas before 1800.

2

Nowhere in the Victorian Empire was the commercial impact of the Scots more noted and celebrated than in British North America.[34] The story usually begins with the barons of the fur trade, moves to the creation of the Bank of Montreal and the great Canadian Pacific Railway, in which Scots were to the fore, and ends with the establishment of Scottish hegemony in industry and commerce: 'The narrative of the enterprising, nation-building Scot is central even to critical muckraking accounts of Canadian history.'[35]

Fortunately, also, Canada is one country where the conventional wisdom of the successful Scot has been recently tested and challenged by serious historical enquiry. Thus analysis of the late nineteenth- and early twentieth-century Canadian industrial elite suggests Scots were indeed prominent in the higher circles of business. Using one test of ethnic background – birthplace of fathers – they were the leading group in both 1885 and 1910, at around 30 per cent, although only 16 per cent of the Canadian population in 1881 and 1911 were of Scottish origin.[36]

The dominant role of Scots in the fur trade has been already discussed. The Hudson's Bay Company (HBC) drew most of its servants from the Orkney Islands, and by 1800 it had become virtually an Orkney dominion, with no less than 78 per cent of its overseas payroll from that single archipelago.[37] On the other hand, only a handful of Orcadians made it up the company ladder from the lowly ranks of labourers, apprentices, tradesmen and clerks to the more elevated positions of Chief Trader and Chief Factor. Even fewer came to be numbered among the names of the HBC's legendary elite, most of whom were of Scottish birth. They included Sir George Simpson, the so-called 'Emperor of the Plains' and lord of what amounted to 'an independent beaver republic', trading across 3 million square miles of territory. Other notable figures were Sir James Douglas and Donald Smith, who ruled the company in Victorian times; the explorers Robert Campbell and John McLean, who unlocked and mapped the Yukon and Ungava territories respectively; John Stuart from Strathspey, who first traversed the distant wilderness of what is now northern British Columbia; and James Leith, a native of Aberdeenshire, who left half his fortune to spread the Protestant faith among the Indian tribes.[38]

The rival North West Company (NWC) was also a virtual Scottish fiefdom. From the start of the first partnership in 1783, it was dominated by Highland Scots and their kindred over successive generations. The original prime movers were Simon McTavish and his nephew William McGillivray. The other great names in the history of the company – the explorers Alexander Mackenzie and Simon Fraser – were from the same Gaelic background.[39] Of the 225 men active in the firm in the early nineteenth century, 62 per cent hailed from the counties of Inverness, Banff and Aberdeen, and were normally from military, farming or small landed backgrounds.[40] By 1821, after a long period of vicious and violent rivalry and a succession of hard-fought legal battles with the HBC, the two concerns were united, so confirming Scottish dominance in the greatest nineteenth-century Canadian trade of all. Between 1824 and 1870, 64 per cent of the

Table 5: Scots in Canadian business circles, selected evidence

Place	Years	Group	Number in group	Born in Scotland %	Rank of Scots born	Number of categories	Origins of highest rank
Halifax	to 1850	Merchants	370[1]	18	2	6	Nova Scotia
Quebec	1800–30	Marchands	34[2]	32	1	4	
Saint John	1820–50	Great merchants	40	n.a.	2	4	Loyalist
Saint John	1851	High-status positions	66[3]	15	2, ties	8	New Brunswick
Montreal	1837–53	Business community	n.a.	1	6		
Hamilton	1851–2	Entrepreneurial class	143[4]	23	2	6	England
Brantford	1852	Self-employed	237	11	5	5	England

				Father born in Scotland			
Canada	1885	Industrial elite	151	28	1	8	7
Canada	1910	Industrial elite	175	30	1	9	7

Sources: David Sutherland, 'The Merchants of Halifax, 1815–1850: A Commercial Class in Pursuit of Metropolitan Status', PhD dissertation University of Toronto (1975), pp. 470–81 (Halifax); George Bervin, *Québec au XIXe siècle: L'activité économique des grands marchands* (Sillery, 1991), pp. 263–4 (Quebec); T. S. Acheson, *Saint John: The Making of a Colonial Urban Community* (Toronto, 1985), pp. 50, 261 (Saint John); Gerald Tulchinsky, *The River Barons: Montreal Businessmen and the Growth of Industry and Transportation, 1837–53* (Toronto, 1977), pp. 19–20 (Montreal); Michael B. Katz, *The People of Hamilton, Canada West: Family and Class in a Mid-Nineteenth-Century City* (Cambridge, Mass., 1975), p. 180 (Hamilton); David Burley, *A Particular Condition in Life: Self-Employment and Social Mobility in Mid-Victorian Brantford, Ontario* (Kingston and Montreal, 1994), p. 79 (Brantford); T. S. Acheson, 'Changing Social Origins of the Canadian Industrial Elite, 1880–1910', in Glenn Porter and Robert Cuff, eds., *Enterprise and National Development: Essays in Canadian Business and Economic History* (Toronto, 1973), p. 57 (Canada).

1 Number for which the birthplace in known
2 Number for which the birthplace is known
3 Sample, class 1
4 Number for which the birthplace is known

From: Douglas McCalla, 'Sojourners in the Snow? The Scots in Business in Nineteenth Century Canada', in Peter E. Rider and Heather McNabb, eds., *A Kingdom of the Mind. How the Scots helped to make Canada* (Montreal, 2006), p. 81.

company's employees were Scots-born, with those from Canada the next largest group at 12 per cent.[41]

Yet the Scottish factor in Canadian business also needs to be kept in perspective. Table 5, based on the wide-ranging researches of Douglas McCalla on the ethnic background of selected business groups, is important in this respect. It suggests that though prominent, the Scots were not always in the majority. There was also considerable variation in their influence between different towns and cities. In Montreal and Quebec, the Scottish-born were pre-eminent but did not have an absolute majority. In Halifax, they ranked second behind locally born businessmen, though some of the latter may have been of Scottish ancestry, and in Brantford they were bottom of the hierarchy. The Scots were clearly not the only ethnicity with entrepreneurial flair. A final salient conclusion from these Canadian data is the modest numbers which can be included among the elite business groupings. Some Scots may have achieved prominence in these circles but the vast majority of their fellow countrymen were not members of these relatively small charmed coteries, though some niche sectors were indeed strongly associated with Scots. One such was banking. Into the twentieth century Scottish bank clerks were preferred in Canada for their 'sternest frugality and industry'.[42] In addition, they were experienced practitioners of the Scottish system of branch banking 'that seemed so well suited to Canada's vast expanses'.[43]

Scots also made their mark in banking, accounting and insurance in South Africa, and the ubiquitous Scottish engineer was a familiar feature of the mining and railway industries there. Examples of Scottish enterprise can also be found in the retail and mercantile trades of the Cape. But the sense from the available evidence is that Scots did not achieve the same degree of pre-eminence in the South African economy which was so marked in Canada.[44] Again, this is an important corrective to notions of worldwide Scottish business achievement, a record which must be qualified and conditioned by local circumstances, connections and business structures.

The pattern seems to have been different again in Australia and New Zealand, though unlike the case for Canada, existing scholarship does not yet always allow for precise conclusions.[45] Nevertheless, there are pointers to sectors where their influence and role were disproportionate. In North Queensland, a significant Scottish presence in trade, coastal shipping, agriculture and mining was well established, and South Australia also had strong Caledonian connections, especially in the expansion of the big sheep ranches.[46]

By the early nineteenth century, as Scotland emerged as the world's second industrial nation, its economy had a cutting edge not simply in manufacturing but in agriculture too.[47] The new class of Lowland capitalist farmers had waxed rich on the booming profits of the Napoleonic Wars. Later they were driven to look abroad not simply to invest capital but to escape the scarcity of rentable farms in Scotland, the post-1815 depression in prices and in order to secure opportunities for non-inheriting younger sons. Flockmasters in the great sheep estates of the Highlands and the Lowlands quickly grasped the potential attractions of the vast stretches of cheap Australian land to establish even greater pastoral empires in the southern hemisphere. Indeed, not only were huge land grants readily available after c.1810, but government was also able to provide cheap labour to help run the sheep ranches by assigning convicts to substantial farmers through a system widely condemned by some as more akin to slavery. Soon Scottish pastoral princes became prominent in the outback. They included men like Lachlan Macallister, who arrived in New South Wales in 1817 as an ensign in the 48th Regiment. He started with a grant of 2,000 acres and soon developed a ruthless reputation for the relentless pursuit of any Aboriginal tribes and bushrangers who dared to stand in the way of his expanding empire. By 1838, he owned a property over eight times the size of his original land grant, which he named 'Strathaird' after the family estate in Skye.

The story of Major Donald Macleod, a tacksman (or leaseholder) also from Skye, reveals the same patterns of Highland background, military career and determined ambition in Australia. It also underscores the point about the entrepreneurial energies of the Gaelic gentry and their ability to respond to the contraction of their position in the Highlands by seeking opportunities in the overseas Empire. Macleod served many years in the 56th Regiment before sailing with his family of nine to Van Diemen's Land. He was allocated a grant of 2,000 acres (which he named 'Talisker'), but the family's fortune was really made when they moved to Sydney and Port Phillip. Eventually, after a series of bloody battles with the Aborigines, which climaxed in the decimation of the local tribes, Macleod annexed over 20,000 acres for sheep farming. It was an even more draconian 'Highland Clearance' than any which occurred in the homeland but this time perpetrated by Gaels on the indigenous population of the Antipodes.

It was a similar story in commerce. Here the new Australian connection was partially forged through the long relationship between the East India Company and the Scots. Two of the most significant early Australian merchants, Robert Campbell and Alexander Berry, were both Scots and each had strong connections in the East Indies trade. The Campbell family were deeply involved in commerce between Glasgow and Calcutta while Berry was a surgeon in the East India Company, where he learnt the rudiments of commerce and left for Australia in 1808. Their careers show how India became a bridge between Scotland and the Antipodes. 'Merchant Campbell', as he is known to history, was able to demonstrate that Australia could have a mutually beneficial economic relationship with the rest of the Empire through exportation of its staples to external markets. This vision was the key to the country's escape from its function as a penal colony. Campbell saw the immense potential of Australia's vast reserves of whales and seals. Every season countless numbers of sperm whales came north from Antarctica to mate and calve along the coasts of south-eastern Australia and Van Diemen's Land. It was said in the early 1800s that the estuary around Hobart was too dangerous for small boats at these times because of the masses of pregnant and calving whales which gathered there. The kill rate by fishermen could easily rise to thousands a year. Despite the opposition of the East India Company, which held the monopoly, Campbell was exporting skins and whale oil directly to London from 1805. He defied the Company for another decade until free trade to and from Australia was eventually conceded in 1815.

Other examples could be provided of Scottish enterprise but until more comparative research is carried out on other ethnic groups its real significance in Australia cannot be fully understood and measured. What is often forgotten or overlooked in the historiography, for instance, is the extent of failure – much less easily identifiable in the record than success or achievement. Also less visible was the proletarian migration of Scots. Between 1853 and 1880, 138,036 Scots arrived in Australia. Overwhelmingly, they were described as domestic servants and general labourers, many of whom reached Australia with the assistance of colonial governments. Males out-numbered females by almost three to two. This pattern suggests that it was not simply the Irish who provided the basic bone and sinew of the colonization of the continent.[48]

The evidence is somewhat more solid for New Zealand and so allows for less tentative conclusions. There was particular Scottish prominence in pastoralism, banking, foundries, engineering works and woollen mills.[49] But the evidence also suggests that this contribution, though significant, ought not to be overstated.[50] The *Dictionary of New Zealand Biography* database suggests that Scots were moderately over-represented among those noted for business success. The figure was 25.1 per cent, compared to 21.3 per cent which was the Scottish representation among all UK-born in the database. Over-representation therefore existed but, equally, it was far from overwhelming.[51] Similarly, of the 1,042 settlers in Otago and Canterbury who left five-figure fortunes, places of birth are known for 425 of them. Exactly one-third were born in Scotland, although 57 per cent of rich Otago settlers were of Scottish birth against only 22.5 per cent of Canterbury settlers.[52] Once again, these data suggest that, while recognizing the Scottish factor, care must be taken not to exaggerate its significance across all the colonies of settlement in the nineteenth century.

Nevertheless, despite the necessary qualifications, Scots immigrants did leave a distinctive economic mark in the Empire, especially in Canada and New Zealand and, to a lesser extent, Australia. Why was this? The answers given here question the Victorian stereotypes of the hard-working, ambitious and able Scot, uniquely fashioned with religious convictions suited to material success and capitalist accumulation. If this had indeed been the case the Scots would surely have carried all before them, rather than achieving fame only in certain areas, sectors and at specific points in time. Hard and unrelenting work was the vital precondition for colonial achievement, whatever the ethnic background of the settler. Moreover, those Scots who did very well are acknowledged to have been but a tiny fraction of the immigrant group as a whole. Nor was Scottish success in any way unique.[53] Even in New Zealand, where Scots had considerable visibility, the English were also very well represented among the ranks of the high achievers.[54]

Scottish migration had a relatively high-skill and professional profile compared to other nationalities. This factor, and the fact that they had come from an advanced and vibrant economy, gave many Scots a competitive edge. Their remarkable success in the colonial banking, insurance and accounting sectors was one result. More generally, and especially in pastoralism and agriculture, they were often sons of tenant farmers who ventured abroad with some capital to spare.[55] Equally critical in large-scale pastoralism, both in Australia and New Zealand, was the fact that many of the enterprises were owned in Scotland itself while at the same time being managed by expatriate Scots in the Antipodes.[56] Throughout the settlement colonies, therefore, a decisive Scottish advantage was the personal and family linkages to sources of capital in the homeland. As Chapter 11 demonstrates in detail, a capital-rich Scotland was aggressively investing unprecedented amounts overseas after c.1860. Often the principal beneficiaries of these loans and credit were Scottish adventurers with kin and friendship connections to banks and investment houses in the mother country. The economic histories of the colonies also show that an important advantage could be gained by those immigrants who arrived in the early stages of settlement, when opportunities were greatest and competition most limited. A classic example were the Scottish shepherds who worked in the early sheep runs of New Zealand. Many were able to move to ownership of farms before the opportunities were closed off as the price of land rocketed in later decades.[57]

3

The issue of Scottish ethnic community and identity after emigration is another controversial field which has yet to produce anything approaching a scholarly consensus. For some, like the Harvard historian David Armitage, 'the Scots were "invisible ethnics" in North

America and Australia, the stalwart supporters of Empire, predominantly Protestant and eager to assimilate'.[58] Another noted writer on Scottish emigration to Australia, Eric Richards, argued that ethnic origins after settlement were forgotten fairly rapidly as powerful forces of integration and assimilation intensified.[59] Yet, in his recent study of Scots in South Africa, the imperial historian John Mackenzie states bluntly that his book is 'dedicated to [the] overturning' of propositions such as those of Armitage and Richards.[60]

There are good reasons for supposing that at least for the first generation of emigrants Mackenzie has the better of the argument and that his perspective can also be applied to the other colonies of settlement in addition to South Africa. One striking feature, for instance, is how the Scots were often picked out by observers as a specific ethnic group and not simply described as part of a general British diaspora, moulded into uniformity by the experience of settlement in distant lands. Sir Charles Lucas, in his *Historical Geography of the British Colonies*, published in 1897, concluded that 'the annals of the dark continent are rich with Scottish names'.[61] Similarly, and much earlier, Sir Joseph Banks, President of the Royal Society, described how 'the serious mind of a Scotch education fits Scotsmen to the habits of industry' and helped to explain their profound impact on imperial expansion.[62] In addition, throughout the settlement colonies Scots developed a rich associational culture of Burns clubs, Caledonian societies, Masonic lodges, Highland games and the like, perhaps more so than any other ethnicity apart from the Irish, but without their emphasis on the politics of the mother country.[63] The export of integral parts of Scottish civil society to the Empire, such as education and Presbyterianism, also left a distinctive mark and elicited considerable contemporary comment from non-Scots. The Scottish military tradition was equally deeply influential as kilted regiments, modelled on their Scottish counterparts, were raised throughout the colonies. In South Africa by the time of the Great War, for instance, the Transvaal Scottish and the Cape Town Highlanders were both lauded as elite formations, with their origins instantly recognizable by tartan regalia supported by the inevitable pipes and drums.[64] 'Highland' regiments were even more popular in Canada. One writer describes how, after the Great War, 'the Canadian Army had never been more "Scottish"', with formations like the Cameron Highlanders of Ottawa, the Calgary Highlanders and the Toronto Scottish, to name but a few of the units of the period.[65]

The flowering of Scottishness in the countries of settlement in large part reflected the contemporaneous re-invention of Scottish identity in the homeland. The age of the mass emigration of the Scots was also the seminal era when national identity evolved within the Union state. Several leading intellectuals, such as Sir Walter Scott, Henry Cockburn and Sir John Sinclair, had feared for 'the death of Scotland' and its transformation into 'North Britain' as English economic, cultural and political forces became ever more influential.[66] The reality was, however, that loyalty to Britain proved to be complementary to the maintenance of a robust Scottish national identity. The Union had allowed Scottish talents to be displayed on the global stage through the contribution of the nation to the development of the greatest territorial dominion on earth. Arguably, therefore, the British Empire did not so much dilute the sense of Scottishness but strengthened it, by powerfully reinforcing a sense of national esteem and confirming that the Scots had become equal partners with the English in the imperial mission. It was commonly said at the time that the Empire was born *after* 1707 and could only have been achieved through a joint enterprise between the two nations. Empire for the Scots before 1914 was therefore a route to self-respect (and even overwhelming self-confidence) as well as to enhanced prosperity. Linda Colley points out that English and foreign observers were wont to refer to the island of Great Britain as 'England' but rarely described the Empire as anything other than 'British'.[67] Within the imperial relationship the Scots could feel that they were the peers of the English. Not only that but, as has been seen, the Scots could see themselves conspicuously successful as Empire builders. As one contemporary observer put it: 'Scotsmen, whether as soldiers, statesmen, financiers, bankers, scientists, educators, engineers, or merchants have in all our Colonies fully held their own, nay, risen to positions of eminence'.[68] Here indeed were ample opportunities for displays of ethnic conceit.

Scottish Presbyterianism exported dedicated missionaries throughout the world, as Scottish religious colonies blossomed in Canada, Australasia and Africa; David Livingstone, the explorer and missionary, became one of the great national heroes of Victorian times. The Scots were equally proud of their proven abilities as imperial governors and administrators. A third of the colonial governor-generals between 1850 and 1939 were Scots. The Glasgow-born Sir John A. Macdonald dominated Canadian politics for over two decades after the establishment of the federal dominion in 1867. In 1884 Robert Stout, a teacher from Orkney, became Prime Minister of New Zealand, while in 1908, in Australia, Andrew Fisher, a miner from Ayrshire, became the world's first Labour Prime Minister.

Empire-building was therefore depicted as something peculiarly Scottish and the fulfilment of a national destiny. Historical links were drawn with the Jacobite movement. The '45 was recognized as a heroic failure, but it was also depicted as a glorious feat of arms which epitomized the essential Scottish martial qualities of courage, loyalty, trust and fidelity that were now so vital to the achievement of the imperial mission. The exploits of the Scottish regiments, which played such an important part in the expansion of empire, were recounted in detail in innumerable press reports, children's comics, regimental histories and military biographies, all designed to appeal to a wide audience and to personify and reinforce the notion of the Scots as a truly martial race. New national heroes were constantly created: the men of the 'Thin Red Line', the 93rd Highlanders at Balaclava, Sir Colin Campbell in the Indian Mutiny and General Gordon at Khartoum in 1885, whom the chroniclers depicted as saving the Empire from barbarian enemies through his martyr's death. The military glamour of empire was colourfully displayed at home by the numerous companies of Volunteers, the part-time soldiers who drilled and paraded at the weekends dressed in the full uniform of their shadow regular regiments while marching to the stirring music of the pipes and drums and responding to the pride and delight of local audiences.

This was also the time when the idea of Scotland as a national entity was being reinforced through an appeal to the nation's distinctive past, which some thought was threatened with destruction by the sheer scale of urban and industrial transformation. Sir Walter Scott himself, who feared that Scotland might become invisible, helped to pioneer (with others) major collections of Scottish ballads and folk tales. P. F. Tytler's monumental multi-volume and scholarly *History of*

Scotland, published over a span of fifteen years from 1828, reached a wide middle-class readership and testified to the continuing interest in the nation's heritage. Scottish history loomed large in the most popular working-class paper of the later nineteenth century, *The People's Journal*. It contained frequent series on the Scottish past and also had a pioneering interest in folklore and social history that went far beyond the old interest in kings, queens and national heroes. Presbyterian religious history attracted wide interest. Thomas McCrie's biographies of John Knox (1811) and Andrew Melville (1819) were best-sellers. The Reformation, the Covenanters and the Presbyterian heroes were commemorated in the paintings of Sir George Harvey and immortalized in numerous monuments in stone erected in Scottish towns. This was the culture baggage which the emigrants took with them to the new lands.

Even more potent were mythical and semi-mythical personalities and stories, set in the times before industrialization. Here again Scott had led the way. Through his Waverley novels and *Tales of a Grandfather* he invested the Scottish past with a magical appeal and satisfied the powerful emotional needs for nostalgia in a society experiencing unprecedented changes. Scott was a brilliant pioneer in the invention of tradition, a process which helped to develop a new set of national symbols and icons while at the same time renewing others of venerable antiquity in the contemporary image of Victorian Scotland. The tartan and kilt of the Highlands had been appropriated even before 1830 as the national dress. But its adoption was given further impetus by the heroic and well-publicized deeds of the kilted regiments in the Empire, by the growing number of Caledonian societies in the emigrant communities abroad, with their support for pipe bands and tartan dress, and, not least, by Queen Victoria's love affair with the Highlands. The monarch built a residence at Balmoral on Deeside and, from 1848, spent every autumn there on holiday. By comparison, she visited Ireland only four times in her entire reign. The fact that Victoria showed such fascination with the Highlands and was sometimes even heard to proclaim herself a Jacobite at heart was bound to have a major effect. Highlandism had now been given wholehearted royal approval and tartan recognized as the badge of Scottish identity. When a company of radical volunteers was established to fight for

Garibaldi in Italy, they were dressed in tartan shirts and bonnets topped with a Scottish thistle. At the same time, Scottish landscape painting developed a fascination with 'the land of the mountain and the flood' in the work of such artists as Horatio McCulloch (1805–67), with his pictures of lochs, corries and waterfalls and, above all, the archetypal and hugely popular *My Heart's in the Highlands* (1860).

Most importantly, the cult of national heroes became one of the most popular ways of linking urban Scotland with its history. Prominent in this respect were Robert Burns and William Wallace. In the period after *c.*1840, Burns was venerated as never before. In one Burns Festival in 1844 an estimated 80,000 were in attendance, and of this multitude 2,000 sat down to eat lunch, accompanied by numerous toasts to the poet. The enormous influence of the National Bard was seen in the countless attempts at imitations of his verse which dominated the 'poetry corners' of local newspapers throughout Scotland. But the historic Burns and his remarkable literary achievement were also moulded to suit the political tastes of a Victorian middle-class readership. He was depicted as anti-aristocratic and as a man who had succeeded by his own individual talent rather than through inherited privilege or noble birth. Burns became the apotheosis of 'the lad o' pairts', a key element in the most influential Victorian Scottish myths, that personal ability alone was enough to achieve success in life. But he was also praised because he linked the Scots with their rural past – it was often said that the blood of the Ayrshire Covenanters flowed in his veins – and preserved the ancient vernacular language by his genius. As Lord Rosebery put it in a speech at Dumfries at the centenary of Burns' death:

> For Burns exalted our race: he hallowed Scotland and the Scottish tongue . . . The Scottish dialect as he put it, was in danger of perishing. Burns seemed at this juncture to start to his feet and reassert Scotland's claim to national existence; his Scottish notes range through the world, and he has thus preserved the Scottish language forever – for mankind will never allow to die that idiom in which his songs and poems are enshrined.[69]

The cult of William Wallace in the nineteenth century was equally complex, and bears little relation to the raw nationalism of Hollywood's *Braveheart* of the 1990s. There can be little doubt that Wallace was one of the supreme Victorian icons. Magnificent statues to the hero of the Wars of Independence were erected overlooking the Tweed and in Lanark, but these paled before the grandest of all of these projects, the 220-foot-high tower of the National Wallace Monument, built near Stirling between 1859 and 1869. This colossal edifice overlooked the country where the Scots at Stirling Bridge and Bannockburn had fought their most decisive battles against the English in the fourteenth century. Wallace was not only remembered in statuary and monuments. Blind Harry's fifteenth-century epic, *The Wallace*, which was vehemently anti-English in language and tone, maintained its popularity, while tales of Bruce and Wallace were always familiar features in the local press. Those who left Scotland in the nineteenth century carried these myths and traditions as markers of identity with them to the new lands, littering the landscape in far-off territories with names, myths, commemorations and statues from the homeland.[70]

8

Settlers, Traders and Native Peoples

Mass European settlement in the new lands of the Americas, Africa and Australasia could not have been achieved without the extensive dispossession and expropriation of the land of the native peoples, often carried out by brutal and violent means. Scots were in the vanguard of white expansion throughout the colonies, and Scottish regiments were a military spearhead of empire in America, India, Asia and the African territories (see Chapter 10). Despite this record, some writers view the relationship of Scots with native peoples through somewhat rose-tinted spectacles. John Buchan, Scottish novelist and sometime Governor of Canada, has one of his fictional characters assert that 'the truth is we are the only race on earth that can produce men capable of getting inside the skins of remote peoples'.[1] Arthur Herman, author of a relentlessly optimistic book on the impact of the Scots on the modern world, can conclude: 'In one colonial setting after another, Scots proved themselves far better able to get along with people of another culture and colour than their English counterparts.'[2] There is almost a sense here that Scottish settlers in the New World saw native peoples in terms of Robert Burns' famous song in praise of human equality: 'A Man's a Man for A' That'. Michael Fry succumbs to the same seductive romanticism, proclaiming that 'there was nothing more striking than the affinity of Scots and native Americans' and then musing that 'the generosity and freedom of both peoples made a mutual appeal to them across the racial barrier'.[3]

In part, some of this rhetoric derives from the feeling that Scots, and especially Highland Scots, were more accustomed to clanship and tribalism in their own society and hence more like native peoples in social structure and cultural tradition than other immigrants. Also, not surprisingly, lone males from Europe living on the eighteenth-century colonial frontiers invariably married Indian women and in effect often became Indians themselves in culture. It has been shown how, by the nineteenth century, in western Canada, eastern New York and the mountains of Tennessee and Montana one could hear Cree, Mohawk, Cherokee and Salish spoken with Gaelic accents.[4] Much has been made of these connections in some recent writings but Scottish pioneers were not unique in this respect.[5] In Indian country, Gaels were but one of several ethnic groups, including French, Spanish, English and Africans.[6] Rigorous historical research suggests that their relations with native peoples were not significantly more generous or benevolent than the British or European norm. In a very wide-ranging study of North America in the eighteenth and nineteenth centuries, Colin G. Calloway delivers a stark verdict:

> ... Highland traders, soldiers and settlers often displayed the same prejudices, sentiments and behaviour as other European traders, soldiers and settlers when dealing with Indians and Scots took on the role of colonising and civilising Indians with zeal. Highland governors, soldiers and traders were probably just as likely as their English or American counterparts to exploit, shoot and cheat Indians, and Highland settlers proved as eager as anyone else to occupy Indian land. Indians in turn knew that Scots came to their country as part of a colonial endeavour that always subordinated and sometimes sacrificed Indian interest to British benefit. The notion that peoples were less prone to abuse or kill each other because they shared similar tribal structures does not stand up to historical scrutiny anywhere in the world.[7]

Again, in South Africa, recent scholarship suggests that Scots were as complicit as other nationalities in racial domination, not least by stressing their affinities and connections with the Afrikaans people.[8] In Australia, too, Scots were as heavily involved in 'the quasi-genocidal aspects' of the take-over of Aboriginal lands as any other immigrants from Britain.[9] Hence, far from being 'victims' of English imperialism, as some have asserted in the past, the Scots were prime instruments of British expansion across the globe. This chapter explores three aspects of this process: Ulster Scots in eighteenth-century American colonies;

Scottish settlers in nineteenth-century Australia; and the fur traders of the Canadian wilderness.

I

Analysis of emigration from the British Isles to the Americas in the seventeenth and eighteenth centuries reveals two contrasting trends. Between 1600 and 1700 the movement to the transatlantic colonies was overwhelmingly English in composition. After 1700, but more especially after c.1750, there was a radical change in the ethnic composition of the emigrant flows and the pattern of earlier decades was reversed. Now, between 1700 and 1780, around 70 per cent of all British settlers arriving in America were from Ireland and Scotland.[10]

Earlier chapters have described the major Scottish contribution to the formation of this new British Atlantic. If anything, however, the exodus from Ireland was even greater: from 1700 to 1820 between a quarter of a million and half a million emigrants came from Ireland to America. They accounted for 30 per cent of all European immigrants in the period and constituted the largest single nationality group from Europe to cross the Atlantic up to c.1800.[11] By way of comparison, and even by the most generous estimates, Scotland was probably able to muster around 90,000 emigrants to America between 1700 and 1815. Even when Ireland's greater national population is taken into account it is still clear that the Irish rate of emigration was significantly higher than that of the Scots. At certain periods the differences were palpable. For instance, in the period after the American War of Independence, when Scottish levels of emigration were in the doldrums, the Irish outflow surged ahead. From 1783 to 1814 perhaps as many as 100,000–150,000 Irish men, women and children left for the United States.[12]

Apart from scale, the other main distinguishing feature of Irish emigration at this time was its remarkable regional diversity. The biggest element between 1700 and the 1790s were Protestants from Ulster. Indeed, from 1717 to 1776 perhaps two out of every three Irish emigrants came from that province.[13] They came from different faith traditions. Some were of English descent and adherents of the Church of Ireland. Most, however, were Presbyterians, many of whom could directly trace their ancestry back to the seventeenth-century migrations of Lowland Scots to Ulster.[14] They can be seen as an identifiable ethnic group, a hybrid people with their territorial roots in Ireland but also partly Scottish in terms of religious loyalties, cultures, speech and intellectual heritage. They are variously known as the 'Scots Irish', 'Scotch-Irish' and 'Ulster Scots'. The sheer magnitude of the Ulster Scots diaspora and its widespread geographical impact across the American colonies demands attention. In 1790 something like 14 to 17 per cent of the white population of the United States were of identifiable Irish origin. This was around 440,000 to 520,000 individuals out of 3.17 million whites. Upwards of 350,000 are reckoned to have been first-generation Ulster Scots immigrants or the descendants of earlier arrivals.[15] Their diffusion within the American colonies, and after 1783 throughout the USA, was remarkable. New England was the magnet for many of the first emigrants. Soon, however, they were also moving into Maine, New Hampshire, present-day Vermont and then western Massachusetts, where for the first time they acted as human buffers between the regions of British influence and areas populated by American Indians. The Ulster Scots were to become famous (or infamous) as frontiersmen in the backcountry from Pennsylvania to Georgia. Philadelphia became their first capital with 100,000 people of Ulster origin or descent living there in 1790. As immigration accelerated, waves of land-hungry Ulster Scots crossed the Allegheny Mountains, settling first in the area where Pittsburgh now stands, then across the Potomac River into western Maryland and the Shenandoah Valley. From there they pressed on to the Carolinas and Georgia. At the same time many thousands of their compatriots penetrated westward through the Cumberland Gap into the territories that became the states of Kentucky (1789) and Tennessee (1790).[16] More than any other ethnic group the Ulster Scots were responsible for the expansion of European settlement on the American frontier at this time. Already on the eve of the Revolution in 1776 they had managed to colonize much of the southern backcountry.[17]

In this wilderness the Ulster Scots made up a high proportion of the first European farmers and soon became typecast as the archetypal American pioneers who won the West for future generations. Such legendary figures as Davy Crockett and Jim Bowie, both of Ulster Scots stock, came to personify this story. Theodore Roosevelt, in his *The Winning of the West*, burnished the myth and set the Ulster Scots epic against their ethnic and religious background in Scotland and Ireland:

> That these Irish Presbyterians were a bold and hardy race is proved by their at once pushing past the settled regions, and plunging into the wilderness as the leaders of the white advance. They were the first and last set of immigrants to do this; all others have merely followed in the wake of their predecessors. But, indeed, they were fitted to be Americans from the very start; they were kinsfolk of the Covenanters; they deemed it a religious duty to interpret their own Bible, and held for a divine right the election of their own clergy.[18]

In this semi-mythical tradition they were seen as brave, God-fearing pioneers who 'settled the frontier ... founded the Kirk and ... built the school'.[19]

It is intriguing to turn from this later legend to reports of contemporary eighteenth-century attitudes to the Ulster Scots. Here the commentaries were much less favourable, especially those from their religious rivals. One writer described them as 'the scum of two nations'. An Anglican cleric went even further in spatial range and called them 'the scum of the universe'.[20] Charles Woodmason, 'Anglican Itinerant' in North Carolina, referred to 'the herd of vile Irish presbyterians'.[21] Even the tolerant Quakers of Philadelphia found the Ulstermen subversive and uncouth and 'a pernicious and pugnacious people'.[22] In Pennsylvania they were constantly at odds with the neighbouring German settlers. Indeed, disturbances became so frequent that the Quaker authorities instructed their agents not to sell any more land to Ulster Scots in areas of German settlement, and even to offer them generous relocation terms to move further west. It could be that their assertiveness, not to say aggressiveness, which many contemporaries saw as their distinguishing characteristic, may well have been the product of their embattled religious position in Ulster itself.[23]

However, it was as implacable enemies of the Native Americans that the Ulster Scots made their bloodiest and most notorious impact on the west, although the cruelty and ferocity of the Indian wars came relatively late. In the first half of the eighteenth century, despite the progress westwards of Ulster Scots and German settlers, few major incidents occurred, partly due to the absence of significant Indian concentrations in the Shenandoah Valley. As the white settlers steadily migrated to their lands, most natives quietly moved away further into the interior. Again in Pennsylvania, the policy of the Quaker government was crucial. Their religious convictions ensured that they treated the Indians as equals, giving a fair price when their land was purchased and avoiding the building of forts and the creation of armed militias.[24] But trouble was inevitable. The insatiable land hunger of the Ulster Scots would brook no interference from those they regarded as pagan savages. They could easily justify the subjugation of the red men as a Christian crusade, the 'smiting of the enemies of the Lord'. In Ulster, the occupation of the lands of dispossessed natives had been an integral part of their earlier history. On the American frontier, too, the existing inhabitants were deemed an obstacle to the advance of Christian civilization. Official complaints against their ruthless encroachment on Indian territory elicited the response that 'it was against the laws of God and nature that so much land should be idle while so many Christians wanted it to labour on and to raise their bread'.[25] Colonial officials recognized the aggressive Ulster Scots ethos. Massachusetts and South Carolina recruited them as human shields against the threat of Indian attack. In 1756, for instance, the colony of South Carolina offered Ulster Scots inducements to settle in the backcountry after the Cherokee uprising of that year, in order to provide a defence against the Indians and their French and Spanish allies.[26] It was, therefore, probably only a matter of time before armed conflict broke out between land-hungry pioneers and native peoples.

In the end the catalyst was the start in 1756 of the Seven Years War between France and Britain. Significantly this is known in American history as the 'French and Indian War'. The French had no difficulty in persuading the Indian tribes to be their allies as, after victory against the British, the Shawnees, Cherokees, Tuscaroras, Creeks, Choctaws and Chickasaws were promised restoration to their former territories and that the white men would be driven back to the sea. The rout of General Braddock's redcoats at the battle of Monongahela River by a joint French and Indian force in the summer of 1755 unleashed a furious Indian assault on frontier settlements from southern Virginia to Canada. One French officer wrote: 'It is incredible what a quantity of scalps they bring us . . . These miserable English are in the extremity of distress.'[27]

This was a new kind of war far removed from the elaborate codes which governed set-piece battles in eighteenth-century Europe. Civilians were fair game. Houses were burnt, women and children were slaughtered without mercy, and hideous torture employed routinely against the enemy. In 1760, a party of some 250 Ulster Scots left their homes to seek refuge in Augusta, Georgia. They were ambushed by over a hundred mounted Cherokee and lost about forty killed or captured. One of those who died was the grandmother of John C. Calhoun, the most famous spokesman for the South in the years before the Civil War. In all, the Calhouns lost twenty-three of their number in the Cherokee attack. Indian raids became endemic across the frontier during the Seven Years War and then continued after 1763 in the uprising known as Pontiac's War. During this over 2,000 settlers were killed in Pennsylvania alone.[28]

The Ulster Scots retaliated with equal ferocity and in the process enthusiastically adopted the Indian methods of butchering women and children, the firing of villages and the ritual scalping of the fallen enemy. They carried the war far into Indian territory and wrought extensive devastation in the tribal heartlands. In the set battles of the Seven Years War the regular British line regiments did most of the fighting. But the brunt of the brutal guerrilla warfare against the Indian allies of the French was borne by the Ulster Scots levies. German settlers, especially in Pennsylvania, mainly retreated eastwards rather than fight. The Quaker-dominated authority in Philadelphia refused for reasons of conscience to take up arms and the British army was fully stretched against the French. The Ulster Scots were left, on the whole, to defend themselves and this they did with a combination of courage, cruelty and unparalleled ruthlessness.[29]

2

Until about 1845 there were probably more Aborigines in the Australian continent than whites. They had lived off the land and the sea as hunter-gatherers for between forty and sixty millennia. Neither stock-rearing nor agriculture were practised, but the Aborigines had developed such a remarkably intimate relationship with the land and its plants, animals and watercourses that they were able to survive even in this most hostile of environments. At almost every point their culture and way of life was radically different from, and therefore incomprehensible to, European settlers. The numerous tribes spoke many languages and had minimal material possessions. Even the territories where they hunted were considered accessible to all clan members in common. They saved nothing and lived entirely in the present. Men, women and children roamed the outback, apparently aimlessly, in search of food. They did not build houses or have recognizable forms of government. To Europeans they were not simply different, but primitive, inferior and savage: 'No greater contrast could exist with the incessant digging, enclosing and building activities of the newcomers, determined to conquer their environment, and using military discipline and individual ownership as a means to that end.'[30] The relationship between settlers and natives was therefore one of mutual incomprehension. The Aborigines were shocked by the white skins and pale eyes of Europeans, thinking at first they were the spirits of the dead come to haunt them. The newcomers in their turn were revolted by the rumours of cannibalism associated with the blacks, the ritual ornamentation of their bodies, their colour and their nakedness.

The first contacts seemed peaceable enough in and around Botany Bay. In addition, every governor, from Phillip in 1788 to Brisbane in 1822, had instructions from London that the Aborigines had to be well treated. The objective was to develop 'amity and kindness' between the races. The Aborigines were even given the status of British subjects: anyone who killed them or caused 'any unnecessary interruption of their several occupations' merited punishment with the utmost severity of the law. The first Scottish governor, John Hunter, in the course of his early explorations of New South Wales, noted in his *Historical Journal* that 'we wished to live with them on the most friendly footing, and . . . to promote, as such as might be in our power, their comfort and happiness'.[31] Lachlan Macquarie, the famous and influential Governor of New South Wales, born in Ulva in the Inner Hebrides, hoped to encourage the Aborigines from their 'rambling naked state' and transform them into farmers. In 1815 he experimented with sixteen native men cultivating a smallholding on Sydney Harbour, but they soon wandered off into the bush. Sir Thomas Brisbane, another Scot, born in Ayrshire, was at first equally solicitous. On his arrival as governor he proclaimed his concern for 'these poor, distressed creatures' who unless they were supported, would surely become extinct.

However, there was a yawning gap between this benevolent policy of officialdom, which itself abruptly changed in the later 1820s, and actual practices in the bush. Relations between the races rapidly deteriorated and European diseases soon took a horrific toll of the Aboriginal populations. As early as 1789 an outbreak of smallpox carried off half the natives in the Sydney area. Convicts also became increasingly hostile to the Aborigines. They contrasted the cruel punishments meted out to prisoners who had committed even minor offences with the conciliatory treatment of the blacks by the penal authorities. Some took their revenge when they completed their sentences and moved into the interior in the search for land. Between 1800 and 1830 settlement pushed outwards as the Australian sheep economy, with its insatiable appetite for more and more territory, started to develop. Conflict between the white culture of private property and the black ethic of communal possession became inevitable. Nor did the Aboriginal clans accept the European invasion passively.[32] Instead, fierce battles were fought across the expanding frontier, with natives making devastating attacks on isolated homesteads and shepherds' huts in acts of reprisal and revenge. This in turn produced – and for some justified – genocidal retaliation by whites, secure in the knowledge that in the outback they were far from the powers of the colonial judiciary.

At the same time, intellectual arguments for the 'dispersal' of the Aborigines (as mass killing was euphemistically described) began to be advanced. When *Two Years in New South Wales* by the Scottish explorer Allan Cunningham was published in 1828, the commentator in the *Quarterly Review* expressed the view emanating from the colony that the Aborigines were 'among the lowest, if not the very lowest, in the scale of human beings'. Others at the time considered them 'many degrees below even the worst of the Zealanders' and 'among the most hideous of all the living creatures of humanity'.[33] Horror stories also circulated of the Aboriginal appetite for cannibalism and human banquets. 'Scales of Civilization' put them near the bottom of the hierarchy of native peoples, with American Indians at the top, followed by Maori and Zulus. Not everyone agreed. Scottish explorers such as Cunningham and, later, Sir Thomas Livingston Mitchell praised the adaptability, ingenuity and skills of the Aborigines, which they had experienced for themselves on many trips into the interior. Mitchell, who also had shot blacks in his time, was largely responsible for retaining Aboriginal place-names in eastern Australia. But theirs were lonely voices among the growing chorus of racist propaganda. During the long frontier war it is reckoned that perhaps 2,000 to 2,500 Europeans were killed and upwards of 20,000 Aborigines.[34] The overall death rates among the native population were, however, much higher, as disease imported by the white men, malnutrition and the lethal effect of alcohol consumption were, in the final analysis, even greater killers.

For much of the twentieth century the dispossession of the Aborigines was virtually written out of Australian history in both popular and academic texts. As late as the 1970s, a much used university primer, Frank Crowley's edited collection, *A New History of Australia* (1974), entirely omitted reference to Aboriginal peoples. A wide-reaching survey of the Scottish impact on Australia, Malcolm D. Prentis's *The Scots in Australia* (1983), contains only one reference to Aborigines in the index – not concerned with expropriation, but how the Scots-born Premier of colonial New South Wales, Sir Alexander Stuart, presided over the establishment of the Board for the Protection of the Aborigines in 1883.[35] Their 'disappearance' from history was paralleled by the development of a dominant narrative which stressed the hard struggle of the British settler communities against an unforgiving land and the menace of drought, heat and flood. The eventual achievement of mastery of the territory gave legitimacy in this perspective to its possession and ownership. The result was that Australian history became depicted as beginning with the arrival of the first Europeans.[36]

The irony was that some writers in the nineteenth century had actually detailed the white onslaught on the traditional peoples in unsparing detail. Henry Melville, in his *History of Van Diemen's*

Land, noted that in the 1820s the 'natives . . . were massacred without mercy . . . they were slaughtered in cold blood'. He went on, 'The historian must ever lament, that he has to record outrages so inhuman and so unjust on the part of a British community.' G. W. Rusden's *History of Australia* (1883) similarly described the extent of the killing as 'a sin crying aloud to the covering heavens and the stars the silent witnesses [which] can be denied by none who know the course of Australian history'. John West's *History of Tasmania* (1852) was equally critical in its vigorous condemnation of the cruelty and brutality visited upon the indigenous peoples by the white settlers there.[37] These unpalatable realities of the colonial past eventually began to be recaptured from the 1970s, not only by historians, but also by novelists, dramatists and film-makers, as political concerns about racism blended with growing demands for social justice for the Aboriginal peoples. The so-called 'great Australian silence' came to an end.

The evidence currently to hand confirms that Scots were just as deeply implicated as any other white immigrants in the tragedy of the Aborigines.[38] After all, Scots were over-represented in those very sectors of the frontier economy – large-scale pastoralism and land-squatting – where interracial violence was most endemic. Defining the 'average' Australian squatter of the middle decades of the nineteenth century, one author concluded, 'the mixture is Scotch, somewhat military, and intolerant alike of obstacles and authorities'.[39] Thus, Angus McMillan from Glenbrittle in Skye built up a great personal fortune in Victoria by sheep-farming, 'though in the process, he disposed of the Aborigines with hideous savagery'.[40] The murder by natives of a kinsman named Ronald Macalister, in 1843 in Gippsland, led to the formation of the so-called 'Highland Brigade', when 'every Scotchman who had a horse and gun' gathered and which then led to one of the worst single massacres in Aboriginal history.[41] At Warrigal Creek over a hundred men, women and children were slaughtered by the 'Brigade' in retaliation for the killing of Macalister.[42] Inevitably, there are conflicting accounts of this incident. However, it appears that the initial catalyst for this chain of events was that Macalister's murder had been an act of revenge for the killing of an Aboriginal boy either by Macalister himself or by one of his stockmen.[43]

An alternative impression of Scottish-Aboriginal relations might be given by the evidence of the foundation of *An Comunn na Feinne* (The Fingalian Society) of Geelong, Victoria in 1856. Its main purpose was to preserve Gaelic culture and traditions in the new land but the additional focus on charitable activities soon expanded to support for the wider community, both settler and native. Local Aborigines were not only provided with material goods but became involved in the society's Highland games. The apparent racial harmony was confirmed in the detail of *An Comunn*'s insignia which featured a Highlander and an Aborigine in traditional dress, the former carrying broadsword and targe, the latter spear and boomerang.[44] The anthropologist Paul Basu has said:

> The temptation is to thus imagine Highlander and Aborigine standing on equal footing, united in a brotherhood of *noblesse sauvage*, and to forget that the Wathaurong tribe, which, it is estimated, had occupied the *iDjillongi*/Geelong region for twenty-five millennia, was, within fifty years of European settlement, on the verge of extinction – displaced, not least, by the heroic 'Fingalians' among the thousands who flocked to *fearann an òir* to seek their fortunes in the gold diggings of 1852 or the no less lucrative woollen industry of which Geelong became the capital.[45]

3

By the early nineteenth century in British North America, the fur trade was controlled by the Hudson's Bay Company (HBC) and the North West Company (NWC) and both in turn were dominated by Scots: Orcadians in the former and Gaels in the latter. When the two organizations merged in 1821, Scots continued to hold sway, notably when George Simpson became Governor of the enormous expanse of the Northern Department, which stretched from the Arctic to the United States border and from Hudson Bay to the Rockies and beyond. It was a territory of 'wintry lakes and boundless forests . . . almost equal to that of the East India Company over the voluptuous chimes and magnificent realms of the Orient'.[46] The American author Washington

Irving painted a memorable picture of the leading personalities of the time:

> They descended the rivers in great state, like sovereigns making a progress: or rather like Highland chieftains navigating their subject lakes. They were wrapped in rich furs, their huge canoes freighted with every convenience and luxury, and manned by Canadian voyageurs, as obedient as Highland clansmen . . . the councils were held in great state alternated by huge feasts and revels, like some of the old feasts described in Highland castles. This was the Northwest Company in its powerful and prosperous days, when it held a kind of feudal sway over a vast domain of lake and forest.[47]

Close encounters with natives were, of course, essential to the effective functioning of the fur trade. It was they who hunted the animals, paddled the canoes, provided local knowledge and acted as guides. They were the labour force of the enterprise while the Scots and mixed race Métis provided the goods in exchange for pelts and the links with the world of international trade and capitalism which lay beyond the tribal frontiers. It was a joint endeavour in which commercial exchange, social links and sexual relations between the two ethnicities were necessary functions and the essential preconditions for profit-making. Sometimes the connections between the two peoples were very positive and harmonious. For instance, an Orcadian, William Thomson, the HBC Chief Factor in the Saskatchewan for nearly two decades, gained the gratitude of the local tribes for his support during the terrible smallpox epidemic of 1781–2.[48] Exploration and the fur trade went hand in hand as company officers sought out new territories for business expansion, and some of the most famous explorers paid generous tribute to the help they had received from Indians during their long treks into unknown lands. They included Alexander Mackenzie, the first European to cross the North American continent above the Rio Grande, who relied heavily on Indian guides and knowledge. Another was Alexander Ross, whose expedition to the Snake River country in 1823 included nineteen Iroquois, Abenakis, Flatheads, Crees and a Shoshone in the party.[49] Dr John Rae, the first European to confirm the existence of the North West Passage from the Atlantic Ocean to the Pacific, developed a remarkably close relationship with the Cree and Inuit peoples which provided him with vital survival and hunting skills. He was said to have been the best white snowshoe walker of his time, covering 1,200 miles on foot in 1844–5 for instance, an achievement which earned him the nickname 'Aglooka' – 'he who takes long strides' – from the admiring tribes.[50] Cross-cultural exchanges of ornaments, trinkets, clothing and shoes were also very common. Indeed, objects garnered from the fur trade enhance museum collections in Scotland to this day. Scots traders widely adopted Indian deerskin bags, moccasins and leggings while Scotch bonnets and tartan shawls were popular among the Cree and Ojibwa peoples.[51]

The primary bond, however, was the relationship between Indian women and Scots men: 'Highland men and Indian women produced Scots Indian children, Scots Indian families and sometimes even Scots Indian communities . . . relations ranged from casual sex to enduring monogamy.'[52] These 'intimate frontiers' of Canadian life had several origins.[53] Predatory sexual behaviour by the white men was one factor. Indian men reciprocated by offering the bodies of their womenfolk in order to affirm closer connections with the traders. In such kin-based societies of matrilineal succession, sexual liaison was a means of extending family allegiances and networks into the world of the Europeans with the possible promise of favours returned in commerce and goods.[54] The strategic value of sex was also recognized from the HBC perspective. As Governor, Sir George Simpson expressly advised 'connubial alliances' with Indian women, arguing that they were 'the best security we can have of the good will of the natives. I have therefore recommended the Gentlemen to form connections with the principal Families immediately on their arrival, which is no difficult matter, as the offer of their Wives and Daughters is the first token of their friendship and hospitality.'[55] By the 1830s almost all officers in the HBC and many lower-level employees had some kind of relationship with Indian women.[56] Simpson himself enthusiastically practised what he preached, fathering at least five children by four different women.[57] Often such alliances did not endure as some traders ended them when they returned home, a practice known as 'turning off'. Simpson and many of his fellow officers found new wives on their return to Britain, referring to the Indian women whom they had abandoned as 'articles', 'commodities' or 'bits of brown'. But not all behaved in this way. Some brought their native wives back to Scotland, paid for their children's education there and made provision for families in their wills.[58] The custom of taking Indian women as wives went into rapid decline by the middle decades of the nineteenth century but even today it is not entirely forgotten. In 2004, twenty-five members of the Saskatchewan First Nations travelled to Orkney as 'a sort of pilgrimage . . . coming to see the home of their grandfathers'.[59]

Nevertheless, such inter-generational loyalties and sentiments cannot disguise the fact that the fur trade where it was most practised in Canada was an historic disaster of epic proportions for Indian culture and society. Diseases imported from beyond the seas had a devastating impact on a population which had little or no resistance to them. Over-hunting drove wildlife to the point of extinction and undermined traditional subsistence economies. In the final analysis, and despite the evidence of cross-cultural human relationships, greed and the lust for profit were the basis of the fur trade. Scots traders, it was said, usually divided Indians 'into two classes, those who have furs and those who have none'.[60] To obtain the valued pelts, the traders were driven to extreme measures, pressing alcohol on the tribes. Soon trade became impossible without the provision of copious supplies of rum to the natives. The country was flooded with alcohol as rival companies competed for business. Enormous Indian drinking binges at company forts often led to violence and deaths. Drinking for twenty-four hours and more at such times was common. Yet, as one leading trader put it cynically, 'When a nation becomes addicted to drinking, it affords a strong presumption that they will become excellent hunters.' As the winter snows melted, so the Indians would come down after winter hunting to the company forts 'to once more pay their devotions at the shrine of Bacchus'.[61] Not all Indian communities in the far north were affected by the European impact in the days of the fur trade, but for those who were the consequences were often tragic.

9

The Missionary Dynamic

Two events, in 1910 and 1913, amply demonstrated Scotland's important religious connections with the outside world. The first, in June 1910, and lasting for ten days, was the World Missionary Conference in Edinburgh, attended by 1,200 delegates representing 160 churches and Christian societies from across the globe. The event can be seen as one of the most important in the history of the missionary movement, and, indeed, of twentieth-century Christianity.[1] It was no coincidence that Scotland's capital should have been chosen to host such an historic gathering. The organizers bestowed the honour because of the prominent role played by Scots in worldwide mission. As *The Scotsman* commented, 'it was a signal honour for Scotland that the greatest missionary conference which has ever been held took place in Edinburgh'.[2] The second key event took place three years later. It was the centenary of the birth of David Livingstone, the nation's so-called 'Protestant saint', internationally renowned missionary and explorer and the most famous Scot of the nineteenth century. Over the course of 1913, a major exhibition was held to commemorate the great man's life at the Royal Scottish Museum, missionary gatherings took place throughout the land, and receptions, lectures and church services, dedicated to Livingstone's memory, were held in numerous towns and villages.[3]

The religious world which supported the immense range of missionary activity before 1914 has now passed away in much of Europe. This is one reason why the sheer scale and significance of the work done in Africa, India, Asia, Australasia and the Pacific Islands by every Christian creed and denomination can easily be underestimated.[4] The importance of missions for the historian is partly because they form an integral part of the wider question of the impact of European thought and values on native peoples across the world. In addition, the size of their activities was remarkable. In 1899, British churches and mission societies supported an army of some 10,000 overseas missionaries. In 1908, Britain alone accounted for around 40 per cent of total global expenditure on Protestant missionary work.[5] The connections between missions and empire also raise fundamental and controversial questions basic to our understanding of the British Empire. How far does J. A. Hobson's famous explanation for imperial expansion convince: 'first the missionary, then the Consul and at last the invading army'[6]? A variant on the same theme from the view of the colonized has it: 'First they had the Bible and we had the land; now we have the Bible and they have the land.'[7] But there is an alternative perspective. In sub-Saharan Islamic Africa literacy was effectively confined to a small elite of learned Muslims. This was not so in the Christian tradition, where teaching, texts and literature became quickly accessible in many African vernaculars. Literary skills, first taught for overtly religious reasons, could therefore easily be put to secular and even political ends. Through such a process, 'missionary education had become the Achilles heel of colonialism'.[8] The missions were also key to the relationship between metropolis and empire.[9] The missions attracted much attention, especially from the devout middle classes, and that spread imperial interest and sentiment widely within influential sections of Scottish society. Not the least effect was the role they provided for women, both married and single, in a project which is often seen in exclusively masculine terms.

But their significance went even deeper and wider than that. The explosive expansion of Christianity in Africa and Asia during the last two centuries can be seen in transformational terms.[10] For Africa there have been two great watersheds in the history of the continent: first the transition to food growing and production and, secondly, the revolution in the means of communication. Christian missions, both Protestant and Catholic, were in the vanguard of this latter development as leading proponents of literacy and education and enthusiastic supporters of exploration and the opening up of Africa to the outside world.[11]

As indicated, missionary activity was a pan-European phenomenon.

In this chapter, the particular role and impact of one nation, Protestant Scotland, is considered, but that broader international context must always be kept in focus. To understand the phenomenon from a Scottish perspective, the domestic religious experience of the nation in the nineteenth century must first be explored, because it was from that background that missionary fervour emerged and flourished in far-off lands.

I

Even the most superficial examination confirms that religious values were fundamental to the ethos of Victorian Scotland, and especially to that of the elites and the middle classes of the nation. The most visible sign of Christian influence was the maintenance of the Sabbath when shops and businesses closed and even most tram services were cancelled. Crucially, the keeping of the Sabbath did not always depend on law. Sunday shopping, for instance, had never been made illegal. It did not happen simply because it was regarded as socially unacceptable until the 1970s to open a shop on a Sunday.[12] The Protestant Churches also had an enormously influential impact on public life. Christian leaders such as Thomas Chalmers, possibly the most famous Scottish cleric of the nineteenth century and first Moderator of the Free Church after it broke with the Established Church in 1843, dominated national debates on the poor law, education and a host of other matters of social policy.[13] Figures of lesser eminence, like James Begg, Norman Macleod and Thomas Guthrie, were all at the centre of public discourse throughout the Victorian period and made major contributions on such varied topics as housing for the working classes, temperance and sanitary reform. The clergy were among the social and intellectual leaders of Scotland and from their families came a constant stream of young men and women reared in a domestic atmosphere of religious duty and educational endeavour who went on to make their mark in the Scottish professions both at home and in the Empire.[14]

Religion also had an effect on most areas of public policy as this was framed, for much of the period, in emphatically moral terms.

Evangelical Presbyterianism, for instance, was the moral dynamic behind the initiative taken by the Scots in the Edinburgh and Glasgow Emancipation Societies during the British agitation against slavery between 1833 and the outbreak of the American Civil War. On the other hand, there was also a tendency to reduce complex economic, social and political problems to a simple matter of personal religion and morality, thus over-emphasizing individual responsibility to the virtual exclusion of environmental factors outwith individual control. As the Free Church newspaper *The Witness* put it in 1841: 'irreligion is the cause of this miserable estate of things, and ... religion is the only cure'.[15] The result was a somewhat myopic commitment for much of the nineteenth century to voluntary effort and passionate religious mission which often went hand in hand with a profound hostility to state intervention in industry and commerce.

From one angle it might appear that the influence of the Churches on social issues was gradually crumbling in the nineteenth century. The Poor Law Amendment Act of 1845 took exclusive responsibility for the care of the poor out of Church hands, thus ending a system which had endured at least from the time of the Reformation. In 1872 came universal state elementary education, which also transferred local power over schools to lay boards outside ecclesiastical control. But to suggest that this effectively terminated the influence of religious values in civic life would be mistaken. The members of these new secular authorities were appointed on the basis of elections, and local democracy therefore allowed churchmen and committed laymen to maintain the relevance of religious ideals in Scottish public life. In fact, far from religious erosion, the Victorian era saw a quite remarkable and hitherto unprecedented fusion between Christian ethos and civic policy. Many of the great urban issues of the day, such as poor housing, sanitation, crime and the provision of public utilities, were dealt with from an overtly religious perspective. Town councillors were also often Kirk elders and were not slow to bring their religious principles to bear on the many problems that confronted them in the urban environment. The influence of evangelical ministers and leading laity has been detected in areas as varied as the free access to public parks in Edinburgh and Glasgow, sanitary legislation in the 1850s, the licensing of public houses and work schemes for the unemployed and hungry in the cities and in the famine-ravaged west Highlands of the 1840s. Much Victorian social policy after 1850 was driven by a religious vision which equated social improvement with moral improvement and placed particular emphasis on the values of hard work, self-help, thrift and temperance.[16] Indeed, religion deeply impacted the entire population from school to family, from leisure to work, all driven by a vigorous spiritual energy.

It was evangelicalism above all which cemented the relationship between religion at home and the overseas missions. Evangelicals took the view that faith was a matter of the heart rather than the mind and was a gift from God through revelation and conversion. Assurance of salvation rested only on the election by God of the repentant sinner. Christ alone could achieve this, but visible symbols of election could also be found in observance of the Sabbath, good works and spiritual exercises in atonement for sin. But the Evangelicals were less interested in theological debate than in action, first to transform individuals and help each human being to make their own personal journey to God, and, secondly, to reform society so as to make that journey easier and less hazardous. This call to action in God's name produced a huge release of missionary energy, the development of which has been termed 'aggressive Christianity'. It was the powerful catalyst for the endless stream of Sunday schools, mission societies, benevolent societies, Bible classes and prayer groups that were part of the fabric of urban Scotland in the nineteenth century.[17]

By the 1830s a coherent focus had been given to these evangelical ideals of mission and conversion by Thomas Chalmers. He himself had experienced an intense evangelical conversion in 1811 and tried to put his ideas into practice as minister of the rural parish of Kilmany in Fife. His principles were based on those of the sixteenth- and seventeenth-century ideal of the 'godly commonwealth', in which there was no separation of Church and State. Both were bound in sacred partnership to create a society which conformed to the word of God. Kilmany became almost a laboratory for the evangelical method: preaching, schooling, systematic visitation and effective organization of poor relief all combined to mould the community in God's image. An even greater opportunity came when Chalmers was appointed to the Tron parish in Glasgow. In 1819 a new parish of

St John's was created out of this larger area and here Chalmers began his famous experiment to transform the religious beliefs, morals and social values of a poor inner-city community. Four schools were established, poor relief was radically altered and came to be based on voluntary giving rather than compulsory assessment, and an active ministry was created with dedicated lay visitors and Sunday school teachers. Despite its superficial short-term success, however, the experiment miserably failed in its primary objective of transforming the community of St John's into a 'godly' society. In fact, the whole exercise might have been counterproductive. Chalmers was convinced that poverty was the consequence of personal moral failure. His rigorous experiment of imposing character tests as a prerequisite before the distribution of meagre doles to the poor at the bottom of trade depressions could have done little to enhance his appeal among the city's working classes.[18]

Nevertheless, the St John's scheme was of fundamental importance in the later development of 'aggressive Christianity'. Chalmers and others believed it to be a success and that the method employed would have had a deep impact on urban irreligion if only Glasgow Town Council had given more support. A true partnership between civil and religious authorities would ensure that Christianity could rise to the challenge of an industrial society, and the 'godly commonwealth' would indeed be brought about. These views struck a chord with many of the urban middle classes. In part this was because Chalmers was by far the most outstanding preacher and the most charismatic church leader of the age. His pre-eminence was graphically demonstrated when he died in 1847. An estimated 100,000 mourners attended his funeral in Edinburgh. But Chalmers had also produced an apparently effective blueprint for evangelical action which might resolve one of the most daunting and insoluble social problems of the age. Above all, his social ideas were also those of the propertied classes because, like them, he accepted the existing economic order to be divinely ordained, opposed 'democracy' as a sure route to anarchy, condemned trade unions, and believed that the pursuit of self-interest would, through Adam Smith's 'invisible hand', also promote the general welfare of all citizens. But Chalmers also argued that with the possession of wealth came the heavy responsibility of philanthropic action. This also generated a deep response among his middle-class audience:

> The effect was to turn the cities into the vibrant focus of aggressive Christianity with endless and very successful appeals for money for building churches, manses and mission stations, for mounting foreign missions, and for the publication of tracts. Equally, though, urban evangelicalism demanded personal commitment through voluntary effort in Sunday schools, Bible classes, tract distribution, home visiting, the temperance soiree, and hundreds of other related activities.[19]

It was not long before some of this energetic impulse began to be channelled abroad in Christian mission.

2

Overseas missions were not entirely a nineteenth-century phenomenon. Indeed, even Scottish ministers sent on the ill-fated Darien expedition of the 1690s were enjoined to instruct the native inhabitants in the gospels. Two missionary organizations, the Society for the Propagation of the Gospel in Foreign Parts (established in 1701) and the Society in Scotland for Propagating Christian Knowledge (1709), emerged in the early eighteenth century. But both had only limited impact. The established Church of Scotland had a major theological problem at this time as far as attempts to convert the heathen were concerned. The idea was in direct conflict with the core belief in Calvinism that God had already predestined some to salvation and others to damnation. Not surprisingly, therefore, the Moderate-dominated General Assembly was for the most part hostile to foreign missions. In 1796 it declared that the preaching of the Gospel 'among barbarians and even natives to be highly preposterous in so far as it anticipates, nay even reverses, the order of Nature'.[20]

Nowhere was this opposition more strongly felt than in the case of India. Enlightenment thinkers such as the historian and former Moderator William Robertson, and Scottish Orientalists, including Alexander Duff, James Mackintosh and Alexander Hamilton, advanced the idea of tolerance for and non-interference with traditional Indian culture rather than any overt attempt to assimilate the peoples of the subcontinent to the norms of Western Christianity.[21]

Thus, although missionary societies were founded in Glasgow, Edinburgh and Paisley in 1790, most Scottish missionaries in the early days were sponsored by agencies in England such as the famous London Missionary Society (LMS), founded in 1795 by groups of Congregationalists and some evangelical Anglicans.[22] A year later, the LMS, inspired in large part by Captain Cook's voyages of discovery in the South Pacific, sent its first party of some thirty missionaries to Tahiti and the neighbouring islands. This pioneering venture was soon followed by further forays into South Africa (1798), Ceylon (1804), Canton (1807), Demerara (1808), Malacca (1815) and Madagascar (1818). These laid the foundations for the extraordinary endeavours which were to come.[23]

In the Scottish context, a key factor was the declining appeal of the concept of Predestination and belief in the Elect. Only if this fundamental principle was abandoned, or significantly diluted, could the message to mission in Matthew 28:19 became the catalyst for action: 'Go ye therefore, and teach all nations, baptizing them in the name of the Father, and of the Son, and of the Holy Ghost.' Already several ministers in the Scottish dissenting churches were preaching the doctrine of universal salvation through good works and a pious life. By 1824, an Act of the Church of Scotland recognized the new attitudes: decreeing that 'Christ died for the elect' while acknowledging that 'His death has also a relation to mankind sinners, being suitable to all'.[24] This acknowledgement was to be of critical importance in the history of Scottish overseas missions.

To that was added the awakening of evangelicalism, which caused a new urgency to convert, both at home and overseas. It became a moral imperative to save 'the heathens' throughout the world from the torments of hell and ensure their eternal bliss in heaven. The 'Great Commission' given by the risen Christ to His disciples – 'Go ye into all the world, and preach the gospel to every creature' (Mark 16:15) – was now of first importance. The remarkable outpouring of domestic evangelical energy finally started to flow overseas. Indeed, 'home mission' and 'foreign mission' became intimately connected. The 'lapsed masses', the 'home heathens' of the urban slums and the pagans abroad, were all part of the same enormous challenge to the evangelical mind.

Also feeding into the new popularity for overseas mission were the established anti-slavery campaigns. The anti-slavery movement in Scotland went through two major phases, the first from the 1780s to the early 1790s and the second over the period from the 1820s to the 1860s. The struggle was for the abolition of the slave trade, the emancipation of slaves in the British Empire and, finally, the abolition of slavery in the USA.[25] Overlaps in the membership of anti-slavery and missionary societies were common. Women, for instance, were deeply involved in both.[26] The anti-slavery movement prepared the ground for the missionary societies which became ever more dominant from the middle years of Victoria's reign. In the late 1830s the campaigns became linked, when anti-slavers started to develop bold new plans to eradicate the human traffic in Africa itself. The idea was to Christianize Africa, stimulate trade and agriculture and so destroy the need for slavery: 'It is the Bible and the plough that must regenerate Africa.'[27] It was an idea which was subsequently given even more prestige and influence when David Livingstone took it up during his travels in Africa.

Profound forces also helped the missionary cause. In the early nineteenth century at least there was little evidence of an overtly imperial dynamic. Instead, the thinking of the Evangelicals at this time was dominated by the belief in the workings of Providence as the divine plan for the course of world history. From the 1760s and for several decades thereafter, the providential view insisted on the rapid approach of Christ's 1,000-year reign on earth, which was predicted to begin in the new century. Advocates pointed to 'the signs of the times' which 'heralded the new dawn': the American and French Revolutions; the long wars of 1793 to 1815; and the profound economic changes now transforming Britain. All these portents, believers argued, were indicative of Christ's Second Coming and so gave an enormous incentive for those already baptized to Christianize the world in order to confirm His dominion in all corners of the globe.[28] There was also the firm conviction that Britain above all other nations had been chosen to carry out this sacred task. That was the reason, so some Evangelicals argued, for the unprecedented success of British arms against the might of France and the parallel achievements of pre-eminence in manufactures and commerce. Britain, in other words, was an 'elect nation' with consequential Christian responsibilities and duties to be undertaken in return for God's favour.[29]

In Scotland, however, the key event came later, following the disagreement that resulted in the Disruption of the Established Church in 1843. The Evangelicals who walked out to form the Free Church in that year had always been more committed to overseas mission than their rivals in the Moderate camp. Once liberated, the Free Church embarked on the planning and promotion of foreign missions with the same passion and commitment as they had already demonstrated in the campaigns of 'aggressive Christianity' in the Scottish cities. Just over a decade later, in India, the Mutiny, or Rising, of 1857 seemed to confirm the moral vision of their cause. That crisis destroyed the old belief that Indian religious culture should be left to exist uncontaminated by Christian interference. The atrocities associated with the Mutiny were seen as conclusive proof that those who advocated the Christianization of the subcontinent had been proven correct. In a series of letters to *The Witness* in 1857 and 1858, the most famous Scottish missionary in India, Alexander Duff, now argued that the massacres were the awful signs of God's displeasure for the failure to carry out Britain's responsibility to convert the Indian nation. *The Scotsman* supported the same view.[30] Others were more extreme. For one preacher, the slaughtered Britons were 'India's Martyrs For England's Sins'.[31] Some other commentators, however, stressed that the Mutiny was not simply a calamity but an opportunity. The territories of the East India Company had for some time been opened up to missionary activity by parliamentary legislation, the so-called 'pious clause' of 1813. The timid advances made since then, so it was argued, should now be replaced by much more zealous and determined action.[32]

Certainly, by the middle decades of the nineteenth century, the Scottish missionaries seem to have made a considerable mark on the imperial world. One scholar has summarized the impact of the Free Church in South Africa by the 1860s:

In Kaffuaria there were thirteen missions and eighty-one Scots missionaries, twenty-eight 'native staff' and seventy-three day schools with

4,000 pupils (a Christian community of 9,500). In the Transkei, four-teen missions, forty-five Scots missionaries, seventy-one African staff, 202 schools with 10,650 pupils (a community of 17,712). And in Natal, five missions, eighteen Scots missionaries, eighteen African staff, 202 schools and 1,845 pupils (and a community of 10,985).[33]

The Scots had also been responsible for the Lovedale mission which, from 1841, became the setting for the development of the most important educational establishment in that region, if not – in terms of black education – South Africa as a whole.[34] The Lovedale Seminary (later Institution) was designed to transform Africans into work-ers on the European model, with the expertise, skills and attitudes to contribute to economic improvement. It was in South Africa, too, that John Philip, a former weaver from the burgh of Kirkcaldy, did signal work. Philip was a classic product of the Evangelical Revival who, after his conversion, became a Congregational minister in 1802 and was sent by the London Missionary Society to South Africa in 1819. His social background gave him a particular empathy for ordinary African people. Drawing on the intellectual traditions of the Enlight-enment, he had a deep hatred of slavery and saw its abolition as the first step towards achieving full human dignity for the black man. Like all evangelicals, his attitudes also stemmed from the firm belief that 'all humans are equal in sin and guilt before God, the redeemed are also made equal in the eyes of God by their conversion'.[35] Philip soon became a deep thorn in the flesh of both colonial administra-tions and Boer settlers, who were often bitterly hostile to his values.

When missionaries were allowed to enter India after 1813, several Scots, including John Stevenson, John Wilson and Alexander Duff, were sent to Calcutta, Madras and Nagpur. From the start the strat-egy was not to attempt conversion of the Indian masses to Christianity, not least because the resources to have any impact on a society of countless millions would have been enormous. Instead, the missions targeted the Indian elites, whom they sought to transform through Western education in the hope that this process would eventually fil-ter down to the lower orders.[36] The Scots were not alone. By the 1850s, British missionaries in India numbered around 400, represent-ing 25 Protestant churches and societies; in the same decade it was reckoned that 14,000 boys and 11,500 girls were attending mission schools.[37] All shared the same strategy: undermining faith in Hindu beliefs through Christian conversion among the young of the elite. By 1850, to a large extent because of the influence of the charismatic Duff, a pupil of Thomas Chalmers at St Andrews, the General Assembly of the Church of Scotland had approved three higher educational institutions, in Bombay (1832), Madras (1837) and Nagpur (1844). These were intended to build on Duff's own success in Calcutta, where his emphasis on teaching through the medium of English had proven to be spectacularly successful among those Indians of higher castes who aspired to commercial careers.[38]

The energies expended on these various endeavours cannot be underestimated. Yet, on balance, the results of their efforts did not always match the commitment of those men and women who fought bravely against inhospitable and alien environments to deliver what they believed to be the good news. Certainly, by the 1860s, the yawning gulf between aspiration and result was not only apparent but attracted criticism from contemporary observers. In South Africa the energetic founding of mission stations was not matched by rapid conversions, and in India there were only an estimated 3,359 converts after fifty years' work.[39] This last figure was the background to the recriminations among missionary interests at the time of the Indian Rising.[40]

3

David Livingstone was born in humble circumstances in 1813 in Blantyre, Lanarkshire and, aged ten, went to work in the local cotton mill. When he died fifty years later he had become a national hero and the most celebrated Scot of the Victorian era. He was given what almost amounted to a state funeral. Livingstone's body lay in the headquarters of the Royal Geographical Society in London to allow the public to show their respects and the coffin was then borne, with due pomp, to Westminster Abbey through massive crowds to its final burial among the greatest of the British nation in an atmosphere of patriotic emotion not experienced since the death of Nelson. Queen Victoria herself followed the cortège in the royal carriage to mark the deep respect and sadness felt by the monarch at the passing of a national hero. His fame lived on as a combination of Protestant saint, icon of imperialism and, paradoxically, as a patron of modern African nationalism. President Kenneth Kaunda of Zambia described him as 'the first freedom fighter' and this image explains why, unlike other African towns which have lost their European names, Blantyre in Malawi and Livingstonia in Zambia are retained as confirmation of the enduring appeal and status of David Livingstone in the new Africa. On the centenary of his death in 1973, thirty-four African countries issued memorial stamps in his honour.[41]

While at work in the Blantyre mill Livingstone pursued his education at night school and then attended the Andersonian Medical School in Glasgow where he trained as a doctor. A Congregationalist, he was accepted for service by the London Missionary Society, which eventually sent him to South Africa, where he was posted to the edge of the Kalahari Desert. Livingstone was soon convinced of his own personal mission to reach the peoples of the interior of Africa, in order both to spread the Christian gospel among them and, at the same time, bring an end to the slave trading which still flourished in those areas. The missionary now also became an explorer. In 1849 and 1851, he travelled across the Kalahari; then, from 1852, started a trek which lasted for four years to find a route from the upper Zambesi River to the coast. The mouth of the great river was finally reached on the Indian Ocean in May 1856. Livingstone had become the first European to cross the entirety of southern Africa. His exploits made headlines across the Western world.

After a brief sojourn in Britain, where he enjoyed the adulation of a hero's welcome, Livingstone left for Africa again in 1858 and for five years carried on exploring, sponsored by the British government, in the eastern and southern regions of the continent. This was the least successful part of his career and it was also marred by personal tragedy when his wife, Mary, died of malaria in 1862. Livingstone returned to Britain, an apparent failure, in 1864. Nevertheless, two years later he had secured enough private support to return to Africa to search for the source of the Nile and report further on the infamous slave trade. It was to be his longest and last expedition, including a period when he disappeared entirely from public view. Livingstone's wanderings lasted for seven years until his death, aged sixty, on 1 May 1873.

In many ways, Livingstone failed miserably in several of his missionary and exploration endeavours. His Zambesi expedition in particular was a disaster, leading at least one contemporary Scottish missionary to describe him as an unreliable dreamer.[42] But the years of disappointing achievement hardly dulled the superstar image he held by the end of his life. Livingstone had a powerful appeal at several levels of the Victorian consciousness.[43] He was a Protestant saint, acclaimed for his attacks on the evils of African slavery, his Christian courage in the face of endless tribulations and his final sufferings and death. Also, Livingstone's own faith was tolerant and non-sectarian, and as a Congregationalist he could appeal to those who followed the largely rival Scottish churches. Significantly, the leading promoter of the Scottish National Memorial at Blantyre referred to it as 'a place of pilgrimage, a shrine'. One of the chapters in his recollections of the birth of the Memorial was even entitled 'The Gathering of the Relics'.[44] Equally, Livingstone's rise from humble origins to the status of international celebratory was seen as a classic tale of Victorian self-help, confirming the value of hard work, moral worth and iron commitment and so reinforcing the belief among the middle classes that personal effort and will could transform lives for the better, while also instructing the masses that self-help, rather than protest and revolution, was the route to social betterment.[45]

In addition, by famously promoting 'Commerce and Christianity' as the solution for the eradication of slavery and bringing civilization to the benighted, Livingstone appealed to the imperial mind. In his public lectures and very readable *Missionary Travels and Researches* he presented an alluring prospect of adventure, discovery and Christian mission. Until his explorations it was commonly believed that the African interior was parched desert inhabited by bloodthirsty savages. Instead, Livingstone presented it as a land suitable for cultivation, settlement and economic development, the whole penetrated by the great Zambesi River along which an immense trade might one day flow.[46] Not surprisingly, not only British but leading imperialist politicians throughout Europe seized on this seductive vision. It helped to drive the so-called 'Scramble for Africa' between 1885 and 1895, when European states divided the continent up into their own colonial possessions and statesmen often legitimized their predatory behaviour as their response to Livingstone's famous appeal to intervene in order to rid Africa of the obscenities of the slave trade. Even King Leopold of the Belgians, creator of the Congo Free State which was to become synonymous with appalling abuse and cruelty, invoked Livingstone.[47] Yet, though some might describe him as such, Livingstone was no crude imperial propagandist. His later renown and respect among African nationalists was soundly based on his opposition to white rule, colonization and his commitment to the equality of all mankind. In his view, native Africans were no better or worse than Europeans. What condemned them to poverty and barbarism were basically defective social and economic institutions, which could be improved through the joint forces of Commerce and Christianity.[48]

Livingstone was also fortunate in the early promoters of his legend. Horace Walter, the first editor of the *Last Journals*, carefully bowdlerized them by removing all references to the great man's volatile moods, the physical punishment visited on some of his followers and the open threats to shoot those who obstructed his aims. Walter created a saintly figure, devoid of the flaws which made Livingstone such a complex personality. In the process, Sussi and Chuma, the devoted followers who carried his body to the coast for shipment to England, came to be seen as the faithful disciples of a Christ-like character.[49] Perhaps even more influential was Henry Morton Stanley's book, *How I Found Livingstone* (1872), memorably described by Florence Nightingale as 'the very worst book on the very best subject I ever saw in my life'.[50] It went through three editions by the end of 1872 and remained in print for several decades to come. As the man who had 'found' Livingstone after his mysterious disappearance in the depths of Africa, Stanley himself attracted huge interest, not simply through his writings but in his many nationwide speaking tours.[51] The stage was now set for a veritable bonanza of popular publications in the form of biographies, pamphlets and newspaper articles, which kept Livingstone's name and fame before the public well beyond the grave.

There can be little doubt that David Livingstone, both the man and the myth, virtually single-handedly raised the popular profile of overseas missions. The tales of his endeavours infused them with glamour and excitement. Some of the biographies read in parts like travelogues, colourfully describing the exotic scenery and wildlife of Africa to a fascinated Victorian readership, while at the same time burnishing the story of Christian mission with thrilling episodes and heroic adventures. With some exaggeration, indeed, some scholars have claimed that Livingstone alone deserves the credit for the sudden expansion of missions to central Africa in the 1870s and 1880s. The exploits of his last expedition were seen as crucial here: the false report of his death by murder, the historic meeting with Stanley, and finally the lonely death at Ilala all stimulated renewed and massive interest in his work. Horace Walter was able to inform Livingstone in October 1869, three years before the famous Stanley meeting, 'the interest in this country about you is intense as I ever could wish it to be . . . The Geographical Society might in short be called the Livingstone Society for the last two years.'[52]

The missionary fervour unleashed by Livingstone's status as Scotland's hero led in due course to the foundation of the two settlements, at Livingstonia in 1875 and Blantyre in 1876 by the Free and Established Churches respectively. The Livingstonia Mission did not develop to preach theology to uncomprehending natives. Rather it was devised as an attempt to construct a community of African Christians who could replace the immoral economy of slavery with a new and more 'civilized' society.[53] This blend of Christian evangelism and the drive towards economic progress had immediate appeal for pious businessmen, primarily in Glasgow but also in other Scottish cities, who wished not only to commemorate the great explorer but to do so in highly practical ways.[54] As a correspondent to the *Church of Scotland Missionary Record* put it in October 1876:

> The complaint that missions are a burden or a waste ought for ever to cease; for just the opposite of this is true. They are profitable in every way; they are a grand outlying business investment – in the way of protecting commerce, of promoting manufactures and of stimulating trade. They bring up savage men to a higher appreciation of themselves, to realise their wants and needs, and thus awaken in them healthful tastes. So this grand missionary movement is being felt in our markets that supply the new and increasing wants of the world. In this way profits are reaped and business is benefited.

From this perspective, missions, capitalism and empire were not only compatible but reinforced each other.

The other great legacy of Livingstone was to enhance the distinctive Scottish contribution to overseas mission and strengthen the perception at home that the Scots had a special status in the missionary endeavour. At one level, he did indeed personify British values and Britishness: buried in Westminster Abbey, sponsored by the Foreign Office and the Royal Geographical Society, a loyal servant of the Queen. But both contemporary and later biographers played up Livingstone's Scottishness, which he himself did not deny, notably in his visit to his ancestral home on the island of Ulva in 1864. In that sense, he easily personified the dual world of identity which most Scots inhabited by the Victorian era. Much was made of Livingstone's joint Highland and Lowland ancestry. His great-grandfather was a Gael who was said to have fought at Culloden. On his mother's side, however, he was descended from Lowland Covenanters. It was common to explain his sympathy for the African people by recourse to his Highland heritage as the Scottish clan system was portrayed as similar to the tribal structures of Africa. Thus, so it was said, Livingstone the Scot would understand African society in a way that no Englishman could. The myth fortified Scottish beliefs in the nation's special ethnic contribution to empire. In the centennial year of his birth, 1913, the principal speaker at the Royal Geographical Society, Lord Curzon, lauded him as 'the invincible Scotsman [who] hewed his way through the world and carved his name deep in the history of mankind'. When he added that the giant of missions had been born 'with no social advantages, possessing no prospects, backed by no powerful influence', Livingstone's fellow countrymen would doubtless have enthusiastically voiced their approval of these sentiments.[55]

4

Outside the colonies of white settlement women played a minor role in the imperial enterprise as few were active in trade, military service and administration. In Christian missions, however, women were not only present but, over the course of the nineteenth century, became dominant numerically. By 1900, 66 per cent of Church of Scotland missionaries were female, and of these the clear majority, by a factor of 2:1, were single women. Similarly, in the same year 51 per cent of Free Church missionaries were women, although in that body the balance of married and single was more equal. In addition, at home, women had long been crucial to the success of missionary fund-raising and support activities. By the 1820s a number of Ladies and Female Missionary Societies had emerged. With the creation of the Church of Scotland's Women's Guild in 1887, their core role in missions achieved an even higher profile. The Free Church admitted the massive contribution of 'the honourable Christian women', describing them as 'busy bees', in its success. Periodical missionary literature designed specifically for women appeared from the 1840s, and by the 1860s they were addressing meetings of missionary supporters of both sexes. Missionaries and their supporters at home came overwhelmingly from the middle classes and this dominance paralleled the pattern of leadership of women from that social background in domestic voluntary and philanthropic societies. Indeed, in all the Scottish cities, similar female networks exerted major influence in both home and overseas missionary activity. Increasingly, too, single female missionaries were often professional women with teaching or medical qualifications. A detailed study of the careers of Aberdeen University female graduates reveals that seventy-nine became missionaries between 1860 and 1900, of whom nearly half worked in India.[56] Missionary wives were first in the field because it had become apparent by the early nineteenth century that sending men abroad alone carried considerable risks that they would develop liaisons with native women. Disturbing news reached the London Missionary Society that some male missionaries in the Pacific islands had taken 'heathen' Polynesian women as partners. Similar accusations were made of men attached to the Church Missionary Society in New Zealand. Moreover, wives were increasingly viewed as useful in the missionary field, providing living exemplars of the virtues of monogamous Christian marriage in polygamous societies as well as helping to run mission schools, which were regarded by all Protestant mission societies as central to the overall project of evangelization. It also became apparent that females were better suited for missionary work than men in societies such as India where it was not thought appropriate for males from alien races and religions to become too close to mature women. By the later nineteenth century, for instance, the societies at home realized that conversion was unlikely unless heathen women were specifically targeted, and that female missionaries were best suited to carry out that role.[57]

Factors on the home front also boosted female missionary recruitment. As noted earlier, the popularity of foreign missions in part grew out of the anti-slavery movement of the early nineteenth century. Women had become increasingly important in this campaign, signing petitions, joining Female Emancipation Societies and attending public meetings.[58] Mission in far-off lands was also a more adventurous and glamorous extension of the voluntary philanthropic activity in Scottish towns in which middle-class women were already heavily engaged. Indeed, not only were the same individuals and social groups involved in both, but the same language was used to describe native peoples in colonial territories and the urban poor in Scotland itself.[59] These relationships, however, could operate in both directions. One explanation given for the difficulties in the recruitment to and financing of foreign missions in the years before the Great War was the much greater perceived need at the time for philanthropic endeavour at home.[60]

Role models of the Livingstonian variety were also widely available for young women who were keen to commit to the cause. The missionary lives of Margaret Wilson, Mrs Sutherland, Mary Moffat and Louise Anderson were widely reported and celebrated in the periodical press. By far the most famous and charismatic was Mary Mitchell Slessor, who worked with the Scottish Presbyterian Mission in Calabar in East Nigeria from 1876. Like David Livingstone, she came from unusually humble circumstances as a former mill-girl in Dundee. Like him too, she gained a professional qualification (in her case in teaching) at night school. In Africa, she not only built schools in the familiar way but also established particularly close relations with native peoples, especially the Efik, who encouraged her to expand her work beyond the colonial frontier. A woman of great courage and conviction, Slessor confronted the Efik on their 'barbarous' practices, particularly polygamy, and established refuges for women and children who left their husbands and fathers. In 1883, as a single white woman, she adopted the first of several Efik girls. By the end of her life Slessor was dubbed Ma Akamba (Great Mother). Not many were as adventurous as her but Mary Slessor's remarkable life inspired others to follow in the mission fields of Africa.[61]

Judging the significance of the female role in missions for the overall development of women in Scottish society in general is not easy.[62] The foreign mission movement was undeniably part of a much wider process in the late Victorian era whereby philanthropic activity allowed some women to redefine their role in society. A similar trend can be detected in the contemporary campaigns for greater access to professional work in teaching, medicine and nursing.[63] Nevertheless, some perspective is needed here. Throughout the period 1830 to 1930 only a few hundred Presbyterian women took part directly in the missionary enterprise and the overwhelming majority were drawn from the upper and middle classes. Moreover, even this small minority ought not to be regarded as forming some kind of vanguard in the struggle for women's rights. While missionary work gave some opportunities to take responsibilities which were still not readily available at home, the motivation to go overseas remained based firmly on deep Christian conviction rather than any conscious aspiration towards female emancipation and advancement.[64]

An even livelier debate is centred on the controversial issue of the relationship between empire and missionary enterprise. Were Scottish missionaries advocates of imperialism and agents, however unconsciously, for the destruction of indigenous cultures? Certainly, Protestant Christian culture for them was the final standard of excellence and so, inevitably, heathen patterns of behaviour were judged inferior and often even repulsive. They had to be changed and improved by 'the civilizing mission'. All missionaries were confident in their moral superiority and so bent on the destruction of such native 'customs' as slavery, polygamy and child marriage. Equally, the enormous publicity afforded missionary endeavours overseas – and especially the feats of such cult figures as Livingstone and Slessor – through sermons, reports, the press, biographies and speaking tours, doubtless helped to spread domestic awareness of empire and, especially, the distinctive role of the Scots in it. Indeed, a striking feature of the propaganda was the stress placed on 'Scottishness', particularly in the areas of elementary and higher education in mission territories, thus confirming Scotland's individual contribution to the imperial project.[65]

Yet, to see missionaries as the ideological advance guard of imperial expansion would perhaps be to go too far.[66] From the days of John Philip in the Cape in the early 1800s there was a long tradition of tension and conflict between white settlers and Scottish missionaries sympathetic to the rights of native peoples. In addition, European missionaries generally achieved very little in the way of Christian conversion either in India or Africa in the course of the nineteenth century. If they can be depicted as agents of a 'cultural imperialism' they were not particularly successful in that project.[67] Perhaps the most enduring mark left by the Scots missionaries was in the foundation of schools and colleges that not only empowered native peoples through the spread of literacy but, in some cases, contributed to the emergence of new Indian and African elites.

In 1894, for instance, Dr Robert Laws, an Aberdeen graduate, drew up plans for the Overtoun Institution in Livingstonia. He wished to include science and technology to promote technical training. But the rest of the curriculum was built on that of the Scottish university, with a strong philosophical structure. Indeed, sometimes the subject matter was distinctively Scoto-centric. Scottish geography and the exploits of William Wallace were both incorporated in the teaching and Laws proposed to top the new building with a replica of the Crown Tower of King's College, Aberdeen. From one perspective this might be regarded as a strategy for cultural assimilation. From another, however, the curriculum was indeed designed to teach African students to think critically, and in the longer-term to contribute to the advancement of their own people.[68]

10

Soldiers of Empire

Some battles can change the course of human history. Among these, the defeat of Napoleonic France at Waterloo in 1815 must stand as an epoch-making event. Seven times between 1689 and 1815 Britain and France had fought each other in successive wars for global dominance. The allied victory at Waterloo settled the conflict for the rest of the nineteenth century. Britain became Europe's most powerful state and the foundations for territorial expansion of its Empire across the world were securely laid.

The collapse of France inevitably brought in its train nationwide celebrations. A year after Waterloo, Scotland's capital welcomed back one of the Scottish regiments which had fought at the decisive battle. In March 1816, the 42nd Regiment, the Black Watch, entered Edinburgh to joyful acclaim from the citizenry. As they marched towards the city, the *Caledonian Mercury* reported that 'nothing could exceed the enthusiasm with which these gallant veterans were welcomed in every town and village through which their route lay'. In Edinburgh itself there were unprecedented scenes:

> House tops and windows were also crowded with spectators, and as they passed along the streets, amidst the ringing of bells, acclamations of thousands, their red and white plumes, tattered colours and glittering bayonets, were all that could be seen of these heroes, except by the few who were fortunate in obtaining elevated situations. The scene, viewed from the windows and house tops, was the most extraordinary ever witnessed in this city. The crowds were wedged together across the whole breadth of the street, and extended in length as far as the eye could reach; and this motley throng appeared to move like a solid body slowly along till the gallant Highlanders were safely lodged in the Castle.[1]

Public acknowledgement and appreciation for the troops of a victorious army were nothing new. What was remarkable about this triumphant return was the public tribute given to a Highland regiment, and this a mere two generations after the failure of the '45 rising. The praise for the Gael as hero-warrior, representing the ancient martial traditions of the Scottish nation, was now apparent for all to see. A poem published to celebrate the event was entitled 'Caledonia's Welcome to the Gallant 42nd'. In its first stanza, the author proclaimed: 'All hail to the land of the moor and the mountain' from where had come the warriors who had shattered the myth of Napoleonic invincibility. Not only were the Highlanders represented as true and brave Scots, but they were also worthy of high praise from 'Britons who will sing "Gallant heroes for ever"'.[2] Elsewhere in the Scottish press, other Highland regiments, such as the 93rd, 92nd and 79th, attracted glowing tributes from all quarters.[3] The previous year the kilted battalions had taken pride of place in the allies' march of triumph through Brussels.

The age-old Lowland perception of Gaeldom as a benighted region of primitives and savages which had spawned a succession of rebellions against the state between 1689 and 1746 had been transformed. Now the Highlands were eulogized as a land of heroes. In a famous song of the time, 'The Garb of Old Gaul', the courage of the Highland soldier was incorporated into a *Scottish* tradition of valour stretching back through the ages. It was deeply significant in this respect that Walter Scott's first novel and runaway best-seller, *Waverley*, was published in 1814, the year before Waterloo. The book is rightly regarded as a landmark text in the military rehabilitation of the Highlanders and their metamorphosis from faithless rebels to imperial warriors.[4] Scott portrayed their failure in the '45 as the result of misplaced loyalty to a romantic, though hopeless cause, not because of any intrinsic barbarity or savagery. In truth, this capacity for loyal allegiance, coupled with the legendary fighting abilities of the clans, could be of enormous value if employed in the service of the British state. Scott was, however, writing at the end of an earlier process of rehabilitation which had been ongoing during the wars for empire of the second half of the eighteenth century.

I

In the tradition of the Highland regiments of the British army, 1740 is a seminal date. In that year the six Independent Companies created by General Wade to police or 'watch' the disaffected Jacobite areas of the Highlands were embodied as the 43rd of Foot. The new regiment then became the 42nd of Foot, the 'Gallant Forty-Twa', in 1749 but became even more celebrated in fame, song and story as the Black Watch, 'Am Freiceadan Dubh', the name given because of its characteristic dark colours of tartan which set these Highland troops apart from the 'Saighdearan Dearg', the 'Red Soldiers', of the rest of the regular army. The early years of service were not auspicious. In March 1743 the regiment was sent to England, the intention being to transport it from there to Flanders. Discontent spread among the rank and file at being forced to leave the Highlands. This soon changed to anger and aliena-tion when the rumour spread that they were to be shipped to the dreaded West Indies, known as the graveyard of the ordinary sol-dier. One hundred and twenty men mutinied and deserted. Three were condemned to death and executed. The rest were then dispersed among other regiments, many of them ending up in the Caribbean and Georgia. In time, however, the reorganized Black Watch served with great distinction in the War of the Austrian Succession, the Seven Years War and subsequent imperial conflicts. In 1758 it was decided to honour the corps with the title 'Royal Highland Regiment' and to raise a second battalion.

But Highland soldiers were no strangers to imperial warfare before 1740. By 1745 the Scots Brigade in Holland had risen to over 5,000 men and it was common for cadres there to move back and forth between the Low Countries and service in the British army. Highland officers served in the expedition led in 1740 to the West Indies under the command of Lord Charles Cathcart. From the 1720s, too, East India Company military posts were being offered through the influence of the Company Director (and Scottish financier) John Drummond of Quarrell to Jacobite families in Perthshire and Ross-shire to counter disaffection. Long before the concept of the 'Highland regiments', decked out in tartans and kilts, became popular, the clan gentry were sending their sons into Lowland and English regiments. Even the first systematic use of Highland troops on the colonial frontier predated by a few years the foundation of the Black Watch. Clansmen from the central and northern Highlands were recruited to Georgia by Scottish imperial officials in the 1730s, where they formed a defensive barrier against the incursion of Spanish forces on the bitterly contested frontier territories.[5]

But the boom time for the Highland regiments as such only really started after the defeat of the '45 rebellion and, in particular, during the Seven Years War, the American War of Independence and, most crucially of all, during the long years of conflict with France after 1793. Six regiments of the line were mobilized between 1753 and 1783, including Fraser's and Montgomery's formations. Around 12,000 men were involved during the Seven Years War, almost the same size as the Highland army of the biggest Jacobite uprising at the time in 1715, and more than twice that of the force of Prince Charles Edward Stuart in the '45. It was indeed a great irony that after the death of clanship Gaeldom became even more militarized than in its recent past. By the French Revolutionary and Napoleonic Wars the number of recruits was unprecedented. The most recent careful estimate suggests totals ranging from 37,000 to 48,000 men in regular, fencible and volunteer units. This is an extraordinary figure, given that the population of the Highlands was only around 250,000 to 300,000 during the second half of the eighteenth century.[6] The region had now become the most intensely recruited region of the United Kingdom. Perhaps not surprisingly Scotland had the highest density of those famous retired veterans the Chelsea Pensioners within the British Isles, and the Highland counties had the largest proportion of all.[7]

In some areas recruitment reached unparalleled levels. Between the years 1793 and 1805, 3,680 men were under arms from the Skye estates of Lord Macdonald, MacLeod of MacLeod and MacLeod of Raasay. From 1792 to 1837 the numbers included no fewer than 21 lieutenant generals or major generals, 48 lieutenant colonels, 600 other officers and 120 pipers.[8] The west coast parish of Gairloch in 1799 was nearly stripped of its menfolk. A survey for the Lord

Lieutenant of Ross-shire concluded that the parish now mainly consisted of children, women and old men, so intensive had the recruitment of young men become. One other calculation suggests that on the vast territories of the Earl of Breadalbane, which straddled Argyllshire and Perthshire, as many as three farm tenancies out of every five had experienced some level of recruitment in the 1790s.[9] Fort George at Ardersier, east of Inverness, the most formidable bastion fortress in Europe and built to control the clans after Culloden, quickly developed a different function. By the time of the American War of Independence it had become 'the great drill square' where the Highland levies were trained for overseas duties.[10] Clanship had mutated into imperial service. The Gaels now pioneered a role in the British military which was later to be assumed by conquered peoples of the Empire with a martial tradition, such as the Gurkhas, Sikhs and Pathans.

Why the Highlands should supply so many soldiers for the British army for much of the second half of the eighteenth century is an intriguing question. After all, Gaeldom was portrayed in the 1740s as the very heartland of treachery, the region which had spawned a series of rebellions culminating in the '45 which came close to overthrowing the Protestant succession itself. Loyal Whigs responded hysterically. 'Scoto-Britannicus' depicted Highlanders as being beyond the pale of civilization. Charles Edward Stuart had landed in the most remote and wild recesses of the kingdom 'amidst dens of barbarous and lawless ruffians' and 'a crew of ungrateful villains, savages and traitors'.[11] The Young Pretender was the agent of Popery, the 'limb of Antichrist' and his clansmen were 'a Hellish Band of Highland Thieves'.[12] With enormous relief, Presbyterian Lowland Scotland celebrated the happy deliverance at Culloden from these pernicious forces of darkness.[13] In the aftermath, the forces of the Crown took a terrible revenge, unleashing a reign of terror throughout the disaffected areas of the north and west which endured for several years.[14]

Yet a mere few years after Culloden, the British state started to deploy Highlanders as a military spearhead of imperial expansion. Not only that, but these former rebels were to be regimented in distinctive concentrated units, permitted to wear the banned Highland dress and encouraged to develop their own particular *esprit de corps*. These were privileges not afforded the Irish (who vastly outnumbered the Scottish Gaels in the service of empire) or the Lowland battalions. In fact, the martial value of the Highlander was already being recognized some time before the Young Pretender landed in the Hebrides at the beginning of his ill-fated adventure. Just before the '45, prominent Whig politicians in the Highlands, such as Duncan Forbes of Culloden and the Duke of Argyll, had suggested raising regiments among the Jacobite clans. Military posts in the British army for the clan gentry would, it was argued, help to cure disaffection. The appointment of a new Prime Minister, William Pitt, in 1756 signalled a more overt commitment to 'a blue water policy' which preferred colonial expansion to European commitments. A fresh and reliable military supply was now vital, not least because of the outbreak of the Seven Years War with France, a conflict which more than any other was to be fought in the colonial theatre. The catastrophic defeat inflicted by the French and their Indian allies on General Edward Braddock on the Monongahela River in Maryland, with the loss of two-thirds of his command killed or wounded, concentrated Pitt's mind. The 'Great War for Empire' was going very badly, and the Prime Minister was also known for his resolute opposition to the use of foreign mercenaries. The only alternative was to expand domestic supply. By early 1757 two additional Highland battalions were sanctioned, commanded by Simon Fraser, son of the executed Jacobite Lord Lovat, and Archibald Montgomery, later Earl of Eglinton. By the end of the war, ten more Highland regiments had been created. They were the first of many which served during the long American Revolutionary and Napoleonic campaigns. In 1766 Pitt looked back on his policy in a famous speech:

> I sought for merit wherever it was to be found; it is my boast that I was the first minister who looked for it and found it in the mountains of the north. I called it forth and drew into your service a hardy and intrepid race of men, who, when left by your jealousy, became a prey to the artifice of your enemies, and had gone nigh to have overturned the state in the war before the last. These men in the last war were brought to combat on your side; they served with fidelity, as they fought with valour and conquered for you in every part of the world.[15]

A sea-change had taken place in government attitudes. In part this was because the destruction of the Jacobite threat was now recognized to be so complete. The Highlands, unlike Ireland, were no longer perceived to be an internal menace and mass recruitment to the crown forces could therefore proceed. At the same time, however, some of the ingrained fear of disaffection took time to dissipate. The solution was not to allow Highland troops to linger long in Scotland after training but to have them dispatched overseas with all speed. Thus it was that the Highlanders became, perforce, the crack troops of imperial warfare, with wide experience in North America, the West Indies and India, encountering long and arduous tours of duty lasting for several years. In the view of Lord Barrington, they should even be enlisted for life, to prevent battle-hardened veterans causing trouble when they came back home.[16] The perception of the '45 was also relevant. The Highlanders first impressed themselves on the British state as warriors, and formidable ones at that. The terrifying charge and slashing broadswords which routed Cope's regulars at Prestonpans were not easily forgotten. Even in the carnage of Culloden the following year the rebel army had performed with remarkable courage and an almost suicidal tenacity.

Over time the myth hardened and deepened. It was argued that the Jacobite soldiers had followed the wrong cause but they had done so only at the behest of their chiefs. Throughout they had displayed not only heroism in battle but undying loyalty. In such best-selling publications as *Young Juba or the History of the Young Chevalier* and *Ascanius or the Young Adventurer*, attention was focused on the story of the 'Prince and the Heather' when the Young Pretender was never betrayed by his followers despite the high price on his head. The Crown assumed that all these virtues were founded on the ethic of clanship, the martial society which had long disappeared from the rest of Britain. For this reason the government wished to keep Highlanders together in 'Highland regiments' under their 'natural' leaders. Fraser's Highlanders (the 71st of Foot) had no fewer than six chiefs of clans among its officers as well as many clan gentry. Ironically, while the state was bent on destroying clanship as a threat to the state, it was also at the same time committed to reinforcing clan allegiances through regimental recruitment. This happened while the clan ethos itself was dying rapidly through a cycle of inevitable decline, which was soon accelerated in the later eighteenth century by the commercialization of estates and clearance of people. But the state hardly doubted that the Highlander was nonetheless a natural warrior, not least because landowners seeking to establish family regiments constantly milked the glamorous image of clanship in order to gain a favourable response from their political paymasters.

The foundation had thus been laid for a spectacular expansion of Highland recruitment between 1775 and 1783 and, then, on an even more colossal scale in the years 1793 to 1815. The higher echelons of the British military were increasingly coloured by German military concepts which stressed that the people of mountainous areas were especially suited to the martial way of life. David Stewart of Garth's *Sketches of the Character, Manners and Present State of the Highlands of Scotland, with Details of the Military Service of the Highland Regiments*, first published in 1822, was the most influential text on the Highland soldier of the period. Stewart contended that 'nature' had honed the qualities of the perfect warrior:

> Nursed in poverty he acquired a hardihood which enabled him to sustain severe privations. As the simplicity of his life gave vigour to his body, so it fortified his mind. Possessing a frame and constitution thus hardened he was taught to consider courage as the most honourable virtue, cowardice the most disgraceful failing.[17]

Enlightenment thought further fortified the legend. The 'stage' theory of the development of human civilization, propounded by such Scottish intellectuals as Adam Ferguson and John Miller, fitted perfectly with the stereotype of the Highlander as a soldier. The region was seen to be still located in the feudal period where militarism was a way of life. Ferguson, for instance, argued that the Gaels were not interested in the 'commercial arts' but were rather by their very nature disposed to make war.[18] The parallel notion soon also became popular, that the Highlander could be spared from ordinary manual labour for military activity because the regional economy was so underdeveloped compared to other more advanced areas of the British Isles.[19]

There can be little doubt that in the early years of their formation, the Highland battalions had a strong sense of identity based on their distinctive dress, language, common heritage and culture and, often, on the same name. Imperial war came as a godsend for the *daoine uaisle*, the clan gentries, whose status on many Highland estates was being steadily undermined by rising rentals and the breaking up of holdings to create crofting townships. The army became an escape route for many members of this class from the irresistible forces of agrarian modernization. In this period they virtually became a professional military cadre of full-pay and half-pay officers who only returned to farming in the years between wars. Their traditional leadership role and influence on the localities where their regiments recruited must also have been a factor of significance in enhancing *esprit de corps*. Indeed, the bond between the native Highlander and his officer does seem to have been much closer than the relationship between English soldiers and their superiors.[20]

Yet any intimate connection between the clans and the regiments was at best superficial. This was hardly surprising since recruitment boomed at the very time when the Highlands were being transformed from tribalism to capitalism. The mania for raising family regiments fits well into the prevailing context of rampant commercialism. Landowners were primarily military entrepreneurs rather than patriarchal chieftains. They harvested the population of their estates for the army to make money in the same way as they established sheepwalks, cattle ranches and kelp shores. But such profiteering had to be done behind the façade of clan loyalties and martial enthusiasms because it was these very attributes which gave the Highlands its competitive brand in the military labour market. Even sophisticated and experienced politicians like Henry Dundas, Scotland's most powerful figure, were taken in. During the Napoleonic Wars he exuded praise for the clansmen and their 'chiefs', enthusiastically approved of the great scheme to embody even more of them in 1797 and applauded the Highland warriors for their hostility to the 'levelling and dangerous principles' of the urban radicals of the time.[21]

Successful recruitment could provide many benefits for the Highland elites. Raising a regiment furnished commissions for a magnate's own kinsmen and associates, but also conferred influence and patronage in the neighbourhood among other impoverished minor gentry, who desperately sought commissions and the secure incomes and pensions which came with them. Local power and standing were increased, and military service also consolidated connections with government. The rewards could be substantial. Sir James Grant, whose estates were heavily encumbered, achieved a sinecure worth £3,000 a year and the lord lieutenancy of Inverness in 1794. Mackenzie of Seaforth who, like most Highland landowners, had financial difficulties, did even better. In quick succession he became Lord Lieutenant of Ross in 1794, Lord Seaforth in the English peerage in the same year and, in 1800, Governor of Barbados. But there were also more direct and equally lucrative benefits to recruitment. Allocating land to soldiers could provide an estate with more regular rentals than were likely to accrue from the small tenantry, whose payments were notoriously volatile because of harvest failures and market fluctuations. Soldiers had a secure income not only when on active service but also (at a lower level) through their small pensions when they retired. There is evidence that several proprietors showed a clear preference for such 'military' tenants as a result of this advantage.[22]

There was also on these properties the assumed expectation that men were obliged to serve. When this was in doubt, systematic coercion was employed. Estate records teem with examples of the practice. Alexander Macdonell of Glengarry ordered his agent to 'warn out' a list of small tenants from his Knoydart property, they 'having refused to serve me'. Similarly, Maclaine of Lochbuie on the island of Mull threatened to remove seventy-one tenants, cottars and their families in 1795 because they had not provided sons for service. On several estates, the tradition of 'land for sons' was widespread. In the Lord Macdonald papers relating to his extensive lands in Skye, a document is headed '*List of Tenants who have been promised Lands and an exchange of lands for their sons*'.[23] These contracts were often very specific, indicating the length of leases and the tenurial arrangements as a result of sons traded for land. In the long run, however, they generated angry controversy. Many recruits did not return home but lay buried in foreign graves through death in battle or, more likely, from disease. To the families, therefore, their holdings had often been acquired, quite literally, through the blood of their kinfolk. When these obligations were ended, for whatever cause, the people felt a sense of gross breach of trust. Recruitment was of immense profit to the landed classes of the Highlands. But its consequences often brought down great opprobrium on their successors and gave a special emotional edge to the contentious saga of the Highland Clearances.[24]

2

The storming of Quebec, in 1759, the defeat of Napoleon's army in Egypt in 1801 (which for the first time shattered the myth of French invincibility on land) and the signal achievements in the Peninsular War, at Quatre Bras and, finally, at Waterloo, all combined to celebrate the legend of the valorous Highlander. But behind the façade of glorious triumph all was not as it seemed. Land clearance and emigration in the north of Scotland made recruitment to the regiments increasingly more challenging. As early as the 1770s some struggled to make up numbers, and by the end of the eighteenth century 'the well had run dry'.[25] When the 79th or Cameron Highlanders were reconstituted in 1798, after their rank and file was decimated by disease, the battalion comprised more non-Scots than Scots.[26] Even the most prestigious formations were forced to extend the geographical range of their recruitment. It was reckoned that at least a third of the Black Watch who fought at Waterloo were drawn from the Scottish Lowlands, the Borders and even England.[27] The spectacular expansion of the levies drawn mainly from the indigenous Gaelic population had come to an end as early as 1800. The manpower resources of the Highlands were virtually exhausted by over-recruitment, death in battle, discharges and natural attrition.

In addition, the popular belief that the Gael was a natural warrior was, in large part, a myth. As has been already noted, there is abundant evidence of the systematic use of coercion of the tenantry to make up numbers in the family regiments. When a battalion of the 78th Seaforth Highlanders was raised, a kinsman of its colonel, Sir George Mackenzie, concluded in his *General View of the Agriculture of the Counties of Ross and Cromarty* (1813) that the young recruits had joined in order to save their parents being turned out of their farms.[28] Hostility to the hazards of army life, low pay (no more than that of a casual labourer) and many years spent far from home were as common in some parts of the Highlands as among the population in general. Thus, in the parish of Blair Atholl, in Perthshire, in the 1790s it was said that 'many had learned to despise a soldier's pay and hate a life of servitude'.[29] Even in poorer counties, such as Ross-shire, one observer argued that by 1813, 'it was notorious that the inhabitants have now a strong aversion to a military life'.[30]

It seemed then that at the very pinnacle of their glory the future of the Highland units was beset by serious doubt. In 1809 the problems of recruitment became so acute that the kilt was abandoned in five regiments, leaving only five whose social composition merited the wearing of the famous Highland dress. These were the only survivors by 1815 from the total of fifty-nine regular and fencible (home defence) units which had been raised between 1740 and 1800.[31] Scotland as a whole had contributed disproportionately to the armies which fought Napoleon, but in subsequent decades recruiting fell dramatically. In 1830, when Scots contributed 10 per cent of the UK population, they made up 13 per cent of the army. By 1870 this had fallen to 8 per cent, and to 7.6 per cent in 1913.[32] In the 1850s, senior army officers continued to complain that not enough Scots, far less Gaels, could be found for the 'kilted regiments'.[33] By the end of the nineteenth century, some observers denounced them as 'cultural forgeries' since they were more likely to recruit from the poorer working classes of the towns and cities than the Highland crofts and glens of the past.[34] Not only did the British army contract in size in the decades of peace after 1815 but the number of Highland formations declined even more dramatically. At the beginning of Victoria's reign they represented a minute part of the armed forces, with a mere five units surviving demobilization after the end of the Napoleonic Wars: the 42nd (Royal Highland Regiment of the Black Watch), the 78th (Ross-shire Buffs), the 79th (Cameron Highlanders), the 92nd (Gordon Highlanders) and the 93rd (Sutherland Highlanders).[35] Paradoxically, however, it was in the Victorian era they not only managed to maintain their traditional fame and public profile but, if anything, became even more celebrated as national icons of Scotland.

One historian in the second half of the nineteenth century has noted how Highlanders were 'the most feted of all Victorian soldiers', while another refers to 'the Victorian cult of the Highlander'. The regiments, out of all proportion to their actual numbers in the British army, attracted the lion's share of publicity in contemporary art, advertising, the press and reports from the front, much to the envy and jealous pride of other units which often performed just as gallantly in action.[36] Gradually, indeed, Scottish military activity in general became 'high-landized'. The climax came in 1881 when Scottish Lowland regiments were outfitted with Highland doublets and tartan trews, although some units had already been maintaining pipers in Highland dress for some decades before that.[37] The cult also spread overseas to the Scottish diaspora. Local, part-time volunteer defence forces in Canada, Australia, New Zealand and South Africa from the 1860s included 'Scottish regiments', clad in kilt and tartan and uniforms modelled on those of their illustrious parents. In at least one instance, that of the Queensland Scottish in the 1880s, the Australian unit wore uniforms recycled from those cast off by the Gordon Highlanders at home.[38] During the Great War these formations spawned countless additional battalions, each with a Highland designation. Hardly surprisingly, therefore, to this day, all countries of the Commonwealth boast their own military pipe bands.

Why then did Scottish Highland regiments become so popular in the course of the nineteenth century?[39] Some argue it came about because of royal patronage and, in particular, reflected the renowned Scotophilia of Queen Victoria. The Highland enthusiasms of the monarchy had in fact begun in the later eighteenth century under her royal ancestors, and was celebrated with much pageantry in the 'plaided panorama' of George IV's famous visit to Edinburgh, not least because of Major General David Stewart of Garth's (formerly of the Black Watch) influence on the ceremonial during that series of events.[40] But Victoria's royal impact was more powerful. From her first visit to the Highlands in 1842 she developed a long love affair with the region and its people. As part of this, the Queen took a special interest in 'her' Highland regiments. She decorated Scottish soldiers at Balmoral and, in 1873, bestowed a royal title on the 79th (which thereafter became known as the 79th Queen's Own Cameron Highlanders). She regularly presented regimental colours to other kilted battalions during the annual visits to her Scottish castle.[41] The prestige and status which followed such royal approval doubtless enhanced regimental profiles, but it does not alone entirely explain their remarkable celebrity and social standing. The lens needs to be widened considerably to take into account the general changes which affected soldiering in Victorian society, and then to offer an explanation as to why Highland soldiers in particular were able to gain from this transformation.

Public esteem for the army and its role in colonial warfare rose dramatically in the Victorian era and especially after c.1870. 'The rapacious and licentious' soldiery of the old days came to attract a wholly different image in British popular culture.[42] The Crimean War was a key turning point in this process as it generated unparalleled public sympathy for the hardships suffered before Sebastapol, chronicled in emotive detail in the press, especially in the famous reports in *The Times* by William Howard Russell.[43] Soldiers came to be seen as victims who were badly led by incompetent commanders. The patient fatalism of the men was also depicted as proof of their 'high feelings' and even 'their piety and religion'.[44] The fact that a soldier might also be a good Christian had particular appeal for the respectable church-going middle classes. This response helped to lay the foundations for the growth of Christian militarism, which in due course gave rise to the Salvation Army, Boys' Brigade and other organizations with a quasi-military identity.

The Indian Rising (Mutiny) of 1857 further confirmed the more favourable image. The notorious massacre of British women and children at Cawnpore on 15 July 1857 and the siege of the garrison at Lucknow, which threatened another human catastrophe, generated unprecedented interest at home. The supposed depravity and inhumanity of the rebellious sepoys was contrasted with the righteous vengeance and the heroic deeds of the British soldiers who valiantly came to the rescue of defenceless civilians.[45]

Underpinning the extraordinary public impact of the Rising was the contemporaneous revolutionary expansion of the print media which ensured that even conflicts at the remote ends of empire were now reported at length to an interested mass audience at home. By 1841 the delivery of news from India took a month instead of the eight weeks and more which had been the case just a few years previously. During the 1850s, the various taxes on newspapers were abolished, leading to huge increases in circulation of the provincial press and the development of weekly papers specifically designed in price and content for a working-class readership.[46]

There was plenty of copy available for the new army of foreign correspondents. With the exception of the Crimean War, all the conflicts in which Britain was involved in this period were colonial, fought in such faraway places as the African bush, the North-West Frontier in India, Afghanistan and the Sudan. Between 1815 and 1914 there was scarcely a year when the British were not fighting a campaign somewhere in the world.[47] But this fact in itself guaranteed a huge and interested reading public. These wars not only had the attraction of the exotic but were also usually reported as a conflict between civilization and savagery, morality and barbarity, with the British soldier as the heroic incarnation of righteousness, always victorious over evil and primitive enemies.

The Highland regiments were seen to be at the heart of this triumphal progress. The roll call of their battle honours stretched from the Alma and Balaclava in the Crimean War to Lucknow, Tel-el-Kebir, Dargai and Al-Bara on the frontiers of empire. A legend of martial invincibility was generated which not even their disastrous reverses at Majuba Hill and Magersfontein during the South African War could erase. It was said that the mere appearance of kilted soldiers urged on by the skirl of the pipes struck terror into the enemy. Their fame was magnified in the reports of war correspondents and by artists, sculptors, novelists and composers who delighted in the 'sartorial allure of kilt and tartan'. One of the most successful battle-painters of the Victorian era, Lady Elizabeth Butler, memorably remarked that 'these splendid troops are so essentially pictorial'.[48] They stood out from the khaki-clad ranks of the rest of the army and, of course, the pipes and drums also projected a distinctive musical dimension. Officers of the regiments were determined self-publicists, penning copy from the front for newspapers at home and, in retirement, writing memoirs and histories of the campaigns in which they had fought during their careers. As Alexander Somerville famously remarked in the 1840s in his *Autobiography of a Working Man*, 'it was the *writing* quite as much as the *fighting* of the Scotch regiments which distinguished them'.[49]

Indeed, much of the publicity which the Highland soldier attracted verged on overt propaganda. The news sent back to the press was carefully focused and sanitized. There was little mention in the dispatches of the fate of prisoners in the aftermath of the relief of Cawnpore during the Indian Rebellion or the terrible brutality against both sepoys and civilians in the same period.[50] Victories were also often easily won against opposition which lacked modern weaponry and organization. At least fifteen war correspondents were present at the Anglo-Egyptian battle at Omdurman in the Sudan against the forces of the Mahdi which numbered possibly 53,000 men. Before noon on 2 September 1898 this great host had been annihilated, leaving some 10,000 corpses on the battlefield and a further 16,000 wounded. The Anglo-Egyptians lost a mere forty-eight officers and men.[51] Carnage on this scale, which was not untypical of colonial campaigns, gave the impression to readers at home of war as sport in which British forces would always triumph with minimal loss even against seemingly overwhelming odds. The Boer War, however, fought against a much better armed enemy, deploying 'modern' and superior tactics, brought a reality check. Sir George Younghusband explained the poor showing of the troops, including Highland units, thus:

> The British public, fed by sensational newspapers, were chiefly to blame for this low standard. Easy victories, against ill-armed though brave adversaries, where the enemy lost thousands, and we counted our casualties by tens, or at most hundreds, became to be thought the normal proportion in the wars we waged.[52]

3

Scottish history of whatever period is incomprehensible without an understanding of war and the national martial tradition. For better or worse the identity of the nation has been moulded by these forces over the centuries. But for the sustained struggle for independence in medieval times Scotland would have been conquered and colonized. It is no coincidence that two of the nation's most famous hero figures, William Wallace and Robert the Bruce, are for ever associated with that remarkable period which retains potent resonance to the present day. It was not simply a question, however, of removing the threat of subjugation. Essentially, the Wars of Independence helped to fuse the confused mix of kindreds, clans and tribes into a nation. There is therefore much truth in the saying that Scotland was born fighting.

The place of the Highland regiments in national identity was based on this age-old tradition of the Scots as a martial people. Within the Union they were seen to be at the cutting edge of empire, confirming the Anglo-Scottish relationship as a partnership in which the Scots contributed, quite literally, more than their fair share in blood. Contrasts were often drawn in the late Victorian era with the Irish, who actually contributed many more men to the imperial effort than the Scots ever did but whose absolute loyalty to the union state and empire became questionable at a time of increasing nationalism and agitation for Home Rule. The Scots were not only willing; above all, they were also loyal. It was probably entirely apposite, therefore, when the sun finally set on the greatest territorial empire the world had ever seen, with the handover of the colony of Hong Kong to China in June 1997, it was the pipes and drums of the Black Watch that ended the ceremonial with 'Auld Lang Syne'. Yet the regiments not only helped to cement the Anglo-Scottish relationship between 1750 and 1914, they also sustained a strong sense of Scottish identity within the union state. They were imperial units but their soldiers, strikingly distinctive in dress and appearance, were recognizably and unambiguously Scottish, martial champions of the nation.

From the end of the Napoleonic Wars the number of Scotsmen joining the regular army had declined in proportion to the Scottish share of the national population. Yet in 1914, with the outbreak of the Great War, all that seemed to change. Scots joined up during the volunteering phase of the conflict in 1914–15 in significantly greater numbers than the other three nations of the United Kingdom. By July 1915 the average rate of enlistment for men in Britain was 20 per cent but over 24 per cent in Scotland. A third of a million Scots enlisted voluntarily before conscription was introduced in January 1916.[53] So great was the response that in some parts of the country recruitment had to be temporarily suspended as the agencies could not cope with the flood of numbers. The fact that most Scottish regiments had a local base of recruitment meant that towns and districts, enthusiastically encouraged by the press, vied with one another to stay ahead of the competition as the number of volunteers reached levels never seen before in any previous conflict.[54]

Historians have speculated on the reasons for this new popularity of the profession of arms. Some of the theories advanced include the attractions of a secure income and employment in a period of economic instability; an alternative to emigration, which had been taking place on a very significant scale in the years before the outbreak of war; and the lure of adventure in lives which were often dull and humdrum.[55] But the influence of the martial history of the Scots must also have been crucial. It is remarkable how the rhetoric of recruiting drew heavily on the traditional beliefs of distinctive Scottish fighting prowess in the age-old defence of the Empire.[56] Posters, press comment, public statements and political speeches were all carefully crafted to appeal to a new generation of young men bred on a diet of militarism. The most popular youth organization in Scotland, the Boys' Brigade (founded in Glasgow in 1883), was organized in a quasi-military style and gave its vast membership a taste of the qualities of duty, obedience, loyalty and love of country associated with good soldiering. Adventure stories, school history books and the cigarette cards which many youngsters collected presented war as an adventure, an opportunity to rise above the mundane and engage in heroic deeds. And always at the forefront of the visual images was the iconography of the Highland soldier. An examination of the columns of *The Scotsman* and the *Glasgow Herald* for the first year of the war conveys the distinct impression that the Highland regiments were in fact the sole armed representatives of Scotland in this conflict. The amateur poetry printed in the press consistently made reference to the glens and crofts of the north, the environment which was said to have produced Scotland's crack troops. The Black Watch, Cameron and Gordon Highlanders and others had their 'skirmishes' at the front picked over in minute journalistic detail. Emphasis was placed on the fact that the Germans feared above all the valour and dash of Scotland's kilted regiments. The great battles of the past where the Highlands had distinguished themselves, such as Waterloo, the Alma, Lucknow and Dargai, were also a common point of reference in many reports. Not all commentators were impressed. A. G. Macdonell responded acidly in his *My Scotland* some years after the war:

The Lowlander was to be allowed to wear the coveted panoply, to stand in the ranks of the regiments that bore historic names, to be called a Highlander, and no questions asked. In return he was to do nine-tenths of the fighting, and nine-tenths of the dying, and all the credit was to go to the Highlander, and no stones thrown. Each side made a contribution, the one putting their lives into the common pool, the one an undeserved name and the other an unearned fame.[57]

Several decades before the Great War, in 1859, the volunteer corps which had been raised during the Napoleonic Wars were reborn. These part-time amateur soldiers, drawn mainly from the urban areas and the artisan classes, proved to be remarkably popular in Scotland. The nation raised twice as many per head of the male population as the rest of the United Kingdom in the later Victorian era. The county in Britain which generated most volunteer units was industrial Lanarkshire, with no fewer than 107 formations. Once again, Highlandism had its effect. The simple grey uniforms of the volunteers were decorated with tartan flourishes and some Highland companies wore full Highland military dress. By 1914, the volunteers had been reformed into the Territorial Force, which had made its mark during the Boer Wars, and became the key engine of mobilization during the first eighteen months of the Great War. The link between Highlandism and militarism maintained its remarkable and enduring potency, and the age-old bond between Scottish identity, empire and the martial tradition was not only consolidated during the Great War but emerged intact in 1918 even after the catastrophic loss of life Scotland endured during that terrible conflict.

I I

Funding the New Lands

Scotland had furnished credit and invested abroad since time immemorial. Notable examples were the loans to customers which helped to lubricate commerce in seventeenth-century Poland and the advance of credit by the eighteenth-century Glasgow tobacco lords to the needy planters of Virginia and Maryland. Yet the scale and global spread of Scottish funding overseas between the 1870s and the Great War was a new departure. External lending of such magnitude had never occurred before in Scottish history and would never be matched again. It was nothing less than a financial revolution which helped to mould the development of economies in the Americas, Asia, Africa and Australasia, facilitated emigration to these territories and, at the same time, had profound effects on Scotland itself.

The views of two contemporary publications captured something of the significance of the development. In the 1880s, *The Statist* commented:

> There are investors and speculators of a sort in all communities, but as a rule they are exceptional beings. In Scotland, however, they form so large a percentage of the well-to-do class as to be rather the rule than the exception. In Edinburgh, Dundee and Aberdeen it would be perfectly safe to bet on any man you pass in the street with an income of over three hundred a year being familiar with the fluctuation of Grand Turks, and having quite as much as he can afford staked on prairies, or some kindred gamble. A dividend of twenty per cent, or more is to a Scotchman of this class a bait which he cannot resist.[1]

For *Blackwood's Edinburgh Magazine* Scotland was contributing disproportionately 'to the great stream of British capital which is continually flowing out to foreign countries' and it judged 'this vast exportation of the country's wealth' to be a 'revolution' in the history of Scotland. The journal added, possibly with some exaggeration: 'In proportion to her size and the number of her population, she furnishes far more of it than either of the sister kingdoms. England gives sparingly and Ireland hardly any, *Scotland revels in foreign investment.*'[2]

It had not always been thus. Indeed, the Scots were much slower than the English to exploit opportunities abroad. There was a sporadic beginning in 1837 with the formation of the Illinois Investment Company, which spawned another three ventures in the following few years.[3] Again in the 1830s and early 1840s, Aberdeen interests had become involved in the Australian mortgage market with two investment companies established in that period. Scotland's capital had already broken into Australia in the 1820s with the foundation of the Australian Company of Edinburgh and Leith.[4] However, it was to be another three decades before Scottish finance flowed abroad in substantial and continuous volume. The real origins, in what eventually became a virtual craze, came via the investment and mortgage companies organized during the economic depression in 1873 in the United States. Some Scottish capitalists exploited the low prices for securities on the New York Stock Exchange by wholesale investment in the burgeoning American railroad system. Before that time, most surplus funds were inevitably swallowed up by the demands of the second great phase of domestic Scottish industrialization in mining, iron and steel-making, engineering, shipbuilding and, not least, in the development of Scotland's own national rail network. These first successful forays into the American market in the early 1870s eventually generated an enormous wave of investment which spread quickly into land reclamation and development, gold and silver mining, sheep and cattle farming on a grand scale, city building and expansion and numerous other ventures across four continents. In 1882, one newspaper correspondent could report:

> ... in the summer of 1882 hardly a train came into Edinburgh from the West or the South which did not bring a Yankee with a cattle ranch in one pocket, a 'timber limit' in another, and perhaps an embryo Erie Railway up his sleeve.

The operation, in fact, was often made ridiculously easy for him. The moment he was heard of in Princes Street, a bevy of S.S.C.s – Anglicé, Solicitors before the Supreme Courts – would be after him to hunt him down. Every S.S.C. had his own little syndicate at his back – that is, a group of retired drapers, head clerks, and second-rate accountants, who could club together money enough for the advertising, printing and postages needed to float a Company.[5]

The following year an Australian banker in London described Scotland's capital as 'honeycombed with agencies for collecting money not for use in Australia alone, but for India, China, Canada, South America – everywhere almost and for all purposes, on the security of pastoral and agricultural lands in Texas, California, Queensland and Mexico'.[6]

I

The outflow of Scottish capital in this period needs to be first seen in a British context because it was an integral, albeit a distinctive, part of a more general financial revolution.[7] Over that period British capital holdings abroad quadrupled across the globe, from £1 million in 1870 to £4 million at the outbreak of the Great War. The share of the Empire rose slightly to some 43 per cent in 1913, with the settlement colonies of Canada, Australia, New Zealand and South Africa absorbing just over a third of this vast sum. But this was mainly a global process and not simply an imperial one. Investment in transportation, especially railway construction, in overseas territories was king, accounting for nearly half of the portfolio in 1914, but the holdings covered a remarkable range from agriculture to mining, from public utilities to manufacturing. Especially striking was the fact that in this period Britain became the world's banker.[8] Other European countries and, to a much lesser extent, the United States, did export capital on a significant scale by the Great War but their performance was dwarfed by the United Kingdom. Its overseas investments comprised 44 per cent of the global total of the main investing countries. Only France and Germany came anywhere near this dominant position, but with holdings of 20 per cent and 12 per cent respectively they were a very poor second and third in this league table of world financial power.

In proportion to its population size of nearly 4.5 million people and its relative economic power within the UK, Scotland was a major player in this lucrative field. Estimates of the size of the investment portfolio vary. One suggestion well known in the academic literature is that it grew spectacularly from £60 million in 1870 to £500 million by 1914.[9] If correct, that figure would mean that Scotland was not simply expanding its total capital exports but was doing so at an even faster pace than the UK as a whole. In this scenario its share was rising from 7 to 12 per cent of all British foreign lending over the period.[10] Another commentator could state confidently that, in 1914, overseas investment was equivalent to £110 for every Scot, compared to an average of £90 for the UK.[11] However, the most recent and thorough investigation of the issue reveals the difficulty of coming to precise conclusions. It suggests the possibility of a range of net Scottish foreign lending stretching from somewhere between £390 million at minimum and £520 million at maximum by around 1914.[12] The truth is that a final conclusion is impossible on this matter, given the imponderables of investment that could have been undertaken directly by private individuals and not through financial organizations, such as investment trusts and mortgage companies (from whose records researchers gather much of their evidence), the unknown number of Scottish capitalists who worked through the Stock Exchange in London and, by no means least, the potentially immense sums taken out of the country by emigrant Scots from their personal funds and savings accounts as they set out for new lives across the Atlantic or in the Antipodes. Nevertheless, although final totals might prove elusive, we do still know a great deal about Scottish overseas investment after c.1870.

Overwhelmingly capital went to the USA, Canada, Australasia, India and Ceylon, with only limited outflows to the rest of the world. Up to half the investment was destined for the Empire, in which the Scottish contribution per head was about 60 per cent above the British average.[13] In certain periods, countries and sectors the Scottish factor was often decisive. Between 1873 and 1890, for instance, investment in US railroads doubled, running into many millions of pounds. One estimate suggests that two-thirds of the British funds invested in American stock markets and mortgages were of Scottish origin.[14] Similarly, in the 1880s in Australia, at least a third of pastoral, mortgage and investment company securities (and an even higher proportion of deposit receipts issued by banks) were taken up in Scotland. Indeed, in the years prior to the Antipodean financial crisis of 1893, Scotland was very much the dominant source of loanable funds from the UK.[15] In New Zealand English capital was pre-eminent, but Scottish funds in the 1860s to the 1890s (usually accounting for around one-fifth of the total in the country) were second in significance and much greater than any other source after England by a considerable margin. The Scots had a particular niche interest in pastoral development and in areas of Scottish migrant settlement in New Zealand where their concentration of capital was unmatched.[16]

When financial markets in general are considered, it is now apparent that in Scotland there was a decisive swing away from home to overseas investment in the last quarter of the nineteenth century. Remarkably, nearly half (44 per cent) of the increase in Scottish capital between 1885 and 1910 took the form of investment overseas and the share of new income devoted to that market had become almost a third of the total.[17] A new era in the economic history of the nation had begun. The big Scottish insurance companies were also moving in the same direction. By 1900 Scottish Widows had around £6 million placed in foreign assets and a similar trend can also be identified in the investment policies of Standard Life Assurance.[18] In 1880, the company had only £0.5 million in overseas railway and government bonds, as well as mortgages and property assets. By 1910 this had risen to £7.5 million, which represented well over half of total assets held by Standard Life.[19] If it were assumed that the seven leading Scottish life assurance firms (which owned assets of £81.7 million in 1912–13) held a similar proportion of these abroad to Standard Life, this would amount to around £40–50 million of Scottish holdings overseas from this source alone.[20]

In parallel, some major industrial firms were diversifying their interests. The most spectacular example was that of J. and P. Coats, after 1896 the world's biggest manufacturer of thread, eventually controlling more than 80 per cent of global thread-making capacity. From its home base in Paisley, the firm built up a huge subsidiary empire in the USA, Canada, Russia, Austria-Hungary and Spain.[21] But there were also a number of other instances. Several of the big Dundee jute companies were starting to open mills in India; those doyens of iron-manufacture, the Bairds of Gartsherrie, acquired Spanish ore mines in the 1870s, while the Burmah Oil Company was developing a portfolio of American railway bonds from the later nineteenth century.[22] There is indeed much evidence that while capital investment in domestic industry had dwindled, it was being replaced as the economic dynamo of Scotland by the new craze for overseas lending from the 1870s onwards.

Where that lending came from is an intriguing question. In part, the source was those members of Scottish society who had made personal fortunes out of the country's rapid industrialization earlier in the nineteenth century. Some had made colossal piles and were looking for further good investments with high returns at limited risk to further expand their wealth. Sir Charles Tennant of the chemical empire, Sir James and Peter Coats of the thread-making dynasty and William Weir, coal tycoon and iron manufacturer, were among the elite of forty men in Britain reckoned to be worth £2 million or more in the nineteenth century.[23] Four members of the Baird iron-making dynasty were among the millionaires too.[24] In Dundee, the juteocracy of the Baxters, Coxes, Gilrays and others could also be numbered among the richest in the land. As a later section will show, these jute barons were at the very heart of Dundee's overseas investment boom from the 1870s.[25] Several of the other wealthy tycoons were also very active. The Coats family, for instance, had interests in an impressively large number of these ventures.[26]

Yet, one of the striking features of the sources of lending from Scotland was that it was not confined to the new aristocracy of trade and industry. R. Dudley Baxter's analysis of *National Income of the United Kingdom*, published in 1867, identified the really rich in Scotland (with incomes over £1,000 per annum) as numbering 4,700, or a tiny elite of only 0.33 per cent of 'productive persons' in the country. But he also thought that a further 276,300 individuals by his measure could be included in the middle and professional classes. In all, this group made up nearly one-fifth of 'productive persons'. It was they who were to play a key role in the investment bonanza of the later nineteenth century because, invariably, they would have a margin above daily living costs which might be spared for other purposes.

The growth of a modestly prosperous group below the ranks of the rich is confirmed by the development of the savings bank movement earlier in the nineteenth century. Started in 1810, it was flourishing by the 1850s. By then the savings banks had been joined by the penny banks which were designed to encourage the savings habit among more humble social groups. An analysis of the subscribers to the Glasgow Savings Bank shows the involvement of printers, weavers, mechanics, tradesmen and domestic servants, mainly the artisan classes. A list of new accounts opened in Edinburgh in 1907 demonstrates that over half of them were registered by women – married, widows and spinsters. By that period over 500,000 accounts had been opened in Scotland.[27] This was a striking figure, one for every nine of the population of the country.

It was partly on the basis of these foundations that 'a democratization of foreign investment' began to evolve. Those with financial interests abroad grew dramatically, from around 4,000 in 1867, to 30,000 in 1890 and nearly 80,000 by 1913. Over time, the average individual value of investments declined, another sign that the smaller investors were making their presence felt. Women were also beginning to make their mark. Among probated estates with some foreign assets, the female share rose from just over 6 per cent in 1867 to a fifth in 1890. It was also the case that the new habit of investing overseas spread across the length and breadth of the country. As Table 6 reveals, inhabitants of Edinburgh, Glasgow (from a late start) and, to a lesser extent, Dundee were dominant but the pattern of investment also soon penetrated deeply into the small towns and country areas of the nation.

Table 6: Distribution of probated estates in Scotland containing foreign assets, by Sheriff Court districts, 1867, 1890 and 1914 (excluding Orkney and Shetland Sheriff Courts)

Sheriff Court	1867	1890	1914
EDINBURGH	16	188	374
GLASGOW	8	63	227
CENTRAL SCOTLAND			
Airdrie		3	7
Alloa		4	6
Cupar	6	35	80
Dumbarton	1	15	41
Dunblane		8	9
Dundee		39	79
Dunoon	1	11	18
Forfar	3	21	53
Greenock		5	33
Haddington	2	7	11
Hamilton		8	28
Kilmarnock			22
Kinross		4	4
Lanark		6	14
Linlithgow		1	9
Paisley	6	17	37
Perth	7	45	81
Rothesay		3	7
Stirling	4	19	42
SOUTHERN SCOTLAND			
Ayr	10	30	38
Dumfries	5	22	38

Table 6: (*continued*)

Sheriff Court	1867	1890	1914
Duns	1	7	18
Jedburgh	3	9	25
Kirkcudbright	2	4	20
Peebles	1	3	10
Selkirk		5	9
Wigtown		4	13
NORTHERN SCOTLAND			
Aberdeen	7	42	89
Banff	2	3	8
Dingwall	1	5	7
Dornoch			4
Elgin	3	9	15
Inverness	2	5	17
Nairn			2
Stonehaven		3	9
Wick	1	1	4
Totals	**92**	**654**	**1,508**

Source: Christopher Schmitz, 'The Nature and Dimensions of Scottish Foreign Investment 1860–1914', *Business History*, 39, 2 (1997), p. 56.

Although a larger group than the really wealthy, the investing public still represented a relatively small proportion of the Scottish population as a whole. According to Dudley Baxter's figures of 1867, the middling elements (lawyers, merchants, some tradesmen, doctors, bankers, accountants and farmers) composed 19 per cent of 'productive persons' in Scotland, while the 'manual labour class' (skilled, semi-skilled and unskilled) comprised an overwhelming 81 per cent. Nevertheless, these middle classes, together with the very rich, absorbed well over half of national income and it was mainly from their number that the new investors were drawn. This hardly amounted to 'democratization' – more probably, in fact, a further embedding of the entrenched social divisions and inequalities of wealth in Scotland, which the lucrative returns from overseas investments helped not only to consolidate but to deepen.

Ironically, however, ordinary Scots were often involved in other ways in influencing the export of capital, through the funds taken abroad by the nation's huge army of emigrants. Of course, no figure or even order of magnitude can be given for what must have been a very substantial outflow, given the fact that over 2 million Scots emigrated between the end of the Napoleonic Wars in 1815 and the start of the Great War in 1914, with much of this exodus concentrated in the decades after c.1850. Most of this movement was not a flight of the poor. The majority of emigrants sought to exploit opportunities and had some means, however modest, on their departure.[28] A glimpse into the channelling of savings into other countries which often resulted was given by the Secretary of the Scottish Farm Servants' Union, Joe Duncan, in the early 1900s. He noted 'the steady stream of emigration from the rural districts of Scotland, rising at times into something of a torrent'. Because the unmarried ploughmen were paid only every six months in Scottish agriculture, 'a system of involuntary savings' was in place which then not only paid for passage abroad but helped to provide the funds for resettlement overseas.[29] The occupational profile of emigration also led to resources going to countries of overseas settlement. It was never more than a significant minority but in the years before the Great War up to a fifth of adult men leaving Scotland must have had some means, being described as belonging to the group labelled 'commerce, finance, insurance, professional'.[30] Nor was the financial leakage stemmed by the kind of high levels of return migration which characterized other diasporas and led to remittances to the homeland of significant cash resources. The rates of return of Italian, Swedish and Spanish emigrants averaged around 50 to 60 per cent of those who left from the mid-nineteenth century. The comparative Scottish figure, on the other hand, was closer to a third of the national exodus.[31]

2

In order to understand the scale and remarkable speed of increase in Scottish overseas investment after *c*.1870 the analytical lens must now be extended somewhat. The broad context of the transformation in Scottish capitalism was the revolution in the pattern of world trade, human settlement and the vast expansion in food and raw material production in the New World. In consequence, the United States, Canada, Australasia, south Asia and Latin America developed a huge appetite for European financial resources to sustain their extraordinary rates of economic expansion. The numbers are indeed stunning. Between 1821 and 1915, 44 million emigrants left Europe for North America and Australasia. World trade multiplied tenfold from 1850 to 1913. The world's railway mileage stood at 66,000 in 1860. By 1920 the rate of expansion had brought it to 674,000 miles.[32] As rural producers around the globe reaped richer rewards for their grain, meat, timber, rubber, tea, oil and countless other commodities in European markets, they bought more imports and borrowed more money. It was scarcely surprising that even the most astute minds were seduced by the apparently limitless possibilities for gain around the world. The Edinburgh lawyer William J. Menzies, a Writer to the Signet, was a powerful influence on the formation of the Scottish-American Investment Company in 1873, a pioneering venture in overseas investment. He visited the USA in 1864, 1867 and again in 1872 and was convinced by New York and Chicago bankers on this last trip of the potential for vast profits in that booming country. His preliminary draft of the prospectus for the future captures some of the excitement in the early stages of the financial mania:

> The growth of America in population, resources and wealth, is too well known to require any statement . . . the wonderful fertility of the virgin soil, the multitude and variety of its production and manufactures, the rapid development of its railroad system . . . and the enormous immigration taking place in America, all combine to the development of almost illimitable resources and the creation of material wealth.

The population of the United States is now larger than that of the British Isles, and besides natural increase, receives by immigration an additional half-a-million annually; its territory is twenty-eight times as large. In developing its resources afford ample opportunities for employing capital profitably, *that for many years to come the demand must be greater than the supply, and the rate of interest therefore high.*[33]

Three examples, in the United States and beyond, illustrate the force of Menzies' argument. The Great Plains of the American West experienced a 'beef bonanza' in the 1880s and for a few buoyant seasons cattle ranching seemed for investors at home to be almost a licence to print money. Texan longhorns colonized Montana, Wyoming, Colorado, Nebraska, Kansas and the neighbouring states where the buffalo had once dominated. The cattle were cheap, the land free and the unrelenting spread of American urbanization ensured booming consumer markets for beef. Cattle numbers in the USA as a whole rose by more than a half in the 1880s to an astonishing 60 million head.[34]

Another instance was Canada in the first decade of the twentieth century. The driving force in development there was the rise in agricultural and raw material prices throughout the world. The large stretches of fertile prairie opened up by the ever-expanding railway system enabled Canada to exploit high prices without an immediate risk of an equal rise in costs. At the same time raw material and mineral production boomed. The nation became the leading nickel producer in the world while copper, silver and gold were exported in large quantities. Demand for labour was vast, with 650,000 emigrants settling in Canada between 1901 and 1911, and a further half a million in the following three years. There was simply not enough capital in the country to sustain the inevitable expansion in housing, towns and transport infrastructure. Canada had to borrow on an immense scale. Therefore, in the early 1900s roughly $2.5 million were invested from outside, especially from Britain, which was not far short of Canada's own savings during the period.[35]

In Australia, the main impetus during the boom of the late 1890s was the export to Britain of wool, canned and frozen mutton and beef, together with butter and cheese. Exports increased elevenfold in value between 1890 and 1900. By 1913 Australia and New Zealand combined supplied 260,000 tons of sheep-meat to Britain, about 30 per cent of its consumption. Lending to Antipodean farmers and ranchers became big business.[36]

But the story of overseas investment was far from being a perfect fable of irresistible opportunity and easy profit. On the contrary, the economic cycle fluctuated violently over the period and boom times could be quickly followed by steep slumps, lost capital and ruined investors. As far as the USA was concerned, the years 1870 to 1873 brought handsome returns. But those good years were then followed by seven of depression. Daring investment was replaced by cautious planning, with much capital being withdrawn from the USA and a widespread failure to reinvest holdings on redemption. From c.1880, however, the trend was once again upwards to 1890.[37] By the end

Table 7: Booms in Canada, Australia/New Zealand and South Africa, 1870–1914

Dates	Region
Canada	
1878/85–89/93	Manitoba, British Columbia
1898–1907/13	Prairie Provinces
Australia and New Zealand	
1872–79/91	Inland Victoria
	New South Wales
	Queensland
	New Zealand
1887–1913	Western Australia
South Africa	
1872–82	Cape
1886–99	Transvaal

Source: James Belich, *Replenishing the Earth. The Settler Revolution and the Rise of the Anglo-World 1783–1939* (Oxford, 2009), p. 89.

of the decade, however, there was a collapse in Argentina, a crisis in Australia and soon afterwards a crash in America.[38] When prosperity returned in 1895–6, Scottish capital in the United States never really recovered its previous value. The US economic system was now increasingly able to furnish future financial needs from its own resources. Table 7 confirms similar patterns in other parts of the world.

The Scots often did well through their overseas investments, but the evidence of extreme volatility in the different markets for land, ranching, railways and minerals meant that gains were often elusive. Scottish mortgage and investment trusts and mortgage companies experienced some painful losses in the 1880s and for some years in the following decades. Investment in mining speculation in particular rarely brought instant riches. Moreover, as W. T. Jackson has argued, the whole saga of financial enterprise at this time places a significant question against the stereotype of the 'canny Scots' with their reputation for thrift, prudence and caution, especially in money matters. Jackson's judgement is that with their imaginations fired by the successes of the 1870s they invested too rapidly, in too many schemes, and were in too great a hurry for instant dividends:

> A nation of four million which plunged approximately twenty millions sterling into western lands [in the USA], railroads, mines, ranches and forests within a three year period and then saw their investments lose one million pounds and depreciate in value, at least temporarily, another three million pounds within the twelve months of 1884, must certainly have impaired its reputation for canniness.[39]

3

By the later nineteenth century an extensive system of support was in place for the mobilization and transfer of many millions of pounds from the UK to the developing countries of the world. This enabled overseas investment to increase to levels unthinkable only a generation or two before. In the first instance, an information revolution had occurred by the 1870s, which ensured much easier and faster communication of financial knowledge between donor and receiver countries. The keystones in this transformation were the railway, the steamship and electric telegraph. In consequence, the number of letters flowing between Britain and the USA, which had reached 2 million by 1854, had tripled to 6 million twenty years later. Mail times from the UK to Australia halved between the 1830s and 1850s and halved again in the 1870s as a result of the expansion in steam services and the opening of the Suez Canal.[40] By 1851 telegraph wires traversed the USA and five years later a transatlantic submarine cable successfully linked Britain and America.

A striking feature of the investment saga was how agents and managers from Scottish companies were able to travel abroad regularly to check on the performance of their shareholdings to an extent that would have been impossible in the days of the sailing ship and the horse and carriage.[41] Information on financial markets also became abundant and more detailed in the national and regional press, the periodical literature, such as *The Statist* and *Blackwood's Edinburgh Magazine*, and in specialist pamphlets. Press advertisements in *The Scotsman*, the *Glasgow Herald* and in other papers placed by overseas governments advertising the opportunities in their countries were now commonplace. Twenty-one Australasian banks advertised deposits in *The Scotsman* alone in November 1890. Delegations from the same places appeared as frequent visitors in the Scottish capital. A remarkable example of this came in the aftermath of the great fire in Chicago of October 1871, which destroyed over 12,000 properties and resulted in losses of over £33 million. In the wake of this disaster, the city fathers sought funds from overseas to rebuild Chicago. They do not appear to have spent much time looking for support in the USA, but soon targeted the monied classes of Scotland as a likely source of capital. The delegation which arrived in Edinburgh in the early summer of 1874 brought with it letters of introduction from the great and good of Chicago and the state of Illinois, including the Governor, a US Senator, the city Mayor and the Secretary to the US Treasury.[42] It was confirmation of the high profile already achieved by Scottish financiers in American capital markets by that period. The Americans were not alone. One Australian finance company had eighty agents in Britain, of whom twenty-one were Scottish-based.[43]

Nor should the importance of the ever-growing Scottish diaspora be neglected, as personal and business links between lender and borrowers were often crucial.[44] Some went further and linked their connections abroad to those at home. Robert Burnett from Kincardineshire settled in the United States in the 1860s and did well in ranching. On his return to Britain he became involved in a number of enterprises formed to exploit the agricultural resources of the American West, including the Texas Land and Mortgage Company which derived much of its support from the north-east counties of Scotland, where Burnett was a member of a local landed family.[45] Another example was Andrew McIlwraith from Ayrshire. He became an influential promoter of numerous Australian shipping, pastoral and mining enterprises between 1875 and 1913 by forging relationships between his Scottish connections and the investment needs of his adopted country.[46]

In Scotland itself, the evolution of financial institutions before the 1870s meant that when the opportunities became known for massive investment abroad from that period on, the structures were in place to exploit them. Scottish banking had a long-standing reputation for innovative business practice from the late seventeenth century. By the 1800s, in addition, building societies, friendly societies and mutual savings associations were also said to be especially numerous in Scotland, often encouraged by the Churches. These institutions helped to spread the habit of making small contributions on a regular basis and so creating common and secure funds for investment, a key principle of the later investment trusts which were to become enormously important in mobilizing the savings of many thousands of people for overseas lending. The maturity of the Scottish financial system by the Victorian era was also confirmed by the expansion of the insurance companies. By the 1850s such famous names as Standard Life, Scottish Widows and Scottish Amicable were well established. At mid-century, the policy values of Scottish life assurance offices, at £34 million, were only slightly less than the total of Scottish bank deposits, which stood at £36 million.[47] Later in the nineteenth century, the big insurance companies were to play a full part in the great overseas investment bonanza.

Three other institutions, one traditional and historic, the other two new and innovative, were also vital. At the heart of the business was the Scottish legal profession. The *British Economist* noted in 1888 that 'there is hardly an influential firm of lawyers in the city [Edinburgh] which does not hold an agency for one or other of those colonial investment organisations', while one London-based Australian banker memorably described Edinburgh as 'honeycombed with agencies for collecting money not for use in Australia alone, but for India, Canada, South America – everywhere almost and for all purposes on the security of pastoral and agricultural lands in Texas, California, Queensland and Mexico'.[48] The solicitor in Scotland had always been trusted as the affluent family's 'man of business' who dealt regularly in financial matters such as stockbroking and land transactions. So, in this period, solicitors were able to become a nationwide investment network in Scottish localities, a veritable clearing-house moving surplus funds about to areas of potential opportunity and all within the close-knit world of the legal profession. The colonial agencies searching for investment came to them and also often employed them to represent their interests in Scotland. It was no coincidence, therefore, that lawyers were the prime factors in the formation of the trusts which played such a key role in the history of Scottish overseas investment in this period.

Two institutional developments were also central to the overseas investment boom. The first was the mid-nineteenth-century legislation governing joint stock companies that culminated in the Joint Stock Companies Acts of 1856 and 1862. A previous constraint on individuals of modest wealth investing some of their assets in productive enterprises was the danger of losing all their possessions if the venture collapsed. The joint stock companies legislation came as a godsend because henceforth the investor would only be liable for the nominal shares in the business to which he subscribed. At a stroke, the savings of great and small individuals of means were liberated for investment purposes. By 1900, joint stock pervaded the Scottish economy but did not dominate it.[49]

The second key element was the evolution of the investment trust.

The idea and practice had first been established in Belgium in the 1820s and the first British trust was founded in London in 1868. However, though by no means a Scottish invention, the investment trust became remarkably popular in Scotland, not least because Robert Fleming of Dundee, the main influence on the creation of one of the first, the Scottish American Investment Trust, in 1873, fully demonstrated its value. This was twofold. First, the key principle was to diversify the assets of the trust across a great range of investments in order to minimize risk. Second, expert advice on portfolio management was provided by the management of the trust. This was an essential advantage, especially in overseas markets, and was fundamental to the mobilization of capital from smaller shareholders, the very social group who, as seen earlier in this chapter, were fundamental to the growth of investment overseas on a larger scale than ever before. By 1914, there were 853 Edinburgh-registered general investment trusts, spanning a whole range of economic sectors, as Table 8 shows.[50]

Table 8: Scottish investment trusts, registered 1862–1914: sectoral breakdown

	Companies (number)	Initial capital and Nominal (total – £ million)	Shareholding Paid	Shareholdings (thousands)
Mining, quarrying, oil	376	21.02	9.54	22.6
Gold mining	163	9.19	4.48	12.4
Copper mining	29	4.91	1.98	4.3
Agriculture, ranching	184	20.53	7.49	18.4
Rubber plantation	46	2.33	1.12	7.5
Tea plantation	30	4.72	2.01	3.3
Livestock, ranching	21	5.48	1.57	3.4
Manufacturing	34	2.90	0.93	2.0
Jute spinning	7	1.27	0.20	1.0
Transport, Communications	18	2.71	0.81	0.4

Table 8: (*continued*)

	Companies (number)	Initial capital and Nominal (total – £ million)	Shareholding Paid	Shareholdings (thousands)
Services, utilities	42	2.68	0.70	1.1
General trading, agencies	31	2.67	0.60	0.9
Investment, real estate	148	38.91	10.31	23.1
Investment trusts, general investment	87	19.71	7.67	13.0
Mortgage companies	29	11.55	1.36	6.9
Land, real estate	31	7.45	1.28	3.2
Miscellaneous	10	0.40	0.07	0.4
General, unspecified	41	1.06	0.49	1.7
TOTAL	853	90.21	30.34	69.7

Source: Christopher Schmitz, 'The Nature and Dimensions of Scottish Foreign Investment 1860–1914', *Business History*, 39, 2 (1997), p. 47.

4

The trigger for what one journal of the time called the release of 'the golden flood' streaming out of Scotland to the colonies and the USA was, undeniably, the significantly higher returns which overseas investments for much of this period could earn compared to domestic opportunities.[51] *Blackwood's Edinburgh Magazine* stated in 1884:

> If the question were put, Why have Scottish investors become at once too partial to America and the colonies? The answer would be on the tip of every tongue – 'Because they pay the highest interest' ... Borrowed at 4 per cent and lending at 8 to 10 per cent, looks like an industry which should be encouraged in these dull times![52]

In the aftermath of the Great Fire of Chicago, when Scottish finance helped to rebuild the city, the chairman of the newly formed Scottish American Mortgage Company voiced similar sentiments: 'It does not require a very intimate knowledge of finances to understand that, if we can borrow in this country at 4½ and 5 per cent and advance in Chicago at 8 per cent there is a substantial profit ... any schoolboy can tell you that.'[53] For some sectors, however, even these handsome returns were less than what might be expected. For instance, of the eight Scottish American cattle companies operating in 1883, five returned dividends of between 10 and 20½ per cent.[54]

Expectation of high returns may have been the catalyst but the bonanza of overseas investment also depended on the huge increase of Scottish wealth earlier in the nineteenth century and the comparative prospects for investment in the Scottish economy itself. Scots themselves were fully aware of the radical transformation in their fortunes from earlier times. *Blackwood's Edinburgh Magazine* commented: 'In the course of the first half of the present century Scotland was changed from one of the poorest to one of the most prosperous countries in Europe. From an unknown inaccessible corner of the world it has been transformed within the life of two generations into the favourite haunt of the tourist and the home of merchant prince.'[55]

Precise evidence does not exist but some estimates provide a general guide to the revolution. In 1798, the nation's wealth was considered to be around £120 million. By 1910, the estimated figure was £1,451 million, a twelvefold increase in broad terms. Further, this enormous capital sum was very unevenly distributed.[56] Dudley Baxter's perspective of 1867 was that 0.33 per cent of 'productive persons' controlled a quarter of Scottish national income and just over 8 per cent of the same group absorbed just less than half (46.72 per cent) of national income.[57] This maldistribution ensured there was now a social elite with the capacity to invest on a truly grand scale. Their financial muscle had already been fully demonstrated during the great railway boom of the middle decades of the nineteenth century. By 1887 Scottish railway companies had over £101 million invested in stock. About 75,000 shareholders held an average holding of £1,350 in the system.[58] But by the 1880s the height of railway construction was over. The search was on for new opportunities. Between 1885 and 1910 the estimated national capital stock once again increased from £792 to £1,062 million.[59]

This remarkable pile was the fruit of three generations of Scottish industrialism. An examination of the shareholder lists of the Scottish limited companies reveals that much of the leadership in overseas investment were families that had made their fortunes during the Industrial Revolution before c.1860. The classic exemplars were the Dundee jute barons. It was the Baxters, Gilrays, Coxes and others, for example, who inspired young men of enterprise, such as the legendary Robert Fleming, to take the lead in the investment trusts which made the city a world centre of excellence in financial management.[60] As W. T. Jackson, the pioneering historian of Scottish investment in the American West, put it:

> The funds that were invested came from merchants and tradesmen, from manufacturers and bankers, from clerks, cashiers, and account-ants and from professional people – lawyers, doctors, ministers, teach-ers, and soldiers. Every class and occupation was represented; for this reason the fortunes of these companies, for good or evil, affected the economy and the people of Scotland in an exaggerated way.[61]

The obvious question then begs itself: why was investment at home so neglected in favour of sending the nation's wealth abroad on such a scale in this period? Domestic investment in the second, metal-based phase of Scottish industrialization and during the mid-century rail-way mania had indeed taken place on an unparalleled scale. If signifi-cant demand for funds for home-based industry had existed they would have been delivered. Yet Scottish capital generally lacked domestic outlets in the last three decades of the nineteenth century except for a short property boom and a brief period of manufacturing expansion in the early 1870s.[62] This is confirmed by the sustained decline in the rate of interest and the shift on the part of the big Scot-tish investment companies away from domestic investment because of falling yields.[63]

By the later 1880s, even Glasgow and the west of Scotland, the heartlands of heavy industry, were beginning to move into the over-seas capital markets. Quite simply, it was because there was now a glut of funds at home. As one expert commentator had it in 1884, 'money is a drug at home . . . "What home investments can you offer in their [overseas companies] place?" It is true for the moment, that capital appears to be over-abundant.'[64] An analysis of the investment portfolio of the Cox family, the greatest of all Dundee jute dynasties, reveals little that was Scottish, let alone local. In 1904 the family held shares in sixty-four companies, three-quarters of them were American and railways were pre-eminent. Most of the remainder were English businesses.[65]

The strategic weaknesses of the extraordinarily successful Scottish heavy-industry economy were now revealed in stark detail. The achievement had been built on low wages and the interlocking critical mass of shipbuilding, engineering, coal, iron and steel, which fixed the economy into the past rather than creating fresh opportunities for the future. Despite some attempts, the 'new' consumer-based manufactures (household goods, electrical products, motor cars and cycles), which were expanding south of the Border, did not take off in Scotland because of the levels of relative poverty among the mass of the population and the small size of the domestic market.[66] The nation, therefore, missed out on the next big stage of economic development. It was inevitable that in a private enterprise system capital, now surplus to domestic requirements, would move elsewhere.

Nonetheless, there was one area of Scottish society where the need for large-scale investment was clear, massive and urgent. Scottish housing for the mass of the people was appalling by the European standards of the time. One authority has suggested that in 1914 the country 'stood on the brink of a housing catastrophe'.[67] Nearly half the population lived in one- or two-roomed dwellings compared with just over 7 per cent in England. On the eve of the Great War, over 2 million Scots lived more than two to a room, the contemporary definition of overcrowding. But the opportunity for housing investment was more apparent than real. Indeed, there was even evidence that urban property was becoming even less popular for small investors in this period. Rates of return declined steadily, from 4 per cent per annum in the 1860s to 3.25 per cent per annum in the 1890s. Tenement property was especially unpopular with landlords as many poorer tenants found it difficult to pay rental on a regular basis. In 1890, for instance, the proportion of unlet housing stood at

11.2 per cent in Glasgow and the accumulation of arrears and proceedings for eviction were commonplace. Thus, those with savings to spare increasingly preferred to place their funds in stocks and shares.[68] In a society where private enterprise and the market ethos were dominant and virtually unquestioned, this was also an inevitable process. Thus, the story of overseas investment again recalls a key paradox at the core of Scottish society in the late nineteenth century: a nation of plenty for some coexisting with one of terrible poverty for many. In Dundee, the investment trust capital of Scotland and the source of many millions of pounds channelled abroad, a young academic newly appointed to the city's University College in 1904, recalled how appalled he was by what he saw then:

> Dundee was terribly poor. When I first came here the Greenmarket was full of idle men, walking to and fro, hungry and in rags. Of all those young professors who had come to Town, I doubt if there was one who was not shocked and saddened by the poverty of which Dundee openly displayed . . . Dundee was worse even than the slums of London, Glasgow and Liverpool; the infant mortality in Dundee under one year old was 50 per cent and only one Child in five lived to three years old.[69]

The acute social problems of Glasgow would have undeniably elicited a similar shocked response from any sensitive observer, able to see beyond the architectural magnificence of the urban centre to the human squalor and degradation which was all too close nearby. Despite its record of colossal economic achievement and global preeminence, it was indeed a tragic paradox that Victorian and Edwardian Scotland bequeathed such a baleful social legacy to the twentieth-century nation.

12

Eclipse of Empires

I

On the eve of the Great War Scotland was at the pinnacle of global prominence. Despite growing concerns in the late nineteenth century about international competition and structural weaknesses, the nation's major industries still possessed a world reach. Shipbuilding, the primary motor of the domestic economy, remained pre-eminent as in 1914 the Clyde yards built not only a third of British tonnage but almost a fifth of the world's total output. As George Blake's fictional hero, Leslie Pagan, told his men in the novel *The Shipbuilders*, 'there was not one of [the] yards but had two or three big ships a-building, so that up and down the River the bows of vessels unlaunched towered over the tenement buildings of the workers and people passing could hardly hear themselves speak for the noise of metal upon metal that filled the valley from Old Kilpatrick to Govan'.[1] Then there was the interlinked and massive complex of coal, steel, iron and engineering, employing over a third of a million men or a quarter of the entire Scottish labour force, all dependent on the ebb and flow of overseas markets in the Empire, Europe and a host of other countries. Nor was the global dependency unique to the heavy industries of the west. The other manufacturing sectors – carpets, thread, cotton, jute and woollens – covering the country from the Borders to the north-east Lowlands had a broadly similar orientation. The nation's global economic significance was also confirmed by the continuing success of the great Scottish trading and shipping companies in Asia and Africa.

The outbreak of war confirmed the vital importance of the Scottish economy to the imperial cause. During the years 1914–18 Scottish industry became a vast military arsenal. Unrestricted submarine warfare later in the war destroyed the equivalent of nearly a third of the pre-1914 British merchant fleet and created a prodigious new source of demand for the shipbuilding yards of the Clyde. Engineering and metal production were diverted to the mass delivery of guns and shells. The linen and woollen districts of Scotland supplied huge amounts of canvas for tenting and clothing for troops. Trench warfare, the enduring image of the Great War, would have been impossible without the innumerable sandbags made from Dundee jute. By 1918 over 1,000 million of them had been shipped to the fronts in Europe. Carpet factories were converted to make blankets for the army, with Templetons of Glasgow alone producing over 4 million a year by the end of the war.[2] In the same year the Clyde Valley had become the single most important concentration of munitions production in the United Kingdom, with the great heavy industries of the region under government control, regulation or direction because of their vital importance in the war effort.

Victory in 1918 not only consolidated but extended the Empire into new areas of Africa and the Middle East, as former German colonies and great swathes of the former Ottoman Empire were annexed or became protectorates of the Crown. British rule now encompassed around 700 million of the world's population. The role of the Scots as the key junior partners in Empire was also maintained. As soldiers, missionaries, merchants, doctors, engineers, scientists, planters and administrators, the careers of numerous professional and middle-class Scots continued to be pursued within the imperial domain. In addition, as peace was restored, so the age-old migration of the Scottish people across the Atlantic, to Australasia and elsewhere resumed. Indeed, in the 1920s, the exodus reached unprecedented levels, even by the standards of the migrations of Victorian times.

Ironically, however, this particular exodus was in large part stimulated by an historic crisis which was to begin the unravelling of Scotland's long-established place in global markets. The details of the nation's trauma between the wars and especially in the early 1930s are well-known and require only a brief overview here, though it must be said, of course, that the period was not all doom and gloom for Scottish industry.[3] For those who were in a job, standards of living rose for much of the period. As a result the relatively small part of the manufacturing economy geared to domestic consumers did well. Carpets, linoleum, hosiery and knitwear were especially successful, although they were relatively modest employers of labour. But the giants of the nineteenth-century economy were either in the doldrums in most years or endured acute crisis, which seemed to reinforce the belief of some observers that Scotland was in a state of terminal decline.[4] After a brief post-war boom, jute experienced a drop in demand and encountered savage overseas competition. At the depth of the depression in the early 1930s nearly half the industry's labour force was unemployed. From the mid-1920s demand for coal ceased to grow and employment slumped from 155,000 in 1920 to 81,000 in 1933 as the industry struggled against competition in its traditional markets from the new energy sources of oil, gas and electricity. Steel-making was sluggish throughout the rest of the interwar period and never recovered the position it had attained during the early 1920s. This was hardly surprising since its fortunes depended on the economic anchor of shipbuilding, which was itself in long-term decline. On the one hand, world shipbuilding capacity had more than doubled during the Great War and its immediate aftermath; on the other hand, the trade between primary producers and industrial countries, the basic engine of international commerce which drove demand for new ships before 1914, languished for most of the 1920s and 1930s. A chronic problem of global over-capacity in shipbuilding emerged. One estimate suggests that the difficulties were such that British yards could easily have built all the new tonnage required in the world between 1921 and 1939 and still be left with some spare capacity. The crisis in demand for merchant vessels was aggravated by the termination of many warship orders after the signing of the Washington Treaty for the Limitation of Naval Armaments in 1922. It was cold comfort that the Clyde, because of its expertise in passenger liners, for which the market remained a little more buoyant, was not quite as badly hit as the Tyne and Wear yards.[5]

The Great War also ended the golden age of growth for the Scottish trading companies. The interwar environment became highly unfavourable to their continued business success.[6] The collapse of world trade, their core business, caused unprecedented challenges. The rate of growth of total trade per decade declined from an average of almost 40 per cent between 1881 and 1913 to 14 per cent between 1913 and 1937. Protectionism became rife and reached new heights in the 1930s. In 1932 Britain itself abandoned free trade, and by the end of the decade nearly half the commerce of the world was restricted by tariffs. The growing importance of Japan in the Asian markets further added to the gloom. Profits fell and some firms were pushed to the very edge. Grahams, for instance, an interlinked merchant partnership based in Glasgow, India and Portugal, was badly hit by the recession of 1920–21 and eventually collapsed. Yet, for the most part, the other great Scottish syndicates survived, albeit after experiencing losses in several years. Since the majority were still family-controlled, partners were willing to sacrifice gains in difficult times to ensure the longer-term survival of the business until the hoped-for recovery took place.

As intensive rearmament and the Second World War revived and then expanded the domestic economy, it might have seemed that Scotland had weathered the international storm and the nation's greatest single challenge to domestic manufacturing since the Industrial Revolution. Virtually full employment returned by the early 1940s while post-war retooling and rebuilding, together with the temporary elimination of German and Japanese competition, seemed to bode well for the future. Ironically, by the 1950s, the traditional staple industries of Scotland were even more entrenched within the economic structure of the nation than they had been in 1939. Yet it soon became apparent that the old problems of slow growth and limited diversification into 'new' manufacturing had not gone away. By the end of the 1950s, it was said that Scotland was living in a fool's paradise.[7]

The economic boom was now seen to depend on the temporary conditions of replacement demand after 1945 and the virtual absence of international competition while the ravaged economies of Europe and the Far East recovered from the devastation of war. There had still been precious little industrial diversification in Scotland. In the west of Scotland, heartland of the traditional industries, the rate of entry of new companies in the 1950s was about half that of the 1940s. The most serious concerns were voiced about the condition of the industrial staples. Coal in particular faced a bleak future. The once-rich Lanarkshire field was almost worked out, while many consumers

18. Andrew Carnegie (1835–1919). Born into a family of weavers in Dunfermline, he rose to become America's richest man and later in life a philanthropist without peer.

19. Scottish curling in New York. The impact of Scottish sports in the New World was not confined to the popularity of Highland games.

Jake Grandma Bob Margaret Lizzie
Dave Jim Nap in Arms Carley
Jolly Hous

20. Mrs Jean Jolly, originally from Glenesk in Angus, with her family outside their new home in Deer Trail, Colorado.

21. William Landsborough (1825–86). Scottish explorer of Australia, with his guide, a young Aboriginal boy, 1858.

22. Sir George Simpson (1792–1860) in Vancouver Island, 1855. Simpson, from Dingwall, became a pivotal figure in the Hudson Bay Company, being dubbed 'Emperor of the Plains'.

23. James Augustus Grant (1827–92). Scottish soldier and explorer of Africa. Grant, in the right foreground, is dancing with a woman in an East African village in 1861, during his travels with the explorer J. H. Speke.

24. David Livingstone (1813–73). The supreme Victorian icon of missionary and exploring endeavour.

25. Robert Moffat (1795–1883). Bringing the Gospel to the heathen in Africa.

26. Robert Morrison (1782–1834) with his Chinese
assistants, translating the Bible into Chinese.

27. 91st Highlanders and 2nd Gurkhas storming Gandia Mullah during the
Afghan War, 1877–80. Images such as these confirmed the reputation of the
Highland regiments as the invincible shock troops of imperial expansion.

28. Piper Lang from Aberdour passing on the martial spirit to the next generation. This image was used as a recruiting poster for the Gordon Highlanders until the Great War.

29. Amris Highlanders, 1879. The fighting qualities of the Scottish regiments led to Afghan troops being dressed in kilts to instil in them a similar élan.

30. 'A Highland Regiment on its way to the trenches'. Scots contributed disproportionately to the rapid expansion of the volunteer army in 1914.

31. Soldiers of the Black Watch in Hong Kong, 1997, during the ceremonies of transfer of the colony to China, in which they played a central role.

32. Ten-year-old Billy Neil of Glasgow with his football, en route to Australia on the *Ormonde* in 1947.

33. The Igoe family from Edinburgh awaiting their train in London, en route to a new life in Melbourne in 1955.

34. President Dwight D. Eisenhower signing the drum from the State University of Iowa's Scottish Highlanders Band in 1956, one sign of the renaissance of interest in Scottish heritage in the USA from the 1950s.

35. The 'Kirking o' the Tartan' at Grandfather Mountain Highland Games, 2009: an American addition to a Scottish tradition.

36. Clan Gregor, with the South African flag to the fore, march up the Royal Mile to Edinburgh Castle during The Gathering, 2009.

were moving to electricity, oil and gas. The conversion of locomotives from coal-burning to diesel engines, and steel furnaces from coal to oil-fired, cut deeply into much of the traditional market for coal. Steel was better placed. In 1957 Scotland's first integrated iron and steel works, built at a cost of £22.5 million, was brought into production at Ravenscraig near Motherwell. But by that time Europe had recovered from the war, much more steel was being produced and, with a world surplus building up, price-cutting became a common strategy. Despite the Ravenscraig investment, the Scottish steel industry remained vulnerable because of its inland location and consequent high costs for ore transportation and delivery of the finished products.

Also, even before the late 1950s Scottish shipbuilding was losing much of its world ascendancy as, though global demand for ships was still very buoyant, the Clyde's share of output was already in steady decline. In 1947, Clyde yards launched 18 per cent of world tonnage, but this share had slumped to 4.5 per cent in 1958. Scottish shipbuilding, once a world-class industry, was in a sorry state and it now seemed that the many long-standing problems had simply been concealed by the post-war replacement boom. Certainly German, Dutch, Swedish and Japanese yards had the benefit of more lavish state support, but many of the wounds of Scottish shipbuilders were self-inflicted. While their rivals adopted streamlined assembly-line techniques, invested extensively in mechanization and designed well-planned yards, the Scots stood still, apart from the replacement of riveting by welding and improvements in prefabrication. They were now rapidly losing their competitive edge. In the later 1950s German yards could frequently deliver ships in half the time quoted by Clyde builders. Indecisive management and workers caught up in numerous union demarcation disputes bore a collective responsibility for this state of affairs, which, although by no means inevitable, before too long would bring a once-mighty industry to the brink of total collapse.[8]

In truth, Scotland was no longer the economic superpower it had been in the past. The old commercial empire was in its death throes. The nation's impact on the world economy receded with the continued malaise of the heavy industries, several of which were now kept afloat only by the nationalization of steel and coal in the 1940s, lavish government intervention in the 1960s and the overriding post-war policy by the state of a commitment to full employment. It was not, therefore, surprising that when the government withdrew life support in the 1980s and prioritized the control of inflation over the guaranteeing of employment the traditional pillars of Scottish industry disintegrated with frightening speed.[9] The take-over of Scottish companies by outside interests speeded up so that by 1960 over 60 per cent of all manufacturing firms employing more than 250 people were owned by non-Scottish interests, primarily from England and the USA.[10] Some concluded gloomily that Scotland had sunk to the level of 'a branch-plant economy'. The irony was that as the old ruling families sold up, they often transferred their gains into investment trusts and the like, so helping to boost Scotland's financial sector in later decades.[11] But the tables were now well and truly turned. While Scottish finance had helped to transform the New World in the nineteenth century, overseas companies had now become major players in Scotland. By 1964 direct investment from the USA alone supported 52,000 jobs, and by the 1970s 40 per cent of manufacturing labour in Scotland was employed by English-owned firms. This was also the time which saw the final demise of most of the great Scottish trading companies in the Far East. Acquisitions, mergers and nationalization by post-imperial governments brought to an end the long and independent histories of such illustrious firms as Gray Mackenzie (1960), the Borneo Company (1967), Wallace Brothers (1977) and Guthries (1981).[12]

But perhaps judged against the panorama of the past, the major watershed for Scotland might be seen to have been the rapid collapse of the British Empire. The 700 million imperial subjects of 1945 had fallen to fewer than 5 million but two decades later. Of these, over 3 million were in the last major colony, Hong Kong, which itself returned to Chinese rule in 1997. Scots soldiers had been among the military spearheads of Empire. Now in its twilight years they assumed the role of pallbearers.[13] The British army in India beat the final retreat to the sound of the pipes and drums playing 'Auld Lang Syne' in 1947. Five decades later it was the band of the Black Watch which took centre stage when Hong Kong reverted to Chinese rule in July 1997. The British contingent led by the last Governor, Chris Patten, and the

Prince of Wales, left for *Britannia* to the dirge 'Will ye no' come back again?', first composed for another royal personage, Bonnie Prince Charlie, long after he had fled into exile in France in 1746.

2

Insofar as the subject has attracted attention at all, discussion of the issue of the response of the Scottish people to the retreat from empire has tended to focus on its later impact on Scottish political development.[14] Some have introduced the apparently plausible argument that since the Empire was for Scots in particular the sheet-anchor of the union state its disappearance would also spell the end of the Anglo-Scottish Union. They point to the sustained rise in the popularity of the Scottish National Party (SNP) since the 1960s to support their assertion and the cracks that were starting to appear in the Scottish consensus on Union over the same period. The onset of devolution in 1999, followed in the early years of the new millennium by the first-ever SNP minority government in Edinburgh, might also be seen to give some credibility to this thesis.

But the case is far from proven. Historians are naturally sceptical about any suggestion which might smack of the *post hoc, ergo propter hoc* fallacy, 'after this, therefore because of this'. On the whole, therefore, they have tended to look elsewhere for the root causes of devolution, and have found them in the broader rise of nationalism throughout Europe (which helped to usher in the collapse of the Soviet Union) and the profound disenchantment in Scotland in the later 1960s and 1970s when both Tory and Labour governments seemed incapable of arresting national economic decline while the British state struggled against recurrent currency crises and inflationary pressures in those decades.[15] Even these stresses, however, were not yet enough to trigger a general demand for more Scottish autonomy, as the failed first referendum on Home Rule in 1979 confirmed. It was only in the 1990s, half a century after India left the Empire, that a firm consensus for devolution built up. That seems not to have been fashioned by nostalgia for either lost imperial glory or former colonial material advantage. Rather, it came about because of the acute economic crisis of the 1980s, the so-called 'democratic deficit' caused by the Scots persistently voting Labour but being governed instead by what many regarded as anti-Scottish Tory administrations in London, and those administrations' decisions to abandon supportive corporatist policies which had maintained the survival of much of Scottish industry.[16] It was the political reaction to these developments which fashioned the backbone of the movement for a Scottish Parliament. Hence, Margaret Thatcher has an infinitely greater claim to be the midwife of Scottish devolution than the influence of imperial decline. Critics also point out that in 2010, several decades after the end of Empire, the Union, reformed by devolution, remains, though enthusiasm for even stronger powers of Home Rule persists. But over several years the cause of independence per se has rarely attracted more than between 20 and 30 per cent of the Scottish electorate. Only time will tell whether, in the much longer term, the withdrawal from Empire in the mid-twentieth century might still come to be seen by future historians as a watershed period if indeed a break-up of the United Kingdom does come about.

Yet, two aspects of that period do suggest that the withdrawal from empire in the late 1940s and 1950s did not cause the expected serious reactions in Scotland. Perhaps not surprisingly, Scots-born imperial civil servants and other officials in the bureaucracies of the African empire in particular were, on the whole, opposed to decolonization, not simply as a result of vested career interests, but because many thought that the African colonies were not yet ready for full independence.[17] Those responses apart, it is difficult to find outside the columns of the Empire-leaning Beaverbrook Press's *Scottish Daily Express* any opposition to or anxiety about the retreat from empire in the public press. The files of the *Glasgow Herald* and *The Scotsman* for 1947, when India and Pakistan became independent, do not even mention any likely adverse effect on Scotland. Instead, the tone was one of acceptance, bordering on indifference, some praise for the contribution of the Raj to Indian development and warm good wishes for the future of both India and Pakistan as independent states. The Scottish role in the Indian empire, now well rehearsed by historians, was not discussed or even hinted at in the sympathetic valedictory opinion columns. If there was concern it was about the menace of possible racial tension and conflict between Hindu and Muslim in the subcontinent after the British had gone. Even the *Dundee Courier*, the newspaper of the city with the deepest Scottish connections to India in the past through jute manufacture, did not voice regret and (remarkably) did not even allude to the long historical relationship between Dundee and the newly independent state.

The second intriguing aspect was the post-imperial silence in Scotland concerning empire and the nation's historic central role in its development. Between Andrew Dewar Gibb's *Scottish Empire*, published in 1937, and Michael Fry's *The Scottish Empire*, which appeared in 2001, not a single book was published on what some now regard as a development that can rank with the Reformation, the Enlightenment and the Industrial Revolution as among the key formative influences on the modern nation of Scotland. The imperial historian of Scottish-birth John Mackenzie, who then worked at an English university, published a seminal article on Scotland and Empire in 1993 but even it did not in the short term stimulate much scholarly stirring north of the Border.[18] The 1970s and 1980s were indeed decades of lively advance in Scottish historiography, but this rebirth was paralleled by disinterest in the subject of empire. One historian could write as recently as 1997 that 'Few areas of Scottish history have been as neglected as the contribution made by Scots to British imperialism, in spite of the fact that nineteenth-century Scotland rejoiced in its self-proclaimed status as a nation of "Empire builders".' Instead, some sociologists bizarrely even began to suggest that Scotland was more of a colonized than a colonizing nation, an 'internal colony' of the British state. The nation's imperial past was threatened with premature burial under numerous theories of 'under development' and 'internal colonialism', which purported to show that the relationship with England during the Age of Empire had been one-sided and exploitative for the junior partner.[19] During the same decades, the general Scottish public, if they read much history at all, preferred to devour the Highland trilogy of the popular writer John Prebble, with their immensely dark central narratives of victimhood, loss and a tragic national past.

Doubtless there may be some obvious reasons for this national collective amnesia. The myth of Scotland as an egalitarian society par excellence was fortified as never before as the nation overwhelmingly moved to the political left from the 1970s. That world view obviously sat uneasily with some of the unpleasant realities of an imperial past. But what is striking was not that there was some kind of social and intellectual conspiracy to avoid the history of Scotland and empire. Rather, the mood was one of indifference and disinterest. The topic was simply irrelevant. There is here an intriguing difference with England which reaches down to the present day. One historian of England and empire, in a book published in 2005, noted that 'After years of neglect, the Empire is everywhere today – in novels, newspapers and museums, on radio and television. Indeed, the British appear to be attached to their imperial past like a mooring rope; the further they travel, the more they feel its pull.'[20] Not so in Scotland. Scholarly interest is indeed now at an all-time high but popular engagement still remains at a low level.[21] South of the Border, the 200th anniversary of the abolition of the British slave trade attracted unprecedented attention in schools, exhibitions, conferences and the media. In Scotland, interest was very much more muted. The Scots, on the face of it, therefore, seem to have shed the memory of empire with conspicuous ease and little fuss. Why is this?

3

One possible answer is to question the very premise that the British Empire was ever of central significance to the mass of the Scottish people, a view which has a long pedigree. Some time ago, for instance, the novelist H. G. Wells famously remarked that nineteen citizens out of twenty knew as much about the British Empire as they did about the Italian Renaissance.[22] More recently, however, a powerful and detailed exploration of this thesis has come from the pen of Bernard Porter in his *The Absent-Minded Imperialists: Empire, Society and Culture in Britain* (2004). Despite its subtitle, Porter's focus is almost entirely Anglocentric. In 108 pages of end-notes and 30 pages of 'select' bibliography, there is only one article with a Scottish emphasis. Essentially, therefore, it is for English historians to judge the overall validity of his thesis. Porter argues that 'the ordinary Briton's relationship to the Empire in the nineteenth and early twentieth centuries was complex and ambivalent, less soaked in or affected by imperialism ... to the extent that many English people, at any rate possibly even a majority were almost entirely ignorant of it for most of the nineteenth century'. He readily concedes, however, that 'The Scots may be a different matter.'[23]

In this book and its predecessor, *Scotland's Empire 1600–1815* (2003), it is argued that whatever the English experience, the evidence for Scotland is unambiguous. Indeed, so intense was Scottish engagement with empire that it had an impact on almost every nook and cranny of Scottish life over two centuries: economy, identity, politics, intellectual activity, popular culture, consumerism, religion, demographic trends and much else. In the 1700s the colonial tobacco and sugar trades were two of the key drivers of eighteenth-century Scottish industrialization, while during the Victorian and Edwardian eras the Scottish heavy industrial economy was strongly biased towards export markets and the principal outlets for ships, locomotives and engineering products were the British colonies. Dundee became 'Juteopolis', its booming textile industry founded on the importation of raw jute from India. Gordon Stewart, later an historian who went on to write an important study of jute, recalled the imperial connections of his native city in the 1950s:

I grew up in Dundee and I thought that the Scottish city was the centre of the world jute trade. This impression was dinned into me by my geography lessons at school and by a host of childhood encounters with jute. When I felt depressed by the drabness of life amidst the row of identical, rain-stained buildings on the housing scheme where I lived, I would pedal my bike down to the docks and watch hundreds of bales of jute being unloaded from the holds of great cargo steamers which had sailed half-way round the world from Chittagong and Calcutta. On the way home from school I would sit on city buses crowded with women workers coming off their shifts with wisps of jute sticking to their hair and clothes and their hands roughened red by the handling of jute in the factories ... because of the names on the sterns of the cargo ships and the faces of the crewmen, I understood there was an Indian dimension to jute. I also learned of this connection by listening to family stories about relatives and friends of my parents who had spent time in India.[24]

In Glasgow, the economic connections were equally deep. It arrogated to itself the description 'Second City of Empire' (a term first used as early as 1824), while the broader west of Scotland region was later celebrated as 'The Workshop of the British Empire'. Scottish society more generally had strong ties to empire. As has been seen throughout this book, for much of the nineteenth century Scottish educators, physicians, soldiers, administrators, missionaries, engineers, scientists and merchants relentlessly penetrated every corner of the Empire and beyond, so that in virtually any area of professional employment examined, Scots had a high profile.

This elite emigration was, of course, but one element in a greater mass diaspora. As seen in Chapter 4, between 1825 and 1938 over 2.3 million Scots left their homeland for overseas destinations. These huge levels of emigration generated a vast network of family and individual connections with the colonies and dominions which endured into the later twentieth century. The links were consolidated by return migration (by one estimate averaging more than 40 per cent of the total exodus in the 1890s), chain migration, letter correspondence and widespread coverage of the emigrant experience in the Scottish popular press and periodical literature. The *People's Journal*, the biggest-selling working-class periodical, rarely published an issue without some imperial and/or emigration content, as did *Forward*, the journal of the Independent Labour Party in the early twentieth century.

The British Empire also had a potent influence on Scottish national consciousness and identity. For the elite in the years before 1914 Scottish patriotism was not in conflict with the Union, but rather integrated closely with it. The Empire was the means by which the Scots asserted their equal partnership with England after 1707. As noted earlier, in the Victorian era it was commonplace to assert that substantial imperial expansion only occurred *after* the Union, and hence was a joint endeavour between the partners in which the Scots had played their full part. This was no empty boast. Scottish publicists, through such works as John Hill Burton's *The Scots Abroad* (2 vols., 1864) and W. J. Rattray's monumental four-volume *magnum opus*, *The Scot in British North America* (1880), were easily able to demonstrate the mark that Scottish education (especially at college and university level), Presbyterianism, medicine, trading networks and philosophical enquiry had had on the colonies. Pride in the Scottish achievement was taken even further by those who saw the Scottish people as a unique race of natural empire-builders. Thus Andrew Dewar Gibb argued in 1930:

> ... the position of Scotland as a Mother nation of the Empire is at all costs to be preserved to her. England and Scotland occupy a unique position as the begetters and defenders of the Empire. They alone of all the Aryan peoples in it have never been otherwise sovereign and independent. Ireland and Wales, mere satrapos of England, can claim no comparable place. Scotsmen today are occupying places both eminent and humble throughout the Empire, and Scottish interests are bound up with every colony in it.[25]

Nonetheless, it might be objected that the argument thus far ignores the important factor of differences in the attitudes between social classes to empire. Porter focuses especially on this aspect by suggesting that the upper and middle classes were most committed to the imperial project while the working classes were 'either apathetic towards the Empire or superficial in their attitude to it'.[26] While it is impossible, of course, in the current state of knowledge to determine in precise terms what the ordinary Scot thought about empire, it is nevertheless unlikely that the words 'apathy' and 'ignorance' are at all appropriate terms to use of national public opinion. For a start, exposure to imperial themes started early in Scotland. In 1907 the Scottish Education Department, in its memorandum on the teaching of history in schools, directed that the curriculum should develop from the study of Scotland to British and then international themes, but always throughout stressing the nation's role in the Empire. Textbooks embodying this approach were soon available in schools. The most popular was *Cormack's Caledonia Readers*, which placed very considerable emphasis on empire. The British Empire had a key part to play in late nineteenth-century history teaching because it provided the kind of blend of British and Scottish history which reflected Scotland's position in the union state.[27] Interestingly, this was not apparently the pattern in England, where 'The Empire and empire-related matters were almost never mentioned in schools at any level.'[28]

But this was not all. The early 1900s also saw the widespread celebration of 'Empire Day', when flags were exchanged between Scottish schools and those elsewhere in the Empire.[29] The stories of such imperial heroes as General Gordon, Sir Colin Campbell, Mary Slessor and, above all, David Livingstone would have been very familiar to Scottish schoolchildren. Biographies of Livingstone were widely read and also awarded as prizes in schools and Sunday schools, a practice which continued unabated through to the 1960s. Of course it was not simply children who were taught to respond to these imperial heroes. They were also celebrated by the trade-union movement, working-men's clubs and Labour politicians such as Keir Hardie as models of Scottish virtue and exemplars for the nation. Knowledge of and loyalty to empire was also communicated by such organizations as the Junior Empire League, with around 20,000 members, and the Boys' Brigade. The 'BBs' remained enormously popular among young Protestant Scots boys well into the second half of the twentieth century.[30]

As the cinema developed a huge following, most Scots were brought for the first time face to face with the visual and moving images of the distant and exotic territories of empire. An industrial town like Motherwell had four cinemas by 1914 and Glasgow sixty-six. In 1938, Glasgow's cinemas had increased to an astonishing 104, and going to 'the pictures' became the craze of the age. Admission charges of between 1d. and 6d. were very low compared to the theatre and it was therefore hardly surprising that working-class men, women and children flocked to the cinemas. Film had magical and universal appeal. A survey of children in West Lothian conducted in 1937 found that over a third attended 'the pictures' once a week and a quarter more than once. A mere 6 per cent of interviewees never went.[31] Among the subjects of documentaries and newsreels shown were the Boer War and the great Durbar in Delhi in 1911, possibly the most lavish spectacle ever mounted by the British Raj, with 233 encampments covering 25 square miles and 2 huge amphitheatres, one able to accommodate 100,000 spectators. Commercial films with an imperial theme were also popular, with such action movies as *Gunga Din* (1939), *Lives of a Bengal Lancer* (1935) and *The Four Feathers* (1939) doing specially well at the box-office in the years immediately before the Second World War.[32]

Among the mass of the population, a key symbol of empire were the Scottish regiments. Widely celebrated in music, story, painting and statue as the tartan-clad icons of the Scottish nation, they enjoyed unchallenged prominence in Scottish society as symbols of national self-image. Nowhere else in Britain was there such a profound connection between identity and militarism as the regiments made a remarkable impact on Scottish consciousness. Seen as the heirs of a martial national tradition which went back for centuries, they also acted as important catalysts for the wide diffusion of the military ethic throughout the country. One major spin-off, as has been noted, was the Volunteer movement, which developed into a permanent reserve force for the army and attracted many thousands of young Scotsmen. The Volunteers were a focus for local pride but they also strongly identified with the Empire. Both the Volunteers and the Boys' Brigade adopted army ranks and nomenclature, undertook military drill and were regularly inspected by army officers. The fame and significance of the Scottish military tradition lives on to the present day, as illustrated by the continuing success of the Edinburgh Military Tattoo and the political controversies during the 2005 General Election over the proposed reorganization of the historic Scottish regiments.

There therefore seems to be a huge gap between the imperial enthusiasms of the nineteenth and early twentieth centuries and the apparent equanimity with which Scotland accepted decolonization in the middle decades of the twentieth century. For it is the case that imperial sentiment still flourished in the decade after the Great War. The massive losses suffered by Scotland, officially counted at 74,000 but unofficially reckoned to be over 110,000, were commemorated in the Scottish National War Memorial dedicated at Edinburgh Castle in 1927. It was not simply a remarkable tribute in stone to the nation's fallen but also to the sons and grandsons of Scotland from the Empire. The Roll of Honour included all those who had served in Scottish regiments and in those of the dominions overseas, an eloquent affirmation of the continuing importance of the imperial bond.[33]

The link between empire and the national churches also seemed robust. The cult of David Livingstone reached its apotheosis in the 1920s when numerous small donations by ordinary Scots financed the creation of the Livingstone Memorial Centre in Blantyre, Lanarkshire, at the very cotton-mill complex where the explorer and missionary had worked as a boy. The Centre remained a very popular place of pilgrimage for schools and Sunday Schools until the 1950s. The public face of imperial Scotland also seemed to have changed little. A great imperial exhibition was held in Glasgow in 1938, the fourth in a series that since the 1890s had attracted literally millions of visitors. As late as 1951 a colonial week was held in the same city. Empire was also still very much on the political agenda. In the interwar years factional arguments raged in the Scottish nationalist movement over the nature of the relationship which a self-governing Scotland would have with the Empire. Even the Labour Party temporarily diluted earlier hostility, and some of its leading intellectuals in Scotland, including John Wheatley, argued that through the Empire could come not only economic regeneration but also the hope of protecting a socialist Britain from the menace of international capitalism.[34]

4

Some write as if empire was the main economic anchor of Scotland in the nineteenth and early twentieth centuries, and it is the case that important trade, emigration, investment and market links with the imperial territories cannot be denied. They were very real and they were very significant. But by the end of the Victorian era the imperial connections were no longer the only set of Scottish overseas relationships. The USA, Europe and other non-empire countries were also as important for trade and markets. Moreover, the Empire had not saved Scotland from the great crisis of the interwar period. Indeed, the nation's external markets among the world's primary producers of foods and raw materials were especially badly hit and Canada, Australia, New Zealand and India were among the most significant of these. The most arresting illustration of the new economic context of empire was the experience between the wars of the Dundee jute industry. Already, by the 1890s, Bengal had overtaken its Scottish parent to become the world's dominant manufacturing centre for the jute sacks and hessian cloth which carried the world's foodstuffs. Not surprisingly, in the depressed market conditions of the 1930s, Dundee jute interests pleaded on numerous occasions for tariffs to be imposed on the cheap imports from Calcutta. But their pleas were in vain. Now it was Dundee which looked more like the colony, and Bengal the metropole: 'jute presents an unusual example of a powerful industry emerging in a colonial setting which almost destroyed the rival indus-try back in Britain while the empire was still flourishing'.[35]

Moreover, the experience of the hard times of the 1930s and total war of the 1940s had begun to convince most Scots as never before of the high priority of the domestic social issues of employment, welfare and personal security. This new mood was crystallized after the pub-lication of the Beveridge Report in December 1942. Immediately, the Report and the Summary became best-sellers; large queues formed outside the shops of His Majesty's Stationery Office to buy them and a Gallup Poll discovered that nineteen out of twenty people had heard of the proposals a mere fortnight after their publication. Copies soon found their way to the troops at the fronts and even in POW camps. One soldier recalled: 'I was in a prisoner-of-war camp when the Bev-eridge Report came out. Somebody had a copy sent to them and the excitement that this caused was quite marked and there were big dis-cussions and debates about why we had been fighting. It always seemed clear to me that the army, by and large, was going to vote left.'[36]

Beveridge provided a blueprint for post-war society that would commit government to the conquest of the historic enemies for ordin-ary people of Want, Disease, Ignorance, Squalor and Idleness. Family allowances should be provided for all children, mass unemployment could be avoided by state planning and intervention in the economy and a National Health Service would be established. Citizens would be covered for all their needs from cradle to grave through a single weekly insurance contribution. At the heart of the proposals was the idea of the 'national minimum', a basic level of income below which no one should be allowed to fall. All this had a magical appeal for the mass of the population, although government was less enthusiastic. The War Minister banned discussion of the Report in the army's com-pulsory current affairs classes, while the Cabinet equivocated before agreeing to accept the recommendations in principle, insisting that only a new government elected after the war could implement the necessary legislation. The Tories were therefore regarded as lukewarm on Beveridge's plans and overly concerned about their potential cost. Perhaps this helped to seal their fate in Scotland in the election of 1945. To the 'stupefied surprise' of the *Glasgow Herald*, Labour swept to power in the UK, notched up 17 Scottish seats and attracted nearly 48 per cent of the votes cast north of the border.[37] Thus, when the expected independence of India became a settled fact in 1947, the concerns of the Scots were already more focused on the new welfare reforms in health, social security and pensions and employment prospects in the post-war economy. The Welfare State and the commitment of the Labour government to the pursuit of policies of full employment, rather than nostalgic dreams of empire, now became the new anchors of the union state.

Two other factors were also relevant. First, Scottish emotional links of family and kindred were not mainly with India and the African colonies but rather with the Dominions of Canada, Australia, New Zealand and South Africa, the countries of mass Scottish settlement over many generations. Their autonomy as members of the British Commonwealth of Nations had been confirmed in the Statute of Westminster of 1931. But this 'independence' in no way destroyed the links of kith and kin. On the contrary, the enthusiastic commitment of the Dominion forces to the war against Nazi Germany and their courageous contributions to victory during it, confirmed that the bonds with the mother country still held very fast. The renewal of Scottish emigration after 1945 continued to refresh these links where it really counted – at the human, personal and familial level. Over 300,000 Scots left between 1950 and 1970, the decades when the Dominions were giving very strong encouragement to immigration from Britain.[38] (See Chapter 13.)

Secondly, two influential institutions in Scotland were becoming concerned by the 1950s about the morality of continued imperial rule. This was particularly the case in relation to some of the African colonies which had long had close association with Scotland through missionary networks and where nationalist movements, notably in Kenya during the Mau Mau 'emergency', were resulting in terrible atrocities committed by both ruled and rulers. In the 1950s, the General Assembly of the Church of Scotland enthusiastically advocated the cause of black nationalism and, especially in Nyasaland (modern

Malawi), pronounced against the pressing menace of white racist minority rule.[39] This was at a time when Scotland's 'surrogate parliament' was listened to, its deliberations reported at length in the national press and membership of the Church of Scotland stood at an all-time high, especially among the Protestant business and professional classes. In similar vein, the Scottish Trades Union Congress received regular reports on the colonies and again strongly supported 'the native peoples [who] were entitled to the same freedom, liberty and opportunities as were the people of Britain'.[40] British policy in Kenya came in for special criticism as it was denounced by the STUC as 'a war of extermination' and much else. Some delegates extended specific comment to a general condemnation of British imperialism writ large.[41] If the position of the Church of Scotland and the STUC reflected a wider constituency (and that has yet to be determined), some Scots were ending the imperial connection not only with relief but with overt distaste for the nation's colonial past.

13

Diaspora 1945–2010

I

A few years after the end of the Second World War, a Scottish National Party pamphlet was published with the title 'Beware of Emigration'. It argued that 'nothing has sapped the life of Scotland more in the last 150 years' than mass emigration, and lamented that it was always the lifeblood of the nation, 'the young and enterprising, the skilled craftsmen and . . . the back-bone of industry' who were the first to leave.[1] Few took note of the warning. Yet Scottish emigration, inevitably constrained by six years of global conflict, quickly returned to pre-war levels soon after 1945. Between 1951 and 1981, 753,000 Scots left the country, around 45 per cent of them for England and the rest for new lives overseas. As the table below reveals, there was fluctuation over time in outward movement but emigration at high levels was sustained throughout the period.

Table 9: Net migration from Scotland, 1931–89 (thousands)

Decades	UK	Overseas
1931–51	210	10
1951–61	140	142
1961–71	169	157
1971–81	52	99
1981–9	70	47

Source: Annual Reports of the Registrar General Scotland, 1931–89.

Between 1951 and 2006 net migration loss, defined as the difference in the number of people moving to and leaving a country, was about 825,000, described by one authority as 'a staggering amount' from a nation of little more than 5 million.[2] Most of this haemorrhage occurred before the 1990s as in that decade there began a phase of relative balance, with the number of immigrants coming to Scotland starting to equal the number of emigrants leaving the country. Once again, as in the past, the Scottish experience contrasted with that of England and Wales. Scots continued to supply a disproportionate number of both Britain's internal migrants and also its emigrants.[3] As a result, Scotland's share of the population of the United Kingdom fell from 11 per cent in 1914 to just over 9 per cent by 1981. Between 1921 and 1961 the population of England grew by nearly one third; Scotland by only 5 per cent. Emigration on a substantial scale was also sustained much longer north of the Border. Historians of English emigration describe a post-war surge in the 1950s and 1960s which started to come to an end by the 1970s; not so in Scotland.[4] As late as 2003 to 2006, over 217,000 Scots left for other parts of the United Kingdom or overseas. Those who went abroad numbered 82,200 over that four-year period.[5]

What compounded the Scottish problem until near the end of the twentieth century was that the country failed to attract enough immigrants to compensate for these large emigration losses. The Irish moved in large numbers to England after 1950 but that pattern was not repeated in Scotland. Similarly, the massive Asian migration to Britain tended to peter out as it approached the north of England. In 1966 only 2 of every 1,000 Scots were natives of the New Commonwealth. The figure for England and Wales was over twelve times greater – such a difference of magnitude which suggests that Scotland was not regarded as a land of great opportunity from the immigrant perspective at that time.[6]

In fact, it was the increase in immigration to Scotland that eventually began to make for a more favourable migration balance. By 2004 total in- and out-migration was about 70,000 per year, in each direction, resulting in a net loss of just 2,000 people, a radical reduction compared to most years in the twentieth century. This turned into a favourable balance of over 19,800 in 2005 and 21,600 in 2006.[7] Two factors were influential. First, there was a significant growth in English immigration to Scotland, from 220,000 in 1951 to 408,984 in 2001, a total increase of 86 per cent. The English-born are now by far Scotland's largest immigrant group.[8] Secondly, Scotland shared in the sharp rise in immigration to the United Kingdom from the countries which joined the European Union in May 2004. Poland was the prime, though by no means the only source. The Polish Consulate in Edinburgh considered that the number of Polish immigrants to Scotland rose rapidly to around 50,000 by the end of 2006. Current estimates vary between 75,000 and 85,000.[9]

It could perhaps be predicted that the acute austerity and rationing of necessities in the years after 1945 would have resulted in a new surge of emigration, especially for a generation which still had vivid memories of the profound poverty and insecurities of the 1930s.[10] More difficult to explain was not only the continuation of outward movement for several decades after the 1950s but also its considerable increase in scale. After all, economic recovery and material improvement had proceeded apace in the 1950s. It was in 1957 that Harold Macmillan made his oft-quoted remark: 'Let's be frank about it, most of our people have never had it so good.' His comment had particular relevance to Scotland, which had endured a good deal of pain for much of the interwar period. Unemployment, the curse of the 1930s, fell to historically low levels. Between 1947 and 1957, Scottish unemployment was remarkably stable and only varied between 2.4 per cent and 3 per cent of an insured labour force that had actually increased significantly by over 690,000 between 1945 and 1960. There were now jobs for virtually everyone who wanted to work. Full employment also brought rising incomes. That of the average working-class household in 1953 was reckoned to be two and a half to three times greater than in 1938. For a time, even the gap in average wage levels between England and Scotland narrowed.

The nation's health also improved, not simply because of the new prosperity but also as a result of legislative changes and scientific advances. The National Health Service, established in 1948, extended free treatment to all while by the Education (Scotland) Acts of 1945 and 1947 local authorities could insist on the medical inspection of pupils and provide free treatment. Antibiotics were introduced for the first time on a large scale in the mid-1940s and soon wiped out tuber-culosis, the killer disease of young adults in the very recent past. By 1960, Scotland's infant mortality rate was the same as that of the USA and close to the figures for England and Wales. Rising living standards in the 1950s were shown by the steady increase in the range of new household appliances, such as washing machines, vacuum cleaners and electric cookers, which made homes easier to run. Leisure pat-terns were transformed by the television and, for a long time after its introduction, cinema audience figures tumbled. The number of TV sets in Scotland grew from 41,000 in 1952 to well over 1 million ten years later, fuelled partly by the huge demand for televisions at the time of the Coronation in 1953. The nation's housing crisis was now tackled for the first time on a large scale with the extraordinary total of over 564,000 new houses built in the two decades after 1945. As the urban slums came down, many thousands of Scots now had decent houses, equipped to modern standards with inside toilets.[11]

Yet such gains in living standards failed to stem the flow of emi-grants. Wage levels and real incomes in the 1950s and 1960s, despite the better times, were still marginally behind the English averages, although it is generally agreed that these small differences cannot con-vincingly account for the exodus.[12] The Toothill Committee Report on the Scottish Economy in 1960 was sceptical of any likely connec-tion between economic vicissitudes at home and levels of emigration. They 'could find no clear relationship between unemployment and emigration rates . . . no doubt whatever the conditions at home, many Scots still migrate as they have done even during the most prosperous period'.[13] Indeed, Scots emigrants in this period were on the whole more highly skilled and came from higher social backgrounds than those who moved to England for work.[14]

Much of the movement abroad was therefore aspirational and, ironically, was probably spurred on by the material improvements at home which engendered a new spirit of optimism and desire for even greater opportunities. The mid-twentieth-century communications revolution with television, the telephone and air travel made emigra-tion even easier as well as providing more immediate and appealing information on a higher quality of life abroad. Rising incomes also made emigration affordable for more families. A vital factor was the enthusiastic commitment of Commonwealth governments to encourage white, and especially British, emigration from the late 1940s. The most forceful and successful recruitment campaigns were mounted by Australia.[15] The nightmare scenario of Japanese invasion and occupation had almost become a reality for that country during the war. In the years of peace 'populate or perish' became the new national mantra in an attempt to provide a demographic bulwark against future enemies. The result was legislation in 1947 promising a subsidized fare of £10 for adult emigrants and free passage for children under the age of fourteen. Additional migration offices were opened in British cities. Bureaucracy for potential migrants was cut and countless glossy brochures were distributed depicting sunny outdoor lifestyles in Australia, together with information sheets offering the British settler special support for health and social security. In the 1960s and 1970s Scots (around 10 per cent of the UK population) made up between a quarter and a third of the British exodus to Australia. Only in 1973 was the 'White Australia Policy' abandoned and immigration targets reduced.[16]

Other countries developed their own policies. In 1952 the USA eased immigration restrictions and in subsequent years Scots comprised a quarter to a third of all British emigrants there. Indeed visa allocations to Britain were so generous they were never completely taken up. Canada until 1962 gave preference to immigrants from the United Kingdom, France and the United States while New Zealand offered £10 passages for key workers from 1947 until 1975. However, by that decade overseas immigration policies became much more restrictive, with a consequent decline in the volume of emigration from Britain.[17]

2

By the 1850s there were some 100,000 first-generation Scots in the United States, a number which increased between 1890 and 1920 to a quarter of a million. Four-fifths of them were concentrated in the Northwest and Midwest states. Another one-sixth were located in the far West. Only about one in twenty were settled in the South.[18] These

Scots immigrants to the United States demonstrated and celebrated their ethnic origins in a series of Scottish associations in the same way as other ethnic groups.[19] Between the 1850s and the Great War they founded over 1,200 local societies. They included those named after the national patron, St Andrew, which were long-established, prestigious and devoted to charitable works and good causes, and a useful source of networking for members of the immigrant Scottish elites. Local areas of Scotland had, in addition, their own societies. In 1878, a national fraternal organization, the Order of Scottish Clans (quite unlike the clan societies of later times) was founded. It was followed in 1895 by the female counterpart, the Daughters of Scotia. By 1900 there were over a hundred Burns clubs and statues of the Scottish Bard soon appeared in prominent locations in several American towns and cities. Highland or Caledonian games also become a common fixture. By 1920, they were being held in around 120 different locations. Some argue that modern American track and field athletics evolved directly from these games. They were far from being exclusively ethnic in nature and were open to all in local communities, not simply those of Scottish descent.[20] The gatherings were among the first mass-spectator sports in America.[21] There was also a flourishing Scottish press which included the *Scottish-American Journal* (1857–1919), the *Scotsman* (1869–86) and the *Boston Scotsman*. The readership was never particularly large; the most popular and enduring – the *Scottish-American Journal* – had only 15,000 subscribers.[22]

It is more than likely that the Scottish societies, despite their visibility, attracted no more than a minority even of first-generation immigrants. This may help to explain the notable collapse in Scottish associational activity in the USA from the 1920s, in spite of the huge emigration to America from Scotland in that decade totalling more than 160,000 (see Chapter 4). The older St Andrew societies survived but the number of Caledonian games dwindled to a mere two dozen in the mid-1960s and the Scottish newspapers and journals all went out of business in the 1920s. Robert Burns continued to be celebrated and the Daughters of Scotia flourished but the Order of Scottish Clans became but a shadow of its former self.[23] As the assimilation of second- and third-generation migrants into American society accelerated, memories of the old country, at least as manifested in institutional structures if not in personal and family recollections, seemed destined to fade. Emigration from Scotland to the United States itself fell dramatically in the depressed 1930s and after the Second World War and never again regained the levels of the period 1850 to 1930. Between 1945 and 1970 it amounted to 85,000, less than in any of the four previous decades. By 1970 there were only 170,000 Scots-born in the USA, fewer than at any time since 1860: 'on the average probably older, and on both counts more likely than ever to cling to the remnants of folkways long since outmoded in Scotland'.[24] Against this background, few could have predicted the explosion of 'Scottishness', American-style, that was now about to take place.

The transformation came, not from the dwindling numbers of immigrants from Scotland, but rather from new categories of self-professed Scots, often removed by several generations from the old country and sometimes having the most tenuous direct diasporic connections with Scotland.[25] The statistics speak for themselves. In the early twentieth century around 300 Highland games took place in North America every year. Between the 1960s and 1980, the number in the United States alone tripled, from a mere two dozen to over seventy. From 1985 to 2003 the rate of growth quadrupled. By 2005, 150 Scottish clan societies and 'family associations' had been established and a recent estimate suggests that at the same date, the number of pipe bands in North America was in the region of 1,900 individual ensembles, with the total continuing to grow, year on year.[26]

Another indicator of the Scottish-American ethnic revival is the popularity of Highland dancing. There were reckoned to be 150 Highland dancing schools and over 200 Scottish Country Dance groups across the USA in 2010. Other niche associations cater for special interests, from historical re-enactment to societies for golf, curling and fans of Scottish folk bands, with many of them gathering at annual Highland games to share their enthusiasms with the like-minded.[27] None of the home-based Scottish games can compete with the largest events in the USA in terms of numbers. At the most prestigious in the South, the Grandfather Mountain Highland Games, over 30,000 people gather annually for four days of sport and amusement. Several others can boast numbers in excess of 10,000 and 20,000.[28]

Perhaps the most striking fact about this upsurge in Scottish-American interest is its novelty. It cannot simply be seen as a revival of nineteenth- and early twentieth-century Scottish diasporic traditions, although at its core, the myths and stories of auld Scotia still loom large. In essence, the recent evolution and popularity of Scottish heritage in the United States is an indigenous American development, managed and directed by the transatlantic diaspora and often containing elements which native Scots find risible or even offensive. While all areas of the United States have been affected, much of the dynamic for this new heritage has come from the American South, a region which, ironically, attracted few direct migrants from Scotland throughout the nineteenth and twentieth centuries.[29] In 1979, for instance, less than two-fifths of the enrolled members of clan and family societies lived in the Northeast and Midwest, the regions where, historically, the vast majority of Scottish emigrants had settled. Nearly half and perhaps even two-thirds of these 'neo-clansmen' lived in the South.[30] It was certainly true that some historic connections could be traced in pockets of North Carolina back to eighteenth-century Highland emigration. But, even if this old experience was historically renowned, it was very much an exception rather than the rule. The Scottish societies of recent times in the South may indeed be replete with Scottish names but their ancestral connection is mainly with Ireland rather than Scotland. The South attracted large numbers of Ulster Scots, whose Lowland Scots ancestors had settled in the north of Ireland in the seventeenth century.[31] It is mainly their descendants, friends and families who now flock in large numbers to Highland games and clan societies in the Southern states. Significantly, when the first Grandfather Mountain Highland Games were held on 19 August 1956 (the anniversary of the raising of the Jacobite standard at Glenfinnan in 1745), the location was 'MacRae Meadows' in the heart of Ulster-Scots territory. The Cape Fear area, where Highland immigrants had actually settled, was thought too flat and not sufficiently authentic to represent the romantic mountain country of bonnie Scotland.[32]

Some key features differentiate these Scottish-American associations in the South from those of the Scottish homeland. One innovation is the ceremony of 'The Kirkin' o' the Tartan'. The name was apparently coined by an immigrant Scottish minister in Washington in 1943 and eventually led to the widespread practice of bearing clan tartans into churches to be blessed, with great solemnity, as 'a token of the faith of our fathers'. Not everyone thought it a good thing. One Canadian Scot suggested in 1957, 'Any day we'll be reading about the Blessin' o' the Haggis!'[33] Nonetheless, the 'Kirkin' o' the Tartan' caught on. In some parts, for instance, the ceremony often takes place in open fields to emulate the conventicles of the Scottish Covenanters of the seventeenth century and their struggles against a hostile state.[34] This is all quite extraordinary from an historical perspective, given the visceral hatred of the Covenanting movement of the seventeenth century for Gaelic Scotland, which it associated with Romanism, barbarism, absolutism and the menace of Stuart tyranny.

Equally intriguing is the martial nature of parts of Southern Scottish-American culture. The Scottish-American Military Society (SAMS), for instance, seeks to preserve and promote both Scottish customs and traditions and those of the American Armed Forces. It expresses the view that Scotland has always had a renowned warrior culture which is still manifested in the martial qualities of the children of the diaspora. Emphasis is placed on the nature of the clan as a military unit, encouraging the warrior values of courage, loyalty and obedience. In North Carolina this aspect has considerable appeal. There, at Fort Bragg, one of the most formidable military complexes in the world, is the home of the US Airborne Corps and Special Forces. It occupies 160,000 acres of the old Highland settlements dating from the eighteenth century. Military people, battle re-enactors and army bands in the region, few of whom have any direct Scottish ethnic connection, attach themselves to Scottish events because of the assumption that the Scots come from a strong martial culture. In a sense this is scarcely surprising. Military encampments are commonplace at many American Highland games. The warrior ethos is physically celebrated at Highland games across the South by the proliferation of broadswords, dirks, halberds, spears, Lochaber axes, targes, claymores and chain-mail, an array of weaponry which could result in immediate police intervention in the old country.[35] One Scottish historian has this to say of the members of SAMS he personally encountered:

They ... have almost universally been fiercely patriotic military veterans with only the vaguest notion of Scotland, save for the conviction that they somehow belong to bloodlines of genetically engineered psychopathological warriors dating from time immemorial. Even in the Auld Country the relentless military associations of kilts and ceremonial dress, with overtones of army uniforms, accompanied by bristling weaponry, repels as many people as are attracted.[36]

There is, finally, a key bonding myth in Scottish-American heritage Southern style, and it is, perhaps, the most paradoxical of all. The Scottish identity embraced by American descendants of Highland Scots, Lowland Scots or Ulster Scots is a Highland Gaelic identity which was formed in the nineteenth century in Scotland long after the first great waves of transatlantic emigration from Scotland and Ireland to the South: 'In one's imagined history ... being Scottish meant to be a Highlander.'[37] This is seen most obviously in the rise of numerous clan societies, almost all of which are of recent origin, stretching not much further back than the 1960s. Before the Second World War, the genre was rare. Even the largest and most influential of them all, Clan Donald, was founded as late as 1954. The new clannishness was generated in the USA and in the 1970s little more than a third had ties with Scotland or with Scottish clan associations. At Southern Highland games, though not to the same extent in the rest of the USA, clan tents and displays on clan histories and heritage became very prominent. During the 2003 Grandfather Mountain Games over a hundred clan societies were represented by clan tents, a number not atypical of the bigger events.[38] Again, in this respect, American-Scottish identities dramatically diverge from those of the homeland, where celebrations of kinship and supposed blood relationships formed on a clan name at Highland games are, to say the least, uncommon.

Blending strongly with the attachment to a Highland identity is the belief (also in sharp conflict with the historical evidence) that Scottish migrations to America came about by force. Ancestors were seen to have been driven to leave after the collapse of the Jacobite Risings, by the post-Culloden ethnic cleansing imposed by an avenging British state and, above all, as a result of the Highland Clearances. These beliefs are powerfully embedded, with themes of exile, victimhood, oppression and dispossession strongly absorbed within them.[39] The rhetoric of exile frequently appears on Scottish-interest internet sites. Thus, the lyrics of one song posted, 'We're the Children of the Clearances', has this refrain:

> . . . the wanderers old and young
> And a heart and soul in Scotland just like you
> So when you sing of the great white
> sheep this you must also know
> While Scotland mourns her tragedy it
> was us that had to go.
> In exile now far away from
> the land of our race's birth
> We're the living flag of Andrew
> scattered all across the Earth.[40]

In one internet essay entitled 'Cries of the never born', composed by a Florida-based American Scot, the people are not only burnt out of their homes but even forced into slavery and compulsory assimilation into another culture:

In the last 270 years, more than a quarter of a million indigenous people were forced off their ancestral lands, burned out of their homes, sold into slavery and forcibly assimilated into a foreign culture. But these were not Native Americans, or Black Africans, or Jews; these were the white residents of the Scottish Highlands. Their crime: Occupying land that others coveted.[41]

The new vogue for 'ancestral tourism' has a similar focus. Visit-Scotland figures indicate that about 70 per cent of 'Roots Tourists', whatever their family ancestral background in either Scotland or Ireland, visit the Western Highlands and the Grampians: 'While their actual roots may be in Kelso or Peebles, interviewees often report feeling more "in touch with their Scottish heritage" on the Isle of Skye.'[42] For such returnees the primary interest is not modern Scotland but in the Scotland of three centuries ago. They come to see the battlefields and 'clanscapes' associated with Jacobitism and Jacobite-induced exile. For such pilgrims the Field of Culloden is above all else a sacred place, where the destruction of clanship is seen to have led directly to the displacement of the Clearances and then, inevitably, to the mass migrations of which they are the descendants.[43] Key sources for this understanding of the Scottish past are the books of John Prebble, who is still by far the most influential and widely read writer on Scottish history among the Scottish-American diaspora, closely followed by the historical novelist Nigel Tranter and, more recently, the American fantasy writer Diana Gabaldon, whose *Outlander* series of books recounts time travel between the 1940s and the era of the Jacobite Risings.

Needless to say, as one commentator has put it, 'What the Scottish diaspora conceives as Scottish can be excruciating for Scots.'[44] Academic critics in Scotland have railed against the transatlantic obsession with clans and tartans, condemning it for perpetuating an outdated stereotype of the post-devolution nation and projecting an image of Scottish history which is fabricated and founded on kitsch symbolism.[45] It is said that the American love of Highlandism 'sends Scots into hilarity or sanctimonious diatribes' and 'part of their disgust is that the diaspora still adores the Highlandist vision of Scotland which many Scots disdain'.[46] In truth, however, the origins of these mythologies lie only partly across the Atlantic. Modern Scots who deride aspects of Scottish-American heritage culture would do well to remember that Highlandism is itself a home-grown product, born in the later eighteenth century and coming to full maturity in the decades after 1815.[47] When the emigrants of Victorian times left Scotland, many took with them these new mythical symbols of tartans, kilts, pipes and drums, Highland games and other traditions. These were then embellished in the New World by subsequent generations of the Scottish diaspora. The widespread and relatively recent popularity of wearing Highland dress in today's Scotland at weddings, graduation ceremonies, formal dinners and other public events confirms that the seductive appeal of Highlandism is by no means confined to the descendants of Scots overseas.

Indeed, Scottish heritage has an extraordinary contemporary allure which reaches well beyond the United States and even the countries of traditional Scottish settlement. The twenty-six Highland games held in Canada in 1982 had grown to seventy in 2003 at a time which was supposed to have experienced 'the twilight of European ethnicities' in that country. In the same year there were an estimated 230 games in the USA, and in both Canada and the United States three times the number of such events as in Scotland. Close to thirty annual Scottish heritage meetings take place in Australia and pipe band associations also flourish much more strongly than before in New Zealand and South Africa.[48] Even more remarkable than growth in the countries to which Scots have emigrated for generations is the veritable explosion of interest in Scottish heritage in Europe, often in regions of the Continent untouched by medieval and early modern Scottish migration. The current patterns (2010), based on the pioneering research of David Hesse, are shown in Table 10.[49]

Films such as *Braveheart* and *Rob Roy*, the 'Celtic revival' and the attractions of Highlandism have come together in a powerful alchemy to revive interest among much broader social groups than those European aristocrats who were attracted to romantic Scotland in the later

Table 10: Numbers of European Scottish heritage events and activities, 2010

Pipe and drum bands:	at least 220
Highland games:	at least 160
Total Scottish events (including bagpipe festivals, heritage events and Highland games)	c.300
Main locations:	North-Western Europe (Germany, Netherlands, Belgium, Austria, Switzerland, France) but stretching from Russia to Malta
Largest event:	Scotfest, Tilburg, Netherlands (35,000 people in 2008 according to the organizers – www.scotfest.nl)
Re-enactors:	Several dozen 'Scottish' groups, from medieval warriors to Second World War regiments, to be found at Scottish and other festivals

eighteenth century. The Highland terrain of glens, mountains, castles and lochs has once again become irresistible for many as 'the most romanticized landscapes in Western literature, art, film and photography', an international cultural perception which, predictably, is relentlessly exploited by Scotland's tourist agencies.[50]

In the USA, the heritage revival is often dated from the 1950s, in particular to when Dame Flora MacLeod, the first female chief of Clan MacLeod, visited America in 1953 and made her famous plea to the diaspora to 'Come back to Scotland'. In the same decade the Clan Donald Society USA was founded, destined to become the largest clan association by far in America. But these were but halting first steps.[51] Exponential expansion was more concentrated in the later twentieth century and wider factors were much more relevant by then. The passing by the US Congress in 1974 of the Ethnic Heritage Act to support the funding of initiatives to celebrate the traditions and cultures of the nation's ethnic populations promoted greater interest in cultural pluralism, a trend further stimulated by the bicentennial celebrations of 1976 and the success of such books and TV series as Alex Haley's *Roots*. Genealogy and family history became fast-growing hobbies, which were revolutionized in the 1990s by the internet. Indeed, family history is reputedly second only to pornography as the most common leisure pursuit in cyberspace.[52] One such website, launched in 1999, was reported to be receiving more than 100 million hits a day.[53] *The Scotsman* reported a year later that 'few countries outside the United States are attracting as much attention as Scotland, with thousands of emigrant Caledonians from across the globe using the digital highway to stake their claim in the nation's past'.[54] The launch of the 'Scotland's People' website by the Scottish government, an enormous database of 80 million records available for access and proclaiming itself 'one of the largest online sources of original genealogical information', gave a further boost to the popularity of the internet for Scottish family history.[55]

Scholars have looked for deeper reasons for the new attractions of heritage, defined by one writer not as history but as 'a rhapsody on history':

> We strike the chords we wish to hear. The value of heritage lies in its perennial flexibility and the strength of emotions it evokes. Celebratory

and commemorative reflections on ancestral experience merge histori-cal incidents, folk memories, invented traditions and often sheer fan-tasy to interpret a past in a form meaningful for a particular group or individual at a particular point in time. The bits of the past that seem most significant continuously change relative to the present.[56]

For some, the romantic images of Highlanders created in the Victo-rian era 'feed a modern-day hunger for a connection with an earlier, better, pre-industrial non-capitalist society', with the new interest in ethnicity booming as globalization gathered pace in the later twenti-eth century.[57]

The 1995 Oscar-winning film *Braveheart*, reckoned to have grossed some $204 million at the box-office worldwide, was also of signifi-cance. The Hollywood version of the exploits of the Scottish medieval hero and 'freedom fighter' William Wallace may have verged on the ludicrous as a realistic portrayal of Scottish history, but it had a gal-vanizing impact in Scotland itself and abroad: 'this evocation of Scotland as the original "land of the free, home to the brave" is noth-ing less than a projection of specifically American nationalist ideology onto an old country'. American applications for membership of clan societies boomed after the film was released.[58] Even more importantly, the impact of Braveheartism was key to the passing in the US Senate of Resolution No.155, declaring 6 April (the anniversary of the medi-eval Declaration of Arbroath) to become the official 'National Tartan Day', and so recognizing 'the outstanding achievements and contribu-tions made by Scottish-Americans to the United States' (Congressional Record – Senate 1998a:S2373). The legislation was tabled by the Republican Senator for Mississippi, Trent Lott, who was the Senate Majority Leader at the time. One critic suggested that Lott's oration in support of Resolution 155 'sounds like the script of *Braveheart*, for that execrable film and the constituting of Tartan Day inhabit the same ideological universe'.[59] *Braveheart* confirmed the belief in some Americans that Scotland was indeed the home of warrior culture, a concept dear to the heart of some modern 'tartaneers'. The subse-quent Senate initiative also sought to place the Scottish influence at the very heart of American history: 'The Resolution constructs Scottish-American life as an endless chain of successes that shaped the United States. Scottish-Americans are constructed as heroic, pioneering and indomitable. In short, they are the embodiment of the United States itself.'[60]

Thinking such as this seems to have had special appeal in the American South, especially when embroidered and expanded by popular writers in the 'Scotch-Irish' tradition there. Typical of this genre is Grady McWhiney's *Cracker Culture: Celtic Ways in the Old South* (1988), which argued that the distinctive culture of the deep South originated in a direct line of descent from ancient Celtic society whose traditions were carried across the Atlantic by emigrants from Ulster and Scotland in the eighteenth and nineteenth centuries. Parallels were also drawn between Scottish and Southern identities.[61] Both ethnicities have potent elements of 'lost cause' mythology at the heart of their historical memories: the collapse of Jacobitism, the final defeat at Culloden alongside the Clearances for Scots; the humiliations suffered after the American Civil War for the people of the South. In the view of some authorities, indeed, while history may well be written by the winners, heritage increasingly belongs to the losers.[62] A 'Confederate Memorial Tartan' is now registered and it is not unusual at Scottish gatherings in the South to see some attending wearing combined Highland dress and Confederate garb, 'a kind of Bonnie Prince Charlie meets Robert E. Lee lost-cause combo', yet another confirmation that heritage has less to do with history than the realization of emotions in response to an imagined past.[63]

3

For much of the nineteenth century, articulate opinion in Scotland regarded emigration from the homeland in positive terms. It was a means of maintaining and extending the time-honoured Scottish connection with the British Empire and spreading Scottish Presbyterianism, education, ideas and commercial networks across the globe. After the Great War, perceptions changed. The domestic economic crisis seemed to be mirrored and confirmed by the huge levels of out-migration, which were also portrayed as grievously harming the nation as those who left were viewed as the young and energetic, the most skilled and enterprising, a key resource which a nation seen to be in decline could not afford to lose. There were exceptions to this consensus. A major academic investigation published in 1953 noted that there were some compensations from the exodus: 'Scottish trade ... has at all times been greatly assisted by the migratory habits of the people. The large numbers who came to occupy important positions in industry and commerce overseas or made their homes abroad as permanent emigrants have become reliable customers for Scottish exports.'[64] Yet for the most part, there was hardly any recognition at the time of emigration as a resource which could be of benefit to the mother country.

That indifference changed – at least as far as government and its public agencies were concerned – in the late 1990s and the early years of the new millennium. In September 2010 the Scottish government announced a 'Diaspora Engagement Plan', proclaiming that Scotland was the first European nation 'to develop a formal approach to motivating and engaging its diaspora' (a somewhat exaggerated claim since, although not 'formally' as a plan, Ireland had been busily engaging with its worldwide emigrants since the 1990s). The announcement of the Plan noted that Scotland already had been praised by the World Bank and the UK-based Institute for Public Policy Research as a country 'in the vanguard of diaspora engagement'. Significantly, the press release stressed that the strategy was not simply 'about sentimentality' as diaspora connections could and should be translated into 'mutually beneficial, hard-edged business partnerships'.[65]

The emergence of a coherent strategy on diaspora engagement was novel but Scotland had in fact been moving to such a stage for some years previously. Initiatives such as Global Scot, a business network established to connect highly skilled Scots around the world, and Global Friends of Scotland, a social and community network linking overseas Scots, had been set up earlier by previous Holyrood administrations. The major public affirmations of the new approach included attendance by senior Scottish politicians at Tartan Day ceremonials and events in the United States and, above all, by Homecoming Scotland 2009, an idea first advanced by the Labour administration in Edinburgh but taken up with enthusiasm by the SNP minority government in 2007. A ten-month programme of 400 events culminated in The Gathering in July 2009, which attracted more than 47,000 people of Scottish ancestry. The Minister for Enterprise, Energy and Tourism had stated in 2007: 'Whether you are Scottish or simply love Scotland you are invited to come home – home to the land of your ancestors so you can experience a living culture.' The fundamental objectives were more pragmatic. Its two targets were to produce a total economic impact of at least £40 million through additional tourism visits, and, by engaging the Scottish diaspora, to deliver '50,000 new consumer prospects and 2,500 "gatekeeper" contacts'. Many expatriates and their families did return and current estimates suggest a significant impact overall on tourist numbers. The success, however, was marred by the fact that the company managing The Gathering went into liquidation despite government and other public grants. The Year of Homecoming 2009 celebrations remain controversial and politically divisive.[66]

This new interest in the diaspora had several origins. The establishment of devolution and a Parliament in Scotland in 1999 allowed Edinburgh-based politicians to pursue a specific Scottish agenda in some areas, especially since the new political dispensation coincided with an awakening of interest in Scottish heritage overseas, particularly in the USA with the inauguration of Tartan Day and related celebrations. Moreover, with the end of the old heavy industrial economy in the 1980s, tourism has become a vital sector of the 'new' Scottish economy. In 2009 it contributed £4.1 billion and accounted, directly or indirectly, for 219,000 jobs and some 20,000 businesses across the country.[67] Pursuing closer connections with the diaspora is regarded as a crucial part of the strategy not only to maintain but to expand tourist numbers. The Scots have also taken note of Ireland's economic success in developing rewarding relationships and networks with elite members of its diaspora. Irish Americans became global leaders in the area of diaspora philanthropy from the 1970s. Indeed, since 1976 the Ireland Funds in the USA have raised over $350 million and funded over 1,200 organizations in Ireland and beyond. As this is written, similar philanthropic endeavours by the Scottish diaspora are notable by their virtual absence. The example of Andrew Carnegie in the early twentieth century has not so far been followed by any of his wealthy successors.

Above all, perhaps, the new interest in the Scots who had left

Scotland was driven by growing alarm about demographic trends in the nation. An authoritative research report published in 2004 concluded that the population of the country was ageing and shrinking, falling by 1 per cent between 1995 and 2001.[68] In that period no other part of the EU experienced population decline. Even more worryingly, the researchers concluded that if no action was taken the number of native Scots would not only fall, but would decline faster than the population of any other EU country.

These lugubrious facts concentrated the minds of policy-makers, and one of the options considered and implemented was a strategy to boost the scale of return migration to Scotland. In the event, other factors entered the equation. In the summer of 2008 the Registrar General could report that the population of Scotland had risen to its highest level since 1983 due to an increase in births and migration from England and Eastern Europe. The latter influence was the more critical. More than 63,000 people left Scotland in that year but nearly 90,000 also arrived in the country.[69]

Whether the strategy of developing links with the diaspora will succeed is, of course, problematic. An analysis comparing Scottish and Irish emigration pointed out that Scottish policy-makers have the greater challenge: 'In general, Irish-mindedness – the strength of Irish identity and an allegiance or patriotism to [sic] Ireland – seems better developed than Scottish-mindedness ... the Scottish diaspora is less visible and less well organised than the Irish diaspora.'[70] There is in addition, of course, the challenge of the two versions of 'Scottishness' which prevail among some diasporic and homeland Scots. Against that background, will there be a real convergence of interests and objectives?

Afterword

In examining the nature and impact of the emigrations of one small country over three centuries it is easy to fall victim to the seductive intellectual traps of exceptionalism and boosterism. I have tried to avoid these dangers in the Scottish case, not only by attempting to place context, perspective and comparison at the heart of the analysis, but also through paying due attention to both the positive and negative aspects of the diasporic experience. Readers can decide if this approach has achieved its declared aim of producing a rounded and critical examination of this narrative in the long and rich history of Scotland.

It might be going too far to pick out from the results of the study unique features of Scottish emigration. Emigrant nations shared many experiences in common and the Scots were often little different in several key respects from the Jews, Irish, English, Armenians, Chinese and others. Nonetheless, behind these uniformities there was also a good deal of variation which marked the histories of different ethnicities. This book has suggested that some distinctive characteristics can indeed be associated with the Scottish diaspora.

One feature is the extraordinary numerical scale of the movement. Another is the fact it was sustained without interruption not only over decades and generations but across centuries. The eighteenth-century exodus was built upon the huge migrations of the medieval and early modern epochs, although the destinations of choice became the Americas and Asia rather than Europe. Over the following two centuries the outflows were especially significant in the 1850s, 1870s, in the early 1900s and again in the 1920s. However, unlike other parts of the UK, high levels of emigration persisted until almost the end of the twentieth century. A related point is the worldwide reach of the overseas diaspora:

Scandinavia, Poland-Lithuania, the Low Countries and Ireland before 1700, and the USA, Canada, the Caribbean, Africa, India, Asia and Australasia since then, not forgetting those pockets of emigrants in Latin America and the numerous traders active in China and Japan. For much of the period covered here it was in large part an imperial diaspora, but it eventually became much more than that. These migrations, especially by merchants, teachers, physicians, missionaries, engineers, bankers, professors and accountants, were global in their reach, which is one of several reasons why the end of the British Empire did not immediately cause the expected political or economic waves in Scotland itself. Scots businessmen and professionals by that point had become citizens of the world. Empire was important but no longer crucial to the success of many middle-class careerists. London, New York, Hong Kong and numerous other global cities now replaced the old imperial centres.

There is also the issue of Scottish impact on the new lands. Many Scots emigrants, like those from England, often had a decided advantage over the peasant masses that flocked across the Atlantic in their millions from Ireland, Central and Eastern Europe and the countries of the Mediterranean in the course of the nineteenth century. The economic, social and religious development of Scotland ensured that from the middle decades of the nineteenth century, if not earlier, its emigrants spoke mainly Scots-English, were usually Protestant, literate, and often highly skilled or semi-skilled in the techniques and practices of an advanced industrial and agrarian economy. They were also drawn abroad for the most part, not by crisis or disaster, but by a desire to exploit opportunities and achieve aspirations not easily satisfied in the homeland. Moreover, unlike many other nationalities, the Scots rarely experienced systematic prejudice or discrimination in the new lands and offered to them skills which were much in demand there. If the Scots did punch above their weight, therefore, as some have alleged, then these background factors may provide part of the explanation.

Also to be taken into account is the vitally important Scottish intellectual, professional and military diaspora, as important in the late twentieth century as it was many generations before. This disseminated Scottish philosophical, medical and scientific ideas, educational institutions, Presbyterian tradition, technology, business practices in banking, investment and accounting and the reputation of the Scottish military, primarily and originally throughout the Empire but, in the longer term, also much further afield. In short, the argument here is that any attempt to write comprehensive histories of the new lands without some assessment of the specific Scottish factor in their development would be myopic. It is undeniable that this ethnic influence was part of a broader British impact, but, equally, the narrative did have distinctive Scottish features.

The impact of long-term and large-scale emigration on Scotland itself is a crucial subject that has attracted little academic attention and cries out for more research. This book suggests that in the eighteenth century at least, the migration of Scots sojourners to the American colonies, the West Indies and India, together with the repatriation of profits by some of those who made good, can be considered a key element in the Scottish Leap Forward of the time. This factor may have been of much less significance after c.1830, in part because a rapidly maturing economy was able to generate its own investment funds for future expansion, but also because it was much more attractive for the rich and not-so-rich of Scotland to achieve higher rates of return on their savings by investing in railways, mines, construction projects and cattle ranching in overseas territories than by putting money into the homeland. Thus, while some Scots made great fortunes abroad, Scotland itself in the Victorian decades contained some of the worst slums in Europe and remained a country of deeply entrenched social inequalities, scarred by terrible poverty in its cities. After the Great War, the era of Scottish global commercial hegemony passed away with the slow death of the major industries which had once serviced world markets and the end of the old imperial trading houses, which were swallowed up by company amalgamation, the pull of London and the nationalization policies of newly independent states when they were liberated from the yoke of empire in the 1950s and 1960s.

Yet, one important manifestation of continuity survived these historic changes. Like their ancestors in medieval and early modern times, twentieth-century Scots continued to emigrate in large numbers. Only the two world wars temporarily interrupted the age-old tradition of wandering in search of work, opportunity and new horizons which remains one of the key hallmarks of the Scottish identity.

Notes

I. IMPERIAL SCOTS 1750–1815

1. Linda Colley, *Captives: Britain, Empire and the World 1660–1850* (London, 2002), p. 4; Peter J. Marshall, 'Introduction', in P. J. Marshall, ed., *The Oxford History of the British Empire*. Vol. 2, *The Eighteenth Century* (Oxford, 1998), p. 5. This first chapter is designed as a bridge between my earlier work, *Scotland's Empire 1600–1815* (London, 2003) and this study of the nineteenth and twentieth centuries. It therefore contains some material used in that earlier book.

2. Sir G. Macartney, *An account of Ireland in 1773* (1773) quoted in Thomas Bartlett, '"This famous island set in a Virginian sea": Ireland in the British Empire, 1690–1801', in Marshall, ed., *Oxford History*, p. 262.

3. John Darwin, 'Britain's Empires', in Sarah Stockwell, ed., *The British Empire. Themes and Perspectives* (Oxford, 2008), p. 1.

4. John Brewer, *The Sinews of Power: War, Money and the English State, 1688–1783* (Cambridge, Mass., 1990), p. xvii.

5. Quoted in T. M. Devine, *Scotland's Empire*, p. 65.

6. The pioneering work on this is Brewer, *Sinews of Power*, passim.

7. T. M. Devine, *Exploring the Scottish Past: Themes in the History of Scottish Society* (East Lothian, 1995), pp. 42–3.

8. P. K. O'Brien, 'Inseparable Connections: Trade, Economy, Fiscal State and the Expansion of "Empire"', in Marshall, ed., *Oxford History*, pp. 63–70; P. K. O'Brien, 'The Political Economy of British Taxation, 1660–1815', *Economic History Review*, 2nd Series, XLI (1988), pp. 1–32; Christopher A. Whatley, *Scottish Society 1707–1830* (Manchester, 2000), pp. 195–6.

9. This and the following two paragraphs summarize the arguments in T. M. Devine, 'Scottish elites and the Indian Empire, 1700–1815', in T. C. Smout, ed., *Anglo-Scottish Relations from 1603 to 1900* (Oxford, 2005), pp. 213–31.

10. Neal Ascherson, *Stone Voices. The Search for Scotland* (London, 2002), p. 237.

11. P. J. Marshall, *The Making and Un-making of Empires* (Oxford, 2005), pp. 58–9.

12. P. J. Marshall, *East India Fortunes: The British in Bengal in the Eighteenth Century* (Oxford, 1976), p. 234.

13. Quoted in Devine, *Scotland's Empire*, p. 259.

14. T. C. Smout, 'Introduction', in Smout, ed., *Anglo-Scottish Relations*, p. 2.

15. *Glasgow Journal*, 28 April 1746.

16. R. C. Nash, 'The English and Scottish Tobacco Trades in the Seventeenth and Eighteenth Centuries; Legal and Illegal Trade', *Economic History Review*, 2nd Series, XXV (1982), pp. 354–72; Devine, *Scotland's Empire* pp. 69–93.

17. George McGilvary, *East India Patronage and the British State* (London, 2008), pp. 28–67; A. Mackillop, 'Scots and the Empire in Asia *c.*1695–1813'. Paper presented at the Scotland and Empire Symposium, Scottish Centre for Diaspora Studies, University of Edinburgh, February 2010.

18. John Robertson, *The Scottish Enlightenment and the Militia Issue* (Edinburgh, 1985).

19. Paul Langford, 'South Britons' Perception of North Britons, 1701–1820', in Smout, ed., *Anglo-Scottish Relations*, p. 148.

20. Quoted in Douglas J. Hamilton, 'Patronage and Profit: Scottish Networks in the British West Indies, *c.*1763–1807', unpublished PhD thesis, University of Aberdeen (1999), p. 208.

21. J. E. Cookson, *The British Armed Nation 1793–1815* (Oxford, 1997), p. 128.

22. Langford, 'South Britons' Perception', p. 148.

23. For criticism of the 'national' approach to imperial history see Antoinette Burton, 'Who needs the nation? Interrogating "British History"', in Catherine Hall, ed., *Cultures of Empire: Colonizers in Britain and the Empire in the Nineteenth and Twentieth Centuries* (Manchester, 2000), pp. 138–42. But see also John M. Mackenzie, 'Irish, Scottish, Welsh and English Worlds? A Four Nation Approach to the History of the British Empire', *History Compass*, 6/5 (2008), pp. 1244–63.

24. Andrew Thompson, 'Empire and the British State', in Stockwell, ed., *British Empire*, p. 51.

25. Ibid.

26. See, for example, Kevin Kenny, ed., *Ireland and the British Empire* (Oxford, 2004); David Fitzpatrick, 'Ireland and the Empire', in Andrew

Porter, ed., *The Oxford History of the British Empire*. Vol. 3, *The Nineteenth Century* (Oxford, 1999), pp. 495–522; Keith Jeffery, ed., 'An Irish Empire?' Aspects of Ireland and the British Empire (Manchester, 1996).

27. Devine, *Scotland's Empire*, pp. 94–118, 140–63.
28. Kevin Kenny, 'The Irish in the Empire', in Kenny, ed., *Ireland and the British Empire*, pp. 104–5.
29. Sir M. O'Dwyer, *India as I Knew It, 1885–1925* (London, 1925), pp. 1–8, 17–21; Scott B. Cook, 'The Irish Raj: Social Origins and Careers of Irishmen in the Indian Civil Service, 1855–1919', *Journal of Social History*, 20 (Spring, 1987), p. 509.
30. Compare the evidence in the works cited in n. 26 above with the conclusions in Devine, *Scotland's Empire*, pp. 164–289.
31. Peter C. Newman, *Company of Adventurers*. Vol. 1 (Toronto, 1985), p. 2.
32. J. S. A. Brown, '"A Parcel of Upstart Scotchmen"', *The Beaver*, 68 (1988), p. 4.
33. Ibid.
34. Quoted in Elaine A. Mitchell, 'The Scot in the Fur Trade', in W. S. Reid, ed., *The Scottish Tradition in Canada* (Toronto, 1976), p. 36.
35. Ibid.
36. *Glasgow Journal*, 14 January 1760.
37. Ibid.
38. D. S. Macmillan, 'The "New Men" in Action: Scottish Mercantile and Shipping Operations in the North American Colonies, 1760–1825', in D. S. Macmillan, ed., *Canadian Business History: Selected Studies, 1497–1971* (Toronto, 1972), pp. 44–103.
39. Ibid.
40. J. K. Johnson, *Becoming Prominent: Regional Leadership in Upper Canada 1791–1841* (Kingston and Montreal, 1989), p. 106.
41. J. M. Bumsted, 'The Scottish Diaspora: Emigration to British North America, 1776–1815', in Ned C. Landsman, ed., *Nation and Province in the First British Empire* (London, 2001), pp. 145–6.
42. Ibid., pp. 143–4.
43. Douglas J. Hamilton, *Scotland, the Caribbean and the Atlantic World, 1750–1820* (Manchester, 2005), p. 23.
44. Rajat Kanta Ray, 'Indian Society and the Establishment of British Supremacy, 1763–1818', in Marshall, ed., *Oxford History*, pp. 508–29.
45. Devine, *Scotland's Empire*, p. 203.
46. H. V. Bowen, *Elites, Enterprise and the Making of the British Overseas Empire, 1688–1775* (Basingstoke, 1996), p. 150.

47. Quoted in Alex M. Cain, *The Cornchest for Scotland: Scots in India* (Edinburgh, 1986), p. 7.

48. Philip Lawson and Jim Phillips, '"Our Execrable Banditti": Perceptions of Nabobs in Mid-Eighteenth Century Britain', *Albion*, XVI (1984), p. 230.

49. *Public Advertiser*.

50. J. Drummond of Quarrell to William Drummond, 18 March 1731, quoted in G. K. McGilvary, 'East India Patronage and the Political Management of Scotland, 1720–1774', unpublished PhD thesis, Open University (1989), p. 207.

51. The figures for Scottish recruitment in this paragraph come from the following: John Riddy, 'Warren Hastings: Scotland's Benefactor?', in Geoffrey Carnall and Colin Nicholson, eds., *The Impeachment of Warren Hastings* (Edinburgh, 1989), p. 42; Cain, *Cornchest for Scotland*, p. 13; G. J. Bryant, 'Scots in India in the Eighteenth Century', *Scottish Historical Review*, LXIV, 1/177 (April, 1985), pp. 23–4; G. K. McGilvary, 'Post-Union Scotland and the Indian Connection', *Cencrastus*, 37 (Summer, 1990), pp. 30–4; James G. Parker, 'Scottish Enterprise in India, 1750–1914', in R. A. Cage, ed., *The Scots Abroad* (London, 1985), pp. 197–8; A. Mackillop, '"The Hard Men of the Peripheries", Scotland's Military Elite and the Imperial Crisis, 1754–1784'. Unpublished paper given at the Eighteenth Century Scottish Studies Conference, University of Edinburgh, July 2002 (I am grateful to Dr Mackillop for allowing me to read and quote from his interesting paper); Mackillop, 'Scots and the Empire in Asia c.1695–1813'.

52. Devine, *Scotland's Empire*, p. 260; Bartlett, '"This famous island set in a Virginian sea"', p. 212.

53. Cook, 'The Irish Raj', pp. 509–10.

54. M. McLaren, *British India and British Scotland 1780–1830* (Akron, Ohio, 2001).

55. An excellent overview is Hamish Ferguson, 'Before the Union: Scottish Trade with the American Plantations, 1660–1700', unpublished MA dissertation, University of Edinburgh, 2008.

56. Thomas Bartlett, 'Ireland, Empire and Union, 1690–1801', in Kenny, ed., *Ireland and the British Empire*, p. 63.

57. Ibid., pp. 63–5.

58. Quoted in Thomas M. Truxes, *Irish-American Trade, 1660–1783* (Cambridge, 1988), p. 6.

59. T. M. Devine, 'The English Connection and Irish and Scottish Development in the Eighteenth Century', in T. M. Devine and David Dickson, eds., *Ireland and Scotland 1600–1850. Parallels and Contrasts in Economic and Social Development* (Edinburgh, 1983), pp. 12–16.

60. Bartlett, 'Ireland, Empire and Union', p. 67.

61. T. M. Devine, 'The Golden Age of Tobacco', in T. M. Devine and G. Jackson, eds., *Glasgow*. Vol. 1, *Beginnings to 1830* (Manchester, 1995), pp. 139–83; Philipp R. Rössner, *Scottish Trade in the Wake of Union 1700–1760* (Stuttgart, 2008), pp. 133–56.

62. Quoted in David Armitage, 'The Scottish Diaspora', in Jenny Wormald, ed., *Scotland. A History* (Oxford, 2005), p. 292.

63. Ibid., p. 229.

64. Allan I. Macinnes, *Clanship, Commerce and the House of Stuart, 1603–1788* (East Linton, 1996), p. 100.

65. Steve Murdoch, 'Introduction', in S. Murdoch, ed., *Scotland and the Thirty Years War 1618–1648* (Leiden, 2001), p. 19. See also A. Åberg, 'Scottish Soldiers in the Swedish Armies in the Sixteenth and Seventeenth Centuries', in G. G. Simpson, ed., *Scotland and Scandinavia, 800–1800* (Edinburgh, 1990), p. 91.

66. John M. Mackenzie, 'Foreword', in S. Murdoch and A. Mackillop, eds., *Military Governors and Imperial Frontiers c.1600–1800* (Leiden, 2003), p. xvi.

67. David Allan, *Scotland in the Eighteenth Century* (Harlow, 2002), pp. 165–6.

68. T. M. Devine and D. Hesse, eds., *Scotland and Poland: Historical Encounters, 1500–2010* (Edinburgh, 2011).

69. Angela McCarthy, 'Introduction', in Angela McCarthy, ed., *A Global Clan. Scottish Migrant Networks and Identities since the Eighteenth Century* (London, 2006), pp. 1–18; Allan I. Macinnes, 'The Treaty of Union: Made in England', in T. M. Devine, ed., *Scotland and the Union 1707–2007* (Edinburgh, 2008), pp. 55–60.

70. Douglas Catterall, *Community without Borders. Scots Migrants and the Changing Face of Power in the Dutch Republic, c.1600–1700* (Leiden, 2002), p. 11.

71. Christopher Smout, 'The Culture of Migration: Scots as Europeans, 1500–1800', *History Workshop Journal*, 40 (Autumn, 1995), p. 113.

72. S. Murdoch, 'The Good, the Bad and the Anonymous: A Preliminary Survey of Scots in the Dutch East Indies 1612–1707', *Northern Scotland*, 22 (2002), pp. 1–13.

73. T. M. Devine, 'The Scottish Merchant Community 1680–1740', in R. H. Campbell and A. S. Skinner, eds., *The Origin and Nature of the Scottish Enlightenment* (Edinburgh, 1982), pp. 26–41.

74. Catterall, *Community without Borders*, pp. 344–5.

75. Linda Colley, *Britons: Forging the Nation 1707–1837*, 2nd edn (London, 1996), p. 135.

76. Ned C. Landsman, 'Nation, Migration and Province in the First British Empire: Scotland and the Americas, 1600–1800', *American Historical Review*, 104 (April, 1999), p. 471, n. 17.

77. James McLachlan, 'Education', in John Carter Brown Library, *Scotland and the Americas 1600–1800* (Providence, R. I., 1955), pp. 65–75.

78. What follows in this paragraph is based on Richard Saville and Paul Auerbach, 'Education and Social Capital in the Development of Scotland to 1750'. Paper prepared for the Economic History Society Conference, University of Reading, March/April 2006, and Richard Saville, 'Intellectual Capital in Pre-1707 Scotland', in Stewart J. Brown and Christopher A. Whatley, eds., *The Union of 1707. New Dimensions* (Edinburgh, 2008).

79. Saville, 'Intellectual Capital', p. 47.

80. T. M. Devine, *The Scottish Nation 1700–2007* (London, 2006), pp. 77–80.

81. T. C. Smout, N. C. Landsman and T. M. Devine, 'Scottish Emigration in the Seventeenth and Eighteenth Centuries', in N. Canny, ed., *Europeans on the Move. Studies on European Migration 1500–1800* (Oxford, 1994), p. 99.

2. DID SLAVERY HELP TO MAKE SCOTLAND GREAT?

1. Eric Williams, *Capitalism and Slavery* (London, 1944; 1964 edn). An earlier version of this chapter was published in *Britain and the World*, 4, 1 (2011), pp. 40–61.

2. Williams, *Capitalism and Slavery*, p. v.

3. See *inter alia*, R. P. Thomas, 'The Sugar Colonies of the Old Empire. Profit or Loss for Great Britain', *Economic History Review*, 21 (1968), pp. 30–45; S. L. Engerman, 'The Slave Trade and British Capital Formation in the Eighteenth Century: A comment on the Williams Thesis', *Business History Review*, 46 (1972), pp. 430–43; Roger I. Anstey, *The Atlantic Slave Trade and British Abolition, 1760–1810* (London, 1965), pp. 38–57; R. P. Thomas and N. Bean, 'The Fishers of Men: The Profits of the Slave Trade', *Journal of Economic History*, 34 (December, 1974), pp. 885–914; C. H. Feinstein, 'Capital Accumulation and the Industrial Revolution', in R. Floud and D. McCloskey, eds., *The Economic History of Britain since 1700*. Vol. 1 (Cambridge, 1981), p. 131.

4. David Richardson, 'The British Empire and the Atlantic Slave Trade, 1660–1807', in P. J. Marshall, ed., *The Oxford History of the British Empire*. Vol. 2: *The Eighteenth Century* (Oxford, 1998), p. 461.

5. See *inter alia*, B. L. Solow, 'Caribbean Slavery and British Growth. The Eric Williams Hypothesis', *Journal of Development Economics*, 17 (1985), pp. 99–115; Joseph E. Inikori and Stanley L. Engerman, eds., *The Atlantic Slave Trade* (Durham, N. C., 1992); R. Blackburn, *The Making of New World Slavery* (London, 1997); Barbara L. Solow and Stanley L. Engerman, eds., *British Capitalism and Caribbean Slavery: The Legacy of Eric Williams* (Cambridge, 1987).

6. David Eltis and Stanley L. Engerman, 'The Importance of Slavery and the Slave Trade to Industrialising Britain', *Journal of Economic History*, 60 (March, 2000), pp. 123–44.

7. Ibid., p. 141.

8. Joseph E. Inikori, *Africans and the Industrial Revolution in England* (Cambridge, 2002).

9. Ibid., p. 482.

10. 'Roundtable' on Inikori's work in *International Journal of Maritime History*, 15 (2003), pp. 279–361.

11. C. D. Rice, *The Scots Abolitionists, 1833–1861* (Baton Rouge, La., 1981); Iain Whyte, *Scotland and the Abolition of Black Slavery, 1756–1838* (Edinburgh, 2006).

12. Michael Lynch, ed., *The Oxford Companion to Scottish History* (Oxford, 2001).

13. M. Duffill, 'The Africa Trade from the Ports of Scotland, 1706–66', *Slavery and Abolition*, 24 (December 2004), pp. 102–22; David Hancock, 'Scots in the Slave Trade', in Ned C. Landsman, ed., *Nation and Province in the First British Empire* (London, 2001), pp. 61–2; Douglas Hamilton, *Scotland, the Caribbean and the Atlantic World, 1750–1820* (Manchester, 2005); Eric Graham, 'Scots in the Liverpool Slave Trade', *History Scotland* (March, 2007); Whyte, *Scotland and the Abolition of Black Slavery*, pp. 18–20; T. M. Devine, *Scotland's Empire 1600–1815* (London, 2003), pp. 221–49.

14. C. D. Rice, *The Rise and Fall of Black Slavery* (London, 1975), p. 155.

15. Jacob M. Price, 'The Rise of Glasgow in the Chesapeake Tobacco Trade, 1707–1775', reprinted in Peter L. Payne, ed., *Studies in Scottish Business History* (London, 1967), pp. 299–318.

16. Gomer Williams, *History of the Liverpool Privateers and Letters of Marque, with an Account of the Liverpool Slave Trade* (London, 1897), p. 674; Graham, 'Scots in the Liverpool Slave Trade'.

17. Hamilton, *Scotland, the Caribbean and the Atlantic World*, pp. 88–92.

18. David Richardson, ed., *Bristol, Africa and the Eighteenth Century Slave Trade to America*. Vol. 3 (Bristol, 1991).

19. Hancock, 'Scots in the Slave Trade', p. 63.

20. Ibid., pp. 63–83.

21. Quoted in A. Herman, *The Scottish Enlightenment* (London, 2002), p. 138.

22. T. M. Devine, 'The Golden Age of Tobacco', in T. M. Devine and G. Jackson, eds., *Glasgow*. Vol. 1. *Beginnings to 1830* (Manchester, 1995), pp. 140ff.

23. I. C. C. Graham, *Colonists from Scotland: Emigration to North America 1707–1783* (Ithaca, N. Y., 1956), p. 127.

24. Devine, 'The Golden Age of Tobacco', pp. 139–83.

25. Glasgow City Archives (GCA), Speirs Papers, TD 131/10-12, Diary of Alexander Speirs, 2 March 1778.

26. Andrew Brown, *History of Glasgow* (Glasgow, 1795), vol. 2, p. 143.

27. T. M. Devine, 'Sources of Capital for the Glasgow Tobacco Trade, *c.*1740–80', *Business History*, 16 (1974).

28. Trevor Burnard, 'European Migration to Jamaica, 1655–1780', *William and Mary Quarterly*, 53, 4 (1996), pp. 769–96; A. L. Karras, *Sojourners in the Sun: Scottish Migrants in Jamaica and the Chesapeake 1740–1800* (Ithaca, N. Y., 1992), pp. 43–5; Hamilton, *Scotland, the Caribbean and the Atlantic World*, pp. 23–4.

29. National Archives, Customs 14 and 17/12. Copies in National Archives of Scotland (NAS), RH 2/4/22 and 40

30. Adam Smith, *The Wealth of Nations* (1776; London, 1937), p. 366.

31. J. R. Ward, 'The British West Indies in the Age of Abolition', in Marshall, ed., *Oxford History*, p. 427.

32. Ibid.

33. Quoted in R. B. Sheridan, 'The Formation of Caribbean Plantation Society, 1689–1748', in Marshall, ed., *Oxford History*, p. 402.

34. Ward, 'British West Indies', p. 433.

35. Philip D. Morgan, 'The Black Experience in the British Empire, 1680–1810', in Marshall, ed., *Oxford History*, p. 470.

36. See *inter alia*, Michael Craton, *Testing the Chains: Resistance to Slavery in the British West Indies* (Ithaca, N. Y., 1982); Elsa V. Coreia, *Slave Society in the British Leeward Islands at the End of the Eighteenth Century* (New Haven, Conn., 1965); Jerome S. Handler and Frederick W. Lange, *Plantation Slavery in Barbados: An Archaeological and Historical Investigation* (Cambridge, Mass., 1978); R. B. Sheridan, *Doctors and Slaves* (Cambridge, 1985), *passim*; Morgan, 'The Black Experience', pp. 467–73.

37. B. W. Higman, *Plantation Jamaica, 1750–1850* (Kingston, 2005).

38. Charles Leslie, *A new and exact History of Jamaica* (Edinburgh, *c.*1740), p. 353.

39. Trevor Burnard, '"Prodigious Riches": The Wealth of Jamaica before the American Revolution', *Economic History Review*, LIV, 3 (2001), p. 508.

40. Higman, *Plantation Jamaica*, p. 5.

41. Edward Long, *A History of Jamaica* (London, 1774), vol. 2, pp. 286–92.

42. R. B. Sheridan, 'The Role of the Scots in the Economy and Society of the West Indies', in V. Rubin and A. Tuden, eds., *Comparative Perspectives on Slavery in New World Plantation Societies*. Annals of the New York Academy of Sciences, Vol. 292 (New York, 1977).

43. Long, *History of Jamaica*, 2, p. 286.

44. Devine, *Scotland's Empire*, pp. 233–4.

45. Quoted in Higman, *Plantation Jamaica*, pp. 77–9.

46. R. B. Sheridan, 'The Wealth of Jamaica in the Eighteenth Century', *Economic History Review*, 18 (1963), p. 158.

47. J. C. Vardin, *La Mise en valeur de l'isle de Tobago, 1673–1783* (Paris, 1969), p. 23; Hancock, 'Scots in the Slave Trade', p. 64.

48. Sir W. Forbes, *Memoirs of a Banking House* (London and Edinburgh, 1869), p. 39.

49. This paragraph summarizes T. M. Devine, 'An Eighteenth Century Business Elite: Glasgow West India Merchants, *c.*1750–1815', *Scottish Historical Review*, LVII, 163 (April, 1978).

50. GCA, West India Association Minutes, Miscellaneous Papers, 3290–3294.

51. Quoted in Whyte, *Scotland and the Abolition of Black Slavery*, p. 86.

52. Burnard, '"Prodigious Riches"', p. 506.

53. Joel Mokyr, 'Accounting for the Industrial Revolution', in R. Floud and P. Johnson, eds., *The Cambridge Economic History of Modern Britain*. Vol. 1. *Industrialisation, 1700–1860* (Cambridge, 2004), pp. 1–27.

54. N. F. R. Crafts and C. K. Hanley, 'Output, Growth and the British Industrial Revolution', *Economic History Review*, 43 (1992), pp. 103–30; M. M. Postan, 'Recent Trends in the Accumulation of Capital', *Economic History Review*, 6, 1 (October, 1935). For an opposing perspective see Inikori, *Africans and the Industrial Revolution*, pp. 405–72.

55. Compare, for instance, the content of my chapter, 'Scotland', in Floud and Johnson, eds., *Cambridge Economic History of Modern Britain*, pp. 388–416, with the rest of the volume.

56. Christopher A. Whatley, 'The Issues facing Scotland in 1707', in S. J. Brown and C. A. Whatley, eds., *The Union of 1707. New Dimensions* (Edinburgh, 2008), p. 13.

57. T. M. Devine, *The Scottish Nation 1700–2007* (London, 2006), pp. 105–23.

58. T. M. Devine, 'Urbanisation', in T. M. Devine and Rosalind Mitchison, eds., *People and Society in Scotland*. Vol. 1, *1760–1830* (Edinburgh, 1988), pp. 27–52.

59. T. M. Devine, *The Transformation of Rural Scotland. Social Change and the Agrarian Economy, 1660–1815* (Edinburgh, 1994, 1999); T. M. Devine, *Clanship to Crofters' War. The Social Transformation of the Scottish Highlands* (Manchester, 1994).

60. R. H. Campbell, 'The Making of the Industrial City', in Devine and Jackson, eds., *Glasgow*, pp. 184–213.

61. J. Butt, 'The Scottish Iron and Steel Industry before the Hot-Blast', *Journal of the West of Scotland Iron and Steel Industry*, 73 (1966); Christopher A. Whatley, *The Industrial Revolution in Scotland* (Cambridge, 1997), p. 31.

62. Norman Murray, *The Scottish Handloom Weavers, 1790–1850* (Edinburgh, 1978), p. 23.

63. National Library of Scotland, MS8793, Letter Book 'E' of Alexander Houston and Co., *passim*; T. M. Devine, 'A Glasgow Tobacco House during the American War of Independence', *William and Mary Quarterly*. XXXIII, 3 (July, 1975); Whatley, *Industrial Revolution in Scotland*, p. 42.

64. Inikori, *Africans and the Industrial Revolution*, pp. 377–8.

65. Eltis and Engerman, 'The Importance of Slavery', p. 125.

66. E. A. Wrigley and R. S. Schofield, *The Population History of England, 1541–1871* (Cambridge, 1986), pp. 208–9.

67. Census 1971 Scotland: Preliminary Report.

68. Inikori, *Africans and the Industrial Revolution*, pp. 192–5.

69. Jacob M. Price, 'New Time Series for Scotland's and Britain's Trade with the Thirteen Colonies and States, 1740–1791', *William and Mary Quarterly*, XXXII, 2 (April, 1975), pp. 301–25.

70. Alastair J. Durie, *The Scottish Linen Industry in the Eighteenth Century* (Edinburgh, 1979), pp. 158–60.

71. John Naismith, *Thoughts on Various Objects of Industry pursued in Scotland* (Edinburgh, 1790), p. 93.

72. Durie, *Scottish Linen Industry*, pp. 151–2.

73. Devine, *Scotland's Empire*, pp. 336–7.

74. T. M. Devine, 'The Colonial Trades and Industrial Investment in Scotland, *c.*1700–1815', in P. Emmer and F. Caastra, eds., *The Organisation of Interoceanic Trade in European Expansion, 1450–1800* (Aldershot, 1996), pp. 299–312.

75. James Finlay and Co., Glasgow, Balance Book of J. Finlay and Co. 1789–1800: the firm's capital rose from £30,000 in 1795 to £75,000 in 1810.

76. NAS, GD64/1/274, (Copy) Contract of Copartnery of New Lanark Co., 5 Oct. 1810.

77. GCA, Campbell of Hallyards Papers, Minute of the Meeting of the Trustees of Alexander Campbell, 16 Apr. 1819; Trustees of R. Dennistoun to Campbell's trustees, 15 Dec. 1823.

78. NAS, Particular Register of Sasines (Renfrew), 42/217.

79. *Glasgow Courier*, 31 December 1812.

80. GCA, Bogle MSS, Genealogy of the Bogle family; Minute Books of West India Association of Glasgow, Individual and Firm Subscriptions.

81. NAS, GD237/134, Minute of a Meeting of the Creditors of the House of A. Houston and Co., 23 Sept. 1806; Signet Library, Court of Session Process 368/21, Petition of Robert Dunmore, 1-4.

82. T. M. Devine, *Clearance and Improvement. Land, Power and People in Scotland, 1700–1900* (Edinburgh, 2006), pp. 54–92.

83. Based on a preliminary survey by my research assistant, Alex Hendrickson, in 2008 of records of landed families with eighteenth-century Scottish West India interests held in both public and private archives.

84. For the Irish comparisons see Nini Rodgers, *Ireland, Slavery and Anti-Slavery: 1612–1865* (Basingstoke, 2009), pp. 82–118 and Davie Dickson, *Old World Colony. Cork and South Munster* (Cork, 2005).

85. George McGilvaray, *East India Patronage and the British State* (London, 2008), pp. 180–202.

86. An important start in advancing current knowledge was made in March 2010 at the Royal Society of Edinburgh Workshop on Scottish connections to the slave trade and slavery, sponsored by both Edinburgh and Glasgow universities. It involved Scottish historians, archivists and key researchers from both sides of the Atlantic with expertise on the subject from non-Scottish perspectives.

87. Rice, *Black Slavery*, p. 167.

88. Adam Smith, *The Theory of Moral Sentiments* (London, 1804), vol. 1, p. 345.

89. Whyte, *Scotland and the Abolition of Black Slavery*, pp. 55–60.

90. Quoted in Rice, *Black Slavery*, p. 176.

91. Quoted in C. D. Rice, 'Abolitionists and Abolitionism in Aberdeen: A Test Case for the Nineteenth-century Anti-slavery Movement', *Northern Scotland*, 1 (December, 1972), p. 70.

3. INDUSTRIAL AND FINANCIAL SINEWS OF SCOTTISH GLOBAL POWER

1. John Darwin, *The Empire Project. The Rise and Fall of the British World-System 1830–1970* (Cambridge, 2009).
2. S. B. Saul, *Studies in British Overseas Trade 1870–1914* (Liverpool, 1960), p. 7.
3. Andrew Porter, 'Introduction: Britain and the Empire in the Nineteenth Century', in Andrew Porter, ed., *The Oxford History of the British Empire*. Vol. 3, *The Nineteenth Century* (Oxford, 1999), p. 4.
4. Quoted in Darwin, *Empire Project*, p. 58.
5. Werner Schlote, *British Overseas Trade from 1700 to the 1930s* (Oxford, 1952), p. 88.
6. Darwin, *Empire Project*, p. 122.
7. Saul, *Studies*, p. 228.
8. Schlote, *British Overseas Trade*, p. 88.
9. Quoted in Porter, 'Introduction', p. 9.
10. W. Woodruff, *The Impact of Western Man* (London, 1966), p. 253.
11. C. A. Bayly, *The Birth of the Modern World 1780–1914* (Oxford, 2004), p. 173.
12. J. H. Clapham, *An Economic History of Modern Britain: The Early Railway Age 1820–1850* (Cambridge, 1939), p. 211.
13. Darwin, *Empire Project*, p. 37.
14. Saul, *Studies*, pp. 9–10.
15. Michael Greenberg, *British Trade and the Opening of China 1800–42* (Cambridge, 1951), pp. 196–215.
16. A. M. Carr-Saunders, *World Population* (London, 1936), p. 30.
17. P. J. Cain and A. G. Hopkins, 'The Political Economy of British Expansion Overseas, 1750–1914', *Economic History Review*, XXXIII, 4 (November, 1980), p. 479.
18. T. M. Devine, *The Scottish Nation, 1700–2007* (London, 2006), p. 249.
19. M. S. Moss and J. R. Hume, *Workshop of the British Empire* (London, 1977); John Butt, 'The Industries of Glasgow', in W. H. Fraser and Irene Maver, eds., *Glasgow*. Vol. 2, *1830–1912* (Manchester, 1996), pp. 96–140.
20. William Knox, *Hanging by a Thread: The Scottish Cotton Industry 1850–1914* (Preston, 1995).
21. Don-Woon Kim, 'The British Multinational Enterprise in the United States before 1914: The Case of J and P Coats', *Business History Review*, 72 (Winter, 1998), pp. 523–51.

22. Gordon Stewart, *Jute and Empire* (Manchester, 1998), pp. 38–92.

23. Devine, *Scottish Nation*, p. 251; C. Gulvin, *The Tweedmakers: A History of the Scottish Fancy Woollen Industry, 1600–1914* (Edinburgh, 1973).

24. S. G. E. Lythe and J. Butt, *An Economic History of Scotland 1100–1939* (London, 1975), pp. 168–80.

25. M. Anderson and D. J. Morse, 'The People', in W. H. Fraser and R. J. Morris, eds., *People and Society in Scotland*. Vol. 2, *1830–1914* (Edinburgh, 1990), pp. 8–45.

26. T. M. Devine, C. H. Lee and G. C. Peden, eds., *The Transformation of Scotland* (Edinburgh, 2005), pp. 92–8.

27. Bruce Lenman, *An Economic History of Modern Scotland 1660–1976* (London, 1977), p. 193.

28. Unless otherwise stated, the following pages are based on Devine, Lee and Peden, eds., *Transformation of Scotland*, pp. 34–70, 128–59 and Devine, *Scottish Nation*, pp. 255–61.

29. James Cleland, *Enumeration of the Inhabitants of the City of Glasgow* (Glasgow, 1843), p. 151.

30. Quoted in A. Slaven, *The Development of the West of Scotland 1750–1960* (London, 1975).

31. W. Knox, 'The Political Workplace Culture of the Scottish Working Class, 1832–1914', in Fraser and Morris, eds., *People and Society in Scotland*, p. 147.

32. Edward Young, *Labor in Europe and America* (Washington, D. C., 1876).

33. See P. J. Cain and A. G. Hopkins, *British Imperialism: Innovation and Expansion, 1888–1914* (London, 1993) and *British Imperialism: Crisis and Deconstruction, 1914–1990* (London, 1993) which gather material published previously in article form.

34. J. Forbes Munro, *Maritime Enterprise and Empire* (Woodbridge, 2003), pp. 8, 34, 505.

35. See, *inter alia*, M. J. Daunton, '"Gentlemanly Capitalism" and British Industry, 1820–1914', *Past and Present*, 122 (1989), pp. 119–58; A. Porter, '"Gentlemanly Capitalism" and Empire: The British Experience since 1750?', *Journal of Imperial and Commonwealth History*, 18 (1990), pp. 265–95; R. E. Dumett, ed., *Gentlemanly Capitalism and British Imperialism: The New Debate on Empire* (London, 1999).

36. J. Forbes Munro and Tony Slaven, 'Networks and Markets in Clyde Shipping', *Business History*, 43, 2 (2001), pp. 22–3; Gordon Jackson and Charles Munn, 'Trade, Commerce and Finance', in Fraser and Maver, eds., *Glasgow*, pp. 62–70.

37. Michael Fry, *The Scottish Empire* (Edinburgh, 2001), p. 265.

38. Munro, *Maritime Enterprise and Empire*, p. 490.

39. Ibid., pp. 485–511.

40. Peter L. Payne, *The Early Scottish Limited Companies 1856–1895: An Historical and Analytical Survey* (Edinburgh, 1980), p. 66.

41. F. E. Hyde, *Cunard and the North Atlantic 1840–1973* (London, 1975), pp. 8–24.

42. Anthony Slaven and Sydney Checkland, eds., *Dictionary of Scottish Business Biography 1860–1960.* Vol. 2 (Aberdeen, 1990), pp. 262–5.

43. Ibid., pp. 274–6, 286–9, 290–2; Jackson and Munn, 'Trade, Commerce and Finance', pp. 65–70.

44. Munro, *Maritime Enterprise and Empire*, pp. 493–4.

45. P. L. Robertson, 'Shipping and Shipbuilding: The Case of William Denny and Brothers', *Business History*, 16 (1974), pp. 36–47.

46. Munro, *Maritime Enterprise and Empire*, pp. 493–4.

47. Stanley Chapman, *Merchant Enterprise in Britain* (Cambridge, 1992), pp. 254–5.

48. Greenberg, *British Trade and the Opening of China*, pp. 37–8.

49. Chapman, *Merchant Enterprise*, p. 113.

50. Neal Ascherson, *Stone Voices. The Search for Scotland* (London, 2002), p. 233.

51. Chapman, *Merchant Enterprise*, p. 271.

52. C. Brogan, *James Finlay and Co. Ltd.* (Glasgow, 1951), chs. 1–6.

53. Cain and Hopkins, *British Imperialism: Innovation*, pp. 433–9.

54. Information from *Forbes Magazine*.

55. Darwin, *Empire Project*, p. 57; Chapman, *Merchant Enterprise*, p. 26.

56. Darwin, *Empire Project*, p. 38.

57. Unless otherwise noted the details which follow on Jardine Matheson come from Robert Blake, *Jardine Matheson. Traders of the Far East* (London, 1999); Maggie Keswick, ed., *The Thistle and the Jade* (London, 1982); Greenberg, *British Trade and the Opening of China*, chs. 4–8; and Geoffrey Jones, *Merchants to Multinationals* (Oxford, 2000).

58. Fry, *Scottish Empire*, p. 307.

59. J. Phipps, *A Practical Treatise on the China and Eastern Trade* (1836), Introduction.

60. Quoted in Greenberg, *British Trade and the Opening of China*, p. 105.

61. Blake, *Jardine Matheson*, p. 121.

62. Quoted in Greenberg, *British Trade and the Opening of China*, pp. 213–14.

63. T. M. Devine, *The Great Highland Famine. Hunger, Emigration and the*

Scottish Highlands in the Nineteenth Century (Edinburgh, 1988), pp. 212–25.

64. Quoted in Stephanie Jones, *Two Centuries of Overseas Trading. The Origins and Growth of the Inchcape Group* (London, 1986), p. 38.

65. Ascherson, *Stone Voices*, pp. 233–4.

66. Quoted in Blake, *Jardine Matheson*, p. 36.

67. Slaven and Checkland, eds., *Dictionary of Scottish Business Biography*, *passim*; Jones, *Two Centuries of Overseas Trading*, p. 41; Munro, *Maritime Enterprise and Empire*, p. 510.

4. THE GREAT MIGRATION

1. M. Flinn, ed., *Scottish Population History from the Seventeenth Century to the 1930s* (Cambridge, 1977), pp. 441–2.

2. Ibid., p. 442.

3. T. C. Smout, N. C. Landsman and T. M. Devine, 'Scottish Emigration in the Seventeenth and Eighteenth Centuries', in Nicholas Canny, ed., *Europeans on the Move: Studies on European Migration 1500–1800* (Oxford, 1994), pp. 90–111.

4. Nicholas J. Evans, 'The Emigration of Skilled Male Workers from Clydeside during the Interwar Period', *International Journal of Maritime History*, XVIII (2006), pp. 255–80; Marjory Harper, *Emigration from Scotland between the Wars* (Manchester, 1998).

5. T. M. Devine, 'The Paradox of Scottish Emigration', in T. M. Devine, ed., *Scottish Emigration and Scottish Society* (Edinburgh, 1992), p. 1.

6. Rosalind R. McClean, 'Scottish Emigrants to New Zealand 1840–1880', unpublished PhD thesis, University of Edinburgh (1990), p. 434.

7. Jock Phillips and Terry Hearn, *Settlers. New Zealand Immigrants from England, Ireland and Scotland 1800–1945* (Auckland, 2008), p. 107.

8. John M. Mackenzie, *The Scots in South Africa* (Manchester, 2007), pp. 64–5.

9. R. A. Cage, ed., *The Scots Abroad* (London, 1985), pp. 191–271; Marjory Harper, *Adventurers and Exiles* (London, 2003), pp. 71–111; Robert Harvey, *Cochrane: The Life and Exploits of a Fighting Captain* (London, 2002); Ian Grimble, *The Sea Wolf: The Life of Admiral Cochrane* (Edinburgh, 2000); Alexander McKay, *Scottish Samurai: Thomas Blake Glover 1838–1911* (Edinburgh, 1997); Michael Gardener, *At the Edge of Empire. The Life of Thomas Blake Glover* (Edinburgh, 2008).

10. Dudley Baines, *Migration in a Mature Economy* (Cambridge, 1985), p. 10.

11. Evans, 'Emigration of Skilled Male Workers', pp. 255–79.

12. Edwin Muir, *Scottish Journey* (London, 1935), p. 94.

13. John Bodnar, *The Transplanted. A History of Immigrants in Urban America* (Bloomington, Ind., 1985), p. 4.

14. Eric Richards, *Britannia's Children. Emigration from England, Scotland, Wales and Ireland since 1600* (London, 2004), pp. 118, 180, 236.

15. Walter Nugent, *Crossings. The Great Transatlantic Migrations, 1870–1914* (Bloomington, Ind., 1992).

16. I. Levitt and T. C. Smout, *The State of the Scottish Working Class in 1843* (Edinburgh, 1979).

17. See, for instance, McClean, 'Scottish Emigrants to New Zealand', pp. 122, 157, 175–6, 436–7.

18. Devine, 'Paradox of Scottish Emigration', pp. 6–8.

19. Charlotte Erickson, *Leaving England. Essays on British Emigration in the Nineteenth Century* (Ithaca, N. Y., 1994), p. 58.

20. Nugent, *Crossings*, pp. 95, 104. For Italian emigration see also Donna R. Gabaccia, *Italy's Many Diasporas* (Washington, D. C., 2000).

21. T. M. Devine, *Scotland's Empire, 1600–1815* (London, 2003), pp. 94–139; Levitt and Smout, *State of the Scottish Working Class*, pp. 91–2.

22. Bodnar, *The Transplanted*, p. 4.

23. Nugent, *Crossings*, p. 47.

24. Devine, 'Paradox of Scottish Emigration', pp. 3–4; Charlotte Erickson, 'Who were the English and Scots Emigrants to the United States in the late Nineteenth Century?', in D. V. Glass and R. Revelle, eds., *Population and Social Change* (London, 1972).

25. I. Frenczi and W. F. Willcox, *International Migrations* (New York, 1929–31), pp. 236–88.

26. Quoted in James Belich, *Replenishing the Earth. The Settler Revolution and the Rise of the Anglo-World, 1783–1939* (Oxford, 2009), p. 148.

27. Quoted in Amy J. Lloyd, 'Popular Perceptions of Emigration in Britain, 1870–1914', unpublished PhD thesis, University of Cambridge (2009), pp. 247–9.

28. Ibid.

29. Richards, *Britannia's Children*, p. 122.

30. Ibid., p. 421.

31. Devine, *Scotland's Empire*, pp. 119–39.

32. Quoted in A. J. Youngson, *After the '45* (Edinburgh, 1982), p. 12.

33. Frank Broeze, 'Private Enterprise and the Peopling of Australia, 1831–1850', *Economic History Review*, 35 (1982), pp. 235–53.

34. Belich, *Replenishing the Earth*, p. 179.

35. Richards, *Britannia's Children*, p. 122.

36. Belich, *Replenishing the Earth*, p. 109.

37. McClean, 'Scottish Emigrants to New Zealand', p. 22.

38. C. K. Harley, 'Ocean, freight rates and productivity, 1740–1913', *Journal of Economic History*, 48 (1988), pp. 851–76.

39. M. Anderson and D. J. Morse, 'The People', in W. H. Fraser and R. J. Morris, eds., *People and Society in Scotland*. Vol. 2, *1830–1914* (Edinburgh, 1990), p. 16.

40. McClean, 'Scottish Emigrants to New Zealand'.

41. Quoted in M. Harper, *Emigration from North-East Scotland* (Aberdeen, 1988), Vol. 2, p. 22.

42. Ibid., *passim*.

43. Bodnar, *The Transplanted*, pp. 53–4.

44. Harper, *Emigration from North-East Scotland*, Vol. 2, pp. 1–41.

45. Belich, *Replenishing the Earth*, *passim*.

46. T. M. Devine, *The Scottish Nation, 1700–2007* (London, 2006), pp. 486–522.

47. Charles W. J. Withers, *Urban Highlanders. Highland–Lowland Migration and Urban Gaelic Culture, 1700–1900* (East Linton, 1998).

48. T. M. Devine, *The Transformation of Rural Scotland. Social Change and the Agrarian Economy 1660–1815* (Edinburgh, 1994), pp. 36–164.

49. R. A. Houston, 'The Demographic Regime', in T. M. Devine and R. Mitchison, eds., *People and Society in Scotland*. Vol. 1, *1760–1830* (Edinburgh, 1988), p. 20.

50. For these points see T. M. Devine, ed., *Farm Servants and Labour in Lowland Scotland, 1770–1914* (Edinburgh, 1984), *passim*.

51. Anderson and Morse, 'The People', pp. 19, 22.

52. R. H. Campbell, 'Scotland', in Cage, ed., *Scots Abroad*, p. 10.

53. Jeanette M. Brock, *The Mobile Scot. A Study of Emigration and Migration, 1861–1911* (Edinburgh, 1999), pp. 178–209.

54. Quoted in Harper, *Emigration from North-East Scotland*, Vol. 2, p. 55.

55. T. C. Smout, *A Century of the Scottish People, 1830–1950* (London, 1986), pp. 109–13.

56. R. D. Anderson, *Education and Opportunity in Victorian Scotland* (Edinburgh, 1983), p. 152.

57. R. H. Campbell, *The Rise and Fall of Scottish Industry, 1707–1939* (Edinburgh, 1980), pp. 76–101; Smout, *Century of the Scottish People*, p. 112.

58. R. G. Rodger, 'The Invisible Hand: Market Forces, Housing and the Urban Form in Victorian Cities', in D. Fraser and A. Sutcliffe, eds., *The Pursuit of Urban History* (London, 1980), pp. 190–211.

59. J. D. Gould, 'European Intercontinental Emigration 1815–1914: Patterns and Causes', *Journal of European Economic History*, 8 (1979).

60. Devine, ed., *Farm Servants and Labour*, pp. 119–20, 251–3.

61. Flinn, ed., *Scottish Population History*, p. 442.

62. C. H. Lee, 'Modern Economic Growth and Structural Change in Scotland: The Service Sector Reconsidered', *Scottish Economic and Social History*, 3 (1983), pp. 5–35.

63. J. H. Treble, 'The Occupied Male Labour Force', in Fraser and Morris, eds., *People and Society in Scotland*, pp. 195–6.

5. HUMAN SELECTION AND ENFORCED EXILE

1. Unless otherwise stated, the information in this section is drawn from my book *The Great Highland Famine. Hunger, Emigration and the Scottish Highlands in the Nineteenth Century* (Edinburgh, 1988, 1996).

2. *Witness*, 21 November 1846.

3. *The Scotsman*, 12 December 1846.

4. National Archives of Scotland (NAS), HD6/2, Treasury Correspondence, Trevelyan to Baird, 19 March 1847.

5. Ibid.

6. Thomas Mulock, *The Western Highlands and Islands of Scotland Socially Considered* (Edinburgh, 1850), pp. 81–2.

7. T. M. Devine, 'Why the Highlands Did Not Starve. Ireland and Highland Scotland During the Potato Famine', in C. Ó Gráda, R. Paping and E. Vanhaute, eds., *When the Potato Failed: Causes and Effects of the 'Last' European Subsistence Crisis, 1845–1850* (Turnhout, Belgium, 2007), pp. 111–22; T. M. Devine, *Clearance and Improvement. Land, Power and People in Scotland, 1700–1900* (Edinburgh, 2006), pp. 218–28.

8. NAS, HD16/101, Minutes of Committee appointed to watch the progress of events connected with the potato failure.

9. *The Scotsman*, 30 July 1850.

10. Parliamentary Papers (PP), *Report to the Board of Supervision by Sir John McNeil on the Western Highlands and Islands*, XXVI, 1851, Appendix A, pp. 93–5.

11. Inveraray Castle (IC), Argyll Estate Papers, Bundle 1522, Abstract of Accounts, 1843–9.

12. PP, *Return of Population and Poor Rates (Scotland), 1853*, XLVI (1854–5).

13. Anon., *The Depopulation System in the Highlands* (Edinburgh, 1849), p. 23.

14. D. Clark, 'On the Agriculture of the County of Argyll', *Transactions of the Highland and Agricultural Society*, 4th Series, X (1878), p. 95; Mulock, *Western Highlands*, p. 66.

15. NAS, HD7/76, Trevelyan to W. Skene, 26 June 1848.

16. W. Orr, *Deer Forests, Landlords and Crofters* (Edinburgh, 1982), p. 155.

17. Devine, *Great Highland Famine*, p. 185.

18. Stephen P. Walker, 'Agents of Dispossession and Acculturation. Edinburgh Accountants and the Highland Clearances', *Critical Perspectives in Accounting*, 14 (2003), pp. 819–20.

19. *The Scotsman*, 25 August 1849.

20. Quoted in Walker, 'Agents of Dispossession', p. 820.

21. John Pinkerton, *An Inquiry into the History of Scotland Preceding the Reign of Malcolm III* (Edinburgh, 1790), p. 339.

22. Krisztina Fenyö, *Contempt, Sympathy and Romance. Lowland Perceptions of the Highlands and the Clearances during the Famine Years, 1845–1855* (Edinburgh, 2000), pp. 29–31.

23. Colin Kidd, 'Race, Empire and the Limits of Nineteenth-Century Nationhood', *Historical Journal*, 46, 4 (2003), pp. 873–92.

24. Fenyö, *Contempt, Sympathy and Romance*, pp. 40–1.

25. Reginald Horsman, 'Origins of Racial Anglo-Saxonism in Great Britain before 1850', *Journal of the History of Ideas*, XXXVII (1976), p. 387.

26. *The Times*, 1 and 7 October 1846.

27. Devine, *Great Highland Famine*, p. 217.

28. NAS, HD4/1, Letterbook of H.I.E.S. (1), Trevelyan to Miss Neave, 20 January 1852.

29. NAS, HD4/2, Letterbook of H.I.E.S. (2), Trevelyan to Sir J. McNeil, 14 August 1852 and Commissary-General Miller, 30 June 1852.

30. *The Scotsman*, 26 July 1851.

31. Devine, *Great Highland Famine*, pp. 192–9.

32. Ibid.

33. MS Diary of J. M. Mackenzie, 1851, Chamberlain of Lewis, 5 April 1851.

34. PP, *Report and Evidence of the Commissioners of Inquiry into the Condition of the Crofters and Cottars in the Highlands and Islands of Scotland*, 1884, XXXII–XXXVI, QQ 1430, 16967–8.

35. Diary of J. M. Mackenzie, *passim*.

36. NAS, HD7/47, William Skene to Sir Charles Trevelyan, 21 February 1848.

37. NAS, Sheriff Court Processes (Tobermory), SC 59/2/4–14.

38. NAS, Sheriff Court Processes (Stornoway), SC 33/17/26–34.

39. *Destitution Papers*, Second Report of the Edinburgh Section (1849). Sir E. P Coffin to W. Skene, 29 June 1848.

40. NAS, AF49/6, Report of T. G. Dickson as acting for the trustee on Sir James M. Riddell's estate; Diary of J. M. Mackenzie, 1851; IC, Argyll Estate Papers, Bundles 1522–1531.

41. IC, Argyll Estate Papers, Bundle 1558, Duke of Argyll to (J. Campbell?), 5 May 1851.

42. Ibid., Bundle 1805, J. Campbell to Duke of Argyll, 27 February 1849.

43. Walker, 'Agents of Dispossession', p. 820.

44. PP, *Papers Relative to Emigration to the North American Colonies*, XXII (1852), Sir J. Matheson to A. C. Buchanan, 10 October 1851.

45. IC, Argyll Estate Papers, Bundle 1804, List of tenants and cottars warned of removal, 1850; Bundle 1523, Campbell to Duke of Argyll, 25 April 1854.

46. All examples come from T. G. Dickson's report in NAS, AF49/6.

47. Donald E. Meek, ed., *Tuath is Tighearna. Tenants and Landlords* (Edinburgh, 1995), p. 204.

6. IN THE LAND OF THE FREE

1. Essays by Louis Cullen and T. C. Smout, N. C. Landsman and T. M. Devine in N. Canny, ed., *Europeans on the Move. Studies on European Migration 1500–1800* (Oxford, 1994).

2. T. M. Devine, *Scotland's Empire, 1600–1815* (London, 2003), pp. 140–63.

3. Dudley Baines, *Migration in a Mature Economy* (Cambridge, 1985), p. 10.

4. Cathal Pórtéir, ed., *The Great Irish Famine* (Cork, 1995); Kerby A. Miller, *Emigrants and Exiles: Ireland and the Irish Exodus to North America* (Oxford, 1985); Andy Bielenberg, ed., *The Irish Diaspora* (Harlow, 2000), pp. 111–38.

5. Jay P. Dolan, *The Irish Americans* (New York, 2008), p. 75.

6. Ibid., p. 74.

7. Cormac Ó Gráda, *Ireland's Great Famine: Interdisciplinary Perspectives* (Dublin, 2006), pp. 190–1.

8. Brenda Collins, 'The Origins of Irish Immigration to Scotland in the

Nineteenth and Twentieth Centuries', in T. M. Devine, ed., *Irish Immigrants and Scottish Society in the Nineteenth and Twentieth Centuries* (Edinburgh, 1991), p. 1.

9. David Fitzpatrick, *Irish Emigration, 1801–1921* (Dublin, 1984), p. 1.

10. Kevin Kenny, *The American Irish, A History* (Harlow, 2000), p. 99.

11. Miller, *Emigrants and Exiles*, p. 295.

12. Kenny, *American Irish*, p. 109.

13. Richard Jensen, '"No Irish Need Apply": A Myth of Victimisation', *Journal of Social History*, 36 (2002), pp. 405–29.

14. Miller, *Emigrants and Exiles*, is the largest scale study of this thesis.

15. Quoted in Dolan, *Irish Americans*, p. 76.

16. Timothy Guinnane, *The Vanishing Irish: Households, Migration and the Rural Economy in Ireland 1850–1914* (Princeton, N. J., 1997), p. 107; John Bodnar, *The Transplanted: A History of Immigrants in Urban America* (Bloomington, Ind., 1985), p. 53.

17. Kenny, *American Irish*, p. 141.

18. Dolan, *Irish Americans*, p. 81.

19. Miller, *Emigrants and Exiles*, p. 81.

20. Patrick Blessing, 'Irish', in Stephan Thernstrom, ed., *Harvard Encyclopedia of American Ethnic Groups* (Cambridge, Mass., 1980), pp. 530–40.

21. D. N. Doyle, 'The Irish as Urban Pioneers in the United States 1850–1870', *Journal of American Ethnic History*, 10 (1990–1), pp. 36–53; Patrick J. Blessing, 'Irish Emigration to the United States, 1800–1920: An Overview', in P. J. Drudy, ed., *Irish in America: Emigration, Assimilation, Impact* (Cambridge, 1985), pp. 23–7.

22. Dolan, *Irish Americans*, p. 85.

23. L. P. Curtis Jr, *Apes and Angels: The Irishman in Victorian Caricature*, rev. edn (Washington, D. C., 1977), pp. 3–5, 18–29.

24. Kenny, *American Irish*, pp. 115–16.

25. Tyler Anbinder, *Nativism and Slavery: The Northern Know Nothings and the Politics of the 1850s* (New York, 1992), pp. 103–26.

26. John Higham, *Strangers in the Land: Patterns of American Nativism, 1860–1925* (New York, 1965), pp. 61–87.

27. Kenny, *American Irish*, p. 123.

28. Jay P. Dolan, *The Immigrant Church* (Baltimore, Md., 1975).

29. Emmett Larkin, 'The Devotional Revolution in Ireland', *American Historical Review*, 77 (1972), pp. 625–52; Patrick Corish, *The Irish Catholic Experience: A Historical Survey* (Dublin, 1985).

30. Dolan, *Irish Americans*, p. 109.

31. Blessing, 'Irish', p. 534.

32. Quoted in Dolan, *Irish Americans*, p. 112.

33. Jay P. Dolan, *The American Catholic Experience: A History from Colonial Times to the Present* (New York, 1985), pp. 270–4.

34. Dolan, *Irish Americans*, p. 87.

35. Kenny, *American Irish*, p. 181.

36. Jensen, '"No Irish Need Apply"', pp. 415–18.

37. Stephan Thernstrom, *The Other Bostonians: Poverty and Progress in the American Metropolis, 1860–1970* (Cambridge, Mass., 1973), pp. 130–2. See also Timothy J. Meagher, *Inventing Irish America: Generation, Class and Ethnic Identity in a New England City 1880–1928* (Notre Dame, Ind., 2001), pp. 111–12 for similar evidence from a smaller urban area.

38. Bodnar, *The Transplanted, passim*.

39. Stephen P. Erie, *Rainbow's End: Irish Americans and the Dilemmas of Urban Machine Politics, 1840–1985* (Berkeley, Calif., 1988).

40. Dolan, *Irish Americans*, p. 141.

41. Francis M. Carroll, 'America and Irish Political Independence', in Drudy, *Irish in America*, pp. 276–8; Kenny, *American Irish*, pp. 194–5.

42. See, for example, G. F. Black, *Scotland's Mark on America* (1921; reprinted Charleston, S. C., 2008); Wallace Notestein, *The Scot in History* (New Haven, Conn., 1946); Duncan Bruce, *The Mark of the Scots. Their Astonishing Contributions to History, Science, Democracy, Literature and the Arts* (New York, 1996).

43. Quoted in George Shepperson, 'Writings in Scottish-American History: A Brief Survey', *William and Mary Quarterly*, 3rd Series, XI (1954), p. 163.

44. Quoted in Andrew Hook, 'Troubling Times in the Scottish-American Relationship', in Celeste Ray, ed., *Transatlantic Scots* (Tuscaloosa, Ala., 2005), p. 217.

45. Ibid., p. 218.

46. Quoted in Andrew Hook, *Scotland and America: A Study of Cultural Relations, 1750–1835* (Glasgow, 1975), p. 69.

47. Julian P. Boyd, *The Declaration of Independence and the Evolution of the Text* (Princeton, N. J., 1945), pp. 34–5.

48. Wallace Brown, *The King's Friends* (Providence, R. I., 1965), p. 260.

49. Hook, *Scotland and America*, p. 51.

50. Wallace Brown, *The Good Americans. The Loyalists in the American Revolution* (New York, 1969), p. 46.

51. Brown, *The King's Friends*, p. 259.

52. W. R. Brock, *Scotus Americanus* (Edinburgh, 1982), p. 129.

53. Emory G. Evans, 'Planter Indebtedness and the Coming of Revolution

in Virginia', *William and Mary Quarterly*, 3rd Series, XIX (1962), pp. 511–33.

54. Ned C. Landsman, 'The Legacy of British Union for the North American Colonies: Provisional Elites and the Problem of Imperial Union', in John Robertson, ed., *A Union for Empire: Political Thought and the British Union of 1707* (Cambridge, 1995), pp. 301–2.

55. Brown, *The King's Friends*, pp. 205–7.

56. Allan I. Macinnes, *Clanship, Commerce and the House of Stuart, 1603–1788* (East Linton, 1996), pp. 159–8, 247.

57. Duane Meyer, *The Highland Scots of North Carolina* (Chapel Hill, N. C., 1957), pp. 147–56.

58. Hook, *Scotland and America*, pp. 51–64.

59. Quoted in ibid., p. 62.

60. William E. Van Vugt, 'British (English, Welsh, Scots, Scotch-Irish)', in E. B. Barkan, ed., *A Nation of Peoples. A Sourcebook on America's Multicultural Heritage* (Westport, Conn., 1999), p. 80.

61. See the list in Rowland Tappan Berthoff, *British Immigrants in Industrial America 1790–1950* (Cambridge, Mass., 1953), p. 251, n. 88.

62. Peter Ross, *The Scot in America* (New York, 1890), pp. 1–2.

63. Quoted in ibid., p. viii.

64. Ferenc Morton Szaz, *Scots in the North American West, 1790–1917* (Norman, Okla., 2000), p. 78. See also, Celeste Ray, 'Transatlantic Scots and Ethnicity', in Ray, ed., *Transatlantic Scots*, p. 33.

65. Andrew Hook, *From Goosecreek to Gandercleugh. Studies in Scottish-American Literary and Cultural History* (East Linton, 1999), pp. 25–43, 94–116.

66. Devine, *Scotland's Empire*, pp. 164–87.

67. Quoted in Hook, *Goosecreek to Gandercleugh*, p. 99.

68. Ibid., p. 102.

69. Shirley Foster, *American Women Travellers to Europe* (Keele, 1994), *passim*.

70. US Department of Commerce, *Fifteenth Census of the United States, 1930: Population* (Washington, D. C.), Vol. 2, p. 245.

71. Szaz, *Scots in the North American West*, p. 211.

72. T. M. Devine, 'Irish and Scottish Development Revisited', in D. Dickson and C. Ó Gráda, eds., *Refiguring Ireland: Essays in Honour of L. M. Cullen* (Dublin, 2003), pp. 37–51.

73. T. M. Devine, *The Scottish Nation 1700–2007* (London, 2006), p. 394.

74. T. M. Devine, 'Why the Highlands Did Not Starve. Ireland and Highland Scotland During the Potato Famine', in C. Ó Gráda, R. Paping and

E. Vanhaute, eds., *When the Potato Failed: Causes and Effects of the 'Last' European Subsistence Crisis, 1845–1850* (Turnhout, Belgium, 2007), pp. 111–22.

75. L. M. Cullen and T. C. Smout, 'Economic Growth in Scotland and Ireland', in L. M. Cullen and T. C. Smout, eds., *Comparative Aspects of Scottish and Irish Economic and Social History 1600–1900* (Edinburgh, 1977), p. 3.

76. Alexander Murdoch, *British Emigration, 1603–1914* (Basingstoke, 2004), p. 122.

77. Berthoff, *British Immigrants*, p. 262.

78. Charlotte J. Erickson, 'Who were the English and Scots Emigrants to the United States in the late Nineteenth Century?', in D. V. Glass and R. Revelle, eds., *Population and Social Change* (London, 1972), pp. 360–2; B. Thomas, *Migration and Economic Growth* (Cambridge, 1973), p. 62; Jeanette M. Brock, 'The Importance of Emigration in Scottish Regional Population Movement 1861–1911', in T. M. Devine, ed., *Scottish Emigration and Scottish Society* (Edinburgh, 1992), pp. 104–26.

79. T. M. Devine, 'The Paradox of Scottish Emigration', in Devine, ed., *Scottish Emigration and Scottish Society*, p. 3.

80. Berthoff, *British Immigrants*, pp. 27–8, 49–50, 69–70, 72, 79–81.

81. Ibid., pp. 31–2.

82. Quoted in ibid., p. 72.

83. Murdoch, *British Emigration*, p. 111.

84. Szaz, *Scots in the North American West*, pp. 91–2, 96, 100.

85. Ibid.

86. Louise Shadduck, *Andy Little: Idaho Sheep King* (Caldwell, 1990).

87. Nicholas J. Evans, 'The Emigration of Skilled Male Workers from Clydeside during the Interwar Period', *International Journal of Maritime History*, XVIII (2006), pp. 255–80.

7. THE EMIGRANT EXPERIENCE
IN THE NEW LANDS

1. Quoted in John M. Mackenzie, 'A Scottish Empire? The Scottish Diaspora and Interactive Identities', in Tom Brooking and Jennie Coleman, eds., *The Heather and the Fern. Scottish Migration and New Zealand Settlement* (Dunedin, 2003), p. 27.

2. Quoted in Eric Richards, 'Australia and the Scottish Connection 1788–1914', in R. A. Cage, ed., *The Scots Abroad* (London, 1985), p. 126.

3. Sir C. W. Dilke, *Greater Britain* (London, 1872), p. 533.

4. W. Stanford Reid, ed., *The Scottish Tradition in Canada* (Toronto, 1976), p. ix.

5. L. A. Murray, 'On the high toby', *Sunday Morning Herald*, 18 October 1975, quoted in Malcolm D. Prentis, *The Scots in Australia. A Study of New South Wales, Victoria and Queensland, 1788–1900* (Sydney, 1983), p. 284.

6. J. Collier, *The Pastoral Age in Australia* (London, 1911), p. 81.

7. Anthony Trollope, *Australia* (London, 1873), p. 420.

8. Quoted in Prentis, *Scots in Australia*, p. 284.

9. Quoted in Richards, 'Australia and the Scottish Connection', p. 126.

10. Margaret Kiddle, *Men of Yesterday: A Social History of the Western District of Victoria 1834–1890* (Melbourne, 1961), p. 44.

11. Edward J. Cowan, 'The Myth of Scotch Canada', in Marjory Harper and Michael E. Vance, eds., *Myth, Migration and the Making of Memory. Scotia and Nova Scotia, c.1700–1990* (Edinburgh, 1999), p. 66.

12. Quoted in Tanja Bueltmann, '"Brither Scots Shoulder tae Shoulder": Ethnic Identity, Culture and Associationism among the Scots in New Zealand to 1930', unpublished PhD thesis, Victoria University of Wellington (2008), p. 1.

13. Quoted in Marjory Harper, 'Exiles or Entrepreneurs? Snapshots of the Scots in Canada', in Peter E. Rider and Heather McNabb, eds., *A Kingdom of the Mind. How the Scots Helped to Make Canada* (Montreal, 2006), p. 34.

14. Quoted in Cowan, 'Myth of Scotch Canada', p. 58.

15. T. M. Devine, *Scotland's Empire 1600–1815* (London, 2003), pp. 190–1, 212–13.

16. Harper and Vance, eds., *Myth, Migration and the Making of Memory*, pp. 16–17.

17. Prentis, *Scots in Australia*, p. 182.

18. John Butt, *John Anderson's Legacy* (Glasgow, 1996).

19. J. M. Bumsted, *The Scots in Canada* (Ottawa, 1982), p. 5.

20. Cairns Craig, *Intending Scotland. Explorations in Scottish Culture since the Enlightenment* (Edinburgh, 2009), pp. 102–30; Cairns Craig, 'Empire of Intellect: The Scottish Enlightenment and Scotland's Intellectual Migrants', in John M. Mackenzie and T. M. Devine, eds., *Scotland and the British Empire* (Oxford, 2011).

21. Helen Meller, *Patrick Geddes: Social Evolutionist and City Planner* (London, 1990).

22. J. M. Bumsted, 'The Scottish Diaspora: Emigration to British North America 1763–1845', in Ned C. Landsman, ed., *Nation and Province in the First British Empire* (London, 2001), pp. 145–6.

23. Devine, *Scotland's Empire*, p. 193.

24. John M. Mackenzie, *The Scots in South Africa* (Manchester, 2007), p. 194.

25. Ibid., p. 196.

26. Prentis, *Scots in Australia*, pp. 182, 185.

27. Tom Brooking, 'Sharing out the Haggis: The Special Scottish Contribution to New Zealand History', in Brooking and Coleman, eds., *The Heather and the Fern*, pp. 60–1, 64.

28. I owe much of what follows in these paragraphs to the seminal work of John Mackenzie, especially *Empires of Nature and the Nature of Empires* (Edinburgh, 1997); 'Scotland and Empire: Ethnicity, Environment and Identity', *Northern Scotland*, 1 (2010), pp. 12–29; *Scots in South Africa*, pp. 204–16.

29. Richard H. Grove, 'Scotland in South Africa: John Crombie Brown and the roots of settler environmentalism', in T. Griffiths and L. Robin, eds., *Ecology and Empire* (Keele, 1997), p. 139.

30. T. M. Devine, *The Transformation of Rural Scotland. Social Change and the Agrarian Economy 1660–1815* (Edinburgh, 1994), pp. 36–110.

31. Mackenzie, *Scots in South Africa*, p. 216.

32. T. C. Smout, 'Woodland History before 1850', in T. C. Smout, ed., *Scotland since Prehistory: Natural Change and Human Impact* (Aberdeen, 1993), pp. 45–7.

33. Richard H. Grove, *Ecology, Climate and Empire: Colonisation and Global Environmental History, 1400–1940* (Knapwell, 1997), p. 27.

34. Michael Bliss, *Northern Enterprise: Five Centuries of Canadian Business* (Toronto, 1987), p. 110.

35. Douglas McCalla, 'Sojourners in the Snow? The Scots in Business in Nineteenth-Century Canada', in Rider and McNabb, eds., *A Kingdom of the Mind*, p. 77.

36. T. W. Acheson, 'Changing Social Origins of the Canadian Industrial Elite, 1880–1910', in G. Porter and R. Cuff, eds., *Enterprise and National Development: Essays in Canadian Business and Economic History* (Toronto, 1973), p. 57. It should, however, be noted that only 7 per cent of the 'industrial elite' had actually been born in Scotland.

37. Peter C. Newman, *Company of Adventurers*. Vol. 1 (Toronto, 1985), pp. 47–9, 179–80; J. S. A. Brown, ' "A Parcel of Upstart Scotchmen" ', *The Beaver*, 68 (1988), p. 4.

38. Devine, *Scotland's Empire*, pp. 197, 204.

39. Quoted in Elaine A. Mitchell, 'The Scot in the Fur Trade', in Reid, ed., *Scottish Tradition in Canada*, p. 36.

40. Ibid.

41. Michael Payne, *The Most Respectable Place in the Territory. Everyday Life in Hudson's Bay Company Service* (Ottawa, 1989), pp. 34–5.

42. McCalla, 'Sojourners in the Snow?', pp. 79–81.

43. Ibid., pp. 91, 96.

44. Mackenzie, *Scots in South Africa*, pp. 223ff.

45. Richards, 'Australia and the Scottish Connection', p. 139.

46. Ian Donnachie, 'The Making of "Scots on the Make": Scottish Settlement and Enterprise in Australia, 1830–1900', in T. M. Devine, ed., *Scottish Emigration and Scottish Society* (Edinburgh, 1992), p. 139.

47. What follows in based on Devine, *Scotland's Empire*, pp. 282–3.

48. Eric Richards, 'Scottish Australia 1788–1914' in Anon., *That Land of Exiles. Scots in Australia* (Edinburgh, 1988), pp. 11–12.

49. Tom Brooking, '"Tam McCanny and Kitty Clydeside": The Scots in New Zealand', in Cage, ed., *Scots Abroad*, p. 180.

50. Ibid., p. 172.

51. Jock Phillips and Terry Hearn, *Settlers. New Zealand Immigrants from England, Ireland and Scotland 1800–1945* (Auckland, 2008), p. 174.

52. Jim McAloon, '"In the colonies those who make money are generally Scotchmen": Scottish Entrepreneurs in Colonial New Zealand'. Paper presented to the Celtic Connections, Irish-Scottish Studies Down Under Conference, Victoria University of Wellington, October 2007. See also his *No Idle Rich. The Wealthy of Canterbury and Otago 1840–1914* (Dunedin, 2002).

53. McCalla, 'Sojourners in the Snow?', p. 92.

54. McAloon, *No Idle Rich*, pp. 154–5.

55. Eric Richards, 'Scottish Voices and Networks in Colonial Australia', in Angela McCarthy, ed., *A Global Clan. Scottish Migrant Networks and Identities since the Eighteenth Century* (London, 2006), pp. 151, 154–8.

56. Donnachie, 'Making of "Scots on the Make"', pp. 140, 147–8.

57. Bumsted, 'Scottish Diaspora', p. 130; James Belich, *Making Peoples: A History of the New Zealanders to 1900* (London, 2002), pp. 400–1.

58. David Armitage, 'The Scottish Diaspora', in Jenny Wormald, ed., *Scotland. A History* (Oxford, 2005), p. 297.

59. Richards, 'Scottish Australia'.

60. Mackenzie, *Scots in South Africa*, p. 7.

61. Quoted in ibid., p. 4.

62. Ibid.

63. See, for example, Tanja Bueltmann, Andrew Hanson and Graeme Morton, eds., *Ties of Bluid, Kin and Countrie. Scottish Associational Culture in the Diaspora* (Markham, Ontario, 2009).

64. Jonathan Hyslop, 'Cape Town Highlanders, Transvaal Scottish: Military "Scottishness" and Social Power in Nineteenth and Twentieth Century South Africa', *South African Historical Journal*, 47 (2002), pp. 96–114.

65. H. P. Klepak, 'A Man's a Man because of That: The Scots in Canadian Military Experience', in Rider and McNabb, eds., *A Kingdom of the Mind*, p. 52.

66. What follows in this and subsequent paragraphs in based on T. M. Devine, 'The Invention of Scotland', in D. Dickson, Seán Duffy, Cathal Ó Háinle and Ian Campbell Ross, eds., *Ireland and Scotland. Nation, Region, Identity* (Dublin, 2001), pp. 18–25.

67. Linda Colley, *Britons: Forging the Nation 1707–1837* (London, 1994).

68. Quoted in Richard J. Finlay, *A Partnership for Good? Scottish Politics and the Union since 1880* (Edinburgh, 1997), p. 26.

69. Quoted in Richard J. Finlay, 'The Burns Cult and Scottish Identity in the Nineteenth and Twentieth Centuries', in Kenneth Simpson, ed., *Love and Liberty* (Edinburgh, 1997), p. 71.

70. For example, Bueltmann, Hanson and Morton, eds., *Ties of Bluid*; Angela McCarthy, *For Spirit and Adventure: Personal Narratives of Irish and Scottish Migration, 1921–65* (Manchester, 2007); Mackenzie, *Scots in South Africa*, pp. 240–67.

8. SETTLERS, TRADERS AND NATIVE PEOPLES

1. Quoted in David Armitage, 'The Scottish Diaspora', in Jenny Wormald, ed., *Scotland. A History* (Oxford, 2005), p. 299.

2. Arthur Herman, *The Scottish Enlightenment* (London, 2002), p. 323.

3. Michael Fry, *'Bold, Independent, Unconquer'd and Free'* (Ayr, 2003), p. 145.

4. Colin G. Calloway, *White People, Indians and Highlanders* (Oxford, 2008), p. 4.

5. See, for instance, James Hunter, *Glencoe and the Indians* (Edinburgh, 1977).

6. Robbie Ethridge, *Creek Country: The Creek Indians and their World* (Chapel Hill, N. C., 2003).

7. Calloway, *White People, Indians and Highlanders*, p. 18.

8. John M. Mackenzie, *The Scots in South Africa* (Manchester, 2007), p. 20.

9. Eric Richards, 'Leaving the Highlands: Colonial Destinations in Canada

and Australia', in Marjory Harper and Michael E. Vance, eds., *Myth, Migration and the Making of Memory: Scotia and Nova Scotia, c.1700–1990* (Edinburgh, 1999), p. 107.

10. James Horn, 'British Diaspora: Emigration from Britain, 1680–1815', in P. J. Marshall, ed., *The Oxford History of the British Empire*, Vol. 2, *The Eighteenth Century* (Oxford, 1998), p. 31. See also essays by L. M. Cullen, T. C. Smout, N. C. Landsman and T. M. Devine in N. Canny, ed., *Europeans on the Move. Studies on European Migration, 1500–1800* (Oxford, 1994); Henry A. Gemery, 'European Emigration to North America 1700–1820: Numbers and Quasi-Numbers', *Perspectives in American History*, 1 (1984), pp. 283–342.

11. David Noel Doyle, 'Scots-Irish or Scotch-Irish', in Michael Glazier, ed., *The Encyclopedia of the Irish in America* (Notre Dame, Ind., 1999), pp. 42, 47, summarizing the work of R. J. Dickson, L. M. Cullen, M. Wokeck and G. Kirkham.

12. Kerby A. Miller, *Emigrants and Exiles: Ireland and the Irish Exodus to North America* (Oxford, 1985), p. 169.

13. David N. Doyle, *Ireland, Irishmen and Revolutionary America, 1760–1820* (Dublin and Cork, 1981), p. 51.

14. R. J. Dickson (with Introduction by G. E. Kirkham), *Ulster Emigration to Colonial America 1718–1775* (Belfast, 1997), pp. xvi–xvii.

15. T. L. Purvis, D. H. Akenson, F. McDonald and E. McDonald, 'The Population of the United States, 1790: A Symposium', *William and Mary Quarterly*, 3rd Series, XLI (1984), pp. 85–135; D. Noel Doyle, 'The Irish in North America, 1776–1845', in W. E. Vaughan, ed., *A New History of Ireland*. Vol. 5, *1801–1870* (Oxford, 1989), p. 692.

16. Kevin Kenny, *The American Irish: A History* (Harlow, 2000), pp. 23–5.

17. E. Estyn Evans, 'The Scotch-Irish: Their Cultural Adaptation and Heritage in the American Old West', in E. R. R. Green, ed., *Essays in Scotch-Irish History* (London and New York, 1969), pp. 75–6.

18. Quoted in James G. Leyburn, *The Scotch-Irish* (Chapel Hill, N. C., 1962), p. 318.

19. Esmond Wright, 'Education in the American Colonies: The Impact of Scotland', in Green, ed., *Essays in Scotch-Irish History*, p. 21.

20. Quoted in David Hackett Fischer, *Albion's Seed: Four British Folkways in America* (Oxford, 1989), p. 813.

21. Richard J. Hooker, ed., *The Carolina Backcountry on the Eve of the Revolution: The Journal and Other Writings of Charles Woodmason, Anglican Itinerant* (Chapel Hill, N. C., 1953), p. 116.

22. Estyn Evans, 'The Scotch-Irish', p. 76.

23. M. A. Jones, 'Scotch-Irish', in Stephan Thernstrom, ed., *Harvard Encyclopedia of American Ethnic Groups* (Cambridge, Mass., 1980), p. 295.

24. Daniel K. Richter, 'Native Peoples of North America and the Eighteenth-Century British Empire', in Marshall, ed., *The Oxford History of the British Empire*, Vol. 2, pp. 347–72.

25. Quoted in Leyburn, *Scotch-Irish*, pp. 223–4.

26. Jones, 'Scotch-Irish', p. 296.

27. Ibid., pp. 295–6.

28. Fischer, *Albion's Seed*, p. 646.

29. Jones, 'Scotch-Irish', p. 296.

30. Glydwyr Williams, 'The Pacific: Exploration and Exploitation', in Marshall, ed., *The Oxford History of the British Empire*, Vol. 2, p. 570.

31. Quoted in Anon., *That Land of Exiles. Scots in Australia* (Edinburgh, 1988), p. 52. See also Ann Curthoys, 'Indigenous Subjects', in D. M. Schreuder and S. Wards, eds., *Australia's Empire* (Oxford, 2008), pp. 78–102.

32. H. Reynolds, *The Other Side of the Frontier. Aboriginal Resistance to the European Invasion of Australia* (Ringwood, 1982).

33. Quoted in Don Watson, *Caledonia Australis. Scottish Highlanders on the Frontier of Australia* (Sydney, 1984), p. 100.

34. Reynolds, *Other Side of the Frontier, passim*.

35. Malcolm D. Prentis, *The Scots in Australia. A Study of New South Wales, Victoria and Queensland, 1788–1900* (Sydney, 1983), p. 143.

36. Ann Curthoys, 'Expulsion, exodus and exile in white Australian historical mythology', *Journal of Australian Studies*, 23, 61 (1999), pp. 1–19.

37. All citations from ibid., pp. 13–14.

38. Ian L. Donnachie, 'The Making of "Scots on the Make": Scottish Settlement and Enterprise in Australia, 1830–1900', in T. M. Devine, ed., *Scottish Emigration and Scottish Society* (Edinburgh, 1992), p. 140.

39. Stephen Roberts, *The Squatting Age in Australia* (Melbourne, 1935), p. 307.

40. Eric Richards, 'Scottish Australia 1788–1914', in Anon., *That Land of Exiles*, p. 36.

41. T. M. Devine, *Scotland's Empire 1600–1815* (London, 2003), p. 282.

42. Watson, *Caledonia Australis*, p. 166.

43. Ibid., pp. 165–6.

44. P. Wood, *Some Geelong Scots* (Geelong, Victoria, n.d.).

45. Paul Basu, *Highland Homecomings* (Abingdon, 2007), p. 203.

46. Quoted in J. M. Bumsted, 'The Curious Tale of the Scots and the Fur Trade: An Historiographical Account', in Peter E. Rider and Heather McNabb, eds., *A Kingdom of the Mind. How the Scots Helped Make Canada* (Montreal, 2006), p. 64.

NOTES

47. Washington Irving, *Astoria or Anecdotes of an Enterprise beyond the Rocky Mountains* (Norman, Okla., 1964 edn), p. 13.
48. Devine, *Scotland's Empire*, p. 203.
49. Calloway, *White People, Indians and Highlanders*, p. 130.
50. http://orkneyjar.com/history/historicalfigures/johnrae/index.html; I. Bunyon, J. Calder, D. Idiens and B. Wilson, *No Ordinary Journey: John Rae, Arctic Explorer, 1813–1893* (Edinburgh, 1993).
51. Christopher L. Miller and George R. Hamell, 'A New Perspective on Indian–White Contact: Cultural Symbols and Colonial Trade', *Journal of American History*, 73 (1986), pp. 311–28.
52. Calloway, *White People, Indians and Highlanders*, p. 150.
53. Albert L. Hurtado, *Intimate Frontiers: Sex, Gender and Culture in Old California* (Albuquerque, N. Mex., 1999).
54. Peter C. Newman, *Company of Adventurers*, Vol. 1 (Toronto, 1985), pp. 203–4.
55. Quoted in ibid., p. 203.
56. Jennifer S. A. Brown, *Strangers in Blood: Fur Trade Families in Indian Country* (Norman, Okla., 1980), p. 51.
57. E. E. Rich, ed., *Journal of Occurrences in the Athabasca Department by George Simpson* (Toronto, 1938), p. 392.
58. Calloway, *White People, Indians and Highlanders*, pp. 161–4.
59. '200 years on, Cree Indians go home to Orkneys', http://nativevillage.org/Archives/2004>/Sep/News; *Independent*, 6 September 2004.
60. Quoted in Calloway, *White People, Indians and Highlanders*, p. 139.
61. A. S. Morton, ed., *The Journal of Duncan McGillivray of the North West Company at Fort George on the Saskatchewan 1794–5* (Toronto, 1929), pp. 30–6.

9. THE MISSIONARY DYNAMIC

1. Stewart J. Brown, *Providence and Empire 1815–1914* (Harlow, 2008), p. 439.
2. *The Scotsman*, 14 June 1910.
3. Esther Breitenbach, *Empire and Scottish Society. The Impact of Foreign Missions at Home c.1790 to c.1914* (Edinburgh, 2009), pp. 159–60.
4. See, for example, in the British case, Norman Etherington, ed., *Missions and Empire* (Oxford, 2005); Andrew Porter, *Religion versus Empire? British Protestant Missionaries and Overseas Expansion, 1700–1914* (Manchester, 2004).
5. A. Porter, 'Religion and Empire: British Expansion in the Long

Nineteenth Century, 1780–1914', *Journal of Imperial and Commonwealth History*, 20 (1992), p. 372; A. Porter, '"Cultural Imperialism" and Protestant Missionary Enterprise, 1780–1914', *Journal of Imperial and Commonwealth History*, 25 (1997), p. 371.

6. J. A. Hobson, *Imperialism: A Study* (London, 1938), p. 204.

7. Quoted in Norman Etherington, 'Introduction', in Etherington, ed., *Missions and Empire*, p. 2.

8. Richard Gray, *Black Christians and White Missionaries* (New Haven, Conn., 1990), pp. 95–7.

9. Breitenbach, *Empire and Scottish Society*, p. 81.

10. Etherington, 'Introduction', p. 1.

11. Gray, *Black Christians*, pp. 96–7.

12. T. M. Devine, *The Scottish Nation 1700–2007* (London, 2006), p. 364.

13. Stewart J. Brown, *Thomas Chalmers and the Godly Commonwealth* (Oxford, 1982).

14. Stana Nenadic, 'The Victorian Middle Classes', in W. Hamish Fraser and Irene Maver, eds., *Glasgow*. Vol. 2, *1830 to 1912* (Manchester, 1996), pp. 278–9.

15. Quoted in A. C. Cheyne, *The Transforming of the Kirk* (Edinburgh, 1983), p. 114.

16. Devine, *Scottish Nation*, pp. 365–6.

17. D. W. Bebbington, *Evangelicalism in Modern Britain* (London, 1989).

18. Brown, *Thomas Chalmers*, *passim*; R. A. Cage and E. O. A. Checkland, 'Thomas Chalmers and Urban Poverty: The St. John's Experiment in Glasgow 1819–1837', *Philosophical Journal*, 13 (1976).

19. Callum Brown, *The Social History of Religion in Scotland since 1730* (London, 1987), p. 141.

20. Quoted in Etherington, 'Introduction', pp. 15–16.

21. Philip Constable, 'Scottish Missionaries, "Protestant Hinduism", and Early Twentieth-Century India', *Scottish Historical Review*, LXXXVI, 2, 222 (October, 2007), pp. 386–7.

22. John M. Mackenzie, *The Scots in South Africa* (Manchester, 2007), p. 102.

23. Brown, *Providence and Empire*, p. 32.

24. Quoted in J. R. Fleming, *A History of the Church of Scotland 1843–1874* (Edinburgh, 1927), p. 10.

25. Iain Whyte, *Scotland and the Abolition of Black Slavery, 1756–1838* (Edinburgh, 2006).

26. C. D. Rice, *The Scots Abolitionists, 1833–1861* (Baton Rouge, La., 1981), pp. 203–5.

27. Quoted in Brown, *Providence and Empire*, p. 141.

28. Andrew Porter, 'An Overview, 1700–1914', in Etherington, ed., *Missions and Empire*, p. 47.

29. Catherine Hall, *Civilising Subjects: Metropole and Colony in the English Imagination* (Cambridge, 2002), pp. 292–301.

30. Breitenbach, *Empire and Scottish Society*, p. 155; *The Scotsman*, 28 September 1857.

31. Quoted in Brown, *Providence and Empire*, p. 199.

32. Ibid., pp. 199–200.

33. Mackenzie, *Scots in South Africa*, p. 123.

34. Ibid., pp. 110–11.

35. Andrew Ross, *John Philip, 1775–1851* (Aberdeen, 1986), p. 221.

36. Constable, 'Scottish Missionaries', pp. 287–8.

37. E. Storrow, *India and Christian Missions* (London, 1859), p. 43.

38. Alexander Duff, *The Church of Scotland India Missions* (Edinburgh, 1835).

39. Mackenzie, *Scots in South Africa*, p. 108.

40. Patricia Grimshaw, 'Faith, Missionary Life and the Family', in Philippa Levine, ed., *Gender and Empire* (Oxford, 2004), pp. 267–8.

41. Andrew Ross, *David Livingstone. Mission and Empire* (London, 2002), pp. 239–40; P. J. Westwood, *David Livingstone: His Life and Work as Told Through the Media of Postage Stamps and Allied Material* (Edinburgh, 1986).

42. Andrew C. Ross, 'Scotland and Malawi, 1850–1984', in Stewart J. Brown and George Newlands, eds., *Scottish Christianity in the Modern World* (Edinburgh, 2000), p. 284.

43. John M. Mackenzie, 'David Livingstone: The Construction of the Myth', in Graham Walker and Tom Gallagher, eds., *Sermons and Battle Hymns* (Edinburgh, 1990), pp. 27–8.

44. James Macnair, *The Story of the Scottish National Memorial to David Livingstone* (Glasgow, n.d.).

45. Mackenzie, 'David Livingstone', p. 32.

46. Brown, *Providence and Empire*, pp. 202–3.

47. Ross, *David Livingstone*, p. 241.

48. John McCracken, *Politics and Christianity in Malawi 1875–1940* (Cambridge, 1977), p. 17.

49. Dorothy O. Helly, *Livingstone's Legacy: Horace Walter and Victorian Mythmaking* (Columbus, Ohio, 1987).

50. Quoted in Mackenzie, 'David Livingstone', p. 29.

51. Frank McLynn, *Stanley: The Making of an Explorer* (London, 1989).

52. Quoted in McCracken, *Politics and Christianity*, pp. 25–6.

53. John D. Hargreaves, *Aberdeenshire to Africa* (Aberdeen, 1981), pp. 23–4.

54. Andrew C. Ross, 'Scottish Missionary Concern 1874–1919: A Golden Era?', *Scottish Historical Review*, 1 (1972), pp. 52–72.

55. Mackenzie, 'David Livingstone', pp. 36–7.

56. Breitenbach, *Empire and Scottish Society*, pp. 58–91; Lesley Orr Macdonald, *A Unique and Glorious Mission: Women and Presbyterianism in Scotland 1830–1930* (Edinburgh, 2000), pp. 115–16; Hargreaves, *Aberdeenshire to Africa*, pp. 20–39; John D. Hargreaves, *Academe and Empire* (Aberdeen, 1994), pp. 5–32.

57. Grimshaw, 'Faith, Missionary Life and the Family', pp. 264–6; Etherington, 'Introduction', pp. 8–9.

58. Clare Midgley, *Women against Slavery: The British Campaign, 1780–1870* (London, 1992), p. 24.

59. Breitenbach, *Empire and Scottish Society*, p. 80.

60. Brown, *Social History of Religion*, pp. 140–68; Ross, 'Scottish Missionary Concern', pp. 53–72.

61. W. H. Taylor, *Mission to Educate: A History of the Educational Work of the Scottish Presbyterian Mission in East Nigeria, 1846–1960* (New York, 1996), ch. 7; Elizabeth Robertson, *Mary Slessor* (Edinburgh, 2001).

62. Breitenbach, *Empire and Scottish Society*, p. 79.

63. Eleanor Gordon, 'Women's Spheres', in W. H. Fraser and R. J. Morris, ed., *People and Society in Scotland*, Vol. 2 (Edinburgh, 1990), p. 226.

64. Macdonald, *Unique and Glorious Mission*, pp. 155–6.

65. Mackenzie, *Scots in South Africa*, pp. 104, 109–11.

66. Porter, '"Cultural Imperialism"', pp. 367–91.

67. Etherington, 'Introduction', p. 7; Gray, *Black Christians and White Missionaries*, pp. 80–1.

68. Hargreaves, *Aberdeenshire to Africa*, pp. 25–6.

10. SOLDIERS OF EMPIRE

1. *Caledonian Mercury*, 21 March 1816.

2. Ibid.

3. Ibid., 29 June 1815; 23 March 1816; *Glasgow Herald*, 30 June 1815; 10 July 1815; 28 July 1815; 13 November 1815.

4. Robert Clyde, *From Rebel to Hero. The Image of the Highlander 1745–1830* (East Linton, 1995), p. 186.

5. W. C. Cooper, *The Story of Georgia* (New York, 1938), Vol. 1, p. 1.

6. By Andrew Mackillop, see his '*More Fruitful than the Soil'. Army, Empire and the Scottish Highlands, 1715–1815* (Edinburgh, 2000), p. 236.

7. Ibid., p. 150.

8. S. E. M. Carpenter, 'Patterns of Recruitment of the Highland Regiments of the British Army, 1756 to 1815', unpublished MLitt thesis, University of St Andrews (1977), p. 75.

9. Mackillop, 'More Fruitful than the Soil', p. 115.

10. Bruce Lenman, The Jacobite Clans of the Great Glen 1650–1784 (London, 1984), p. 212.

11. Quoted in W. Donaldson, The Jacobite Song (Aberdeen, 1988), p. 46.

12. Ibid.

13. Glasgow Journal, 28 April 1746.

14. Geoffrey Plank, Rebellion and Savagery. The Jacobite Risings of 1745 and the British Empire (Philadelphia, 2006).

15. Quoted in Carpenter, 'Patterns of Recruitment', p. 33.

16. Lenman, Jacobite Clans, p. 190.

17. David Stewart of Garth, Sketches of the Character, Manners and Present State of the Highlands of Scotland, with Details of the Military Service of the Highland Regiments (Inverness, 1885 edn), p. 288.

18. Mackillop 'More Fruitful than the Soil', pp. 216–17.

19. Clyde, From Rebel to Hero, p. 161.

20. Stephen Brumwell, Redcoats. The British Soldier and War in the Americas 1755–1763 (Cambridge, 2002), pp. 281–2.

21. J. E. Cookson, The British Armed Nation 1793–1815 (Oxford, 1997), pp. 137–8.

22. Ibid., pp. 132–3.

23. Eric Richards, A History of the Highland Clearances: Agrarian Change and the Evictions, 1746–1886 (London, 1982), pp. 152–3.

24. T. M. Devine, 'Social Responses to Agrarian Improvement: The Highland and Lowland Clearances in Scotland', in R. A. Houston and I. D. Whyte, eds., Scottish Society, 1500–1800 (Cambridge, 1989), pp. 160–1.

25. Hew Strachan, 'Scotland's Military Identity', Scottish Historical Review, LXXXV, 2, 220 (October, 2006), p. 324.

26. Lenman, Jacobite Clans, pp. 207, 211–16.

27. Carpenter, 'Patterns of Recruitment', pp. 103–4.

28. Sir George S. Mackenzie, General View of the Agriculture of the Counties of Ross and Cromarty (London, 1813), p. 298.

29. Quoted in Leah Leneman, Living in Atholl 1685–1785 (Edinburgh, 1986), p. 140.

30. Mackenzie, General View, p. 298.

31. A. Mackillop, 'For King, Country and Regiment? Motive and identity within Highland soldiering 1746–1815', in S. Murdoch and A. Mackillop,

eds., *Fighting for Identity: Scottish Military Experience c.1550–1900* (Leiden, 2002), pp. 198–200.

32. H. J. Hanham, 'Religion and nationality in the mid-Victorian society', in M. R. D. Foot, ed., *War and Society* (London, 1973), pp. 163–6.

33. Diana Henderson, *Highland Soldier: A Social Study of the Highland Regiments 1820–1920* (Edinburgh, 1989), pp. 25, 38.

34. Heather Streets, 'Identity in the Highland Regiments in the Nineteenth Century: Soldier, Region, Nation', in Murdoch and Mackillop, eds., *Fighting for Identity*, p. 222.

35. Edward M. Speirs, *The Scottish Soldier and Empire, 1854–1902* (Edinburgh, 2006), p. 3.

36. Heather Streets, *Martial Races. The Military, Race and Masculinity in British Imperial Culture 1857–1914* (Manchester, 2004), p. 180; John Mackenzie, ed., *Popular Imperialism and the Military 1850–1950* (Manchester, 1992), p. vii.

37. Stuart Allan and Allan Carswell, *The Thin Red Line. War, Empire and Visions of Scotland* (Edinburgh, n.d.), p. 30.

38. Ibid.

39. Streets, 'Identity in the Highland Regiments', p. 213.

40. John Prebble, *The King's Jaunt* (London, 1988).

41. Richard J. Finlay, 'Queen Victoria and the Cult of Scottish Monarchy', in Edward J. Cowan and Richard J. Finlay, eds., *Scottish History. The Power of the Past* (Edinburgh, 2002), pp. 209–24.

42. John M. Mackenzie, 'Introduction', in Mackenzie, ed., *Popular Imperialism and the Military*, p. 1.

43. Olive Anderson, 'The Growth of Christian Militarism in Mid-Victorian Britain', *English Historical Review*, 86, 338 (1971), pp. 46–50.

44. Ibid.

45. Streets, *Martial Races*, pp. 35–42.

46. Allan Lee, *The Origins of the Popular Press 1855–1914* (London, 1976); Lucy Brown, *Victorian News and Newspapers* (Oxford, 1985), pp. 27, 31.

47. Mackenzie, 'Introduction', p. 3.

48. Quoted in Speirs, *Scottish Soldier*, p. 14.

49. Alexander Somerville, *The Autobiography of a Working Man* (London, 1848), p. 188.

50. Streets, *Martial Races*, p. 39.

51. Speirs, *Scottish Soldier*, p. 144.

52. Quoted in Mackenzie, 'Introduction', p. 17.

53. P. E. Dewey, 'Military recruiting and the British labour force during the First World War', *Historical Journal*, 27 (1984), pp. 199–223; D. R.

Young, 'Voluntary Recruitment in Scotland, 1914–1916', unpublished PhD thesis, University of Glasgow (2001).

54. Richard Finlay, *Modern Scotland, 1914–2000* (London, 2004), pp. 6–7.

55. Ibid.

56. E. W. McFarland, 'Introduction: "A Coronach in Stone"', in Catriona M. M. Macdonald and E. W. McFarland, eds., *Scotland and the Great War* (East Linton, 1999), p. 6.

57. Quoted in Strachan, 'Scotland's Military Identity', p. 329.

11. FUNDING THE NEW LANDS

1. 'Scottish Investors in the Dumps', *The Statist. A Weekly Journal for Economists and Men of Business*, XV, 10 January 1883, p. 36.

2. Anon., 'Scottish Capital Abroad', *Blackwood's Edinburgh Magazine*, CXXXVI (1884), p. 468 (my italics).

3. W. Turrentine Jackson, *The Enterprising Scot. Investors in the American West after 1873* (Edinburgh, 1968), p. 8.

4. David S. Macmillan, *Scotland and Australia, 1788–1850: Emigration, Commerce and Investment* (Oxford, 1967), p. 352.

5. 'Scottish Investors in the Dumps', p. 37.

6. Quoted in J. D. Bailey, 'Australian Borrowing in Scotland in the Nineteenth Century', *Economic History Review*, New Series, 12, 2 (1959), p. 272.

7. John Darwin, *The Empire Project. The Rise and Fall of the British World System, 1830–1970* (Cambridge, 2009), p. 117.

8. M. Edelstein, *Overseas Investment in the Age of High Imperialism* (London, 1982), p. 48; R. C. Michie, *The City of London* (London, 1992), p. 72; C. H. Feinstein, 'Britain's Overseas Investments in 1913', *Economic History Review*, 2nd Series, 43, 2 (1990), pp. 288–95.

9. Sydney Pollard, 'Capital Exports, 1870–1914: Harmful or Beneficial', *Economic History Review*, 2nd Series, 38, 4 (1985), p. 492.

10. B. Lenman, *An Economic History of Modern Scotland 1660–1976* (London, 1977), p. 193.

11. C. Harvie, *Scotland and Nationalism: Scottish Society and Politics 1707–1994* (2nd edn, London, 1994), p. 70.

12. Christopher Schmitz, 'The Nature and Dimensions of Scottish Foreign Investment 1860–1914', *Business History*, 39, 2 (1997), pp. 42–68.

13. Ronald Michie, *Money, Mania and Markets: Investment Company Formation and the Stock Exchange in Nineteenth Century Scotland* (Edinburgh, 1981), p. 248.

14. Liza Giffen, *How Scots Financed the World. A History of Scottish Investment Trusts* (Edinburgh, 2009), p. 54.

15. Bailey, 'Australian Borrowing in Scotland', p. 269.

16. T. Brooking, '"Tam McCanny and Kitty Clydeside": The Scots in New Zealand', in R. A. Cage, ed., *The Scots Abroad* (London, 1985), pp. 165–8.

17. C. H. Lee, 'Economic Progress: Wealth and Poverty', in T. M. Devine, C. H. Lee and G. C. Peden, eds., *The Transformation of Scotland* (Edinburgh, 2005), p. 139.

18. Michie, *Money, Mania and Markets*, p. 154.

19. J. H. Treble, 'The Pattern of Investment of the Standard Life Assurance Company 1875–1914', *Business History*, 22 (1980), pp. 170–88.

20. Schmitz, 'Nature and Dimensions of Scottish Foreign Investment', p. 66, n. 48.

21. Dong-Woon Kim, 'The British Multinational Enterprise in the United States before 1914: The Case of J. and P. Coats', *Business History Review*, 72 (Winter, 1998), pp. 523–55.

22. Bruce Lenman and Kathleen Donaldson, 'Partners' Income, Investment and Diversification in the Scottish Linen Area 1850–1921', *Business History*, 21 (1971), pp. 1–18; M. Wilkins, *The History of Foreign Investment in the United States to 1914* (Cambridge, Mass., 1989), pp. 217–18; Michie, *Money, Mania and Markets*, p. 154.

23. W. D. Rubenstein, *Men of Property* (London, 1981).

24. Robert D. Corrins, 'The Scottish Business Elite in the Nineteenth Century: The case of William Baird and Company', in A. J. G. Cummings and T. M. Devine, eds., *Industry, Business and Society in Scotland since 1700* (Edinburgh, 1994), p. 76.

25. G. A. Stout, 'Robert Fleming and the Trustees of the First Scottish-American Investment Trust', *Friends of Dundee City Archives*, 1 (1999), pp. 13–22; Bill Smith, *Robert Fleming 1845–1933* (Haddington, 2000).

26. Jackson, *Enterprising Scot*, pp. 192, 202, 221, 229, 307.

27. M. Moss and A. Slaven, *'From Ledger to Laser Beam': A History of the TSB in Scotland from 1870 to 1990* (Edinburgh, 1992), pp. 28, 32, 52, 74; Lee, 'Economic Progress: Wealth and Poverty', p. 138.

28. T. M. Devine, *The Scottish Nation 1700–2007* (London, 2006), pp. 468–85.

29. Richard F. Anthony, *Herds and Hinds: Farm Labour in Lowland Scotland, 1900–1939* (Edinburgh, 1997), p. 94.

30. T. M. Devine, 'The Paradox of Scottish Emigration', in T. M. Devine, *Scottish Emigration and Scottish Society* (Edinburgh, 1992), p. 3.

31. James Belich, *Replenishing the Earth. The Settler Revolution and the Rise of the Anglo-World 1783–1939* (Oxford, 2009), p. 127; Dudley Baines, *Migration in a Mature Economy* (Cambridge, 1985), pp. 128–40.

32. Darwin, *Empire Project*, pp. 114–15.

33. Prospectus, Scottish-American Investment Company, 1873.

34. Terry L. Anderson and Peter J. Hill, *The Not So Wild West. Property Rights on the Frontier* (Stanford, Calif., 2004), p. 156; T. G. Jordan, *North American Cattle Ranching Frontiers* (Albuquerque, N. Mex., 1993), p. 237.

35. A. K. Cairncross, 'Investment in Canada, 1900–13', in A. R. Hall, ed., *The Export of Capital from Britain 1870–1914* (London, 1968), pp. 153–86.

36. Belich, *Replenishing the Earth*, p. 366.

37. Jackson, *Enterprising Scot*, pp. 4–5.

38. C. K. Hobson, *The Export of Capital* (London, 1914), p. 240.

39. Jackson, *Enterprising Scot*, p. 313.

40. Belich, *Replenishing the Earth*, p. 122.

41. Stout, 'Robert Fleming', pp. 13–14. Fleming of Dundee, the so-called 'Father of the Investment Trust', was said to have crossed the Atlantic 128 times in the course of his duties.

42. Giffen, *How Scots Financed the Modern World*, pp. 94–6.

43. L. E. Davis and R. E. Gallman, *Evolving Financial Markets and International Capital Flows: Britain, the Americas and Australia, 1865–1914* (Cambridge, 2001), p. 635.

44. Michie, *Money, Mania and Markets*, pp. 247–8.

45. Schmitz, 'Nature and Dimensions of Scottish Investment', p. 68, n. 69.

46. Giffen, *How Scots Financed the Modern World*, pp. 13–14.

47. S. G. Checkland, *Scottish Banking. A History, 1695–1973* (Glasgow, 1975), p. 368; C. H. Lee, 'The Establishment of the Financial Network', in Devine, Lee and Peden, eds., *Transformation of Scotland*, p. 111.

48. Both quotations come from Bailey, 'Australian Borrowing in Scotland', p. 272.

49. Michie, *Money, Mania and Markets*, p. 155; see also P. L. Payne, *The Early Scottish Limited Companies, 1856–1895: An Historical and Analytical Survey* (Edinburgh, 1980).

50. Schmitz, 'Nature and Dimensions of Scottish Foreign Investment', pp. 47–8.

51. Anon., 'Scottish Capital Abroad', p. 470.

52. Ibid., p. 477.

53. Jackson, *Enterprising Scot*, pp. 19, 87, 90, 94.

54. Ibid.

55. Anon., 'Scottish Capital Abroad', p. 468.

56. Lee, 'Economic Progress: Wealth and Poverty', p. 135; E. Cramond, 'The economic position of Scotland and her financial relations with England and Ireland', *Journal of the Royal Statistical Society*, New Series, 75 (1912), pp. 168–9.

57. R. D. Baxter, *National Income of the United Kingdom* (London, 1867), p. 56.

58. Lee, 'Financial Network', pp. 121–2.

59. Michie, *Money, Mania and Markets*, p. 137.

60. Lenman and Donaldson, 'Partners' Incomes', pp. 1–18.

61. Jackson, *Enterprising Scot*, pp. 313–14.

62. Bailey, 'Australian Borrowing in Scotland', p. 269.

63. Treble, 'Pattern of Investment', pp. 170–85.

64. Anon., 'Scottish Capital Abroad', p. 476. See also n. 66.

65. Lenman and Donaldson, 'Partners' Incomes', pp. 13–16.

66. Devine, *Scottish Nation*, pp. 264–5.

67. C. H. Lee, *Scotland and the United Kingdom* (Manchester, 1995), p. 40.

68. Michie, *Money, Mania and Markets*, pp. 133–6.

69. Sir D'Arcy Wentworth Thompson (speaking in 1938), quoted in Lenman and Donaldson, 'Partners' Incomes', p. 18.

12. ECLIPSE OF EMPIRES

1. Quoted in Peter L. Payne, 'The Economy', in T. M. Devine and R. J. Finlay, eds., *Scotland in the Twentieth Century* (Edinburgh, 1996), p. 15.

2. Richard Finlay, *Modern Scotland 1914–2000* (London, 2004), pp. 8–11.

3. The most recent discussion is in Catriona M. M. Macdonald, *Whaur Extremes Meet. Scotland's Twentieth Century* (Edinburgh, 2009), pp. 34–50.

4. Finlay, *Modern Scotland*, p. 90.

5. T. M. Devine, *The Scottish Nation 1700–2007* (London, 2006), p. 268.

6. This paragraph is based on Geoffrey Jones, *Merchants to Multinationals* (Oxford, 2000), pp. 84–90.

7. By William Ferguson, cited in Devine, *Scottish Nation*, p. 570.

8. Ibid., pp. 570–1.

9. John Scott and Michael Hughes, *The Anatomy of Scottish Capital* (London, 1980), p. 260.

10. Devine, *Scottish Nation*, p. 570.
11. Scott and Hughes, *Anatomy of Scottish Capital*, p. 259.
12. Jones, *Merchants and Multinationals*, p. 121.
13. David Armitage, 'The Scottish Diaspora', in Jenny Wormald, ed., *Scotland. A History* (Oxford, 2005), p. 302.
14. The views are summarized and considered in T. M. Devine, 'The Break-Up of Britain? Scotland and the End of Empire (The Prothero Lecture)', *Transactions of the Royal Historical Society*, 6th Series, XVI (2006), pp. 163–80.
15. I. G. C. Hutchison, *Scottish Politics in the Twentieth Century* (Basingstoke, 2001), pp. 121–2; Keith Webb, *The Growth of Nationalism in Scotland* (Glasgow, 1977), pp. 85–90.
16. David Torrance, *'We in Scotland': Thatcherism in a Cold Climate* (Edinburgh, 2009); Brian Taylor, *The Road to the Scottish Parliament* (Edinburgh, 1999); Christopher Harvie and Peter Jones, *The Road to Home Rule* (Edinburgh, 2000).
17. Paper given by Bryan Glass, a doctoral candidate at the University of Texas (Austin), at the British Scholar Conference there in March 2010.
18. John M. Mackenzie, 'Essay and Reflection: On Scotland and Empire', *The International History Review*, XV, (November, 1993), pp. 661–880.
19. Richard J. Finlay, 'The Rise and Fall of Popular Imperialism in Scotland 1850–1950', *Scottish Geographical Magazine*, 113, 1 (1997), p. 13.
20. Andrew Thompson, *The Empire Strikes Back?* (Harlow, 2005), p. 1.
21. References to recent works can be found in T. M. Devine, 'The spoils of Empire' and 'Imperial Scotland', in T. M. Devine, ed., *Scotland and the Union 1707–2007* (Edinburgh, 2008), pp. 91–122.
22. Bill Nasson, *Britannia's Empire. Making a British World* (Stroud, 2004), p. 208.
23. Bernard Porter, 'Further Thoughts on Imperial Absent-Mindedness', *Journal of Imperial and Commonwealth History*, 36, 1 (2008), p. 102.
24. Gordon Stewart, *Jute and Empire* (Manchester, 1998), p. ix.
25. A. D. Gibb, *Scotland in Eclipse* (London, 1930), p. 187.
26. Porter, 'Further Thoughts', p. 102.
27. R. D. Anderson, *Education and the Scottish People 1750–1918* (Oxford, 1995), pp. 212–13, 218–19.
28. Porter, 'Further Thoughts', p. 102.
29. See, for example, *The Scotsman*, 24 May 1929; 23 May 1930; 25 May 1934.
30. Devine, 'The Break-Up of Britain?', p. 171.
31. Devine, *Scottish Nation*, pp. 316–17, 360–6.

32. Thompson, *The Empire Strikes Back?*, pp. 89–95, 224–5.

33. Elaine W. McFarland, 'The Great War', in T. M. Devine and J. Wormald, eds., *The Oxford Handbook of Modern Scottish History 1500–2000* (Oxford, forthcoming (2012)) is the most up-to-date account.

34. Devine, 'The Break-Up of Britain?', pp. 172–3.

35. Stewart, *Jute and Empire*, pp. 2–4.

36. Quoted in Seona Robertson and Les Wilson, *Scotland's War* (Edinburgh, 1995), p. 188.

37. Quoted in Christopher Harvie, 'The Recovery of Scottish Labour, 1939–51', in I. Donnachie, Christopher Harvie and I. S. Woods, eds., *Forward! Labour Politics in Scotland 1888–1988* (Edinburgh, 1989), p. 77.

38. Isobel Lindsay, 'Migration and Motivation: A Twentieth Century Perspective', in T. M. Devine, ed., *Scottish Emigration and Scottish Society* (Edinburgh, 1992), pp. 155–6.

39. Reports to the General Assembly of the Church of Scotland, 1952–1968.

40. Glasgow Caledonian University Research Collections, The Scottish Trades Union Congress Archive, Annual Reports of the STUC, 1953–55.

41. Ibid., Fifty-Eighth Annual Report (1955), p. 360.

13. DIASPORA 1945–2010

1. Quoted in Catriona M. M. Macdonald, *Whaur Extremes Meet. Scotland's Twentieth Century* (Edinburgh, 2009), p. 115.

2. R. F. Wright, 'The Economics of New Immigration to Scotland', David Hume Institute Occasional Paper, no. 77 (2008), p. 13.

3. Eric Richards, *Britannia's Children. Emigration from England, Scotland, Wales and Ireland since 1600* (London, 2004), pp. 205–6, 271.

4. Ibid.

5. Wright, 'Economics of New Immigration', pp. 15–16.

6. Richard Finlay, *Modern Scotland 1914–2000* (London, 2004), p. 305.

7. 'Demographic Trends in Scotland: A Shrinking and Ageing Population'. *ESRC Seminar Series. Mapping the Public Policy Landscape* (2004), p. 1.

8. Murray Watson, *Being English in Scotland* (Edinburgh, 2003), p. 27.

9. Aleksander Dietkow, 'Poles in Scotland – before and after 2004', in T. M. Devine and David Hesse, eds., *Scotland and Poland: Historical Encounters, 1500–2010* (Edinburgh, 2011), pp. 186–95.

10. A. James Hammerton and Alistair Thomson, *Ten Pound Poms. Australia's Invisible Migrants* (Manchester, 2005), pp. 52, 67.

11. T. M. Devine, *The Scottish Nation 1700–2007* (London, 2006), pp. 562–5.

12. A. K. Cairncross, ed., *The Scottish Economy* (Glasgow, 1953), pp. 1–8.

13. *Report of the Committee of Enquiry into the Scottish Economy* (Toothill Report), Scottish Council for Development and Industry (1961), paragraphs 14.16–14.18.

14. Finlay, *Modern Scotland*, p. 307.

15. Hammerton and Thomson, *Ten Pound Poms*, pp. 40, 45, 68–70.

16. Timothy J. Hatton, 'Emigration from the UK, 1870–1913 and 1950–1998', *European Review of Economic History*, 8 (2004), p. 166.

17. Ibid., pp. 175–8.

18. Rowland T. Berthoff, 'Under the Kilt: Variations on the Scottish-American Ground', *Journal of American Ethnic History*, 1, 2 (1982), p. 7.

19. Ibid., pp. 5–34.

20. Gerald Redmond, *The Caledonian Games in Nineteenth Century America* (Cranbury, N. J., 1971), p. 140.

21. Ibid., p. 8.

22. Rowland Tappan Berthoff, *British Immigrants in Industrial America, 1790–1950* (Cambridge, Mass., 1953), p. 163.

23. Celeste Ray, 'Scottish Immigration and Ethnic Organization in the United States', in Celeste Ray, ed., *Transatlantic Scots* (Tuscaloosa, Ala., 2005), p. 79.

24. Berthoff, 'Under the Kilt', pp. 13–14.

25. Ibid., p. 14.

26. Celeste Ray, 'Transatlantic Scots and Ethnicity', in Ray, ed., *Transatlantic Scots*, pp. 21–47.

27. Ibid.

28. Jenni Calder, *Scots in the USA* (Edinburgh, 2006), p. 205.

29. Celeste Ray, *Highland Heritage. Scottish Americans in the American South* (Chapel Hill, N. C., 2001).

30. Berthoff, 'Under the Kilt', p. 14.

31. An overview of their history can be found in chapter 7 of T. M. Devine, *Scotland's Empire 1600–1815* (London, 2003), pp. 140–63.

32. Ray, *Highland Heritage*, pp. 60, 112.

33. Berthoff, 'Under the Kilt', p. 24.

34. Ray, *Highland Heritage*, p. 49. Apparently this ceremony also takes place in Perth and Sydney in Australia in June each year where it incorporates such symbols as kilts, clan crests and banners, Scottish songs, dancing and pipe band performances as well as the march to the church. Information kindly supplied by Dr Alex Main, Murdoch University, Australia, September 2010.

35. Celeste Ray, 'Bravehearts and Patriarchs', in Ray, ed., *Transatlantic Scots*, pp. 244–5, 248–50.

36. Edward J. Cowan, 'Tartan Day in America', in Ray, ed., *Transatlantic Scots*, p. 327.

37. Colin G. Calloway, *White People, Indians and Highlanders* (Oxford, 2008), p. 263.

38. Ray, 'Scottish Immigration and Ethnic Organization', pp. 69–74.

39. Paul Basu, *Highland Homecomings* (Abingdon, 2007), pp. 67, 191.

40. Paul Basu, 'Roots tourism as return movement: semantics and the Scottish diaspora', in Marjory Harper, ed., *Emigrant Homecomings* (Manchester, 2005), p. 140.

41. Ibid.

42. Celeste Ray, 'Ancestral Clanscapes and Transatlantic Tartaneers'. Paper presented to the Symposium on Return Migration, Scottish Centre for Diaspora Studies, University of Edinburgh, May 2010.

43. Basu, *Highland Homecomings*, especially chapters 6–10.

44. Ray, 'Ancestral Clanscapes and Transatlantic Tartaneers', pp. 6–7.

45. Euan Hague, 'National Tartan Day: Rewriting History in the United States', *Scottish Affairs*, 38 (2002), p. 97; Colin McArthur, 'Scotland may rue the day', *Scotland on Sunday*, 5 April 1998; Andrew Hook, 'Land of the Free lives the Scottish dream', *Sunday Times*, 4 April 1999.

46. Ray, 'Ancestral Clanscapes and Transatlantic Tartaneers', p. 10.

47. Unless otherwise stated, what follows is based on my *Clanship to Crofters' War. The Social Transformation of the Scottish Highlands* (Manchester, 1994), pp. 84–99 and 'The Invention of Scotland', in D. Dickson, S. Duffy, C. Ó Háinle and I. C. Ross, eds., *Ireland and Scotland. Nation, Region, Identity* (Dublin, 2001), pp. 18–24; Devine, *Scottish Nation*, pp. 231–48.

48. Ray, 'Scottish Immigration and Ethnic Organization', pp. 79, 88.

49. David Hesse, a PhD candidate in the Scottish Centre for Diaspora Studies, University of Edinburgh.

50. Basu, *Highland Homecomings*, p. 41.

51. Ray, 'Scottish Immigration and Ethnic Organization', p. 57.

52. *Scotland on Sunday*, 28 November 1999.

53. *Guardian*, 29 June 1999.

54. *The Scotsman*, 13 March 2000.

55. http://scotlandspeople.gov.uk.

56. Celeste Ray, 'Comment on "The Confederate Memorial Tartan"', *Scottish Affairs*, 35 (2001), p. 137.

57. Calloway, *White People, Indians and Highlanders*, p. 271.

58. Basu, *Highland Homecomings*, pp. 87–9; Internet Movie Database 2002; D. Petrie, *Screening Scotland* (London, 2000), pp. 209–11.

59. McArthur, 'Scotland may rue the day'.

60. Hague, 'National Tartan Day', p. 114.

61. For a convincing demolition of the thesis see Rowland Berthoff, 'Celtic Mist over the South', *Journal of Social History*, LII (1986), pp. 523–46.

62. D. Lowenthal, *The Heritage Crusade and the Spoils of History* (Cambridge, 1998).

63. Calloway, *White People, Indians and Highlanders*, p. 267. For the controversy over the suggested (but denied) links between neo-Confederate groups such as the League of the South and Southern Highlandism see Andrew Hook, 'Troubling Times in the Scottish-American Relationship', in Ray, ed., *Transatlantic Scots*, pp. 227–30; E. H. Sebesta, 'The Confederate Memorial Tartan', *Scottish Affairs*, 31 (2000), pp. 55–132; Ray, 'Comment on the "Confederate Memorial Tartan"', pp. 133–8.

64. Cairncross, ed., *Scottish Economy*, p. 5.

65. http://scotland.gov.uk/News/Releases/2010/09/14111014.

66. Alison Morrison and Brian Hay, 'A Review of the constraints, limitations and success of Homecoming Scotland 2009', *Fraser Economic Commentary*, 34 (2010), Fraser of Allander Institute, University of Strathclyde.

67. VisitScotland, Tourism in Scotland 2008; Scottish Government Scottish Tourism Key Sector Report, 2009.

68. 'Demographic Trends in Scotland', p. 1.

69. http://optimumpopulation.org/blog/?p=138.

70. Delphine Ancien, Mark Boyle and Rob Kitchin, 'The Scottish Diaspora and Diaspora Strategy: Insights and Lessons from Ireland', Scottish Government Social Research, 2009, p. 24.

Bibliography of Secondary Texts

Åberg, A., 'Scottish Soldiers in the Swedish Armies in the Sixteenth and Seventeenth Centuries', in G. G. Simpson, ed., *Scotland and Scandinavia, 800–1800* (Edinburgh, 1990).

Acheson, T. W., 'Changing Social Origins of the Canadian Industrial Elite, 1880–1910', in G. Porter and R. Cuff, eds., *Enterprise and National Development: Essays in Canadian Business and Economic History* (Toronto, 1973).

Allan, David, *Scotland in the Eighteenth Century* (Harlow, 2002).

Allan, Stuart and Allan Carswell, *The Thin Red Line. War, Empire and Visions of Scotland* (Edinburgh, n.d.).

Anbinder, Tyler, *Nativism and Slavery: The Northern Know Nothings and the Politics of the 1850s* (New York, 1992).

Ancien, Delphine, Mark Boyle and Rob Kitchin, 'The Scottish Diaspora and Diaspora Strategy: Insights and Lessons from Ireland', Scottish Government Social Research, 2009.

Anderson, M. and D. J. Morse, 'The People', in W. H. Fraser and R. J. Morris, eds., *People and Society in Scotland*. Vol. 2, *1830–1914* (Edinburgh, 1990).

Anderson, Olive, 'The Growth of Christian Militarism in Mid-Victorian Britain', *English Historical Review*, 86, 338 (1971).

Anderson, R. D., *Education and Opportunity in Victorian Scotland* (Edinburgh, 1983).

Anderson, R. D., *Education and the Scottish People 1750–1918* (Oxford, 1995).

Anderson, Terry L. and Peter J. Hill, *The Not So Wild West. Property Rights on the Frontier* (Stanford, Calif., 2004).

Anon., *The Depopulation System in the Highlands* (Edinburgh, 1849).

Anon., 'Scottish Capital Abroad', *Blackwood's Edinburgh Magazine*, CXXXVI (1884).

Anon., *That Land of Exiles. Scots in Australia* (Edinburgh, 1988).

Anon., 'Demographic Trends in Scotland: A Shrinking and Ageing Population'. *ESRC Seminar Series, Mapping the Public Policy Landscape* (2004).

Anstey, Roger I., *The Atlantic Slave Trade and British Abolition, 1760–1810* (London, 1965).

Anthony, Richard F., *Herds and Hinds: Farm Labour in Lowland Scotland, 1900–1939* (Edinburgh, 1997).

Armitage, David, 'The Scottish Diaspora', in Jenny Wormald, ed., *Scotland: A History* (Oxford, 2005).

Ascherson, Neal, *Stone Voices. The Search for Scotland* (London, 2002).

Bailey, J. D., 'Australian borrowing in Scotland in the nineteenth century', *Economic History Review*, New Series, 12, 2 (1959).

Bailyn, Bernard, *Voyagers to the West* (London, 1986).

Baines, Dudley, *Migration in a Mature Economy* (Cambridge, 1985).

Barkan, E. B., ed., *A Nation of Peoples. A Sourcebook on America's Multicultural Heritage* (Westport, Conn., 1999).

Bartlett, Thomas, '"This famous island set in a Virginian sea": Ireland in the British Empire, 1690–1801', in P. J. Marshall, ed., *The Oxford History of the British Empire*. Vol. 2, *The Eighteenth Century* (Oxford, 1998).

Bartlett, Thomas, 'Ireland, Empire and Union, 1690–1801', in Kevin Kenny, ed., *Ireland and the British Empire* (Oxford, 2004).

Basu, Paul, 'Roots tourism as return movement: semantics and the Scottish diaspora', in Marjory Harper, ed., *Emigrant Homecomings* (Manchester, 2005).

Basu, Paul, *Highland Homecomings* (Abingdon, 2007).

Baxter, R. D., *National Income of the United Kingdom* (London, 1867).

Bayly, C. A., *The Birth of the Modern World 1780–1914* (Oxford, 2004).

Bebbington, D. W., *Evangelicalism in Modern Britain* (London, 1989).

Belich, James, *Making Peoples: A History of the New Zealanders to 1900* (London, 2002).

Belich, James, *Replenishing the Earth. The Settler Revolution and the Rise of the Anglo-World 1783–1939* (Oxford, 2009).

Berthoff, Rowland Tappan, *British Immigrants in Industrial America 1790–1950* (Cambridge, Mass., 1953).

Berthoff, Rowland T., 'Under the Kilt: Variations on the Scottish-American Ground', *Journal of American Ethnic History*, 1, 2 (1982).

Berthoff, Rowland, 'Celtic Mist over the South', *Journal of Social History*, LII (1986).

Bielenberg, Andy, ed., *The Irish Diaspora* (Harlow, 2000).

Black, G. F., *Scotland's Mark on America* (1921; reprinted Charleston, S. C., 2008).

Blackburn, R., *The Making of New World Slavery* (London, 1997).

Blake, Robert, *Jardine Matheson. Traders of the Far East* (London, 1999).

Blessing, Patrick, 'Irish', in Stephan Thernstrom, ed., *Harvard Encyclopedia of American Ethnic Groups* (Cambridge, Mass., 1980).

Blessing, Patrick J., 'Irish Emigration to the United States, 1800–1920: An Overview', in P. J. Drudy, ed., *Irish in America: Emigration, Assimilation, Impact* (Cambridge, 1985).

Bliss, Michael, *Northern Enterprise: Five Centuries of Canadian Business* (Toronto, 1987).

Bodnar, John, *The Transplanted: A History of Immigrants in Urban America* (Bloomington, Ind., 1985).

Bowen, H. V., *Elites, Enterprise and the Making of the British Overseas Empire, 1688–1775* (Basingstoke, 1996).

Bowen, Hugh, *The Business of Empire: The East India Company and Imperial Britain* (Cambridge, 2006).

Boyd, Julian P., *The Declaration of Independence and the Evolution of the Text* (Princeton, N. J., 1945).

Breitenbach, Esther, *Empire and Scottish Society. The Impact of Foreign Missions at Home c.1790 to c.1914* (Edinburgh, 2009).

Brewer, John, *The Sinews of Power: War, Money and the English State, 1688–1783* (Cambridge, Mass., 1990).

Brock, Jeanette M., 'The Importance of Emigration in Scottish Regional Population Movement 1861–1911', in T. M. Devine, *Scottish Emigration and Scottish Society* (Edinburgh, 1992).

Brock, Jeanette M., *The Mobile Scot. A Study of Emigration and Migration, 1861–1911* (Edinburgh, 1999).

Brock, W. R., *Scotus Americanus* (Edinburgh, 1982).

Broeze, Frank, 'Private Enterprise and the Peopling of Australia, 1831–1850', *Economic History Review*, 35 (1982).

Brogan, C., *James Finlay and Co. Ltd.* (Glasgow, 1951).

Brooking, T., '"Tam McCanny and Kitty Clydeside": The Scots in New Zealand', in R. A. Cage, ed., *The Scots Abroad* (London, 1985).

Brooking, Tom, 'Sharing Out the Haggis: The Special Scottish Contribution to New Zealand History', in Tom Brooking and Jennie Coleman, eds., *The Heather and the Fern. Scottish Migration and New Zealand Settlement* (Dunedin, 2003).

Brooking, Tom and Jennie Coleman, eds., *The Heather and the Fern. Scottish Migration and New Zealand Settlement* (Dunedin, 2003).

Brown, Andrew, *History of Glasgow* (Glasgow, 1795).

Brown, Callum, *The Social History of Religion in Scotland since 1730* (London, 1987).

Brown, Jennifer S. A., *Strangers in Blood: Fur Trade Families in Indian Country* (Norman, Okla., 1980).

Brown, J. S. A., '"A Parcel of Upstart Scotchmen"', *The Beaver*, 68 (1988).

Brown, Lucy, *Victorian News and Newspapers* (Oxford, 1985).

Brown, Stewart J., *Thomas Chalmers and the Godly Commonwealth* (Oxford, 1982).

Brown, Stewart J., *Providence and Empire 1815–1914* (Harlow, 2008).

Brown, S. J. and M. Fry, eds., *Scotland in the Age of Disruption* (Edinburgh, 1993).

Brown, Stewart J. and George Newlands, eds., *Scottish Christianity in the Modern World* (Edinburgh, 2000).

Brown, Stewart J. and Christopher A. Whatley, eds., *The Union of 1707. New Dimensions* (Edinburgh, 2008).

Brown, Wallace, *The King's Friends* (Providence, R. I., 1965).

Brown, Wallace, *The Good Americans. The Loyalists in the American Revolution* (New York, 1969).

Bruce, Duncan, *The Mark of the Scots. Their Astonishing Contributions to History, Science, Democracy, Literature and the Arts* (New York, 1996).

Brumwell, Stephen, *Redcoats. The British Soldier and War in the Americas 1755–1763* (Cambridge, 2002).

Bryant, G. J., 'Scots in India in the Eighteenth Century', *Scottish Historical Review*, LXIV, 1, 177 (April, 1985).

Bueltmann, Tanja, '"Brither Scots Shoulder tae Shoulder": Ethnic Identity, Culture and Associationism among the Scots in New Zealand to 1930', unpublished PhD thesis, Victoria University of Wellington (2008).

Bueltmann, Tanja, Andrew Hanson and Graeme Morton, eds., *Ties of Bluid, Kin and Countrie. Scottish Associational Culture in the Diaspora* (Guelph, 2009).

Bumsted, J. M., *The People's Clearance* (Edinburgh, 1982).

Bumsted, J. M., *The Scots in Canada* (Ottawa, 1982).

Bumsted, J. M., 'The Scottish Diaspora: Emigration to British North America, 1776–1815', in Ned C. Landsman, ed., *Nation and Province in the First British Empire* (London, 2001).

Bumsted, J. M., 'The Curious Tale of the Scots and the Fur Trade: An Historiographical Account', in Peter E. Rider and Heather McNabb, eds., *A Kingdom of the Mind. How the Scots Helped Make Canada* (Montreal, 2006).

Bunyon, I., J. Calder, D. Idiens and B. Wilson, *No Ordinary Journey: John Rae, Arctic Explorer, 1813–1893* (Edinburgh, 1993).

Burnard, T., 'European Migration to Jamaica, 1655–1780', *William and Mary Quarterly*, 53, 4 (1996).

Burnard, T., '"Prodigious Riches": The Wealth of Jamaica before the American Revolution', *Economic History Review*, LIV, 3 (2001).

Burton, Antoinette, 'Who needs the nation? Interrogating "British" History', in Catherine Hall, ed., *Cultures of Empire: Colonizers in Britain and the Empire in the Nineteenth and Twentieth Centuries* (Manchester, 2000).

Butt, J., 'The Scottish Iron and Steel Industry before the "Hot-Blast"', *Journal of the West of Scotland Iron and Steel Industry*, 73 (1966).

Butt, John, 'The Industries of Glasgow', in W. H. Fraser and Irene Maver, eds., *Glasgow*. Vol. 2: *1830–1912* (Manchester, 1996).

Butt, John, *John Anderson's Legacy* (Glasgow, 1996).

Cage, R. A., ed., *The Scots Abroad* (London, 1985).

Cage, R. A. and E. O. A. Checkland, 'Thomas Chalmers and Urban Poverty: The St. John's Experiment in Glasgow 1819–1837', *Philosophical Journal*, 13 (1976).

Cain, Alex M., *The Cornchest for Scotland: Scots in India* (Edinburgh, 1986).

Cain, P. J. and A. G. Hopkins, 'The Political Economy of British Expansion Overseas, 1750–1914', *Economic History Review*, XXXIII, 4 (November, 1980).

Cain, P. J. and A. G. Hopkins, *British Imperialism: Innovation and Expansion, 1888–1914* (London, 1993).

Cain, P. J. and A. G. Hopkins, *British Imperialism: Crisis and Deconstruction, 1914–1990* (London, 1993).

Cairncross, A. K., ed., *The Scottish Economy* (Glasgow, 1953).

Cairncross, A. K., 'Investment in Canada, 1900–13', in A. R. Hall, ed., *The Export of Capital from Britain 1870–1914* (London, 1968).

Calder, Jenni, *Scots in the USA* (Edinburgh, 2006).

Calloway, Colin G., *White People, Indians and Highlanders* (Oxford, 2008).

Campbell, R. H., *The Rise and Fall of Scottish Industry, 1707–1939* (Edinburgh, 1980).

Campbell, R. H., 'Scotland', in R. A. Cage, ed., *The Scots Abroad* (London, 1985).

Campbell, R. H., 'The Making of the Industrial City', in T. M. Devine and G. Jackson, eds., *Glasgow*. Vol. 1, *Beginnings to 1830* (Manchester, 1995).

Campbell, R. H. and A. S. Skinner, eds., *The Origin and Nature of the Scottish Enlightenment* (Edinburgh, 1982).

Canny, N., ed., *Europeans on the Move. Studies on European Migration 1500–1800* (Oxford, 1994).

Carnall, Geoffrey and Colin Nicholson, eds., *The Impeachment of Warren Hastings* (Edinburgh, 1989).

Carpenter, S. E. M., 'Patterns of Recruitment of the Highland Regiments of the British Army, 1756–1815', unpublished MLitt thesis, University of St Andrews (1977).

Carroll, Francis M., 'America and Irish Political Independence', in P. J. Drudy, ed., *Irish in America: Emigration, Assimilation, Impact* (Cambridge, 1985).

Carr-Saunders, A. M., *World Population* (London, 1936).

Catterall, Douglas, *Community Without Borders. Scots Migrants and the Changing Face of Power in the Dutch Republic, c.1600–1700* (Leiden, 2002).

Chapman, M., *The Gaelic Vision of Scottish Culture* (London, 1978).

Chapman, Stanley, *Merchant Enterprise in Britain* (Cambridge, 1992).

Checkland, S. G., *Scottish Banking. A History, 1695–1973* (Glasgow, 1975).

Cheyne, A. C., *The Transformation of the Kirk* (Edinburgh, 1983).

Clapham, J. H., *An Economic History of Modern Britain: The Early Railway Age 1820–1850* (Cambridge, 1939).

Clark, D., 'On the Agriculture of the County of Argyll', *Transactions of the Highland and Agricultural Society*, 4th Series, X (1878).

Cleland, James, *Enumeration of the Inhabitants of the City of Glasgow* (Glasgow, 1843).

Clyde, Robert, *From Rebel to Hero. The Image of the Highlander 1745–1830* (East Linton, 1995).

Cockburn, Henry, *Journal*. Vol. 2 (Edinburgh, 1879).

Colley, Linda, *Britons: Forging the Nation 1707–1837* (London, 1994).

Colley, Linda, *Captives: Britain, Empire and the World 1660–1850* (London, 2002).

Collier, J., *The Pastoral Age in Australia* (London, 1911).

Collins, Brenda, 'The Origins of Irish Immigration to Scotland in the Nineteenth and Twentieth Centuries', in T. M. Devine, ed., *Irish Immigrants and Scottish Society in the Nineteenth and Twentieth Centuries* (Edinburgh, 1991).

Constable, Philip, 'Scottish Missionaries, "Protestant Hinduism", and Early Twentieth-Century India', *Scottish Historical Review*, LXXXVI, 2, 222 (October, 2007).

Cook, Scott B., 'The Irish Raj: Social Origins and Careers of Irishmen in the Indian Civil Service, 1855–1919', *Journal of Social History*, 20 (Spring, 1987).

Cookson, J. E., *The British Armed Nation 1793–1815* (Oxford, 1997).

Cooper, W. C., *The Story of Georgia* (New York, 1938).

Coreia, Elsa V., *Slave Society in the British Leeward Islands at the End of the Eighteenth Century* (New Haven, Conn., 1965).

Corish, Patrick, *The Irish Catholic Experience: A Historical Survey* (Dublin, 1985).

Corrins, Robert D., 'The Scottish Business Elite in the Nineteenth Century: The case of William Baird and Company', in A. J. G. Cummings and T. M. Devine, eds., *Industry, Business and Society in Scotland since 1700* (Edinburgh, 1994).

Cowan, Edward J., 'The Myth of Scotch Canada', in Marjory Harper and

Michael E. Vance, eds., *Myth, Migration and the Making of Memory. Scotia and Nova Scotia, c.1700–1990* (Edinburgh, 1999).

Cowan, Edward J., 'Tartan Day in America', in Celeste Ray, ed., *Transatlantic Scots* (Tuscaloosa, Ala., 2005).

Cowan, Edward J. and Richard J. Finlay, eds., *Scottish History. The Power of the Past* (Edinburgh, 2002).

Crafts, N. F. R. and C. K. Hanley, 'Output, Growth and the British Industrial Revolution', *Economic History Review*, 43 (1992).

Craig, Cairns, *Intending Scotland. Explorations in Scottish Culture since the Enlightenment* (Edinburgh, 2009).

Craig, Cairns, 'Empire of Intellect: The Scottish Enlightenment and Scotland's Intellectual Migrants', in John M. Mackenzie and T. M. Devine, eds., *Scotland and the British Empire* (Oxford, 2011).

Cramond, E., 'The economic position of Scotland and her financial relations with England and Ireland', *Journal of the Royal Statistical Society*, New Series, 75 (1912).

Craton, Michael, *Testing the Chains: Resistance to Slavery in the British West Indies* (Ithaca, N. Y., 1982).

Cullen, L. M. and T. C. Smout, 'Economic Growth in Scotland and Ireland', in L. M. Cullen and T. C. Smout, eds., *Comparative Aspects of Scottish and Irish Economic and Social History 1600–1900* (Edinburgh, 1977).

Cummings, A. J. G. and T. M. Devine, eds., *Industry, Business and Society in Scotland since 1700* (Edinburgh, 1994).

Curthoys, Ann, 'Expulsion, exodus and exile in white Australian historical mythology', *Journal of Australian Studies*, 23, 61 (1999).

Curthoys, Ann, 'Indigenous Subjects', in D. M. Schreuder and S. Wards, eds., *Australia's Empire* (Oxford, 2008).

Curtis, L. P. Jr, *Apes and Angels: The Irishman in Victorian Caricature* (Washington, D. C., 1977).

Darwin, John, 'Britain's Empires', in Sarah Stockwell, ed., *The British Empire. Themes and Perspectives* (Oxford, 2008).

Darwin, John, *The Empire Project. The Rise and Fall of the British World System, 1830–1970* (Cambridge, 2009).

Daunton, M. J., '"Gentlemanly Capitalism" and British Industry, 1820–1914', *Past and Present*, 122 (1989).

Davis, L. E. and R. E. Gallman, *Evolving Financial Markets and International Capital Flows: Britain, the Americas and Australia, 1865–1914* (Cambridge, 2001).

Devine, T. M., 'Sources of Capital for the Glasgow Tobacco Trade, c.1740–80', *Business History*, 16 (1974).

Devine, T. M., 'A Glasgow Tobacco House during the American War of Independence', *William and Mary Quarterly*, 3rd Series, XXXIII (July, 1975).

Devine, T. M., 'An Eighteenth Century Business Elite: Glasgow West India Merchants, *c.*1750–1815', *Scottish Historical Review*, LVII, 163 (April, 1978).

Devine, T. M., 'The Scottish Merchant Community 1680–1740', in R. H. Campbell and A. S. Skinner, eds., *The Origin and Nature of the Scottish Enlightenment* (Edinburgh, 1982).

Devine, T. M., 'The English Connection and Irish and Scottish Development in the Eighteenth Century', in T. M. Devine and David Dickson, eds., *Ireland and Scotland 1600–1850. Parallels and Contrasts in Economic and Social Development* (Edinburgh, 1983).

Devine, T. M., ed., *Farm Servants and Labour in Lowland Scotland, 1770–1914* (Edinburgh, 1984).

Devine, T. M., 'Urbanisation', in T. M. Devine and Rosalind Mitchison, eds., *People and Society in Scotland. Vol. 1, 1760–1830* (Edinburgh, 1988).

Devine, T. M., *The Great Highland Famine. Hunger, Emigration and the Scottish Highlands in the Nineteenth Century* (Edinburgh, 1988).

Devine, T. M., 'Social Responses to Agrarian Improvement: The Highland and Lowland Clearances in Scotland', in R. A. Houston and I. D. Whyte, eds., *Scottish Society, 1500–1800* (Cambridge, 1989).

Devine, T. M., ed., *Irish Immigrants and Scottish Society in the Nineteenth and Twentieth Centuries* (Edinburgh, 1991).

Devine, T. M., 'The Paradox of Scottish Emigration', in T. M. Devine, ed., *Scottish Emigration and Scottish Society* (Edinburgh, 1992).

Devine, T. M., ed., *Scottish Emigration and Scottish Society* (Edinburgh, 1992).

Devine, T. M., *The Transformation of Rural Scotland. Social Change and the Agrarian Economy, 1660–1815* (Edinburgh, 1994, 1999).

Devine, T. M., *Clanship to Crofters' War. The Social Transformation of the Scottish Highlands* (Manchester, 1994).

Devine, T. M., *Exploring the Scottish Past: Themes in the History of Scottish Society* (East Linton, 1995).

Devine, T. M., 'The Golden Age of Tobacco', in T. M. Devine and G. Jackson, eds., *Glasgow. Vol. 1, Beginnings to 1830* (Manchester, 1995).

Devine, T. M., 'The Colonial Trades and Industrial Investment in Scotland, *c.*1700–1815', in P. Emmer and F. Caastra, eds., *The Organisation of Interoceanic Trade in European Expansion, 1450–1800* (Aldershot, 1996).

Devine, T. M., 'The Invention of Scotland', in D. Dickson, Seán Duffy, Cathal Ó Háinle and Ian Campbell Ross, eds., *Ireland and Scotland. Nation, Region, Identity* (Dublin, 2001).

Devine, T. M., 'Irish and Scottish Development Revisited', in D. Dickson and C. Ó Gráda, eds., *Refiguring Ireland: Essays in Honour of L. M. Cullen* (Dublin, 2003).

Devine, T. M., *Scotland's Empire 1600–1815* (London, 2003).

Devine, T. M., 'Scotland', in R. Floud and P. Johnson, eds., *The Cambridge Economic History of Modern Britain.* Vol. 1, *Industrialisation, 1700–1860* (Cambridge, 2004).

Devine, T. M., 'Scottish elites and the Indian Empire, 1700–1815', in T. C. Smout, ed., *Anglo-Scottish Relations from 1603 to 1900* (Oxford, 2005).

Devine, T. M., 'The Break-Up of Britain? Scotland and the End of Empire', The Prothero Lecture, *Transactions of the Royal Historical Society*, 6th Series, XVI (2006).

Devine, T. M., *Clearance and Improvement. Land, Power and People in Scotland 1700–1900* (Edinburgh, 2006).

Devine, T. M., *The Scottish Nation 1700–2007* (London, 2006).

Devine, T. M., 'Why the Highlands did not starve. Ireland and Highland Scotland during the potato famine', in C. Ó Gráda, R. Paping and E. Vanhaute, eds., *When the Potato Failed: Causes and Effect of the 'Last' European Subsistence Crisis, 1845–1850* (Turnhout, Belgium, 2007).

Devine, T. M., 'Imperial Scotland', in T. M. Devine, ed., *Scotland and the Union 1707–2007* (Edinburgh, 2008).

Devine, T. M., 'The spoils of Empire', in T. M. Devine, ed., *Scotland and the Union 1707–2007* (Edinburgh, 2008).

Devine, T. M., ed., *Scotland and the Union 1707–2007* (Edinburgh, 2008).

Devine, T. M. and David Dickson, eds., *Ireland and Scotland 1600–1850. Parallels and Contrasts in Economic and Social Development* (Edinburgh, 1983).

Devine, T. M. and R. J. Finlay, eds., *Scotland in the Twentieth Century* (Edinburgh, 1996).

Devine, T. M. and D. Hesse, eds., *Scotland and Poland: Historical Encounters, 1500–2010* (Edinburgh, 2011).

Devine, T. M. and G. Jackson, eds., *Glasgow.* Vol. 1, *Beginnings to 1830* (Manchester, 1995).

Devine, T. M. and Rosalind Mitchison, eds., *People and Society in Scotland.* Vol. 1, *1760–1830* (Edinburgh, 1988).

Devine, T. M. and J. Wormald, eds., *The Oxford Handbook of Modern Scottish History 1500–2000* (Oxford, forthcoming (2012)).

Devine, T. M., C. H. Lee and G. C. Peden, eds., *The Transformation of Scotland* (Edinburgh, 2005).

Dewey, P. E., 'Military recruiting and the British labour force during the First World War', *Historical Journal*, 27 (1984).

Dickson, D., *Old World Colony. Cork and South Munster* (Cork, 2005).

Dickson, D. and C. Ó Gráda, eds., *Refiguring Ireland: Essays in Honour of L. M. Cullen* (Dublin, 2003).

Dickson, D., Seán Duffy, Cathal Ó Háinle and Ian Campbell Ross, eds., *Ireland and Scotland. Nation, Region, Identity* (Dublin, 2001).

Dickson, R. J., *Ulster Emigration to Colonial America 1718–1775* (Belfast, 1997).

Dietkow, Aleksander, 'Poles in Scotland – before and after 2004', in T. M. Devine and D. Hesse, eds., *Scotland and Poland: Historical Encounters, 1500–2010* (Edinburgh, 2011).

Dilke, Sir C. W., *Greater Britain* (London, 1872).

Dobson, David, *Scottish Trade with Colonial Charleston, 1683 to 1783* (Glasgow, 2009).

Dolan, Jay P., *The Immigrant Church* (Baltimore, Md., 1975).

Dolan, Jay P., *The American Catholic Experience: A History from Colonial Times to the Present* (New York, 1985).

Dolan, Jay P., *The Irish Americans* (New York, 2008).

Donaldson, W., *The Jacobite Song* (Aberdeen, 1988).

Donnachie, Ian L., 'The Making of "Scots on the Make": Scottish settlement and enterprise in Australia, 1830–1900', in T. M. Devine, ed., *Scottish Emigration and Scottish Society* (Edinburgh, 1992).

Donnachie, I. L. and C. A. Whatley, eds., *The Manufacture of Scottish History* (Edinburgh, 1992).

Donnachie, I. L., Christopher Harvie and I. S. Wood, eds., *Forward! Labour Politics in Scotland 1888–1988* (Edinburgh, 1989).

Doyle, David N., *Ireland, Irishmen and Revolutionary America, 1760–1820* (Dublin and Cork, 1981).

Doyle, D. Noel, 'The Irish in North America, 1776–1845', in W. E. Vaughan, ed., *A New History of Ireland*. Vol. 5, *1801–1870* (Oxford, 1989).

Doyle, D. N., 'The Irish as Urban Pioneers in the United States 1850–1870', *Journal of American Ethnic History*, 10 (1990/1).

Doyle, David Noel, 'Scots-Irish or Scotch-Irish', in Michael Glazier, ed., *The Encyclopedia of the Irish in America* (Notre Dame, Ind., 1999).

Drudy, P. J., ed., *Irish in America: Emigration, Assimilation, Impact* (Cambridge, 1985).

Drummond, A. L. and J. Bulloch, *The Church in Late Victorian Scotland 1874–1900* (Edinburgh, 1978).

Duff, Alexander, *The Church of Scotland India Missions* (Edinburgh, 1835).

Duffill, M., 'The Africa Trade from the Ports of Scotland, 1706–66', *Slavery and Abolition*, 24 (December 2004).

Dumett, R. E., ed., *Gentlemanly Capitalism and British Imperialism: The New Debate on Empire* (London, 1999).

Durie, Alastair J., *The Scottish Linen Industry in the Eighteenth Century* (Edinburgh, 1979).

Edelstein, M., *Overseas Investment in the Age of High Imperialism* (London, 1982).

Eltis, David and Stanley L. Engerman, 'The Importance of Slavery and the Slave Trade to Industrialising Britain', *Journal of Economic History*, 60 (March, 2000).

Emmer, P., and F. Caastra, eds., *The Organisation of Interoceanic Trade in European Expansion, 1450–1800* (Aldershot, 1996).

Engerman, S. L., 'The Slave Trade and British Capital Formation in the Eighteenth Century: A comment on the Williams Thesis', *Business History Review*, 46 (1972).

Erickson, Charlotte J., 'Who were the English and Scots Emigrants to the United States in the late Nineteenth Century?', in D. V. Glass and R. Revelle, eds., *Population and Social Change* (London, 1972).

Erickson, Charlotte, *Leaving England. Essays on British Emigration in the Nineteenth Century* (Ithaca, N. Y., 1994).

Erie, Stephen P., *Rainbow's End: Irish Americans and the Dilemmas of Urban Machine Politics, 1840–1985* (Berkeley, Calif., 1988).

Etherington, Norman, ed., *Missions and Empire* (Oxford, 2005).

Ethridge, Robbie, *Creek Country: The Creek Indians and their World* (Chapel Hill, N. C., 2003).

Evans, E. Estyn, 'The Scotch-Irish: Their Cultural Adaptation and Heritage in the American Old West', in E. R. R. Green, ed., *Essays in Scotch-Irish History* (London and New York, 1969).

Evans, Emory G., 'Planter Indebtedness and the Coming of Revolution in Virginia', *William and Mary Quarterly*, 3rd Series, XIX (1962).

Evans, Nicholas J., 'The Emigration of Skilled Male Workers from Clydeside during the Interwar Period', *International Journal of Maritime History*, XVIII (2006).

Feinstein, C. H., 'Capital Accumulation and the Industrial Revolution', in R. Floud and D. McCloskey, eds., *The Economic History of Britain since 1700*. Vol. 1 (Cambridge, 1981).

Feinstein, C. H., 'Britain's Overseas Investment in 1913', *Economic History Review*, 2nd Series, 43, 2 (1990).

Fenyő, Krisztina, *Contempt, Sympathy and Romance. Lowland Perceptions of the Highlands and the Clearances during the Famine Years, 1845–1855* (Edinburgh, 2000).

Ferguson, Hamish, 'Before the Union: Scottish Trade with the American Plantations, 1660–1700', unpublished MA dissertation, University of Edinburgh (2008).

Finlay, Richard J., 'The Burns Cult and Scottish Identity in the Nineteenth and Twentieth Centuries', in Kenneth Simpson, ed., *Love and Liberty* (Edinburgh, 1997).

Finlay, Richard J., 'The Rise and Fall of Popular Imperialism in Scotland 1850–1950', *Scottish Geographical Magazine*, 113, 1 (1997).

Finlay, Richard J., *A Partnership for Good? Scottish Politics and the Union since 1880* (Edinburgh, 1997).

Finlay, Richard J., 'Queen Victoria and the Cult of Scottish Monarchy', in Edward J. Cowan and Richard J. Finlay, eds., *Scottish History. The Power of the Past* (Edinburgh, 2002).

Finlay, Richard J., *Modern Scotland, 1914–2000* (London, 2004).

Fischer, David Hackett, *Albion's Seed: Four British Folkways in America* (Oxford, 1989).

Fitzpatrick, David, *Irish Emigration, 1801–1921* (Dublin, 1984).

Fitzpatrick, David, 'Ireland and the Empire', in Andrew Porter, ed., *The Oxford History of the British Empire*. Vol. 3, *The Nineteenth Century* (Oxford, 1999).

Fleming, J. R., *A History of the Church of Scotland 1843–1874* (Edinburgh, 1927).

Flinn, M., ed., *Scottish Population History from the Seventeenth Century to the 1930s* (Cambridge, 1977).

Floud, R. and P. Johnson, eds., *The Cambridge Economic History of Modern Britain*. Vol. 1, *Industrialisation, 1700–1860* (Cambridge, 2004).

Floud, R. and D. McCloskey, eds., *The Economic History of Britain since 1700*. Vol. 1 (Cambridge, 1981).

Foot, M. R. D., ed., *War and Society* (London, 1973).

Forbes, Sir W., *Memoirs of a Banking House* (London and Edinburgh, 1869).

Foster, Shirley, *American Women Travellers to Europe* (Keele, 1994).

Fraser, D. and A. Sutcliffe, eds., *The Pursuit of Urban History* (London, 1980).

Fraser, W. H. and Irene Maver, eds., *Glasgow*. Vol. 2, *1830 to 1912* (Manchester, 1996).

Fraser, W. H. and R. J. Morris, eds., *People and Society in Scotland*. Vol. 2 (Edinburgh, 1990).

Frenczi, I. and W. F. Willcox, *International Migrations* (New York, 1929–31).

Fry, Michael, *The Scottish Empire* (Edinburgh, 2001).

Fry, Michael, *'Bold, Independent, Unconquer'd and Free'* (Ayr, 2003).

Gabaccia, Donna R., *Italy's Many Diasporas* (Washington, D. C., 2000).

Gardener, Michael, *At the Edge of Empire. The Life of Thomas Blake Glover* (Edinburgh, 2008).

Gemery, Henry A., 'European Emigration to North America, 1700–1820:

Numbers and Quasi-Numbers', *Perspectives in American History*, 1 (1984).

Gibb, A. D., *Scotland in Eclipse* (London, 1930).

Giffen, Liza, *How Scots Financed the World. A History of Scottish Investment Trusts* (Edinburgh, 2009).

Glass, D. V. and R. Revelle, eds., *Population and Social Change* (London, 1972).

Glazier, Michael, ed., *The Encyclopedia of the Irish in America* (Notre Dame, Ind., 1999).

Gordon, Eleanor, 'Women's Spheres', in W. H. Fraser and R. J. Morris, eds., *People and Society in Scotland*. Vol. 2 (Edinburgh, 1990).

Gould, J. D., 'European Intercontinental Emigration 1815–1914: Patterns and causes', *Journal of European Economic History*, 8 (1979).

Graham, Eric, 'Scots in the Liverpool Slave Trade', *History Scotland* (March, 2007).

Graham, I. C. C., *Colonists from Scotland: Emigration to North America 1707–1783* (Ithaca, N. Y., 1956).

Gray, Richard, *Black Christians and White Missionaries* (New Haven, Conn., 1990).

Green, E. R. R., ed., *Essays in Scotch-Irish History* (London and New York, 1969).

Greenberg, Michael, *British Trade and the Opening of China 1800–42* (Cambridge, 1951).

Griffiths, T. and L. Robin, eds., *Ecology and Empire* (Keele, 1997).

Grimble, Ian, *The Sea Wolf: The Life of Admiral Cochrane* (Edinburgh, 2000).

Grimshaw, Patricia, 'Faith, Missionary Life and the Family', in Philippa Levine, ed., *Gender and Empire* (Oxford, 2004).

Grove, Richard H., 'Scotland in South Africa: John Crombie Brown and the roots of settler environmentalism', in T. Griffiths and L. Robin, eds., *Ecology and Empire* (Keele, 1997).

Grove, Richard H., *Ecology, Climate and Empire: Colonisation and Global Environmental History, 1400–1940* (Knapwell, 1997).

Guinnane, Timothy, *The Vanishing Irish: Households, Migration and the Rural Economy in Ireland 1850–1914* (Princeton, N. J., 1997).

Gulvin, C., *The Tweedmakers: A History of the Scottish Fancy Woollen Industry, 1600–1914* (Edinburgh, 1973).

Hague, Euan, 'National Tartan Day: Rewriting History in the United States', *Scottish Affairs*, 38 (2002).

Hall, A. R., ed., *The Export of Capital from Britain 1870–1914* (London, 1968).

Hall, Catherine, ed., *Cultures of Empire: Colonizers in Britain and the Empire in the Nineteenth and Twentieth Centuries* (Manchester, 2000).

Hall, Catherine, *Civilising Subjects: Metropole and Colony in the English Imagination* (Cambridge, 2002).

Hamilton, Douglas J., 'Patronage and Profit: Scottish Networks in the British West Indies, *c*.1763–1807', unpublished PhD thesis, University of Aberdeen (1999).

Hamilton, Douglas J., *Scotland, the Caribbean and the Atlantic World, 1750–1820* (Manchester, 2005).

Hammerton, A. James and Alistair Thomson, *Ten Pound Poms. Australia's Invisible Migrants* (Manchester, 2005).

Hancock, David, 'Scots in the Slave Trade', in Ned C. Landsman, ed., *Nation and Province in the First British Empire* (London, 2001).

Handler, Jerome S. and Frederick W. Lange, *Plantation Slavery in Barbados: An Archaeological and Historical Investigation* (Cambridge, Mass., 1978).

Hanham, H. J., 'Religion and nationality in the mid-Victorian society', in M. R. D. Foot, ed., *War and Society* (London, 1973).

Hargreaves, John D., *Aberdeenshire to Africa* (Aberdeen, 1981).

Hargreaves, John D., *Academe and Empire* (Aberdeen, 1994).

Harley, C. K., 'Ocean, freight rates and productivity, 1740–1913', *Journal of Economic History*, 48 (1988).

Harper, M., *Emigration from North-East Scotland*, 2 vols. (Aberdeen, 1988).

Harper, Marjory, *Emigration from Scotland between the Wars* (Manchester, 1998).

Harper, Marjory, *Adventurers and Exiles* (London, 2003).

Harper, Marjory, ed., *Emigrant Homecomings* (Manchester, 2005).

Harper, Marjory, 'Exiles or Entrepreneurs? Snapshots of the Scots in Canada', in Peter E. Rider and Heather McNabb, eds., *A Kingdom of the Mind. How the Scots Helped to Make Canada* (Montreal, 2006).

Harper, M. and S. Constantine, *Migration and Empire* (Oxford, 2010).

Harper, Marjory and Michael E. Vance, eds., *Myth, Migration and the Making of Memory. Scotia and Nova Scotia, c.1700–1990* (Edinburgh, 1999).

Harvey, Robert, *Cochrane: The Life and Exploits of a Fighting Captain* (London, 2002).

Harvie, Christopher, 'The Recovery of Scottish Labour, 1939–51', in I. Donnachie, Christopher Harvie and I. S. Wood, eds., *Forward! Labour Politics in Scotland 1888–1988* (Edinburgh, 1989).

Harvie, C., *Scotland and Nationalism: Scottish Society and Politics 1707–1994* (2nd edn, London, 1994).

Harvie, Christopher and Peter Jones, *The Road to Home Rule* (Edinburgh, 2000).

Hatton, Timothy J., 'Emigration from the UK, 1870–1913 and 1950–1998', *European Review of Economic History*, 8 (2004).

Helly, Dorothy O., *Livingstone's Legacy: Horace Walter and Victorian Mythmaking* (Columbus, Ohio, 1987).

Henderson, Diana, *Highland Soldier: A Social Study of the Highland Regiments 1820–1920* (Edinburgh, 1989).

Herman, A., *The Scottish Enlightenment* (London, 2002).

Higham, John, *Strangers in the Land: Patterns of American Nativism, 1860–1925* (New York, 1965).

Higman, B. W., *Plantation Jamaica, 1750–1850* (Kingston, 2005).

Hillis, P., 'Presbyterianism and Social Class in Mid-nineteenth Century Glasgow: A Study of Nine Churches', *Journal of Ecclesiastical History*, 31 (1981).

Hobsbawm, E. J. and T. O. Ranger, eds., *The Innovation of Tradition* (Oxford, 1983).

Hobson, C. K., *The Export of Capital* (London, 1914).

Hobson, J. A., *Imperialism: A Study* (London, 1938).

Hook, Andrew, *Scotland and America: A Study of Cultural Relations, 1750–1835* (Glasgow, 1975).

Hook, Andrew, *From Goosecreek to Gandercleugh. Studies in Scottish-American Literary and Cultural History* (East Linton, 1999).

Hook, Andrew, 'Troubling Times in the Scottish-American Relationship', in Celeste Ray, ed., *Transatlantic Scots* (Tuscaloosa, Ala., 2005).

Hooker, Richard J., ed., *The Carolina Backcountry on the Eve of the Revolution: The Journal and other Writings of Charles Woodmason, Anglican Itinerant* (Chapel Hill, N. C., 1953).

Horn, James, 'British Diaspora: Emigration from Britain, 1680–1815', in P. J. Marshall, ed., *The Oxford History of the British Empire*. Vol. 2, *The Eighteenth Century* (Oxford, 1998).

Horsman, Reginald, 'Origins of Racial Anglo-Saxonism in Great Britain before 1850', *Journal of the History of Ideas*, XXXVII (1976).

Houston, R. A., 'The Demographic Regime', in T. M. Devine and Rosalind Mitchison, eds., *People and Society in Scotland*. Vol. 1, *1760–1830* (Edinburgh, 1988).

Houston, R. A. and I. D. Whyte, eds., *Scottish Society, 1500–1800* (Cambridge, 1989).

Howe, Stephen, 'Minding the Gaps: New Directions in the Study of Ireland and Empire', *Journal of Imperial and Commonwealth History*, 37, 1 (2009).

Howie, Robert, *The Churches and the Churchless in Scotland* (Glasgow, 1893).

Hunter, James, *Glencoe and the Indians* (Edinburgh, 1977).

Hurtado, Albert L., *Intimate Frontiers: Sex, Gender and Culture in Old California* (Albuquerque, N. Mex., 1999).

Hutchison, I. G. C., *Scottish Politics in the Twentieth Century* (Basingstoke, 2001).

Hyde, F. E., *Cunard and the North Atlantic 1840–1973* (London, 1975).

Hyslop, Jonathan, 'Cape Town Highlanders, Transvaal Scottish: Military "Scottishness" and Social Power in Nineteenth and Twentieth Century South Africa', *South African Historical Journal*, 47 (2002).

Inikori, Joseph E., *Africans and the Industrial Revolution in England* (Cambridge, 2002).

Inikori, Joseph E. and Stanley L. Engerman, eds., *The Atlantic Slave Trade* (Durham, N. C., 1992).

Irving, Washington, *Astoria or Anecdotes of an Enterprise beyond the Rocky Mountains* (Norman, Okla., 1964 edn).

Jackson, Gordon and Charles Munn, 'Trade, Commerce and Finance', in W. H. Fraser and Irene Maver, eds., *Glasgow*. Vol. 2, *1830 to 1912* (Manchester, 1996).

Jackson, W. Turrentine, *The Enterprising Scot. Investors in the American West after 1873* (Edinburgh, 1968).

James, Lawrence, *Warrior Race* (London, 2001).

Jeffery, Keith, ed., *'An Irish Empire?' Aspects of Ireland and the British Empire* (Manchester, 1996).

Jensen, Richard, ' "No Irish Need Apply": A Myth of Victimisation', *Journal of Social History*, 36 (2002).

Johnson, J. K., *Becoming Prominent: Regional Leadership in Upper Canada 1791–1841* (Kingston and Montreal, 1989).

Jones, Geoffrey, *Merchants to Multinationals* (Oxford, 2000).

Jones, M. A., 'Scotch-Irish', in Stephan Thernstrom, ed., *The Harvard Encyclopedia of American Ethnic Groups* (Cambridge, Mass., 1980).

Jones, Stephanie, *Two Centuries of Overseas Trading. The Origins and Growth of the Inchcape Group* (London, 1986).

Jordan, T. G., *North American Cattle Ranching Frontiers* (Albuquerque, N. Mex., 1993).

Karras, A. L., *Sojourners in the Sun: Scottish Migrants in Jamaica and the Chesapeake 1740–1800* (Ithaca, N. Y., 1992).

Kenny, Kevin, *The American Irish, A History* (Harlow, 2000).

Kenny, Kevin, 'The Irish in the Empire', in Kevin Kenny, ed., *Ireland and the British Empire* (Oxford, 2004).

Kenny, Kevin, ed., *Ireland and the British Empire* (Oxford, 2004).

Keswick, Maggie, ed., *The Thistle and the Jade* (London, 1982).

Kidd, Colin, 'Race, Empire and the Limits of Nineteenth-Century Nation-hood', *Historical Journal*, 46, 4 (2003).

Kiddle, Margaret, *Men of Yesterday: A Social History of the Western District of Victoria 1834–1890* (Melbourne, 1961).

Kim, Dong-Woon, 'The British Multinational Enterprise in the United States before 1914: The Case of J. and P. Coats', *Business History Review*, 72 (Winter, 1998).

Klepak, H. P., 'A Man's a Man because of That: The Scots in Canadian Military Experience', in Peter E. Rider and Heather McNabb, eds., *A Kingdom of the Mind. How the Scots Helped to Make Canada* (Montreal, 2006).

Knox, W., 'The Political Workplace Culture of the Scottish Working Class, 1832–1914', in W. H. Fraser and R. J. Morris, eds., *People and Society in Scotland*. Vol. 2 (Edinburgh, 1990).

Knox, William, *Hanging by a Thread. The Scottish Cotton Industry 1850–1914* (Preston, 1995).

Landsman, Ned C., 'The Legacy of British Union for the North American Colonies: Provisional Elites and the Problem of Imperial Union', in John Robertson, ed., *A Union for Empire: Political Thought and the British Union of 1707* (Cambridge, 1995).

Landsman, Ned C., 'Nation, Migration and Province in the First British Empire: Scotland and the Americas, 1600–1800', *American Historical Review*, 104 (April, 1999).

Landsman, Ned C., ed., *Nation and Province in the First British Empire* (London, 2001).

Langford, Paul, 'South Britons' reception of North Britons, 1701–1820', in T. C. Smout, ed., *Anglo-Scottish Relations from 1603 to 1900* (Oxford, 2005).

Larkin, Emmett, 'The Devotional Revolution in Ireland', *American Historical Review*, 77 (1972).

Lawson, Philip and Jim Phillips, '"Our Execrable Banditti": Perceptions of Nabobs in Mid-Eighteenth Century Britain', *Albion*, XVI (1984).

Lee, Allan, *The Origins of the Popular Press 1855–1914* (London, 1976).

Lee, C. H., 'Modern Economic Growth and Structural Change in Scotland: The Service Sector Reconsidered', *Scottish Economic and Social History*, 3 (1983).

Lee, C. H., *Scotland and the United Kingdom* (Manchester, 1995).

Lee, C. H., 'Economic Progress: Wealth and Poverty', in T. M. Devine, C. H. Lee and G. C. Peden, eds., *The Transformation of Scotland* (Edinburgh, 2005).

Lee, C. H., 'The Establishment of the Financial Network', in T. M. Devine,

C. H. Lee and G. C. Peden, eds., *The Transformation of Scotland* (Edinburgh, 2005).

Leneman, Leah, *Living in Atholl 1685–1785* (Edinburgh, 1986).

Lenman, Bruce, *An Economic History of Modern Scotland 1660–1976* (London, 1977).

Lenman, Bruce, *The Jacobite Clans of the Great Glen 1650–1784* (London, 1984).

Lenman, Bruce and Kathleen Donaldson, 'Partners' Income, Investment and Diversification in the Scottish Linen Area 1850–1921', *Business History*, 21 (1971).

Leslie, Charles, *A New and exact History of Jamaica* (Edinburgh, c.1740).

Levine, Philippa, ed., *Gender and Empire* (Oxford, 2004).

Levitt, I. and T. C. Smout, *The State of the Scottish Working Class in 1843* (Edinburgh, 1979).

Leyburn, James G., *The Scotch-Irish* (Chapel Hill, N. C., 1962).

Lindsay, Isobel, 'Migration and Motivation: A Twentieth Century Perspective', in T. M. Devine, ed., *Scottish Emigration and Scottish Society* (Edinburgh, 1992).

Lloyd, Amy J., 'Popular Perceptions of Emigration in Britain, 1870–1914', unpublished PhD thesis, University of Cambridge (2009).

Long, Edward, *A History of Jamaica* (London, 1774).

Lowenthal, D., *The Heritage Crusade and the Spoils of History* (Cambridge, 1998).

Lynch, Michael, ed., *The Oxford Companion to Scottish History* (Oxford, 2001).

Lythe, S. G. E. and J. Butt, *An Economic History of Scotland 1100–1939* (London, 1975).

McAloon, Jim, *No Idle Rich. The Wealthy in Canterbury and Otago 1840–1914* (Dunedin, 2002).

McAloon, Jim, '"In the colonies those who make money are generally Scotchmen": Scottish Entrepreneurs in Colonial New Zealand', paper presented to the Celtic Connections, Irish-Scottish Studies Down Under Conference, Victoria, University of Wellington, October 2007.

McCalla, Douglas, 'Sojourners in the Snow? The Scots in Business in Nineteenth-Century Canada', in Peter E. Rider and Heather McNabb, eds., *A Kingdom of the Mind. How the Scots Helped to Make Canada* (Montreal, 2006).

McCarthy, Angela, ed., *A Global Clan. Scottish Migrant Networks and Identities since the Eighteenth Century* (London, 2006).

McCarthy, Angela, *For Spirit and Adventure: Personal Narratives of Irish and Scottish Migration, 1921–65* (Manchester, 2007).

McClean, Rosalind R., 'Scottish Emigrants to New Zealand 1840–1880', unpublished PhD thesis, University of Edinburgh (1990).

McCracken, John, *Politics and Christianity in Malawi 1875–1940* (Cambridge, 1977).

Macdonald, Catriona M. M., *Whaur Extremes Meet. Scotland's Twentieth Century* (Edinburgh, 2009).

Macdonald, Catriona M. M. and E. W. McFarland, eds., *Scotland and the Great War* (East Linton, 1999).

Macdonald, Lesley Orr, *A Unique and Glorious Mission: Women and Presbyterianism in Scotland 1830–1930* (Edinburgh, 2000).

McFarland, E. W., 'Introduction: "A Coronach in Stone"', in Catriona M. M. Macdonald and E. W. McFarland, eds., *Scotland and the Great War* (East Linton, 1999).

McFarland, Elaine W., 'The Great War', in T. M. Devine and J. Wormald, eds., *The Oxford Handbook of Modern Scottish History 1500–2000* (Oxford, forthcoming (2012)).

McGilvary, G. K., 'East India Patronage and the Political Management of Scotland, 1720–1774', unpublished PhD thesis, Open University (1989).

McGilvary, G. K., 'Post-Union Scotland and the Indian Connection', *Cencrastus*, 37 (Summer, 1990).

McGilvary, George, *East India Patronage and the British State* (London, 2008).

Macinnes, Allan I., *Clanship, Commerce and the House of Stuart, 1603–1788* (East Linton, 1996).

Macinnes, Allan I., 'The Treaty of Union: Made in England', in T. M. Devine, ed., *Scotland and the Union 1707–2007* (Edinburgh, 2008).

McKay, Alexander, *Scottish Samurai: Thomas Blake Glover 1838–1911* (Edinburgh, 1997).

Mackenzie, Sir George S., *General View of the Agriculture of the Counties of Ross and Cromarty* (London, 1813).

Mackenzie, John M., 'David Livingstone: The Construction of the Myth', in Graham Walker and Tom Gallagher, eds., *Sermons and Battle Hymns* (Edinburgh, 1990).

Mackenzie, John M., ed., *Popular Imperialism and the Military 1850–1950* (Manchester, 1992).

Mackenzie, John M., 'Essay and Reflection: On Scotland and Empire', *The International History Review*, XV (November, 1993).

Mackenzie, John M., *Empires of Nature and the Nature of Empires* (Edinburgh, 1997).

Mackenzie, John M., 'Foreword', in S. Murdoch and A. Mackillop, eds., *Military Governors and Imperial Frontiers c.1600–1800* (Leiden, 2003).

Mackenzie, John M., 'A Scottish Empire? The Scottish Diaspora and Interactive Identities', in Tom Brooking and Jennie Coleman, eds., *The Heather
and the Fern. Scottish Migration and New Zealand Settlement* (Dunedin,
2003).

Mackenzie, John M., *The Scots in South Africa* (Manchester, 2007).

Mackenzie, John M., 'Irish, Scottish, Welsh and English Worlds? A Four
Nation Approach to the History of the British Empire', *History Compass*,
6/5 (2008).

Mackenzie, John M., 'Scotland and Empire: Ethnicity, Environment and
Identity', *Northern Scotland*, 1 (2010).

Mackenzie, John M. and T. M. Devine, eds., *Scotland and the British Empire*
(Oxford, 2011).

Mackillop, A., 'More Fruitful than the Soil'. *Army, Empire and the Scottish
Highlands, 1715–1815* (Edinburgh, 2000).

Mackillop, A., 'For King, country and regiment? Motive and identity within
Highland soldiering 1746–1815', in S. Murdoch and A. Mackillop, eds.,
Fighting for Identity: Scottish Military Experience c.1550–1900 (Leiden,
2002).

Mackillop, A., '"The Hard Men of the Peripheries": Scotland's Military Elite and
the Imperial Crisis, 1754–1784'. Unpublished paper given at the Eighteenth
Century Scottish Studies Conference, University of Edinburgh, July 2002.

Mackillop, A., 'Scots and the Empire in Asia *c*.1695–1813'. Paper presented
at the Scotland and Empire Symposium, Scottish Centre for Diaspora
Studies, University of Edinburgh, February 2010.

McLachlan, James, 'Education', in John Carter Brown Library, *Scotland and
the Americas 1600–1800* (Providence, R. I., 1955).

McLaren, M., *British India and British Scotland 1780–1830* (Akron, Ohio,
2001).

McLynn, Frank, *Stanley: The Making of an Explorer* (London, 1989).

Macmillan, D. S., *Scotland and Australia, 1788–1850: Emigration, Commerce and Investment* (Oxford, 1967).

Macmillan, D. S., 'The "New Men" in Action: Scottish Mercantile and Ship-
ping Operations in the North American Colonies, 1760–1825', in D. S.
Macmillan, ed., *Canadian Business History: Selected Studies, 1497–1971*
(Toronto, 1972).

Macmillan, D. S., ed., *Canadian Business History: Selected Studies, 1497–
1971* (Toronto, 1972).

Macnair, James, *The Story of the Scottish National Memorial to David
Livingstone* (Glasgow, n.d.).

Magee, Gary B. and Andrew S. Thompson, *Empire and Globalisation* (Cambridge, 2010).

Marshall, P. J., *East India Fortunes: The British in Bengal in the Eighteenth Century* (Oxford, 1976).

Marshall, P. J., ed., *The Oxford History of the British Empire*. Vol. 2, *The Eighteenth Century* (Oxford, 1998).

Marshall, P. J., *The Making and Un-making of Empires* (Oxford, 2005).

Meagher, Timothy J., *Inventing Irish America: Generation, Class and Ethnic Identity in a New England City 1880–1928* (Notre Dame, Ind., 2001).

Meek, Donald E., ed., *Tuath is Tighearna. Tenants and Landlords* (Edinburgh, 1995).

Meller, Helen, *Patrick Geddes: Social Evolutionist and City Planner* (London, 1990).

Mentz, Søren, *The English Gentleman Merchant at Work: Madras and the City of London* (Copenhagen, 2005).

Meyer, Duane, *The Highland Scots of North Carolina* (Chapel Hill, N. C., 1957).

Michie, Ronald, *Money, Mania and Markets: Investment Company Formation and the Stock Exchange in Nineteenth Century Scotland* (Edinburgh, 1981).

Michie, R. C., *The City of London* (London, 1992).

Midgley, Clare, *Women against Slavery: The British Campaign, 1780–1870* (London, 1992).

Miller, Christopher L. and George R. Hamell, 'A New Perspective on Indian-White Contact: Cultural Symbols and Colonial Trade', *Journal of American History*, 73 (1986).

Miller, Kerby A., *Emigrants and Exiles: Ireland and the Irish Exodus to North America* (Oxford, 1985).

Mitchell, Elaine A., 'The Scot in the Fur Trade', in W. S. Reid, ed., *The Scottish Tradition in Canada* (Toronto, 1976).

Mokyr, Joel, 'Accounting for the Industrial Revolution', in R. Floud and P. Johnson, eds., *The Cambridge Economic History of Modern Britain*. Vol. 1, *Industrialisation, 1700–1860* (Cambridge, 2004).

Morgan, Philip D., 'The Black Experience in the British Empire, 1680–1819', in P. J. Marshall, ed., *The Oxford History of the British Empire*. Vol. 2, *The Eighteenth Century* (Oxford, 1998).

Morrison, Alison and Brian Hay, 'A review of the constraints, limitations and success of Homecoming Scotland 2009', *Fraser Economic Commentary*, 34 (2010) (Fraser of Allander Institute, University of Strathclyde).

Morton, A. S., ed., *The Journal of Duncan McGillivray of the North West Company at Fort George on the Saskatchewan 1794–5* (Toronto, 1929).

Moss, M. and J. R. Hume, *Workshop of the British Empire* (London, 1977).

Moss, M. and A. Slaven, *'From Ledger to Laser Beam': A History of the TSB in Scotland from 1870–1990* (Edinburgh, 1992).

Muir, Edwin, *Scottish Journey* (London, 1935).

Mulock, Thomas, *The Western Highlands and Islands of Scotland Socially Considered* (Edinburgh, 1850).

Munro, J. Forbes, *Maritime Enterprise and Empire* (Woodbridge, 2003).

Munro, J. Forbes and Tony Slaven, 'Networks and Markets in Clyde Shipping', *Business History*, 43, 2 (2001).

Murdoch, Alexander, *British Emigration, 1603–1914* (Basingstoke, 2004).

Murdoch, S., ed., *Scotland and the Thirty Years War 1618–1648* (Leiden, 2001).

Murdoch, S., 'The Good, the Bad and the Anonymous: A Preliminary Survey of Scots in the Dutch East Indies 1612–1707', *Northern Scotland*, 22 (2002).

Murdoch, S., *Networks North: Scottish Kin, Commercial and Covert Associations in Northern Europe 1560–1750* (Leiden, 2006).

Murdoch, S. and A. Mackillop, eds., *Fighting for Identity: Scottish Military Experience c.1550–1900* (Leiden, 2002).

Murdoch, S. and A. Mackillop, eds., *Military Governors and Imperial Frontiers c.1600–1800* (Leiden, 2003).

Murray, Norman, *The Scottish Handloom Weavers, 1790–1850* (Edinburgh, 1978).

Naismith, John, *Thoughts on Various Objects of Industry pursued in Scotland* (Edinburgh, 1790).

Nash, R. C., 'The English and Scottish Tobacco Trades in the Seventeenth and Eighteenth Centuries: Legal and Illegal Trade', *Economic History Review*, 2nd Series, XXV (1982).

Nasson, Bill, *Britannia's Empire. Making a British World* (Stroud, 2004).

Nechtman, Tillman, *Nabobs: Empire and Identity in Eighteenth Century Britain* (Cambridge, 2010).

Nenadic, Stana, 'The Victorian Middle Classes', in W. H. Fraser and Irene Maver, eds., *Glasgow*. Vol. 2, *1830 to 1912* (Manchester, 1996).

Nenadic, Stana, ed., *Scots in London in the Eighteenth Century* (Louisburg, Pa., 2010).

Newman, Peter C., *Company of Adventurers*, Vol. 1 (Toronto, 1985).

Noble, Gus, 'The Chicago Scots', in Tanja Bueltmann, Andrew Hinson and Graeme Morton, eds., *Ties of Bluid, Kin and Countrie. Scottish Associational Culture in the Diaspora* (Guelph, 2009).

Notestein, Wallace, *The Scot in History* (New Haven, Conn., 1946).

Nugent, Walter, *Crossings. The Great Transatlantic Migrations, 1870–1914* (Bloomington, Ind., 1992).

O'Brien, P. K., 'The Political Economy of British Taxation, 1660–1815', *Economic History Review*, 2nd Series, XLI (1988).

O'Brien, P. K., 'Inseparable Connections: Trade, Economy, Fiscal State and the Expansion of "Empire"', in P. J. Marshall, ed., *The Oxford History of the British Empire*. Vol. 2, *The Eighteenth Century* (Oxford, 1998).

O'Dwyer, Sir M., *India as I Knew It, 1885–1925* (London, 1925).

Ó Gráda, Cormac, *Ireland's Great Famine: Interdisciplinary Perspectives* (Dublin, 2006).

Ó Gráda, C., R. Paping and E. Vanhaute, eds., *When the Potato Failed: Causes and Effects of the 'Last' European Subsistence Crisis, 1845–1850* (Turnhout, Belgium, 2007).

Orr, W., *Deer Forests, Landlords and Crofters* (Edinburgh, 1982).

Parker, James G., 'Scottish Enterprise in India, 1750–1914', in R. A. Cage, ed., *The Scots Abroad* (London, 1985).

Payne, Michael, *The Most Respectable Place in the Territory. Everyday Life in Hudson's Bay Company Service* (Ottowa, 1989).

Payne, Peter L., ed., *Studies in Scottish Business History* (London, 1967).

Payne, Peter L., *The Early Scottish Limited Companies, 1856–1895: An Historical and Analytical Survey* (Edinburgh, 1980).

Payne, Peter L., 'The Economy', in T. M. Devine and R. J. Finlay, eds., *Scotland in the Twentieth Century* (Edinburgh, 1996).

Petrie, D., *Screening Scotland* (London, 2000).

Phillips, Jock and Terry Hearn, *Settlers. New Zealand Immigrants from England, Ireland and Scotland 1800–1945* (Auckland, 2008).

Phipps, J., *A Practical Treatise on the China and Eastern Trade* (London, 1836).

Pinkerton, John, *An Inquiry into the History of Scotland Preceding the Reign of Malcolm III* (Edinburgh, 1790).

Plank, Geoffrey, *Rebellion and Savagery. The Jacobite Risings of 1745 and the British Empire* (Philadelphia, Pa., 2006).

Pollard, Sydney, 'Capital Exports, 1870–1914: Harmful or Beneficial?', *Economic History Review*, 2nd Series, 38, 4 (1985).

Pórtéir, Cathal, ed., *The Great Irish Famine* (Cork, 1995).

Porter, A., 'Scottish Missions and Education in Nineteenth-Century India', *Journal of Imperial and Commonwealth History*, 16 (1988).

Porter, A., '"Gentlemanly Capitalism" and Empire: The British Experience since 1750?', *Journal of Imperial and Commonwealth History*, 18 (1990).

Porter, A., 'Religion and Empire: British Expansion in the Long Nineteenth Century, 1780–1914', *Journal of Imperial and Commonwealth History*, 20 (1992).

Porter, A., '"Cultural Imperialism" and Protestant Missionary Enterprise, 1780–1914', *Journal of Imperial and Commonwealth History*, 25 (1997).

Porter, Andrew, ed., *The Oxford History of the British Empire*. Vol. 3, *The Nineteenth Century* (Oxford, 1999).

Porter, Andrew, *Religion versus Empire? British Protestant Missionaries and Overseas Expansion, 1700–1914* (Manchester, 2004).

Porter, Andrew, 'An Overview, 1700–1914', in Norman Etherington, ed., *Missions and Empire* (Oxford, 2005).

Porter, Bernard, 'Further Thoughts on Imperial Absent-Mindedness', *Journal of Imperial and Commonwealth History*, 36 (2008)

Porter, G. and R. Cuff, eds., *Enterprise and National Development: Essays in Canadian Business and Economic History* (Toronto, 1973).

Postan, M. M., 'Recent Trends in the Accumulation of Capital', *Economic History Review*, VI, 1 (October, 1935).

Prebble, John, *The King's Jaunt* (London, 1988).

Prentis, Malcolm D., *The Scots in Australia. A Study of New South Wales, Victoria and Queensland, 1788–1900* (Sydney, 1983).

Price, Jacob M., 'The Rise of Glasgow in the Chesapeake Tobacco Trade, 1707–1775', reprinted in Peter L. Payne, ed., *Studies in Scottish Business History* (London, 1967).

Price, Jacob M., 'New Time Series for Scotland's and Britain's Trade with the Thirteen Colonies and States, 1740–1791', *William and Mary Quarterly*, XXXII, 2 (April, 1975).

Purvis, T. L., D. H. Akenson, F. McDonald and E. McDonald, 'The Population of the United States, 1790: A Symposium', *William and Mary Quarterly*, 3rd Series, XLI (1984).

Ray, Celeste, 'Comment on "The Confederate Memorial Tartan"', *Scottish Affairs*, 35 (2001).

Ray, Celeste, *Highland Heritage. Scottish Americans in the American South* (Chapel Hill, N. C., 2001).

Ray, Celeste, 'Transatlantic Scots and Ethnicity', in Celeste Ray, ed., *Transatlantic Scots* (Tuscaloosa, Ala., 2005).

Ray, Celeste, 'Scottish Immigration and Ethnic Organization in the United States', in Celeste Ray, ed., *Transatlantic Scots* (Tuscaloosa, Ala., 2005).

Ray, Celeste, 'Bravehearts and Patriarchs', in Celeste Ray, ed., *Transatlantic Scots* (Tuscaloosa, Ala., 2005).

Ray, Celeste, ed., *Transatlantic Scots* (Tuscaloosa, Ala., 2005).

Ray, Celeste, 'Ancestral Clanscapes and Transatlantic Tartaneers'. Paper presented to the Symposium on Return Migration, Scottish Centre for Diaspora Studies, University of Edinburgh, May 2010.

Ray, Rajat Kanta, 'Indian Society and the Establishment of British Supremacy, 1763–1818', in P. J. Marshall, ed., *The Oxford History of the British Empire*. Vol. 2, *The Eighteenth Century* (Oxford, 1998).

Redmond, Gerald, *The Caledonian Games in Nineteenth Century America* (Cranbury, N. J., 1971).

Reid, W. Stanford, ed., *The Scottish Tradition in Canada* (Toronto, 1976).

Reynolds, H., *The Other Side of the Frontier. Aboriginal Resistance to the European Invasion of Australia* (Ringwood, 1982).

Rice, C. D., 'Abolitionists and Abolitionism in Aberdeen: A Test Case for the Nineteenth-century Anti-slavery Movement', *Northern Scotland*, 1 (December, 1972).

Rice, C. D., *The Rise and Fall of Black Slavery* (London, 1975).

Rice, C. D., *The Scots Abolitionists, 1833–1861* (Baton Rouge, La., 1981).

Rich, E. E., ed., *Journal of Occurrences in the Athabasca Department by George Simpson* (Toronto, 1938).

Richards, Eric, *A History of the Highland Clearances: Agrarian Change and the Evictions, 1746–1886* (London, 1982).

Richards, Eric, 'Australia and the Scottish Connection 1788–1914', in R. A. Cage, ed., *The Scots Abroad* (London, 1985).

Richards, Eric, 'Scottish Australia 1788–1914', in Anon., *That Land of Exiles. Scots in Australia* (Edinburgh, 1988).

Richards, Eric, 'Leaving the Highlands: Colonial Destinations in Canada and Australia', in Marjory Harper and Michael E. Vance, eds., *Myth, Migration and the Making of Memory: Scotia and Nova Scotia, c.1700–1990* (Edinburgh, 1999).

Richards, Eric, *Britannia's Children. Emigration from England, Scotland, Wales and Ireland since 1600* (London, 2004).

Richards, Eric, 'Scottish Voices and Networks in Colonial Australia', in Angela McCarthy, ed., *A Global Clan. Scottish Migrant Networks and Identities since the Eighteenth Century* (London, 2006).

Richardson, David, ed., *Bristol, Africa and the Eighteenth Century Slave Trade to America*, Vol. 3 (Bristol, 1991).

Richardson, David, 'The British Empire and the Atlantic Slave Trade, 1660–1807', in P. J. Marshall, ed., *The Oxford History of the British Empire*. Vol. 2, *The Eighteenth Century* (Oxford, 1998).

Richter, Daniel K., 'Native Peoples of North America and the Eighteenth-Century British Empire', in P. J. Marshall, ed., *The Oxford History of the British Empire*. Vol. 2, *The Eighteenth Century* (Oxford, 1998).

Riddy, John, 'Warren Hastings: Scotland's Benefactor?', in Geoffrey Carnall and Colin Nicholson, eds., *The Impeachment of Warren Hastings* (Edinburgh, 1989).

Rider, Peter E. and Heather McNabb, eds., *A Kingdom of the Mind. How the Scots Helped to Make Canada* (Montreal, 2006).

Roberts, Stephen, *The Squatting Age in Australia* (Melbourne, 1935).

Robertson, Elizabeth, *Mary Slessor* (Edinburgh, 2001).

Robertson, John, *The Scottish Enlightenment and the Militia Issue* (Edinburgh, 1985).

Robertson, John, ed., *A Union for Empire: Political Thought and the British Union of 1707* (Cambridge, 1995).

Robertson, P. L., 'Shipping and Shipbuilding: The Case of William Denny and Brothers', *Business History*, 16 (1974).

Robertson, Seona and Les Wilson, *Scotland's War* (Edinburgh, 1995).

Rodger, R. G., 'The Invisible Hand: Market Forces, Housing and the Urban Form in Victorian Cities', in D. Fraser and A. Sutcliffe, eds., *The Pursuit of Urban History* (London, 1980).

Rodgers, Nini, *Ireland, Slavery and Anti-Slavery: 1612–1865* (Basingstoke, 2009).

Ross, Andrew, 'Scottish Missionary Concern 1874–1919: A Golden Era', *Scottish Historical Review*, 1 (1972).

Ross, Andrew, *John Philip, 1775–1851* (Aberdeen, 1986).

Ross, Andrew, 'Scotland and Malawi, 1850–1984', in Stewart J. Brown and George Newlands, eds., *Scottish Christianity in the Modern World* (Edinburgh, 2000).

Ross, Andrew, *David Livingstone. Mission and Empire* (London, 2002).

Ross, Peter, *The Scot in America* (New York, 1890).

Rössner, Philipp R., *Scottish Trade in the Wake of Union 1700–1760* (Stuttgart, 2008).

Rubenstein, W. D., *Men of Property* (London, 1981).

Rubin, V. and A. Tuden, eds., *Comparative Perspectives on Slavery in New World Plantation Societies*. Annals of the New York Academy of Sciences, Vol. 292 (New York, 1977).

Saul, S. B., *Studies in British Overseas Trade 1870–1914* (Liverpool, 1960).

Saville, Richard, 'Intellectual Capital in Pre-1707 Scotland', in Stewart J. Brown and Christopher A. Whatley, eds., *The Union of 1707. New Dimensions* (Edinburgh, 2008).

Saville, Richard and Paul Auerbach, 'Education and Social Capital in the Development of Scotland to 1750', paper prepared for the Economic History Society Conference, University of Reading, March–April 2006.

Schlote, Werner, *British Overseas Trade from 1700 to the 1930s* (Oxford, 1952).

Schmitz, Christopher, 'The Nature and Dimensions of Scottish Foreign Investment 1860–1914', *Business History*, 39, 2 (1997).

Schreuder, D. M. and S. Ward, eds., *Australia's Empire* (Oxford, 2008).

Scott, John and Michael Hughes, *The Anatomy of Scottish Capital* (London, 1980).

Sebesta, E. H., 'The Confederate Memorial Tartan', *Scottish Affairs*, 31 (2000).

Shadduck, Louise, *Andy Little: Idaho Sheep King* (Caldwell, 1990).

Sheridan, R. B., 'The Wealth of Jamaica in the Eighteenth Century', *Economic History Review*, XVIII (1963).

Sheridan, R. B., *Sugar and Slavery: An Economic History of the British West Indies 1623–1775* (Barbados, 1974).

Sheridan, R. B., 'The Role of the Scots in the Economy and Society of the West Indies', in V. Rubin and A. Tuden, eds., *Comparative Perspectives on Slavery in New World Plantation Societies*. Annals of the New York Academy of Sciences, Vol. 292 (New York, 1977).

Sheridan, R. B., *Doctors and Slaves* (Cambridge, 1985).

Sheridan, R. B., 'The Formation of Caribbean Plantation Society, 1689–1748', in P. J. Marshall, ed., *The Oxford History of the British Empire*. Vol. 2, *The Eighteenth Century* (Oxford, 1998).

Simpson, G. G., ed., *Scotland and Scandinavia, 800–1800* (Edinburgh, 1990).

Simpson, Kenneth, ed., *Love and Liberty* (Edinburgh, 1997).

Slaven, A., *The Development of the West of Scotland 1750–1960* (London, 1975).

Slaven, Anthony and Sydney Checkland, eds., *Dictionary of Scottish Business Biography 1860–1960*, Vol. 2 (Aberdeen, 1990).

Smith, Adam, *The Theory of Moral Sentiments* (1759; London, 1804 edn).

Smith, Adam, *The Wealth of Nations* (1776; London, 1937 edn).

Smith, Bill, *Robert Fleming 1845–1933* (Haddington, 2000).

Smout, T. C., 'Tours in the Scottish Highlands from the eighteenth to the twentieth centuries', *Northern Scotland*, 5 (1983).

Smout, T. C., *A Century of the Scottish People, 1830–1950* (London, 1986).

Smout, T. C., 'Woodland History before 1850', in T. C. Smout, ed., *Scotland since Prehistory: Natural Change and Human Impact* (Aberdeen, 1993).

Smout, T. C., ed., *Scotland since Prehistory: Natural Change and Human Impact* (Aberdeen, 1993).

Smout, T. C., 'The Culture of Migration: Scots as Europeans, 1500–1800', *History Workshop Journal*, 40 (Autumn, 1995).

Smout, T. C., ed., *Anglo-Scottish Relations from 1603 to 1900* (Oxford, 2005).

Smout, T. C., N. C. Landsman and T. M. Devine, 'Scottish Emigration in the Seventeenth and Eighteenth Centuries', in N. Canny, ed., *Europeans on the Move. Studies on European Migration 1500–1800* (Oxford, 1994).

Solow, B. L., 'Caribbean Slavery and British Growth. The Eric Williams Hypothesis', *Journal of Development Economics*, 17 (1985).

Solow, Barbara L. and Stanley L. Engerman, eds., *British Capitalism and Caribbean Slavery: The Legacy of Eric Williams* (Cambridge, 1987).

Somerville, Alexander, *The Autobiography of a Working Man* (London, 1848).

Speirs, Edward M., *The Scottish Soldier and Empire, 1854–1902* (Edinburgh, 2006).

Sriskandarajah, D. and C. Drew, *Brits Abroad: Mapping the Scale and Nature of British Emigration* (London, 2006).

Stewart, Gordon, *Jute and Empire* (Manchester, 1998).

Stockwell, Sarah, ed., *The British Empire. Themes and Perspectives* (Oxford, 2008).

Storrow, E., *India and Christian Missions* (London, 1859).

Stout, G. A., 'Robert Fleming and the Trustees of the First Scottish-American Investment Trust', *Friends of Dundee City Archives*, 1 (1999).

Strachan, Hew, 'Scotland's Military Identity', *Scottish Historical Review*, LXXXV, 2, 220 (October, 2006).

Streets, Heather, 'Identity in the Highland Regiments in the Nineteenth Century: Soldier, Region, Nation', in S. Murdoch and A. Mackillop, eds., *Fighting for Identity: Scottish Military Experience c.1550–1900* (Leiden, 2002).

Streets, Heather, *Martial Races. The Military, Race and Masculinity in British Imperial Culture 1857–1914* (Manchester, 2004).

Szasz, Ferenc Morton, *Scots in the North American West, 1790–1917* (Norman, Okla., 2000).

Taylor, Brian, *The Road to the Scottish Parliament* (Edinburgh, 1999).

Taylor, W. H., *Mission to Educate: A History of the Educational Work of the Scottish Presbyterian Mission in East Nigeria, 1846–1960* (New York, 1996).

Thernstrom, Stephan, *The Other Bostonians: Poverty and Progress in the American Metropolis, 1860–1970* (Cambridge, Mass., 1973).

Thernstrom, Stephan, ed., *The Harvard Encyclopedia of American Ethnic Groups* (Cambridge, Mass., 1980).

Thomas, B., *Migration and Economic Growth* (Cambridge, 1973).

Thomas, R. P., 'The Sugar Colonies of the Old Empire. Profit or Loss for Great Britain', *Economic History Review*, 21 (1968).

Thomas, R. P. and N. Bean, 'The Fishers of Men: The Profits of the Slave Trade', *Journal of Economic History*, 34 (December, 1974).

Thompson, Andrew, *The Empire Strikes Back?* (Harlow, 2005).

Thompson, Andrew, 'Empire and the British State', in Sarah Stockwell, ed., *The British Empire. Themes and Perspectives* (Oxford, 2008).

Torrance, David, *'We in Scotland': Thatcherism in a Cold Climate* (Edinburgh, 2009).

Treble, J. H., 'The Pattern of Investment of the Standard Life Assurance Company 1875–1914', *Business History*, 22 (1980).

Treble, J. H., 'The Occupied Male Labour Force', in W. H. Fraser and R. J. Morris, eds., *People and Society in Scotland*, Vol. 2 (Edinburgh, 1990).

Trevor-Roper, H., 'The Invention of Tradition: The Highland Tradition of

Scotland', in E. J. Hobsbawm and T. O. Ranger, eds., *The Innovation of Tradition* (Oxford, 1983).

Trollope, Anthony, *Australia* (London, 1873).

Truxes, Thomas M., *Irish-American Trade, 1660–1783* (Cambridge, 1988).

Van Vugt, William E., 'British (English, Welsh, Scots, Scotch-Irish)', in E. B. Barkan, ed., *A Nation of Peoples. A Sourcebook on America's Multicultural Heritage* (Westport, Conn., 1999).

Van Vugt, William E., *British Buckeyes. The English, Scots and Welsh in Ohio 1700–1900* (Kent, Ohio, 2006).

Vardin, J. C., *La Mise en valeur de l'isle de Tobago, 1673–1783* (Paris, 1969).

Vaughan, W. E., ed., *A New History of Ireland.* Vol. 5, *1801–1870* (Oxford, 1989).

Walker, Graham and Tom Gallagher, eds., *Sermons and Battle Hymns* (Edinburgh, 1990).

Walker, Stephen P., 'Agents of Dispossession and Acculturation. Edinburgh Accountants and the Highland Clearances', *Critical Perspectives in Accounting*, 14 (2003).

Ward, J. R., 'The British West Indies in the Age of Abolition', in P. J. Marshall, ed., *The Oxford History of the British Empire.* Vol. 2, *The Eighteenth Century* (Oxford, 1998).

Watson, Don, *Caledonia Australis: Scottish Highlanders on the Frontier of Australia* (Sydney, 1984).

Watson, Murray, *Being English in Scotland* (Edinburgh, 2003).

Webb, Keith, *The Growth of Nationalism in Scotland* (Glasgow, 1977).

Westwood, P. J., *David Livingstone: His Life and Work as Told through the Media of Postage Stamps and Allied Material* (Edinburgh, 1986).

Whatley, Christopher A., *The Industrial Revolution in Scotland* (Cambridge, 1997).

Whatley, Christopher A., *Scottish Society 1707–1830* (Manchester, 2000).

Whatley, Christopher A., 'The Issues Facing Scotland in 1707', in Stewart J. Brown and Christopher A. Whatley, eds., *The Union of 1707. New Dimensions* (Edinburgh, 2008).

Whyte, Iain, *Scotland and the Abolition of Black Slavery, 1756–1838* (Edinburgh, 2006).

Wilkins, M., *The History of Foreign Investment in the United States to 1914* (Cambridge, Mass., 1989).

Williams, Glydwyr, 'The Pacific: Exploration and Exploitation', in P. J. Marshall, ed., *The Oxford History of the British Empire.* Vol. 2, *The Eighteenth Century* (Oxford, 1998).

Williams, Gomer, *History of the Liverpool Privateers and Letters of Marque, with an Account of the Liverpool Slave Trade* (London, 1897).

Withers, C. W. J., 'The historical creation of the Scottish Highlands', in I. L. Donnachie and C. A. Whatley, eds., *The Manufacture of Scottish History* (Edinburgh, 1992).

Withers, C. W. J., *Urban Highlanders. Highland–Lowland Migration and Urban Gaelic Culture, 1700–1900* (East Linton, 1998).

Womack, Peter, *Improvement and Romance* (London, 1989).

Wood, P., *Some Geelong Scots* (Geelong, Victoria, n.d.).

Woodruff, W., *The Impact of Western Man* (London, 1966).

Wormald, Jenny, ed., *Scotland. A History* (Oxford, 2005).

Wright, Esmond, 'Education in the American Colonies: The Impact of Scotland', in E. R. R. Green, ed., *Essays in Scotch-Irish History* (London and New York, 1969).

Wright, R. F., 'The Economics of New Immigration to Scotland', David Hume Institute Occasional Paper 77 (2008).

Wrigley, E. A. and R. S. Schofield, *The Population History of England, 1541–1871* (Cambridge, 1986).

Young, D. R., 'Voluntary Recruitment in Scotland, 1914–1916', unpublished PhD thesis, University of Glasgow (2001).

Youngson, A. J., *After the '45* (Edinburgh, 1982).

Index

emigration – *cont.*
 returnees from 93–4, 95–6, 97,
  262, 288
 Scottish and Irish compared 288
 to New World 4–5, 90, 125–48
 as tragedy 152–3
 urban focus of 129
 see also immigration; migration
Emigration Advances Act 119
Empire Day 264
employment 267, 272
 see also unemployment
Encyclopaedia Britannica 158
energy sources 253
engineering 62–3, 69–70, 74, 86,
  105, 162, 165, 249, 251, 252,
  261
 see also shipbuilding
England
 emigration from 88
 and Industrial Revolution 47
 Irish immigration to 127
 returnees from emigration 96
 as state 1–4
 see also Britain
English, in America 174
Enlightenment 22, 116, 155, 198,
  259
 Scottish 31, 34, 54, 157
environmental issues 156, 157–8
'ethnic cleansing' 119
Ethnic Heritage Act (USA, 1974)
  283
Europe
 Central xiv
 emigration from 290
 interest in Scottish heritage 282–3
 Scottish connection 24–6
 trade with 51, 57, 58
evangelicalism 191–8

evictions 120–24
Exchequer, British 81
exile
 rhetoric of 279–80
 sense of 127–8
exploration 7

family history 283
famine 63, 91
 see also Highland Famine; Ireland,
  Great Famine
farm servants 89, 99, 101, 103, 237
farming 6, 15, 16, 29, 43, 48, 64, 89,
  95, 97, 98
 consolidation of 99
 small tenants 91, 101, 127
 see also agriculture; cattle
  farming; sheep farming
Female Emancipation Societies 206
Fenian Brotherhood 134
Ferguson, Adam 216
 Essay on Civil Society 136
Ferrier, J. F. 155
Fife 51, 63, 100
56th Regiment 163
Fiji 76
Finlay, James, and Co. 52, 78
First Fleet 7
First World War *see* Great War
Fisher, Andrew 169
fishing 15, 91, 108, 112, 113, 122
Flanders 26, 211
Flatheads 185
Fleming, Robert, of Dundee 245,
  248
Florida 6
Forbes, Duncan 214
Forbes, Sir William, *Memoirs* 45
Forester, C. S. 86
Fort Bragg, North Carolina 278